PARTIES AND PARTY SYSTEMS IN LIBERAL DEMOCRACIES

PARTIES AND PARTY SYSTEMS IN LIBERAL DEMOCRACIES

EDITED BY STEVEN B. WOLINETZ

ROUTLEDGE
London and New York

First published 1988
by Routledge
11 New Fetter Lane, London EC4P 4EE
29 West 35th Street, New York, NY 10001

Printed and bound in Great Britain by
Biddles Ltd, Guildford and King's Lynn

British Library Cataloguing in Publication Data

Parties and party systems in liberal
    democracies.
    1. Political science
    I. Wolinetz, Steven B.
    320.9182′1   JA66
    ISBN 0-415-01276-7

Library of Congress Cataloging-in-Publication Data

Wolinetz, Steven B., 1943–
        Parties and party systems in liberal democracies / Steven B.
    Wolinetz.
            p.   cm.
        Includes index.
        ISBN 0-415-01276-7
        1. Political parties. 2. Democracy. 3. Comparative government.
    I. Title.
    JF2011.W65   1988   88-15777
    324.2–dc19   CIP

CONTENTS

List of Tables

List of Figures

NOTES ON CONTRIBUTORS

Grant Amyot is Associate Professor of Political Studies at Queen's University, Kingston, Ontario and author of *Italian Communist Party: The Crisis of the Popular Front Strategy.*

Herman Bakvis is Associate Professor of Political Science and Public Administration at Dalhousie University. The author of *Catholic Power in the Netherlands,* he has written on Dutch and Canadian politics and has served as associate editor of the *Canadian Journal of Political Science.*

George Breckenridge is Associate Professor of Political Science at McMaster University.

R.K. Carty is Associate Professor of Political Science at the University of British Columbia. He is the author of *Party and Parish Pump: Electoral Politics in Ireland,* as well as several articles on Irish and Canadian politics.

William M. Chandler is Professor of Political Science at McMaster University. His research and publications include works on German and Canadian political parties, public policy, and federalism.

Maureen Covell is Associate Professor of Political Science at Simon Fraser University and the author of several articles on constitutional change in Belgium and a book on Madagascar

Frederick C. Engelmann is Professor Emeritus of Political Science at the University of Alberta. He has served as President of the Canadian Political Science Association and as chairman of his department. In addition to his work on Canadian politics, he has written extensively on the politics of his native Austria.

Eric S. Einhorn is Associate Professor of Political Science at the University of Massachusetts (Amherst) and is the author of *National Security and Defense Policy in Denmark.*

John Logue is Associate Professor of Political Science at Kent State University and is the author of *Socialism and Abundance: Radical Socialism in the Danish Welfare State.*

Frank L. Wilson is Professor of Political Science at Purdue University. He is the author of *French Political Parties Under the Fifth Republic*, as well as numerous articles on French parties and the French party system.

Steven B. Wolinetz is Associate Professor of Political Science at Memorial University of Newfoundland. In addition to his work on parties, he has written on changing relations among trade unions, business, and government in the Netherlands.

PREFACE

It is not often that one can date the origins of an idea. This book is an outgrowth of the European Politics Group, an intermittent but sometimes active group within the Canadian Political Science Association. Inspiration for this book emerged from a casual meeting on the terrace of the University of British Columbia Faculty Club in June, 1983. A conference on Parties and Party Systems in the 1980's was subsequently held at Dalhousie University in March, 1985. The conference was made possible through grants from the Social Science and Humanities Research Council (Canada) and the Delegation of the Commission of the European Communities in Ottawa. Memorial University of Newfoundland and Dalhousie University provided additional support. Preparation of the manuscript was made possible by the Social Science and Humanities Research Council Conference grant and supplementary grants from the Dean of Arts at Memorial University. I am grateful to the Department of Political Science for support and encouragement, to Administrative Services at Memorial for typing and word-processing, and to Computing Services for their assistance in generating the final copy on their VAX/VMS system. Janet Murphy and Gayle Barton were particularly helpful in modifying the Scribe programme to produce the require formats and ensuring that the manuscript would print properly. My research assistant, Gerald White, laboured to format and process the manuscript. Without either Gerry White or Gayle Barton, an already long process would have taken even longer. The graphics were done by David MacNeil. Undoubtedly, others - spouses, friends, or typists - helped as well. I am particularly indebted to my wife, Karen Lippold, for indexing, moral support, and help in more ways than I can recount, and to my sons, David and Michael, for grudgingly yielding more of their father's time then they should have. Finally, I would like to thank my co-authors for their cooperation and forbearance, particularly when they received yet another request for revisions.

Steven B. Wolinetz
St. John's, Newfoundland
August 1, 1987

Chapter One

Introduction: Party Systems and How They Change

Steven B. Wolinetz

When and how party systems change or remain the same is the central theme of this book. Our concern reflects the reality of a changing world and the centrality of parties in liberal democracies. Despite doubts about their effectiveness, parties define the alternatives which voters consider and provide a device by which citizens can control their governments. But what determines the shape of party systems? Although we commonly assume parties to be products of earlier cleavages, we have less sense of the ways in which party systems change. Too often, party systems are portrayed as fixed elements of the landscape, like mountains, whose features we describe, but whose origins or ends we rarely question.

But are parties and party systems fixed and unchanging? Previously, there were two distinct, but geographically rooted views in the literature. Students of American politics argued that the American party system had been subject to periodic realignments in which issues were redefined and the interests which the parties represented reshuffled and rearranged (Key 1955; Sundquist 1983), lending a new vitality to politics (Burnham 1970). In contrast, students of Western Europe have usually stressed the durability of party systems and electoral alignments. Parties developed in response to deep-seated class and religious cleavages and continued to reflect them, even though formative conflicts had been resolved or ameliorated. Lipset and Rokkan crystallised the prevailing view when they argued that:

> the party systems of the 1960's reflect, with few but significant exceptions, the cleavage structures of the 1920's...the party alternatives, and in remarkably many cases

> the party organisations, are older than the majorities of the
> national electorates (Lipset and Rokkan 1967:50).

Phenomena such as war, affluence or the purported decline of ideology
had had little impact on underlying party configurations, frozen since
the completion of suffrage extension several decades before.

Until recently, there was little impetus to reassess or reconcile
these contrasting views. Party systems on both sides of the Atlantic fit
their respective molds. In the United States, voting studies revealed
durable bases of support for the New Deal party system, while in
Western Europe aggregate analyses confirmed the durability of earlier
electoral alignments (Rose and Urwin 1969, 1970a, 1970b). Although
comparable survey research was barely underway, the concept of party
identification, central to the early voting studies, provided an
explanation of the stability of party alignments. According to the
Michigan school (Campbell, Converse, Miller, and Stokes 1960, 1966;
Converse 1969), voters developed psychological loyalties or identifications with political parties which hardened with age and length of
psychological membership. Transmitted to successive generations,
these attachments provided stable bases of support for established
parties. Exceptions such as France, Italy, and West Germany could be
explained by the disruptions and political turmoil which these countries
had experienced: the absence of stable regimes meant that voters had
had less time to develop strong party identifications (Converse 1969;
Converse and Dupeux 1962).

Developments since the 1960s have raised questions about both
the durability of party systems and the clarity of the lenses through
which we view them. In the United States, increases in the proportion
of independent voters in the 1960s and 1970s fueled speculation about
impending realignment and the emergence of new majorities (see Ladd
and Hadley 1978; Phillips 1969). However, speculation about an
emergent conservative majority, a regrouping of progressive forces, or
a redefinition of the centre around a silent majority proved to be
premature. No definitive realignment occurred. Instead, the
continued erosion of strong party identifications, wider swings in
Presidential elections, and the increasingly visible role of political
action committees gave credence to Burnham's claim that what was
occurring was not a generational realignment but rather a new
phenomenon, the dealignment of the electorate and the decomposition
of the party system. Burnham (1970) argued that parties were losing
many of their previous functions. Voters were increasingly independent, the media played a greater role in defining issues, and

single-issue groups and factions dominated recruitment. This had serious consequences: voters lacked the clear-cut referents which a healthier party system could supply, and the failure to reconstruct parties around a new political agenda deprived the United States of the renewal which previous realignments had provided (Burnham 1970, 1975).

At the same time, changes in Western European party systems prompted speculation about dealignment there. From the 1960s onward, electorates in many countries became more volatile, and new parties appeared in countries as diverse as Belgium, the Netherlands, Denmark, Norway, the United Kingdom and, more recently, Germany. Although some faded almost as rapidly as they emerged, others survived. Increased volatility and the presence of new parties rippled through political systems, forcing changes at other levels. In Belgium and the Netherlands, the presence of a larger number of parties complicated the politics of cabinet formation, while in Denmark, the sudden doubling of the number of parties in the *Folketing* from five to ten in 1973 narrowed the bases on which cabinets could be constructed: minority governments were forced to build broader legislative coalitions in order to pass legislation. Even in Britain - previously considered a prototype of two-party competition - changes began to appear: the resurgence of the Liberals and growth in support for Scottish and Welsh nationalists resulted in a minority Labour government after the February 1974 election. Although a second general election in October produced a narrow Labour majority, after 1977, deaths and by-elections forced the Callaghan government to rely on the Liberals for its survival. Later on, divisions in the Labour Party resulted in the formation of the Social Democratic Party (SDP).

Confronted with unanticipated developments, scholars began searching for rubrics under which to subsume them. However, the variety and complexity of change made it difficult to categorise, let alone account for, the ways in which party systems were changing. New parties rarely reflected any single tendency or concern, but rather included forces as diverse as small religious parties (e.g. Calvinist parties in the Netherlands, the Christian Peoples Party in Denmark), right-wing protest parties (the Progress parties in Denmark and Norway and the Front Nationale in France), centre-left or centrist parties (Democrats '66 in the Netherlands, the Social Democratic Party in Britain), linguistic parties (Belgium), and parties of the left (dissident socialist parties and, more recently, the Greens). Moreover, developments were anything but uniform: some party systems, such as the Dutch and the Danish, became more fragmented and more volatile, while others, such as the Swedish and (until recently) the Austrian, barely changed at all. Moreover, even where changes occurred, older patterns did not disappear. Instead, there were substantial elements of continuity: in most countries, older parties not only survived but also governed.

It is this pattern of continuity amid change, present in different degrees in Western European and North American party systems, with which this book is concerned. In contrast to many approaches found in the literature, which stress either demographic changes or value change (see Dalton, Flanagan and Beck 1984; Inglehart 1977), we consider not only changes in voting behaviour, but also political parties as organisations and actors, and the ways in which their moves and countermoves constrain or enhance change. Moreover, we take a broader definition of change and consider not only changes in electoral alignments or the number and kind of parties competing, but also changes in coalition patterns and the ways in which parties present and define themselves.

The Focus Elaborated

Why focus on parties as organisations and actors? One reason is that parties are intermediate structures lodged between citizens and governments. As such, parties are capable of influencing and being influenced by factors as diverse as the preferences of the electorate, the behaviour of other parties, their internal structure, and the institutional and legal setting in which they operate. Although survey research is a powerful tool for analyzing and explaining the behaviour of electorates, it *alone* cannot capture the complex ways in which parties respond to the environments in which they find themselves or the patterns of continuity and change which result.

To say that parties are organisations and actors may appear to do little more than assert the obvious. However, the obvious is something which we sometimes neglect. Since the inception of wide-scale survey research more than two decades ago, a substantial portion of comparative research effort has focussed on the attitudes and reported behaviour of voters. The cumulation of studies in a large number of countries has produced an indispensable body of data mapping the preferences of the electorate in different settings. However, survey research focusses on 'parties in the electorate' (Sorauf 1972; Key 1964): the task of presenting and analyzing the data makes it difficult to examine the behaviour of parties as organisations or actors in any systematic way.[1] As Sartori (1966, 1969) has pointed out, parties are typically treated as a dependent variable - a product of mass preferences and earlier cleavage structures.

In reality, parties are far more than passive recipients of electoral preferences. Parties are organisations which seek votes in order to influence both the direction of public policy and the distribution of public resources (Schlesinger 1984). As such, they exert considerable control over the recruitment of political elites, the formation and operation of governments, and the distribution of public resources. In their quest for power, parties respond to a variety of forces, both immediate and anticipated, including the structure of the electorate, the pressures of internal factions, the moves and countermoves of other parties, and the institutional and legal setting in which they compete. However, parties also influence the environment in which they operate: In contesting elections, parties choose tactics; in doing so, they help to define the political agenda and shape the choices which voters confront. Equally, the strategies which parties employ - whether, for example, they build and rely on subcultures or cater to a broader clientele (Houska 1985) - not only shape, but can also maintain or undermine previous patterns of cleavage. In a different vein, by manipulating electoral laws or regulations governing election finance - or, alternatively, refusing to do so - parties can influence the legal framework under which the contest takes place.

Focussing on parties as organisations and actors allows us to consider not only the ways in which voters respond to a given set of political alternatives, but also the ways in which parties shape and respond to the strategic environment in which they operate. The principal questions confronting researchers concern the ways and extent to which party systems change in light of social and economic change. Except for the long-standing debate on the impact of electoral laws (which rarely addresses the question of social change), analyses of continuity and change in party systems typically focus on parties and the ways in which they are rooted in cleavage structures.[2] Two approaches have been prevalent in the literature: The first, drawing on established traditions in political sociology, relates variations in support for different parties to urbanisation, changes in class and occupational structure, and changing patterns of religiosity. The second relates changes in electoral alignments to the stresses of advanced industrial societies, particularly generational changes and the entry of younger voters more concerned with 'post-material' rather than 'material' values. In this case, the emphasis is not only on the relative size of social groups, but also on value change, particularly the changing perspectives of younger generations, coming of age in a period of affluence rather than scarcity. (Dalton, Flanagan, and Beck 1984; Inglehart 1977)

Although both approaches provide valuable information on social change and the changing predilections of the electorate, neither is, *by itself*, capable of explaining broader patterns of continuity and change in party systems. Focussing on demographic patterns provides us with a portrait of the electorate and how it has changed. Although this helps to explain shifts in the party balance, we get little sense of the extent to which established parties are able to adapt and respond to social changes or the circumstances under which new parties are likely to appear or succeed. The second approach, emphasising value change, pays greater attention to the need for parties to adapt to a changing value structure, but rarely addresses the question of whether and how they do so.[3]

The ways in which parties respond to the changes in the structure and preference of the electorate are crucial if we are to understand continuity and change in party systems. The presence of substantial change in some countries, but its absence in others, suggests that continuity and change in party systems depends not on social change, *per se*, but rather on political factors, such as the ability of parties to adapt to, or otherwise deflect changes in their societies. Although never infinitely flexible, parties are sometimes capable of developing new positions and blurring old ones in order to win the support of different groups. This ability to adapt - which varies from party to party and place to place - helps to explain the continuity of many party alignments. Equally, the failure of some parties to adapt rapidly enough to changing demands and the claims of new groups may explain the rise of new parties in some countries, but not others, despite similar patterns of social change (Mair 1983).

In focussing on parties as organisations and actors, we draw on venerable traditions in the study of political parties. These extend as far back as Ostrogorski ([1902] 1964), who charted the rise and entrenchment of party organisation, and continue through Michels' ([1915] 1959) work on bureaucratisation and deradicalisation of parties and Duverger's ([1951] 1959) classification of party organisations, which posits relationships between electoral laws and the number and kind of political parties in a system. Emphasis on parties as adaptive organisations is also prominent in the literature on realignment in the American party system: generational realignments are usually regarded as the product not only of social change, but also the ways in which parties respond to divergent groups and the emergence of cross-cutting issues (Sundquist 1983).[4] In addition, although not directly concerned with party realignment, Downs' (1957) model of parties as rational vote-maximising actors laid out the assumptions about party tactics and behaviour implicit in many analyses of two-party and multiparty systems. More recently, Sartori (1969, 1976) has underscored not only the importance of considering parties as independent variables, but also the value of regarding party systems, once they have been established, as an 'independent *system of channelment*, propelled and maintained by its own laws of inertia' (Sartori 1969:90). Finally, Mair (1983) has stressed both the importance and the difficulty of examining the ways in which parties adapt to social and economic change.

In examining continuity and change in contemporary party systems, we draw eclectically on these traditions. No single approach is adequate to account for the very diverse patterns of continuity and change we are considering. Because parties are intermediate structures, lodged between citizens and governments, they can be influenced by a variety of factors, including the behaviour of the electorate, their ties to particular interests or clienteles, and the uses which they make of political power and control of the government. All of these, in turn, can affect the continuity of party alignments. However, the factors which stabilise one party system are not necessarily operative in another.

Our approach to change is necessarily broad. Rather than concentrating on any single facet of change, such as increases or decreases in the number of parties or shifts in the party balance - jointly referred to by Pedersen (1983) and others as the *format* of a party system (see also Sartori 1976) - our chapters catalogue a wider variety of phenomena, present in some party systems but not necessarily in others. These include changes in coalition patterns, party positions and the ways in which parties present themselves to the electorate. This approach has been dictated both by the variety of changes which have occurred and by our emphasis on parties as adaptive organisations. Both the extent and ways in which parties are able adapt to changing circumstances vary within and among party systems. Moreover, the consequences of adaption are not always certain: responding to one set of pressures or demands may either deflect pressures and inhibit more extensive changes, or lead to more extensive changes. For example, modifying party positions in order to take account of new demands could either prevent the formation of new parties, or encourage it because other groups were alienated in the process. Limiting our discussion would prevent us from exploring either the very different ways in which some party systems have changed or the devices and tactics which have enabled others to remain the same.

The essays that follow explore continuity and change in Western European and North American party systems, but they do so in different ways. The book begins by considering party system change in France, Italy, and Germany, the three principal exceptions to Lipset and Rokkan's suppositions about the freezing of Western European party alignments. Extending his earlier work, Frank L. Wilson examines the French party system in the 1980s and considers the extent to which changes discernable in the 1970s have continued through the 1980s. Examining Italy, Grant Amyot takes a longer view of a dominant party system. Here the emphasis is on the Christian Democratic regime, its long and gradual demise, and its impact on other parties. William M. Chandler examines the transformation of the West German party system from a highly fragmented to a moderate multiparty system and considers more recent developments, particularly the shift to a Christian Democratic-Liberal coalition and the rise of Greens.

Chapters Five through Eight consider continuity and change in the smaller democracies, which were the mainstays of Lipset and Rokkan's analysis. In Chapter Five, Frederick C. Engelmann examines the continuing stability of the Austrian party system and explores the incipient signs of change now visible there. In Chapter Six, Maureen Covell considers the Belgian party system, tracing the rise of linguistically based parties and the continuing dominance of the three older parties, now divided into separate French and Flemish organisations, despite it all. In Chapter Seven, I examine continuity and change in the Netherlands, particularly the reorientation of the Dutch Socialists and the formation of the Christian Democratic Appeal, replacing separate Catholic and Protestant parties. In Chapter Eight, John Logue and Eric S. Einhorn compare patterns of continuity and change in Denmark, Norway and Sweden, particularly the weakening of Social Democratic rule and the divergent ways in which these previously similar party systems have changed.

The next four chapters consider continuity and change in Great Britain, Ireland, Canada, and the United States. Although these countries, with broadly-based political parties, differ from the continental Western European countries, they are relevant to our analysis. In Chapter Nine, George Breckenridge traces successive changes in British party alignments from the 1890s to the present. In Chapter Ten, R.K. Carty examines the evolution of the Irish party system from a dominant to a bipolar party system. Factional conflicts and political changes such as the decision of Fine Gael to contest elections seriously are central to his analysis. Next, Herman Bakvis considers the 'Canadian paradox', particularly the stability of the party system despite weak electoral attachments. In Chapter Twelve, I examine the ways in which intra-party competition has reshaped the American party system. Here the emphasis is not only on changes in party positions, but the rise of candidate-centred campaigning, political action committees, and technologically proficient national party bureaucracies. Chapter Thirteen draws these diverse strands together and examines continuity and change in Western Europe and North America.

Notes

1. This is changing to some extent. Confronted with the weakness of party organisations and dramatic changes in the ways in which candidates campaign for their nomination in election, students of American electoral behaviour now devote considerable attention to campaign techniques. See Chapter Twelve of this volume and Jacobson (1983).

2. Daalder and Mair (1983) is an exception. Although the emphasis of the volume (the first of a cross-national study of change in Western European party systems) is on quantitative analysis of parties and party systems, several chapters stress organisational factors. See especially the concluding chapter by Peter Mair.

3. See, for example, Inglehart (1984). Arguing, as he has done in the past, that 'the rise of post-materialism has placed existing party alignments under chronic stress' (68), Inglehart notes this could lead to either dealignment, realignment or a new synthesis. However, aside from the suggestion that post-materialist values are likely to receive fuller expression under proportional representation (28-9), there is little attention to the circumstances under which different outcomes are likely.

4. The work of Carll Everett Ladd is an exception in this regard. In both Ladd (1970) and Ladd and Hadley (1978), generational realignments are treated as the product of social change and a changing political agenda.

References

Burnham, Walter Dean (1970) *Critical Elections and the Mainsprings of American Politics* Norton, New York

Burnham, Walter Dean (1975) 'American Politics in the 1970s: Beyond Party?' in Louis Maisel and Paul M. Sacks (eds.), *The Future of Political Parties*, Sage, Beverly Hills, 238-77

Campbell, Angus, Philip E. Converse, Warren E. Miller, and Donald E. Stokes (1960) *The American Voter*, John Wiley, New York

Campbell, Angus, Philip E. Converse, Warren E. Miller, and Donald E. Stokes (1966) *Elections and the Political Order*, John Wiley, New York

Converse, Philip E. (1969) 'Of Time and Partisan Stability' *Comparative Political Studies, 2*, 139-71

Converse, Philip E. and Georges Dupeux (1962) 'Politicization of the Electorate in the United States and France', *Public Opinion Quarterly 26*, 1-23

Daalder, Hans and Peter Mair, eds. (1983) *Western European Party Systems: Continuity and Change*, Sage, London.

Dalton, Russell J., Scott C. Flanagan and Paul Allen Beck (1984) *Electoral Change in Advanced Industrial Societies: Realignment or Dealignment?*, Princeton University Press, Princeton

Downs, Anthony (1957) *An Economic Theory of Democracy*, Harper and Row, New York

Duverger, Maurice ([1951] 1959) *Political Parties: Their Organization and Activity in the Modern State*, John Wiley, New York

Houska, Joseph (1985) *Influencing Mass Political Behavior*, Institute of International Studies, Berkeley

Inglehart, Ronald (1977) *The Silent Revolution: Changing Values and Political Styles Among Western Publics*, Princeton University Press, Princeton

Jacobson, Gary C (1983) *The Politics of Congressional Elections*, Boston, Little Brown

Key, V.O. (1955) 'A Theory of Critical Elections' *Journal of Politics 17*, 3-18

Key, V.O. (1964) *Politics, Parties and Pressure Groups*, 5th ed., Thomas Y. Crowell, New York

Kirchheimer, Otto (1966) 'The Transformation of Western European Party Systems' in Joseph LaPalombara and Myron Weiner (eds.), *Political Parties and Political Development*, Princeton University Press, Princeton, 177-200

Ladd, Carll Everett (1970) *American Political Parties: Social Change and Political Response*, Norton, New York

Ladd and Hadley (1978) *Transformations of the American Party System: Political Coalitions from the New Deal to the 1970s*, 2nd ed., Norton, New York

LaPalombara, Joseph and Myron Weiner (1966) 'The Origin and Development of Political Parties' in Joseph LaPalombara and Myron Weiner (eds.), *Political Parties and Political Development*, Princeton University Press, Princeton, 3-42

Lipset, Seymour Martin and Stein Rokkan (1967) 'Introduction' in Seymour Martin Lipset and Stein Rokkan (eds.), *Party Systems and Voter Alignments: Cross-National Perspectives*, Free Press, New York

Mair, Peter (1983) 'Adaptation and Control: Towards an Understanding of Party and Party System Change' in Hans Daalder and Peter Mair, eds., *Western European Party Systems: Continuity and Change*, Sage, London, 405-31

Michels, Robert ([1915] 1959) *Political Parties: A Sociological Study of the Oligarchical Tendencies of Modern Political Parties*, Dover Publications, New York

Ostrogorski, M. ([1902] 1964) *Democracy and the Organization of Political Parties*, Doubleday Ancnor, Garden City

Pedersen, Mogens N. (1983) 'Changing Patterns of Electoral Volatility in European Party Systems, 1947-77' in Hans Daalder and Peter Mair, eds., *Western European Party Systems: Continuity and Change*, Sage, London, 29-66

Phillips, Kevin P. (1969) *The Emerging Republican Majority*, Arlington House, New Rochelle, N.Y.

Rose, Richard and Derek Urwin (1969) 'Social Cohesion, Parties, and Regime Strains', *Comparative Political Studies, 2*, 7-67

Rose, Richard and Derek Urwin (1970a) 'Persistence and Change in Western Party Systems Since 1945', *Political Studies, 18*, 287-319

Rose, Richard and Derek Urwin (1970b) 'Persistence and Disruption in Western Party Systems Between the Wars' (paper presented at the World Congress of the International Sociological Association, Varna)

Sartori, Giovanni (1966) 'European Political Parties: The Case of Polarized Pluralism" in Joseph LaPalombara and Myron Weiner (eds.), *Political Parties and Political Development*, Princeton University Press, Princeton, 137-76

Sartori, Giovanni (1969) 'From the Sociology of Politics to Political Sociology' in Seymour Martin Lipset, ed. *Politics and the Social Sciences*, Oxford University Press, New York, 65-100

Sartori, Giovanni (1976) *Parties and Party Systems: A Framework for Analysis*, Cambridge University Press, Cambridge

Schlesinger, Joseph A. (1984) 'On the Theory of Party Organization', *Journal of Politics, 46*, 369-400

Sorauf, Frank J. (1972) *Party Politics in America*, 2nd ed., Little Brown, Boston

Sundquist, James L. (1983) *Dynamics of the Party System: Alignment and Realignment of Political Parties in the United States*, (rev. ed.) Brookings Institution, Washington, D.C.

Chapter Two

The French Party System In The 1980s

Frank L. Wilson

While the party systems in several other European countries were experiencing crises during the 1960s and 1970s, the once troublesome French party system was replaced by a new pattern of party relations more conducive to stable democracy (Wilson 1982). The transformation of French parties resulted in the following new features: (1) the emergence of a dominant majority coalition composed of the Gaullists and their allies; (2) the reintegration of the Communist party into French politics, the renewal and radicalisation of the Socialist party, and the formation of a durable Socialist-Communist alliance; (3) a trend toward a dualist party system based on two stable multiparty coalitions; (4) strengthened party organisation including renewed membership growth, heightened party discipline, hierarchical control, and centrally imposed restrictions on lower level party units; (5) the nationalisation and personalisation of parties and election campaigns; (6) a movement toward the clear-cut government-opposition dialogue characteristic of 'party government'.

French experience suggested several sources of party transformation with direct or indirect effects on the parties (Wilson 1980). As indicated in figure 2.1, socioeconomic change had the most distant impact on party transformation and one that largely consisted of contributing to a general milieu that was favorable to party change. Changes in the political culture were only slightly more likely to affect party transformation. Both socio-economic and cultural changes were more likely to be useful in understanding long-term evolution in voter alignments than in explaining the dramatic and rapid shifts in party styles, organisations, or tactics. Changes in political institutions had a more direct impact on party transformation, but they had their most pronounced effect when they altered the competitive situation - as they did after 1962 with the installation of a popularly elected president. Changes in the competitive situation seemed to have the most decisive effects on party transformation. Entry of new competitors, discovery of new tactics and approaches by a competitor, change in the rules of competition, the addition of new electoral 'prizes', and shifts in the competitive balance of parties were usually the most direct cause of party transformation. The growth of the Gaullists in the 1960s, for example, provided the major impetus for transformation in a number of other parties (Lawson 1981).

Figure 2.1 A Model of Party Transformation

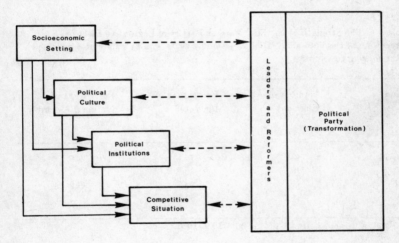

Source: Reprinted from Frank L. Wilson, 'Sources of Party Transformation: The Case of France' in P.H. Merkl (ed.), *Western European Party Systems: Trends and Prospects* (Free Press, 1980).

The new party system that emerged by the mid-1970s provides a reference point for evaluating trends in the French party system. As the changes became evident in the 1970s, one central question which remained was whether the earlier transformations would survive the transfer of power from the Right to the Left. Now, with two transfers, first to the Left in 1981 and then back to the Right in 1986, there is firm evidence of the permanence of these new characteristics of the French party system.

Confirmation of Previous Party Transformations

One of the most significant changes since 1958 has been the replacement of a party system characterised by extreme fragmentation with a party system in which only four parties have national significance: the Gaullists (RPR), the Giscardians (UDF), the Socialists (PS), and the Communists (PCF). These four parties held virtually all seats in the National Assembly and received the vast majority of the votes cast in national elections. As table 2.1 illustrates, the share of votes controlled by the largest four parties jumped dramatically in 1981 from 87.3 per cent to 98.7 per cent. Even the introduction of proportional representation for the 1986 election did not break the dominance of the major parties, who still won 82.4 per cent of the vote and 91.5 per cent of the seats.

Table 2.1 The Strength of the Four Largest Parties in Legislative Elections. (Percentage of the vote and National Assembly seats won by candidates endorsed by the four largest parties.)

Period	Number of Elections	Percentage of the vote[a]	Percentage of National Assembly seats
1946-56	(3)	76.6	72.9
1958-78	(6)	85.3	87.2
1981	(1)	98.7	96.9
1986	(1)	82.4	91.5

Note: a. Based on first ballot results 1956-1981.

Since 1981, the major parties have fended off yet another attempt to revive a centrist party. A much publicised centrist alternative led by several prominent politicians proved an electoral disaster in the 1984 European Parliament elections. The allure of environmental parties such as the Greens in Germany has no parallel in France. The major parties continue to reach out and absorb the voters and sometimes the activists of the remaining smaller parties. Recently, the PS made one more attempt to incorporate the dwindling Unified Socialist Party (PSU). There are now far more ex-PSU members in the PS than active members remaining in the once influential PSU. However, the rise of a new party on the far Right, the National Front, runs counter to the trend.

Nor is the return to proportional representation mandated by the Socialists in 1985 likely to be a serious obstacle to maintaining the reduced number of parties. The threshold for entrance into the National Assembly is set at five percent, but the practical requirement is much greater since the districts are based on *départements* which may have as few as three or four deputies. This kept all the small parties out of parliament in the 1986 elections. In any case, proportional representation is likely to be a passing phenomenon since the new conservative majority pledged an immediate return to a two-ballot majority electoral system.

The Polarisation of the French Party System

A second feature of the Fifth Republic's party system is continued polarisation. The emergence of a genuine government-opposition division to replace the universal opposition of the Third and Fourth Republics has not been accompanied by responsible dialogue between the government and opposition. Dualism has not produced the expected moderation of politics; instead, the Left and Right remain sharply polarised.

In part, the polarisation is due to the continued importance of well-developed party ideologies that offer radically different visions of society for the Left and Right. But often seemingly radical policy differences between Left and Right frequently amount to little more than *blanc bonnet* and *bonnet blanc*: '...the only difference is found in the personality of each of the leaders, a difference that is far from being enormous' (Schonfeld 1983, p. 71). Even if the differences on specific issues are more apparent than real, the psychological distance between party elites produces a near violent political rhetoric. The mistrust and mutual hatred are so intense that they make even ceremonial gestures at cooperation difficult. While the conservatives ruled, the left-wing opposition parties threatened disorder, subversion, and anarchy to discredit the government and attempt to block its policies. When the Left took power, it was the Right which opposed the government as if it were illegal and illegitimate (Rémond, 1983).

The psychological distance between these two camps explains the tense conditions of the changes in power in 1981 and 1986 and the vitriolic exchanges that characterise government/opposition dialogue. After decades in opposition, the parties of the Left saw their return to office as a chance to rectify years of neglect of those they represented and the opportunity to settle some old scores. At the first Socialist party congress after the Left's victory, many activists complained at the slow pace of rectification and one prominent leader demanded that heads fall. In the country of the 'terror', such lurid rhetoric did little to appease the worries of the opposition.

The Socialist government's efforts to move toward a new socioeconomic order accentuated polarisation. Government and party leaders spoke of sweeping reform measures using terminology that fueled apprehensions: a rupture with capitalism, elimination of exploiters, making the wealthy pay, and so forth. Most legislation was rather moderate in content, but some seemed to endanger the existing social order: nationalisation of several large industries and private banks, a wealth tax, new regulations to protect tenants, and several labor relations decrees and laws. Some conservatives, usually from small business circles rather than from the parties, evoked Chilean precedents as a possible resolution of what they saw as a parallel deterioration of the socioeconomic order under socialism. Given the importance of rhetorical and psychological polarisation, it is not surprising that moderation of Socialist policies after 1983 did little to reduce inter-party tensions in France.

Nationalisation of French Parties

During the 1960s and 1970s, nation-wide political parties emerged to challenge the regional party preferences which previously had carved the nation into nearly impregnable partisan fiefdoms. The Gaullists won election in areas where conservatives had rarely been seen; later the Socialists penetrated conservative redoubts. Throughout France, the four major parties were serious contenders in national and local elections.

The 1981 Socialist victory was marked by significant PS penetration of areas long regarded as conservative terrain. Socialist gains tended to be greatest where they had previously been weakest. More evidence of this was seen in the 1986 elections when the pendulum swung back to the Right. The Right's gains were especially important in areas where it had previously been weak, notably in several previously Communist dominated Paris suburbs. These alterations in electoral geography go beyond transitory fluctuations in voter preference; they suggest that voters everywhere see the same party options and give serious consideration to all major parties. The traditional geographic partisan loyalties are still present but no longer exclude challenges from other parties.

Party Change Since 1981

The most significant change in the French party system in the 1980s has been the precipitous decline of the Communist Party. Since the Second World War, the PCF had been the best organised party of the Left and the one with the strongest electoral appeal. By the end of the 1970s, the PCF had lost its electoral advantage to the rapidly growing Socialist party but still retained the loyal support of the 22 per cent of the electorate it had held since 1958. The 1981 election confirmed PCF fears of electoral decline: in the 1978 National Assembly elections, Communist candidates had taken 20.6 per cent of the total votes; three years later, they won only 16.2 per cent. The 1986 election confirmed the decline: PCF strength dropped to 9.8 per cent, the lowest since 1924.

As the PCF's membership has fallen and the level of commitment of many of those who remain has decreased, the party has come to rely more heavily on its militant core. Unfortunately for the party, the number of these activists, who take regular part in cell meetings and political actions, has also decreased. Jenson and Ross (1984) suggest that the number of activists in 1981 had fallen by one-third since 1978-79. With fewer activists, the party must rely on its paid party workers, most of whom come from the party's patronage positions in local government and union officials serving on plant committees. However, the party's heavy losses in municipal elections and the decline of the Communist-dominated General Confederation of Labour (CGT) have reduced their availability.

This is linked directly to the strength of the Socialist Party. For more than twenty years, the PCF had based its appeal on its standing as the most powerful and only significant party of the Left. The rapid growth of the PS during the 1970s changed this situation. No longer the largest party on the Left, it began to see some of its supporters vote Socialist. Mitterrand's Socialist Party had assumed the PCF's old place as the most effective and dynamic party of the Left.

In responding, PCF leaders are trapped by the conflicting preferences of their two key clienteles. The majority of activists favor a return to the hard-line revolutionary posture in the face of an increasingly hostile environment. The remaining Communist voters, however, prefer moderation and renewed cooperation with the Socialist party. The result is near paralysis. From 1981 through 1986, the PCF vacillated between opposition and support for the Socialist government. The survival of the PCF as a major political force in France may well be at stake. Elsewhere in Western Europe during the 1940s and 1950s, the Communist parties that confronted effective socialist parties were quickly marginalised. This change in the French Communist Party's competitive situation *vis-à-vis* the Socialist party is the source of its current crisis. While the PCF is unlikely to

17

disappear completely, it may survive only 'as a declining museum piece' with few traces of its once great power as principal spokesman for the French working class (Jenson and Ross 1984:340).

The Rise of the National Front

Until recently many felt that the incorporation of the often anti-democratic extreme Right in moderate and democratic parties was one of the major accomplishments of the Gaullist era. The stunning rise of the far rightist national front (FN) in the past three years casts this into doubt. In its law and order rhetoric, the FN makes little attempt to disguise its appeal to racist sentiments against the primarily North African and Middle Eastern immigrants.

Racist attitudes exist among the French people but the mainline parties, with only a few temporary lapses, have refused to exploit these sentiments. That has left the field open to the National Front. In the 1984 European elections, the FN won an astounding 2,210,000 votes or 10.95 per cent of the total, only slightly below the PCF figures. This success gave an aura of legitimacy and durability to a movement many had dismissed as on the margins of politics. This brought previously hesitant sympathisers out into the open and the party's organisation began to acquire real substance (Plenel and Rollat 1984). The FN won 9.7 per cent of the vote and elected 35 deputies in 1986.

It is too early to assess the impact of the National Front on the party system. Under the Fourth Republic, 'flash' parties made spectacular entries onto the political scene only to disappear by the next election. It is clear that the FN's law and order and anti-immigrant themes appealed to an important sector of the electorate. But the FN's position on the margins of respectability, with little hope of establishing alliances with the mainline conservative parties will limit its influence. In addition, if the new conservative government restores a majority electoral system, the FN is likely to lose its deputies and face a critical test of its ability to survive.

A Decline of Socialist Ideology?

During the Socialist revival in the 1970s, one expected change that did not occur was the reduction of the party's ideological baggage. French socialists scorned the class compromises of social democrats elsewhere in western Europe and insisted on a pure socialist doctrine. The PS retained a program couched in the terminology of class warfare and called for a revolutionary break with monopoly capitalism.

In its early months, the Socialist government tried to achieve some of its goals by nationalising banks and industries and extending government intervention in the economy. However, PS leaders soon began to back away from some of their ideologically based actions in response to growing economic problems and public disinterest. In addition, the real world exigencies of policy making were fully sensed by Socialist officials getting their first experience in government in 23 years. By 1985, the government's retreat from its doctrine was universal. There was little difference between Socialist 'rigour' and the conservative 'austerity' of the Giscard years. Reform of private schools was shelved and Socialist government officials made an uneasy peace with the business and farm leaders they had earlier scorned as class enemies. Observers began to talk of a new pragmatism on the part of French Socialists produced by the educative effects of the government experience (Thibaud 1983).

It remains to be seen whether this trend will be translated into doctrinal and stylistic changes in the party. Party activists remain much more attached to ideological values than party leaders who held public office; Socialist deputies are still strongly committed to a pure socialism. Demands for ideological consistency limit the leadership's ability to avoid its ideology. As the party revived in the 1970s, one theme shared by all factions was contempt for earlier Socialist government officials who failed to defend party doctrine while in office. Any effort to preach pragmatism within the party must contend with strong sentiment against 'class collaboration'.

It is not clear that Socialist party leaders want to carry out this education of their party. Even while they were governing in a thoroughly non-doctrinaire manner, Mitterrand and his associates still frequently evoked Socialist principles. In doing so, they betrayed a lingering attachment to their principles even if circumstances forced them to act contrary to their beliefs. Out of office, Socialist leaders will likely return to their usual ideological predilections. Ideology serves several useful functions for the party: It offers explanations for their inability to break the hold of capitalism and provides hope for a brighter future and ideological debate has been one of the major animating forces for the Socialist party. Moreover, ideological loyalty is needed to prevent a Communist resurgence based in the Socialist party's 'turn to the Right'. As a result, ideology and factional disputes linked to it will resume importance as the PS struggles to regain momentum after defeat.

The 1981 electoral victories came at a time when the party was committed to a doctrinaire socialist program. They gave the illusion that such appeals are electorally successful and that the oft-hoped for *front de classes* had a basis in reality. During the campaign, Mitterrand deliberately ignored these ideological positions; his victory was due more to voters' dissatisfaction with the conservatives' long rule than his party's ideology. Nevertheless, it is probable that in future disputes over ideology, these victories will be cited by those who seek doctrinal purity and become another impediment to the adoption of a more pragmatic stance by the French Socialist party.

A Breakdown in the Unity of the Two Blocs?

The cohesive coalitions of parties on the Left and Right that had given France a dualist party system during the 1960s and 1970s began to break down by the end of the 1970s. On the Left, PCF Communist leaders redirected their major competitive thrust from attacks on the Right to devastating criticism of the Socialist party and especially of Mitterrand. On the Right, conflict between the Gaullists and Giscardians, which peaked in presentation of several right-wing candidates in the 1981 presidential election, was so bitter that many Gaullist voters either abstained or voted for Mitterrand rather than Giscard on the second ballot after their own candidates were eliminated. The breakdown of the dualist pattern that had been a prominent feature of party change was thus instrumental in the election of Mitterrand (*Le Monde* 1981:139-41).

At first glance, the problems between the PCF and the PS might seem to indicate a collapse of the Left pole of the dualist system. However, despite the Communists' move to the opposition and the deterioration of formal relations between the PCF and the PS, the Left pole remains and voters on all points of the spectrum still perceive the presence of a left-wing bloc as one of the primary political options. However, the Left is increasingly identified with the Socialist Party alone. Some of the PCF's losses in 1986 came from voters who had previously voted PCF on the first ballot and then rallied to the Socialists on the second. With only one ballot in the 1986 electoral system, these people voted directly for the Socialists. More important, Mitterrand, whose political career has been based on left-wing unity, has come to personify the Left. His party's paramount position on the Left maintains the Left bloc even if the PCF has formally abandoned the union of the Left. The persistence of the Left/Right dualism despite Communist efforts to recall their supporters to a more isolated leftism confirms the supremacy of the PS over the PCF and portends further decline for the Communists.

Any hope of rebuilding formal unity between the PCF and the PS disappeared with the adoption of proportional representation. In the past, the two-ballot electoral system made an arrangement for reciprocal withdrawals for the run-off ballot essential for both parties. The new electoral system offers no incentive for cooperation and encourages the two parties to campaign independently. For the PCF, cooperation with the Socialists is now a thing of the past. The Socialists continue to capitalise on the still popular notion of the union of the Left but portray their party as the sole representative of left-wing unity. The likely return to a two-ballot system will renew the electoral incentive for dualism but in a setting where the Communists will be clearly subordinate and fortunate to represent the Left in only a handful of second ballot run-offs.

On the Right, the disunity of the late 1970s was quickly patched up after 1981. The shock of defeat, which they attributed to their squabbling, led the Gaullist and Giscardian parties to put their earlier disagreements behind them in order to organise opposition to the Socialist government. In part, their renewed unity is a natural result of the new balance of party power. Once the Giscardians were ousted from the Elysée Palace, they no longer could challenge the power of the better organised Gaullist Party. The immediate objective of organising to defeat the Left in municipal and legislative elections permitted them to put aside their most contentious division - the presence in their ranks of three would-be conservative presidential candidates.

With few substantive policy differences, unity has been reestablished between Gaullists and Giscardians in the common front against the Socialist 'menace'. Even the potentially divisive proportional electoral system failed to break the unity of the conservative parties in the 1986 elections. In most districts a single list was presented and in those districts where rival Giscardian and Gaullist lists faced each other, there competition was polite and conducive to unity. The rivalry of three presidential aspirants, former president Giscard d'Estaing, former prime minister Raymond Barre, and Gaullist leader and current prime minister Jacques Chirac, remains but the narrow majority the conservatives won in 1986 will force the right to avoid internal divisions.

Divisions on both the Left and the Right have not destroyed the overriding dualism that had emerged during the 1960s and 1970s. The choice between Left and Right remains central and it is supported even by voters whose parties quarrel from time to time. Opinion polls have shown that many French citizens say they prefer to be governed by the centre rather than by either ideological pole. But each time a group claiming the banner of centrism has offered itself at the polls, the same people go on voting for the Gaullists or Giscardians on the Right or the Socialists or Communists on the Left.

French Parties and Their Environment

The breadth and depth of the Socialist majority in 1981 was so impressive that some speculated about a profound reordering of French political life. Socialist leaders, in particular, saw a confirmation of their strategy of building a new leftist electoral coalition based on the notion of a *front de classe*. Aware that socioeconomic changes were making it impossible to base an electoral majority only on the working class, Socialist leaders sought to attract sections of the new middle class: educators, technicians, engineers, clerks, salespeople, farm workers, accountants, professionals, civil servants, and even lower-level managers. These people were presumed to have common interests with the working class in that they too were exploited by their employers and alienated from the large, impersonal bureaucratic organisations in which they typically worked. Once alerted to their oppressed state, they were believed to be ready to join the workers in pressing for a rupture with capitalism.

On the surface, the 1981 results seemed to indicate that this realignment had taken place. The Socialist party polled well in virtually all socioeconomic groups and drew more votes than any other party in all of the major occupational divisions used by French pollsters. However, a more cautious and probably more accurate interpretation would take into account other factors that explain the broad support won by the Socialists (Machin 1982). Divisions within the right-wing coalition alienated many moderate voters and led others to vote for the Left to punish rival rightist parties. Equally importantly, many farmers, small businessmen, middle-level managers, and others voted Socialist because they had legitimate reasons for dissatisfaction with the Giscardian administration and not because of any lasting attachment to the Socialists. This explains the Left's lack of success in consolidating these gains. Despite this swelling of Socialist support in 1981 (Pierce and Rochon 1984), the electoral pattern suggests more continuity than change (Lewis-Beck 1984).

Despite this pattern of electoral stability, there is still considerable fluidity in political behaviour between elections. Over the past decade, French voters have shown a willingness to send messages of disapproval to parties which they have supported in the past and which they intend to support in the future. This represents a major shift; during the first twenty years of the Fifth Republic voters displayed a strong reluctance to vote against the party in power. The party system now permits voters to contemplate a rotation in power and even the cohabitation of a president from one party and a parliamentary majority from another that a decade ago seemed impossible. Even if the older patterns of voting allegiance remain largely intact, some voters on the fringes of both the Left and Right shift back and forth in ways that did not happen before. French voters, like other European electorates, are demonstrating that voting is 'a more volitional and mysterious act than most of us had thought' (Rogowski 1981:649).

Parties and the Economy

There appears to be a clear relationship between the country's economic health and voting patterns (Lewis-Beck and Bellucci 1982; Lewis-Beck 1983). A president's standing with the French public depends primarily on the country's economic performance in terms of real income growth (Hibbs and Vasilatos 1981). Most of the studies were made during the years that the Left was in opposition; as the economy worsened, voters were more likely to vote for leftist parties. The relationship was a strong one, as reliable a predictor of electoral outcomes as a pre-election opinion poll. The proclivity to vote leftist applied not only in the case of a collective judgment of overall national economic decline but also at the microlevel in that individuals who perceived their own economic situation to be deteriorating were more likely to vote for the Left than other voters. The declining economy during the 1970s thus paved the way for the 1981 Socialist victory.

This correlation between economic discontent and a vote for the Left is consistent with French voting patterns in the recent past, but the Left is not the only beneficiary of economic difficulties. The Left paid electorally for the economic problems under its government even though voters did not expect the Right to be any more successful in solving France's economic difficulties (Lewis-Beck 1985). The economic vote is thus more a sanction for past failings than a vote for promising alternatives. There is little evidence to support conservative fears or radical hopes that the continuing economic problems in industrial democracies are producing new backing for major transformation of the socioeconomic order. We have already seen the plummeting support for the PCF; other parties from the far Left have low levels of popular support or are declining. The failure of Socialist economic policies, especially those of the first year in office, which were more in harmony with traditional leftist doctrine than later economic measures, seems to have dispelled any lingering beliefs among the general public that alternative economic orders offer hope for resolving the actual economic problems of advanced industrial democracies. Nor, as we have seen, is the increased appeal of the far Right based on an alternative vision of the economy. Thus, the worst economic crisis in France since the Great Depression had done nothing to promote sympathy for parties advocating radically different social and economic structures.

Parties and Interest Groups

The recent rise of single interest groups that has wreaked havoc on established political parties in other western democracies has not had much effect on France. The close competition between Left and Right has kept public attention focused on the political parties rather than on special interest groups. Some single issue groups have despaired of influencing the parties and have presented their own lists of candidates. Thus, large slates of ecologists and feminists have contested recent parliamentary elections hoping to attract enough voters to call attention to their cause and perhaps to place them in the position of mediating the results of the second ballot run-offs. This strategy has been counter-productive because the audience attracted by their candidates has been too small. The ecologists have never taken more than 4.4 per cent of the vote; the women's candidates in 1978 polled only 1.5 per cent. In addition, these groups have been unsuccessful in controlling the second ballot behaviour of their voters so that they cannot trade crucial run-off support for pledges to pay attention to their causes. The demonstrations of electoral weakness by such groups reduce their ability to influence the parties. Since they are political rivals and have not helped the electoral efforts of the major parties, the parties feel no obligation after the elections to pay heed to their demands. This was particularly obvious in the case of the ecologists after the victory of the Left. Their influence declined despite the presence in office of a party presumably more attuned to environmental issues that the conservatives had been.

Many expected the trade unions to gain in political influence with the victory of the Left. This did not turn out to be the case; the unions had no more influence than they did under conservative governments (Wilson 1985). Initially, the Socialists encouraged the trade unions to take a more active part and to permit their leaders to assume governmental positions. But early optimism about a greater role for trade unions soon faded. One reason was the crisis that the trade union movement was experiencing. The labour movement was divided more deeply than it had been for 20 years. The unions most closely associated with the government parties were losing membership and those members that remained were less dedicated. The divisions and organisational problems meant that the unions were not in a position to take advantage of the more favourable government. The government found the unions too divided to give it either support or useful suggestions on policy matters.

The neo-corporatist trend observed elsewhere in Europe has not made much headway in France (Wilson 1983). The Socialists talked a great deal about their desire to promote more dialogue but concrete steps toward greater group participation in the policy process were few and hesitant. Early and costly confrontations with the farmers and business community were replaced with cautious efforts to get along in public. But the key decision powers remained in the hands of the administrators and political leaders who consulted with and paid heed to only those whom they chose.

In contrast to the vulnerability of parties to pressure group politics during the Fourth Republic, parties now are much better able to resist this influence. Under the Socialists, the major challenge came from the powerful public education lobby. Since the educators' involvement in the disastrous battle over subsidies to private education, even these interests are now muted. Much of the reduction in the role of the interest groups came earlier in the Fifth Republic as the parties increased their central control and discipline. The lessened political effect of groups also reflects the shift of policy-making power away from the parliament and to the administration with a resulting loss of influence for both groups and parliament.

The Relevance of Parties

The revitalisation of French parties during the 1960s and 1970s did not bring with it a strengthened role for parties in the policy process. De Gaulle's mistrust of even those parties who proclaimed allegiance to him kept them at a distance from the policy process. De Gaulle and his conservative successors drew on the party leaders and their supporters in parliament to fill the various ministerial posts but once in government, the ministers were expected to be on holiday from their parties. They frequently bypassed the parties and named senior civil servants and other non-political figures to top government offices. Neither the Gaullists nor the Giscardians were interested in formulating programs that went beyond a simple pledge to support the action and policy of their president. Only on rare occasions were party leaders consulted for advice on policy matters. Even the crucial issues of cabinet formation and the distribution of portfolios among the majority parties were imposed by the president without party leaders. Individually and collectively, Gaullist and Giscardian party figures were able to bring new ideas or point out problems to the executive; but the executive steadfastly resisted bargaining with parties *per se* over programs or policies or ministerial portfolios.

It was widely expected that this situation would change when the

Socialists took power. The PS had long criticised its conservative rivals for their puppet status and its leaders had insisted that democratic procedures required greater respect for the ideas of the government parties and their parliamentary groups. In practice, Mitterrand and his prime minister worked to increase dialogue with their party colleagues. Twice a week, they met with Socialist leaders to discuss current policy and political issues. These regular meetings drew the government's attention to the concerns of rank-and-file party members and aided the government in deflecting opposition from within its parliamentary majority. On occasion, the impact of the party on policy was important. The most dramatic, and ultimately disastrous, party intervention was its joining the education lobby to pressure the government into toughening the proposed restrictions on private schools.

The role of parties in forming the cabinet seems to have been slightly expanded. This was first evident in the Socialist government formed in 1981 when the entrance of the Communist party into the government was prepared by lengthy negotiations between PCF and PS leaders; however, Mitterrand retained final power to determine which Communist leaders were actually named and which portfolios to give them. But the Elysée Palace under Mitterrand jealously guarded its powers of cabinet making. Socialist party leader Lionel Jospin described the party's tasks as 'informing, criticising and pricking' the government but added in an almost Gaullist voice that 'to defend [the government's] policies is to defend our policies' (*Le Monde*: 23 October 1981).

In 1986, with a parliamentary majority different from his own allegiance, Mitterrand was forced to concede important powers over the formation of the government to the majority political parties. The conservative parties' designation of Jacques Chirac as the most acceptable prime minister virtually dictated his selection. In the deliberations over the composition of the government, Mitterrand was able to exercise a veto over the key ministries of defense and foreign affairs and over certain persons he deemed offensive. In effect, the process by which the 1986 Chirac government was formed reversed the usual pattern and resulted in important influence for the majority parties. But this was due to the exceptional circumstances of a Socialist president and a conservative majority sharing power. If political harmony between the president and parliament is restored, it is likely that the president will reassert his power to form governments with little reference to the parties.

Do Parties Make a Difference?

Observers often wonder whether it makes any difference which party controls the government. All governments confront the same international and domestic settings and these environmental conditions are beyond the control of the government. Even socialist governments face these constraints as they accept the imperatives of maintaining consent that their democratic proclivities place upon them (Przeworski 1980). A study of the impact of parties on British policies concluded:

> Much of a party's record in office will be stamped upon it by forces outside its control. British parties are not the primary forces shaping the destiny of British society; it is shaped by something stronger than parties. (Rose 1984:142)

The same might be said of French parties. The international situation, domestic political and social trends, economic forces, administrative processes, tides of public opinion, the prevailing political culture, and the flow of events all affect the policy outcomes more profoundly and less predictably than do party programs and doctrines. Such forces dictate their own policy in some areas. All governments, for example, must impose controls of inflation, budget deficits, and international trade balances. Even in the case of Socialist rule in France, with government leaders ardently committed to a doctrinaire socialism, the attempt to enact distinctive policies reflecting the party's doctrinal positions failed. Economic policy was ultimately dominated by these constraining factors and taken *de facto* out of the hands of Socialists who would have followed other agendas than those forced on them by uncontrollable circumstances. In other policy areas, where governments do act in accord with their programs, these insurmountable forces simply distort the new policies in their implementation stage. Thus, the daring Socialist initiatives in decentralisation and labour-management relations seem destined to fall far short of their aspirations as they are reshaped during the actual enactment phase.

The recognition that there are universal constraints on policy makers does not mean that parties do not make a difference. There remain many important ways in which various parties do things differently in ways that are meaningful to citizens. In France in the 1980s, there can be few citizens who have not in some way, for better or ill, felt the impact of policies inspired by Socialist doctrine. Social benefits are higher than they would have been had the conservatives retained power; rent controls have kept housing costs under control and increased tenants' rights, albeit modestly; many workers enjoy longer paid vacations and nearly all have seen the work week reduced by at least an hour; the costs of public services, such as transportation, housing, and medical care, have been kept at lower levels than otherwise would have been the case; a wealth tax, admittedly riddled by loopholes, hits private fortunes which were previously untaxed; and so on. Such minor policies lack the allure of grand policy but they are not negligible. In many ways, the fact that Paris subway fares have been kept very low has a greater impact in the eyes of citizens than does an abstract policy to combat inflation. The possibility of retirement at 60 is more meaningful for most citizens than the transfer of power in French *départements* from the prefects to the presidents of elected general councils. Thus, parties do make a difference in the issues that are within their control and on many of the issues touching most directly those who make the electoral decisions.

Toward More Party Transformation?

Experience over the past five years seems to confirm the argument made at the beginning of this chapter that party changes come in response to alterations in the competitive situation. The PCF's separation from the Union of the Left and its repudiation of Eurocommunism is attributable to its loss of competitive advantage with respect the its Socialist rival. Its loss of electoral support is due less to socioeconomic changes than to the allure of the Socialist party to once loyal Communist voters. Conflict and disunity on the Right in the late 1970s was also due to changing competitive terms between Gaullists and Giscardians. Ouster from government and the new competitive setting in opposition forced these parties back together. The rise of the National Front is better explained by the major parties' neglect of the immigrant issue and voters' desires to show their ardent opposition to the Socialist government than by cultural changes or even socioeconomic changes. Even a major societal development such as the presence of large numbers of immigrants does not explain the appeal of the far Right: foreign workers have been present in the same numbers for at least ten to fifteen years. The possible shift by the Socialists to a less doctrinaire political style is still very tentative. Even if it does occur, it is less likely to be the result of attitudinal changes in society as a whole - which had taken place much earlier - than the consequence of new competition and hard-knock experience in public office.

Decentralisation may provide attractive new electoral rewards that will lead to party transformation. The enhanced powers of the general councils, the regional assemblies, and the indirectly elected presidents of both these bodies make these elected posts more significant than in the past. The presence of such local prizes might well counter some of the centralising effects of recent years and lead to a resurgence of the influence of local notables. Thus far, the decentralisation reforms have not increased the influence of parties over local policies (Schain 1985:15). Over the long term, local party units may yet emerge as significant actors in their municipalities and departments.

The single most likely source of further change in the party system is the manipulation of the electoral laws. Should the new government fail to return to a majority electoral system, proportional representation would permit the National Front to consolidate its gains and enable the Communist party to survive. But a return to a two-ballot majority system would likely bring the demise of the National Front and probably even the Communist party.

As important as this simplification process has been, the real test for the French party system is the need for reducing polarisation. With a broad consensus on institutions and socioeconomic policies, there is no popular basis for the intense divisions between French parties. The experiment in 'cohabitation' between a Socialist president and a conservative parliamentary majority may mark the beginning of a relaxation of partisan tensions. Or the tensions coming out of that forced marriage of Left and Right may only exacerbate the divisions among the political elite. The tendency of French politicians of all stripes to cling to their ideological shibboleths even as they engage in pragmatic policies and politics suggests that depolarisation is still far off.

References

Hibbs, D. with N. Vasilatos, (1981) 'Economics and Politics in France: Economic Performance and Mass Political Support for Presidents Pompidou and Giscard d'Estaing', *European Journal of Political Research, 9,* 133-45

Hoffmann, S. (1980) 'French Politics: June - November 1979', *The Tocqueville Review, 2,* 146-54

Jenson, J. and G. Ross, (1984) *The View From Inside: A French Communist Cell in Crisis,* University of California Press, Berkeley

Lawson, K. (1981) 'The Impact of Party Reform on Party Systems: The Case of the RPR of France', *Comparative Politics, 13,* 401-19

Le Monde. (1981) *L'Election présidentielle de 1981,* Le Monde, Paris

Lewis-Beck, M. (1983) 'Economics and the French Voter: A Microanalysis', *Public Opinion Quarterly, 47,* 347-60

Lewis-Beck, M. (1984) 'France: The Stalled Electorate', in R.J. Dalton, *et al.*, *Electoral Change in Advanced Industrial Democracies: Realignment or Dealignment*, Princeton University Press, Princeton

Lewis-Beck, M. and P. Bellucci, (1982) 'Economic Influences on Legislative Elections in Multiparty Systems: France and Italy', *Political Behavior, 4*, 93-107

Lewis-Beck, M. (1985) 'Un Modèle de prévision des élections législatives françaises avec une application pour 1986', *Revue Française de Science Politique, 35*, 1080-1091

Machin, H. (1981) 'The *Third Ballot* of 1981: The French Legislative Election of 14 and 21 June', *West European Politics, 5*, 94-9

Pierce, R. and T.R. Rochon, (1984) 'The French Socialist Victories of 1981 and the Theory of Elections', Paper presented at the 1984 Annual Meeting of the American Political Science Association, Washington, D.C.

Platone, R. and J. Ranger, (1981) 'L'Echec du Parti Communiste française aux élections du printemps 1981', *Revue Française de Science Politique, 31*, 1015-37

Plenel, E. and A. Rollat, (1984) *L'Effet Le Pen*, Editions La Découverte - Le Monde, Paris

Przeworski, A. (1980) 'Social Democracy as a Historical Phenomenon', *New Left Review*, 122

Rémond, R. (1983) 'La Droite d'aujourd'hui ressemble-t-elle à l'idée que s'en fait la gauche?', *Projet, 175*, 454-62

Rogowski, R. (1981) 'Social Class and Partisanship in European Electorates: A Re-Assessment', *World Politics, 33*, 639-50

Rose, R. (1984) *Do Parties Make a Difference?* 2nd ed., Chatham House, Chatham, N.J.

Schain, M.A. (1985) *French Communism and Local Power: Urban Politics and Political Change*, St. Martin's, New York

Schonfeld, W.R. (1983) 'Scénes de la vie politique française', *La Revue Tocqueville, 5*, 39-73

Thibaud, P. (1983) 'Le Choix du pragmatisme', *Esprit, 12*, 98-113

Wilson, F.L. (1980) 'Sources of Party Transformation: The Case of France', in P.H. Merkl (ed.), *Western European Party Systems*, The Free Press, New York

Wilson, F.L. (1982) *French Political Parties Under the Fifth Republic*, Praeger, New York

Wilson, F.L. (1983) 'French Interest Group Politics: Pluralist or Neo-Corporatist', *American Political Science Review, 77*, 116-29

Wilson, F.L. (1985) 'Trade Unions and Economic Policy,' in H. Machin and V. Wright (eds.), *Economic Policy and Policy-Making Under the Mitterrand Presidency 1981-1984*, Frances Pinter, London

Chapter Three

Italy: The Long Twilight of the DC Regime

G. Grant Amyot

Students of party systems have constructed two principal accounts of their development and functioning. The first, best formulated in the work of Lipset and Rokkan (1967) and reflecting European experience, emphasises stable and historically rooted cleavages based on relatively fixed demographic characteristics of the electorate, such as religion, class, region, and economic sector. These persistent voting patterns often lead to 'consociational' or 'corporatist' political systems, in which policy is the result of negotiation between the principal social forces, whether these are represented directly in the cabinet or in other forums, such as national negotiations between business associations and trade unions. The second account, more appropriate to the American party system, views parties as actors attempting to create winning coalitions of interests; they are relatively free to direct their appeals to those groups and voters whom they believe can give them a majority. Schumpeter (1942) and Downs (1957) theorised this conception of parties as entrepreneurs, competing to offer the most attractive package to voters; typically this implies 'catch-all' parties (Kirchheimer 1966) and a two-party system with parties alternating in power in the context of a pluralistic system of interest aggregation (Golden 1986).

The Italian party system does not fully correspond to either pattern, and a third type of party system must be constructed to account for its special characteristics. Many scholars, following Sartori (1966, 1976), have classified Italy, along with Weimar Germany and Fourth Republic France, as a case of polarised pluralism.[1] However, despite its ostensible fragmentation (eight parties have regularly been represented in parliament), the Italian party system has been dominated by the two largest parties, the Christian Democrats (DC) and the Communists (PCI), and coalition patterns (though not cabinets) have been remarkably durable. The Christian Democrats, in coalition with the smaller lay parties and, since 1962, the Socialists (PSI), have governed continuously since 1945. The absence of any alternation in government rules out an 'American' interpretation of Italian politics. However, the Italian party system does not fit Lipset and Rokkan's model either. Although Christian Democrats, Communists, and Socialists have roots in distinct subcultures, neither the parties nor the lines of division that emerged in 1945 and solidified after 1948 can be fully explained by the deeply rooted cleavages on which Lipset and Rokkan rely. This is particularly true of the Christian Democratic Party, which dominates and interpenetrates the state and draws on a base of support which extends far beyond the traditional Catholic subculture.

Any account of the Italian party system must consider not only the social bases of parties, but also the Christian Democrats' domination of the state and its effects on the party system. Although the Italian party system appears to be based on relatively stable cleavages, it is better viewed as a regime party system - i.e. a party system in which a dominant party survives in large measure because of the ways in which it has embedded itself within the state apparatus. The entrenchment of the DC regime has stabilised Italian politics, but has not immunised it from change. Since its establishment, Italy has undergone a major economic transformation; this has shaken but not broken up the regime. After tracing the development of the party system and discussing these socio-economic changes and their impact, this chapter will consider the three major parties and their evolution since 1970.

The Origins of the System

We can trace the emergence of the DC regime to Fascism and the Liberation and the ways in which these altered the pre-1922 party system. In the late nineteenth and early twentieth centuries, Italy was governed by shifting parliamentary coalitions of notables. The narrow liberal political class was able to rule despite widespread popular disaffection because of a restricted franchise, corruption and fraud (Gramsci 1971:80n). The introduction of universal male suffrage in 1913 and proportional representation in 1919 allowed mass parties reflecting the religious and class cleavages to emerge. A Catholic party, the Italian Popular Party (PPI), and the Italian Socialist Party (PSI) became important political actors. However, the rise of Fascism interrupted the evolution of a party system which was still adapting to mass politics. Fascism was partly a result of a failure to adapt fast enough: liberal politicians could not command stable majorities while the Socialists and Catholics were not yet ready to govern.

After the Liberation in 1945, the old cleavages and political subcultures reappeared, but in different forms and with very different weights: the PSI now shared the Socialist subculture with the Communist Party, which had vastly expanded its base through its leading role in the struggle against Fascism. The Christian Democratic party, successor of the PPI, emerged as the strongest single party, with 35 per cent of the popular vote (see table 3.1), while the strength of the old lay liberal groups was reduced by the growth of the three mass parties.

The party system has retained the basic characteristics it acquired between 1945 and 1948. Although the Communists have gained and the Socialists have shrunk, the DC, PCI, and PSI remain the principal political forces: they accounted for 74.9 per cent of the popular vote in 1946, and 75.3 per cent in 1987. Moreover, the DC has been in office continuously since 1945, while the PCI has been out of the cabinet since 1947, when the DC, under pressure from the Vatican and right-wing forces in Italy, excluded the Communists and Socialists from the government. Initially, the Communists and Socialists were closely allied. However, the PSI later broke with the PCI and returned to governmental collaboration with the DC in the 'opening to the left' of 1962.

The small Liberal and Republican parties (PLI and PRI), heirs of the lay liberal tradition, have survived, often serving as coalition partners of the DC. The Social Democrats (PSDI), who broke from the PSI in 1947, have played a similar role. The left-wing Radical Party (PR), which first appeared in parliament in 1976, is also an offshoot of the liberal tradition. The Italian Social Movement (MSI), led by neo-fascists, has been formally excluded from government but continues to attract the support of many right-wing voters disgruntled with the more moderate parties; it absorbed the Monarchist party in 1972. Finally, since 1976 the successors of the extra-parliamentary left of 1968, who see the PCI as too moderate, have also been represented in parliament: Proletarian Democracy (DP) are the exponents of this tendency in the present legislature.

Table 3.1 Elections to the Italian Chamber of Deputies, 1946-1987 (in percentage of the popular vote)

	1946	1948	1953	1958	1963	1968	1972	1976	1979	1983	1987
Misc. Left						4.5a	2.6b	1.5c	2.2d	1.5e	1.7e
Greens											2.5
Communists (PCI)	18.9	31.0	22.6	22.7	25.3	26.9	27.2	34.4	30.4	29.9	26.6
Socialists (PSI)	20.7		12.7	14.2	13.8	14.5	9.6	9.6	9.8	11.4	14.3
Social Democrats (PSDI)		7.1	4.5	4.6	6.1		5.1	3.4	3.8	4.1	2.9
Radicals (PR)								1.1	3.5	2.2	2.6
Republicans (PRI)	4.4	2.5	1.6	1.4	1.4	2.0	2.8	3.1	3.0	5.1	3.7
Christian Democrats (DC)	35.2	48.5	40.1	42.4	38.3	39.1	38.8	38.7	38.3	32.9	34.4
Liberals (PLI)	6.8	3.8	3.0	3.5	7.0	5.8	3.9	1.3	1.9	2.9	2.1
Monarchists f	2.8	2.8	6.8	4.9	1.7	1.3					
Italian Social Movement (MSI)		2.0	5.8	4.8	5.1	4.5	8.7	6.1	5.3	6.8	5.9

Sources: Official data, Ministry of the Interior, L'Unita', 29 June 1983 and Le Monde 17 June 1987. Notes: Smaller Marxist Parties: a) Socialist Party of Proletarian Unity (PSIUP) b) PSIUP and Il Manifesto c) Proletarian Democracy (DP) d) Party of Proletarian Unity (PdUP) and United New Left (NSU) e) DP. f) Including various monarchist lists.

The Regime Party System

Although the DC can be called many things - a party of business, a party representing rural interests, a petty-bourgeois party, a catch-all party, as well as a Catholic party - it is best characterised as a 'regime party', a party which has become identified with the state itself because it has occupied the state apparatus and formed a symbiotic relationship with it. In addition to its firm base in the Catholic subculture, the DC aggregates a number of other interests. However, unlike a typical 'catch-all' party, it is linked to these interests (e.g. business groups, peasant associations) *because of* its occupation of the state apparatus, and its links with them are therefore quite permanent.

The term 'regime party' refers not only to the DC, but also to the Japanese Liberal Democratic Party and the Indian Congress.[2] The designation reflects characteristics not only of the parties, but also of the societies in which they operate.[3] All three countries have economic and social structures which are less mature than those of most capitalist democracies: in particular, the petty bourgeoisie remains relatively numerous and politically significant in each of them (see table 3.2) and the bourgeoisie proper lacks real hegemony in society and the state. Hence the capitalist class can rule only by means of a party which can secure the support of the petty bourgeoisie, even if this is at a high price.

Table 3.2 Percentage of the Labour Force Who Are Self-Employed in Some Advanced Capitalist Countries (1985)

Italy	32
Japan	26
France	16
W. Germany	13
U.S.A.	10
U.K.	10

Source: ISTAT data reported in *La Repubblica: Affari e Finanza*, 10 April 1987, 2-3.

The petty bourgeoisie provides the characteristic basis of a regime party. As Suzanne Berger (1981a:85-87) has pointed out, this stratum, in order to survive, looks to the state for favours that will thwart the market's natural tendency to promote concentration. Because it has a low capacity to organise itself, it is available to be organised 'from above', by the state itself. This leads to imbrications of interests of the sort typified by the Italian Small Holders' Federation (the Federazione dei coltivatori diretti, or Coldiretti), an interest group which organises about 85 per cent of the peasantry. The Coldiretti not only controls the powerful public agency (the Federconsorzi) which distributes subsidies in cash and kind to the peasants, but also acts as a faction within the DC (Donolo 1979:173; LaPalombara 1964:235-46). The numerous measures adopted by the DC-controlled Italian state in favour of the petty bourgeoisie include reduced social security payments for the self-employed, the denial of planning permits for new supermarkets, and the toleration of widespread tax evasion by small businesses, an item which alone costs the Treasury tens of billions of dollars annually. In addition to the DC's organisation and aggregation of petty-bourgeois interests, we must note the party's widespread use of patronage (*sottogoverno*), particularly in the South, to win support. Here again, occupation of the state is the basis of the DC system of power, but individual favours (e.g. the massive concession of false disability pensions) often take the place of general measures for entire occupational groups. The importance of patronage is demonstrated by table 3.3, which shows the DC has maintained its strength in Southern regions such as Basilicata, Abruzzo, and Molise: it is now stronger there than in Veneto, the strongest bastion of the Catholic subculture, where its vote has declined in recent elections (see table 3.4). The presence of a large underdeveloped region such as the South, impoverished and eager to accept any favours the ruling party may bestow, facilitates the continuation of the DC regime.

A further source of support for the DC is anti-communism, which is especially strong among the middle classes. The regime owes its origin to the Cold War cleavage between anti-communism and the left, most sharply highlighted in the elections of 18 April 1948. The Christian Democrats then became the home of a heterogeneous amalgam of forces and interests, held together by a common fear of Bolshevism. In this period the party developed close links with organised business and acquired a large following of conservative 'opinion' voters. While the DC's role as principal bulwark against communism continues to bring it many votes of this type, the traditional communist/anti-communist cleavage has been transformed into one separating the regime party from its principal opposition.

The DC, like the Japanese LDP and the Indian Congress, is highly factionalised. This is a result of the vast resources a regime party can command. The earliest factions within the party either reflected ideological divisions within the Catholic subculture (the left-wing dossettiani who challenged De Gasperi's line in the late '40s),

Table 3.3 The DC Vote and the Catholic Subculture: Support for the Popular
Party and Christian Democracy by Region, 1919 and 1983[a]

Vote for Italian Popular Party (PPI) 1919		Vote for Christian Democracy (DC) 1983	
Region	Percentage	Region	Percentage
Veneto[c]	36	Basilicata	46
Lombardy	30	Abruzzo & Molise[b]	46
Marche	27	Veneto[c]	42
Lazio	26	Sicily	38
Liguria	20	Calabria	37
Tuscany	20	Apulia	36
Piedmont	19	Campania[b]	35
Campania[b]	18	Marche	33
Emilia-Romagna[c]	18	Lombardy	33
Calabria	18	Sardinia	32
Umbria	17	Lazio	31
Sicily	12	Piedmont	27
Sardinia	12	Liguria	27
Apulia	11	Umbria	26
Abruzzo & Molise[b]	7	Tuscany	25
Basilicata[d]		Emilia-Romagna[c]	23
Italy	20.6	Italy	32.9

Sources: Italy, Ministero dell'Interno (1963: 114-15) and *L'Unita'*, 29 June 1983.
    Notes: a. The regions of Trentino-Alto Adige and Friuli-Venezia Giulia have
been excluded as they did not participate in the 1919 election. Regions are defined
by their 1919 boundaries.
    b. The Province of Benevento is counted with Abruzzo and Molise rather than
Campania.
    c. The Province of Rovigo is counted with Emilia-Romagna rather than Veneto.
    d. No candidates presented.

or else represented diverse interests within the DC (e.g. the Base,
originally a trade union faction, or the vespisti, representing moderate
Southern notables). However, as the DC systematically occupied the
state in the 1950s, factionalism spread to the entire party and, as
Zuckerman (1979) argues, most factions increasingly lacked either a
clear base in any particular interest or a distinctive ideological

Table 3.4 Mean Percentage of the DC Vote in 16 "White" Provinces, 1948-1983[a]

1948	1953	1958	1963	1968	1972	1976	1979	1983
61.8	54.6	55.8	52.3	52.4	52.5	50.4	48.5	42.2

Source: Caciagli (1985: 108).

Note: a. Asti, Cuneo, Como, Sondrio, Bergamo, Brescia, Trento, Bolzano, Verona, Padua, Vicenza, Treviso, Belluno, Udine, Pordenone, Lucca

position. They were and are 'clientelistic factions', organised because of the rich rewards available to those with political power.

Hierarchical in character, factions often take the name of their chieftain. Factional leaders may have ideological leanings, but their bewildering political shifts show that neither ideology nor a distinct political line is the prime determinant of their actions. For instance, Andreotti's Primavera faction was clearly on the right of the party in the 1950s, but in the late '70s and early '80s the andreottiani were part of the left-wing bloc of factions that favoured a *rapprochement* with the Communists. While the factions' power bases may be in certain regions, institutions, or organisations, this does not mean they represent these interests: though a region or interest group expects some patronage from 'its' faction leader, factional leaders also control and shape their constituencies in order to maximise their support: e.g. bosses in the South may prefer to create temporary jobs that are in the party's control rather than foster long-term development which would end voters' dependence on political patronage.

The Communists

The existence of a regime party such as the DC implies a party of permanent opposition, in this case the Italian Communist Party. Since 1947, a *conventio ad excludendum* has kept it from national office and prevented any alternation in government. The PCI became the principal party of the left by 1948, inheriting the lion's share of the pre-fascist Socialist subculture. Strongest in the 'red' regions of central Italy, this included a network of co-operatives, cultural associations, and other organisations, as well as the largest trade union confederation, the CGIL. The Communists built on this subculture by championing the protests of the victims of the pro-business, labour-repressive policies of the DC regime. By 1953 they had doubled their vote in the South by supporting a radical agrarian reform and the claims of the region for fairer treatment. Nevertheless, the PCI fits the Lipset-Rokkan model of a subculturally rooted party more closely than the DC.

The PCI's firmest base is in the working class, which comprises some 70 per cent of its electorate, but it has to some extent become a coalition of interests, including a large part of the petty bourgeoisie of the red regions (where it controls local and regional government), segments of the trade union movement, and supporters of new social movements, such as feminism, environmentalism, and pacifism. Many of the latter are members of the so-called 'new' middle class, the salaried petty bourgeoisie. Because it retains its privileged relationship with the working class and is still barred from certain segments of the electorate by the Cold War cleavage, the PCI is not a 'catch-all' party. Nonetheless, it has aggregated many groups simply because it is seen as the most powerful force opposing the DC regime. Excluded from the national government, it is not primarily a system of political power like the DC, but rather a channel for the representation of these interests.

The Other Governing Parties

While the DC is a regime party, it, unlike the Japanese Liberal Democrats and the Indian Congress, has had to govern in coalition with other parties. Even in the one legislature (the First, 1948-53) in which it held an absolute majority, it preferred not to rule alone. The Christian Democrats have been able to integrate their smaller partners into the regime, thanks to the ideological cement of anti-communism and the use of patronage. Apart from the PSI, these have become 'external factions' of the DC. In the First Legislature, the typical coalition was 'centrist,' embracing the DC, the PSDI, the PRI and PLI. In the Second (1953-58), governments followed the same formula, but were increasingly unstable, largely because of factional divisions in the DC. The parliamentary situation and the need to re-integrate the working class led to the formation of the first 'centre-left' legislative majority (DC, PSI, PSDI and PRI) in 1962; the Socialists entered the cabinet the following year. With some significant interludes, notably a brief return to a centrist cabinet in 1972-73 and a DC cabinet supported by the PCI, PSI, PSDI, PRI and, for a time, the PLI, from 1976 to 1979, the centre-left has been the predominant formula for the past quarter-century. However, not all governments have included all four parties and, with the readmission of the Liberals to the cabinet in 1979, the formula has been expanded to embrace five parties.

The major change in the coalition pattern, the admission of the

Socialists, will be explained in greater detail below. Unlike the smaller partners, the PSI is not always content with a subordinate role, and can challenge the ruling party. The DC has a stable basis of support, but this very fact hampers it in its competition with the less heavily committed, more free-wheeling Socialists. A weakening of the regime and the spread of American-style competitive politics has placed the DC at a disadvantage.

Economic Development and the Opening to the Left

The rapid maturation of the Italian economy created the conditions for the 'opening to the left' of 1962. A new pattern of economic development required the regime to adapt; its ability to do so, under the leadership of statesmen such as Aldo Moro and Amintore Fanfani, ensured its survival.

The DC regime was a major factor permitting the growth which Italy experienced during the economic miracle of the 1950s and early 1960s (Salvati 1972:7-8). It allowed the exclusion of labour from any role in national decision-making (Golden 1986:7): business interests dominated economic policy, while the DC promoted social policies for its clientele. Wages could be held down to allow the penetration of export markets, particularly by the consumer durables industries (e.g. automobiles, appliances). Italy had not yet advanced to the stage of 'mature Fordism' - i.e. a domestically-centred economy relying on high wages and a buoyant home market, propped up by Keynesian demand-management policies and a modern welfare state - which the most advanced capitalist states had attained in the immediate postwar period.[4] Italian industry used Fordist production techniques and organisation, such as the assembly line, and thus reaped substantial productivity gains, but because wages did not keep pace with productivity, export markets were crucial.

This 'labour-repressive' pattern of economic growth contained the dynamic that led to its own destruction: rapid expansion led to the growth of the industrial proletariat; millions migrated from the South to the Northern cities, causing tremendous social strains. The Communist vote, stagnant since 1953, rose to 25.3 per cent in 1963 and 26.9 per cent in 1968 as a result. Furthermore, the tightening of the labour market in the early 1960s revived trade union strength in the factories: an early wave of strikes at the peak of the boom in 1962-63 foreshadowed the 'Hot Autumn' of 1969-70.

Economic growth led to an increase in the size and strength of both the working class and the new salaried middle class but did not destroy the bases of the DC regime. Although the petty bourgeoisie shrank, it remained large compared to other European nations (see table 3.2); furthermore, the resources generated by growth had allowed further expansion of the DC's power through state agencies and state expenditure, especially in the South. Religiosity declined only slowly, and Communist advances drove more moderate voters into the DC fold. Because historical legacies such as the size of the petty bourgeoisie or the backwardness of the South could not be abolished by a decade of growth, the DC's vote remained stable at 38-42 per cent. However, it felt the need to respond to working-class demands in order to dampen industrial militancy and weaken the political challenge from the left. This provided the basis for the opening to the Socialists.

At the same time, changes were underway in the Socialist camp. In the immediate postwar years, the Italian Socialists had been closely aligned with the Communists. However, the PSI broke its unity of action pact with the PCI in 1957 and later declared its availability as a governmental partner. The Socialists hoped to leave the ghetto of opposition, secure reforms in industrial relations, education, and social services, as well as economic planning, and in the long run replace the PCI as the major party of the left.

Despite opposition on both sides, the 'opening to the left' was consummated in 1963 when the Socialists entered the cabinet, provoking the exit of the Liberals to the right. However, the Socialist hopes for reform were, for the most part, unrealised. Economic policy remained in the same hands as before and the DC's petty-bourgeois clienteles resisted many reforms because these would damage their interests. Rather than spearheading reforms or changing policy, the PSI was quickly integrated into the DC's system of patronage. Those reforms that did occur produced no more than a partial and stunted version of a modern welfare state. The privileged positions of the DC's major clienteles were not attacked but were strengthened. A typical reform was the generous extension of pension benefits approved in 1969: it satisfied the demands of the unions while at the same time providing higher payments to the petty bourgeoisie and opening up greater opportunities for corruption to the Christian Democrats, who could now confer even more valuable favours on able-bodied workers for whom they secured disability pensions. In view of such measures, it is not surprising that Italy, unlike France, saw no petty-bourgeois protest movements in this period.

The 1970s: Crisis of Development

The student movement of 1967-68 and the Hot Autumn strike wave of 1969-70 marked the final end of the previous labour-repressive

41

pattern of economic development. The unions, greatly strengthened in organisation and numbers, finally obtained a voice in public policy-making; however, resistance from the DC, its petty-bourgeois base, and elements of business prevented adoption of fully-fledged Fordist measures. While the new balance of economic and political power meant the old economic system could not continue, the political system was unable to produce consensus on a package re-establishing stability on the basis of Keynesianism and the welfare state. While one wing of business, typified by Fiat Chairman Giovanni Agnelli, wanted to form a 'Manchesterian' alliance (reminiscent of the Manchester-based Anti-Corn Law League) with the workers against 'parasitic' elements, such as the petty bourgeoisie and the bloated public administration, business was disunited and unable to dictate the course of public policy (Martinelli 1980:81-83).

The 1972 elections showed surprisingly little change except for the growth of the neo-fascist MSI. But the 'long wave' of 1968, which was a veritable 'cultural revolution', a far-reaching critique of established values and institutions as well as of the traditional subcultures, became visible in the pro-divorce victory in the 1974 referendum and the spectacular Communist advances in the 1975 regional and local and the 1976 national elections. In 1976, the PCI won 34.4 per cent of the popular vote, while the DC remained unchanged at 38.8 per cent; although the Communists won many first-time voters and gained some others from the DC, the latter gained electors, who feared a Communist victory, from the minor centre-right parties.

At this juncture the PSI, anxious to improve its image by distancing itself from the Christian Democrats, refused to continue supporting governments unless the Communists were also included. A centrist coalition was numerically impossible, so that the DC was forced to bargain for the abstention of five other parties (Communists, Socialists, Republicans, Social Democrats, and Liberals) on a purely DC cabinet led by Andreotti (the government of *non-sfiducia*, or non-non-confidence); in 1978, the first four of the above entered the majority, but not the cabinet, by voting confidence in the government. This quasi-consociational interlude, in which the six (later five) parties met regularly to discuss policy, did not seriously undermine the DC's system of power: while the Communists were admitted to the boards of a few state corporations (notably RAI-TV), the DC continued to hold, in the words of one anonymous wag, '40 per cent of the votes and 80 per cent of the power'. Although the PCI justified its support of a Christian Democratic government by referring to its strategy of 'historic compromise' and arguing that economic crisis and terrorism had created an emergency, the Communists could not sustain the erosion of their support which set in almost as soon as the Andreotti government took office: many of their voters expected radical changes to follow the 'victory' of 1976 and were repulsed by the PCI's preaching of 'austerity' and tough anti-terrorist measures. Furthermore, the DC bloc continued to resist major reform proposals. In the ensuing elections, held in 1979, the PCI declined to 30.4 per cent, losing many youth and working-class votes. The experience of 1976-79 had proven that at least for the time being a consociational solution was unworkable in Italy; governments during the next parliament (1979-83) reverted to the centre-left formula.

The DC regime was shaken but not destroyed by the long wave of 1968. The political system could not produce the policies required for the functioning of a mature Fordist system. This system itself entered into a crisis in 1973, when the mass-production consumer goods industries began to lose ground and shed workers (Lipietz 1984). The new post-Fordist economic systems, which are emerging in the developed world, will require a different mix of policies to regulate them and a new class coalition to support them. The DC regime, if it survives, is unlikely to be able to provide such a policy framework. As a result, Italy may have difficulty entering this next stage of capitalist development.

The Dynamic of Christian Democracy

Some of the most spectacular changes of the past fifteen years have affected the Christian Democrats. There have been two distinct processes at work. On one hand, several long-term trends appear to be weakening the DC's bases of support, although they have not operated with nearly the rapidity that many observers have predicted. On the other, cyclical fluctuations have occurred in response to the perceived danger of a Communist electoral victory and the subsequent waning of this fear. Hence, the predicted decline of the DC has not taken place in any clear or unequivocal way.

In the first place, the size of the petty bourgeoisie has diminished, falling from 44 per cent of the active population to 32 per cent between 1951 and 1985 (table 3.2). Most of this decline has resulted from the exodus from agriculture: urban categories, such as the shopkeepers, have actually increased both absolutely and relatively (Sylos Labini 1974:155-56). Furthermore, the decline of the traditional middle classes has been accompanied not only by the growth of the working class but also by the even more rapid expansion of the salaried middle class. In Italy, however, this class only partially resembles the 'new middle class' which many scholars have identified as a basis of progressive social movements (Inglehart 1977; Therborn 1984:33-35). Instead, the publicly employed new middle class is involved in the clientelistic politics of the regime, and this stratum as a whole retains many of the attitudes of the traditional petty bourgeoisie (Sylos Labini 1974:53-62). Factors such as these have cushioned the impact of the petty bourgeoisie's decline on the DC.

The decline of religious practice has eroded the Catholic base of the DC: this was first evident in the loss of working-class votes in 1970-72 in the aftermath of the Hot Autumn and in the weakening of the ties between the CISL trade union confederation and the Christian Democrats (Barbagli, Corbetta, Parisi, and Schadee 1979:133-34). More recently, traditional 'white' bastions such as the Veneto have seen a fall in DC support not evident in many other regions, notably the South (see tables 3.3 and 3.4). At the same time, the DC, while still a 'party of Catholics' - a 1976 survey showed that 55 per cent of DC voters were regularly practising Catholics, as opposed to only 19 per cent of all other voters (Parisi 1979:110) - is no longer as closely identified with the Church and the Catholic world. After the Second Vatican Council, the Church began to distance itself from Italian politics, a process which has continued even under Pope John Paul II. However, religious sentiment is not simply a residue of a previous age: while regular church-going dropped from 69 per cent in 1956 to 37 per cent in 1976 (Wertman 1981:74) new religious currents have also emerged. For instance, Communion and Liberation, a socially active but religiously conservative Catholic group, became prominent in the '70s as a response to student activism, and later formed a new faction within the DC. However, other politically active Catholic groups are eschewing the Christian Democrats for independent activity.

The severe setbacks of 1974 and 1975 led the DC to adopt a new strategy: Aldo Moro, as party chairman, attempted to guide the party into a 'third phase' in which the PCI would be accepted as a legitimate part of the democratic system; his ally, Benigno Zaccagnini, became party secretary and initiated a parallel programme of renewal. He aimed to 're-found' and revitalise the DC as a popular, mass party and sought to end abuses such as padded membership rolls and factionalism. He made some progress in securing a greater turnover of personnel and in 'moralising' the party: membership fell from 1,733,000 in 1975 to 1,365,000 in 1976 as names copied from telephone directories to augment the power of local bosses were struck off (Caciagli 1985:121). However, opposition from the major factional leaders stalled Zaccagnini's reform programme. He secured only a bare majority at the 1976 Congress, a month before the formation of the PCI-supported Andreotti government. Part of this majority consisted of traditional factional bosses; some disagreed with Moro's policy of *rapprochement* with the PCI and very few were prepared to share their power with the Communists. After Moro's assassination in 1978, the factions realigned according to their position on the historic compromise: Zaccagnini, Andreotti, and their followers in favour, the others opposed. Party reform had already become a dead issue. At the 1980 congress, the right-wing factions, which favoured a preferential relationship with the PSI rather than the PCI, triumphed and elected Flaminio Piccoli secretary.

However, continued uncertainty and conflict about alliances and the reappearance of the 'moral question' in the wake of the P2 scandal led to another attempt to reform the party.[5] An agreement between most factions led to the election in 1982 of Ciriaco De Mita as party secretary. De Mita's objective was to 'modernise' the DC, turning it into moderate party of opinion rather than an ideologically or subculturally based party. He was even prepared to dispense with the traditional cement of anti-communism, admitting that the PCI was a democratic party which could safely be entrusted with the responsibility of government, if it were to win an electoral majority. De Mita suffered a severe setback in the 1983 elections, when the DC fell to an historic low of 32.9 per cent. Several factors contributed to this reversal: these included not only the long-term erosion of the DC's base, but also the end of the Communist danger. Once again moderate voters could abandon the DC for the small centre-right parties, the major beneficiaries in the election. Moreover, many Northern middle-class voters deserted the DC because of the 'moral question' - i.e. the scandals, exemplified by the P2 affair - in which its members had been involved. At the same time, the party's declared intention to 'moralise' itself cost it support in the South, where voters punished it for threatening to reduce the vast system of outdoor relief for the party faithful. The DC's losses in Apulia (8.1 per cent) were greater than those in Veneto (7.9 per cent); similar losses were suffered in other southern regions, e.g. Sicily, -7.3 per cent, Sardinia, -6.6 per cent, Campania, -6.4 per cent.

De Mita, while unable to eliminate clientelism, did reduce large-scale corruption and links to organised crime. Partly as a result of his moralising efforts, the party recovered some of the lost ground in the June 1987 elections, when it received 34.3 per cent of the popular vote. Nevertheless, factions continue to flourish, detracting from the modern image which the secretary seeks to project through the use of external consultants and the mass media. Thus, the DC has survived as a regime party, but its predicament remains unresolved. On one hand, it has retained its petty-bourgeois constituency and remains the channel which entrepreneurs must use to influence the state. On the other hand, it has failed to recapture its 'popular' base or appeal to the 'modern' middle strata. Still dominated by the same factional leaders, the DC appears unable to transform itself from a regime party into a party of a more modern type.

The Transformation of the Socialist Party

In the postwar period, the PSI produced the most important realignment in the party system by crossing the ideological divide between the pro-communist and anti-communist camps. In 1963, after a long internal struggle, the Socialists entered the cabinet in the first centre-left coalition. As we have pointed out, the centre-left's reforms did not meet the expectations of its exponents. Instead the PSI was integrated into the system. In the process, the PSI became much more dependent on patronage for its electoral support; this is reflected in the growth of its vote in the South and its decline in the North and Centre: in 1963, 32.2 per cent of Socialist voters were in the South and Islands; by 1983, 44.7 per cent were (Cazzola 1985:173). The departure of the left-wing factions that had opposed the centre-left, comprising roughly one third of the party's voters and members, facilitated this process.[6] The attempted reunification with the PSDI, which was supposed to produce a rival to the PCI, was a complete failure: the two parties won only 14.5 per cent of the popular vote when they ran a joint list in 1968. The following year the reunified party split into its two original components.

By the 1970s the PSI was in an intolerable position, reduced to less than 10 per cent of the popular vote and ground between the two larger parties. Although they were dissatisfied with government policies, parliamentary arithmetic and the need to support cabinets made it impossible for the Socialists to vote against the government; hence the Communists reaped the benefits of opposition, while the Christian Democrats retained the lion's share of power and the Socialists were tarred by their partners' clientelistic practices. The PSI's refusal to continue in the majority unless the PCI joined them resulted in the governments of national unity from 1976 to 1979. The disappointing 1976 election results also precipitated the designation of Bettino Craxi as party secretary. Craxi was supported by younger leaders of all the major factions and given a mandate to renew the party. Essentially, Craxi has attempted to make the PSI into a 'catch-all' party, or party of opinion, casting it loose from its subcultural moorings in order to gain greater freedom of maneuver.

Under Craxi's leadership, the Socialists distanced themselves from their residual and largely symbolic Marxism. Craxi himself wrote a much-derided article proposing Proudhon rather than Marx as the party's source of ideological inspiration (*L'Espresso*, 27 Aug. 1978). The hammer and sickle on the party's symbol became even smaller, overshadowed by a recently added carnation. The PSI placed more and more emphasis on its leader and its elected representatives and public office-holders, at the expense of the extra-parliamentary party organisation (Mancini and Pasquino 1984); Craxi and his closest collaborators have sought to project a modern 'managerial' image. He also succeeded in reducing the degree of factionalism within the party, first by an alliance with the younger leaders of the left (he himself came from the right-wing Nenni faction) and then by using his control of the party organisation to bring most of the party under the control of his faction.

The new secretary's policies were designed to guarantee the party's autonomy from the two larger formations. During the period of 'national unity' from 1976 to 1979, the major danger appeared to be a consociational-type coalition between the DC and the PCI which would exclude the PSI or at a minimum drastically reduce its bargaining power. At the Turin Congress (1978), the party explicitly rejected this perspective by proposing a 'left alternative' (*alternativa di sinistra*). The Socialists also discussed various suggestions for institutional reforms, such as the French two-ballot electoral system, intended to promote the formation of two clearly opposed camps which would alternate in government. And, while remaining part of the majority supporting the Andreotti government, they expressed sympathy with those civil libertarians and extra-parliamentary leftists who argued that the state's anti-terrorist policies were another manifestation of the reduction of the margins of democracy in the consociational climate of 'national unity'. For instance, the PSI took an ambiguous position on the 1978 referendum requested by the Radicals to repeal the anti-terrorist Reale law, and during the Moro kidnapping Craxi was favourable to some form of symbolic concession to the Red Brigades in order to save the DC leader's life.

The end of the government of national solidarity in 1979 restricted Craxi's room for maneuver and his ability to establish the PSI's autonomy: because PCI support for a government was now ruled out, he was forced to guarantee that the PSI would ensure 'governability'. In effect this meant a return to some form of centre-left coalition. The party gradually abandoned the perspective of a left alternative in favour of immediate reforms; the 1983 election was fought on a five-point programme for a 'great reform'. Heightened rivalry with the PCI contributed to this rightward drift, as did the PSI's return to the cabinet in 1980. All in all, it is doubtful whether Craxi and his closest collaborators saw the socialist alternative as more than a tactical move to recreate a left-wing image for the PSI and distinguish it from the PCI.

These policies produced significant electoral dividends for the PSI. In the regional and local elections of 1980 and 1981, the party made some spectacular gains, winning an average of 12.7 per cent of the popular vote in the fifteen ordinary regions in 1980 (a gain of 2.8 per cent over 1979), with high points such as an unprecedented 23.3 per cent in Bari in 1981 (a gain of 12.1 per cent over 1979). In 1983, the PSI achieved the relatively modest result of 11.4 per cent in the national elections (an advance of 1.6 per cent over 1979), but this was sufficient for Craxi to claim the prime ministership. As Prime Minister, he consolidated the PSI's position with 'decisive' leadership in some fields, such as the struggle against tax evasion and the decree of February 1984 that reduced workers' cost-of-living increases for that year by 27,200 lire per month. Polls suggest that Craxi's style of government made him the most popular postwar prime minister (*L'Espresso*, 13 May 1986), and in the 1987 elections his leadership finally bore fruit, when the PSI advanced to an unprecedented 14.3 per cent of the popular vote, a striking sign of the electorate's approval of his performance. The Socialist party has a smaller loyal electorate than either the PCI or the DC: only some 65-70 per cent of PSI voters have voted for the party in the previous election, in contrast to 85-90 per cent for the two larger parties (Corbetta 1979). PSI supporters include both 'opinion' voters and clientelistic supporters, particularly in the South. For many voters, the PSI is a way station in an evolution from left to right or vice-versa, or a vehicle for temporary protest against the DC or the PCI. In 1987, voters from the minor centre parties accounted for most of its gains. The PSI is becoming a 'catch-all' type of party, offering more competition to the DC than to the PCI. It has the advantage that while much of its support is clientelistic, it lacks the organic relationship with whole social categories which limits the DC's flexibility: Socialist clientelism is more purely political.

At times, the minor parties of the centre and right, especially the Republicans, have also taken advantage of the decline of the DC's electoral base. In 1983, the PRI obtained an unprecedented 5.1 per cent of the popular vote (a gain of 2.1 per cent), placing third in the major centres of Milan (12.3 per cent) and Turin (10.2 per cent). Its gains were in the North, especially in the larger cities, and reflected the support of both the independent and the professional and intellectual middle classes. Moreover, the minor parties of the centre have attracted a much larger share of the support of youth than in the past, and now enjoy more support in the 15-24 age group than in the electorate at large (Ricolfi 1984). Their role in the party system remains that of safety valve for voters discontented with the DC but unwilling to vote Communist; they function principally as subordinate elements in the DC system of power, with a special following among urban, middle-class 'opinion' voters. The 1987 results show they have also acted as the way station in a transfer of votes over two elections from the DC to the PSI. They are in some danger of being absorbed, along with the Radicals, in a 'lay pole' dominated by the Socialists; this is one element of Craxi's long-term strategy, which would allow him to contemplate at least the threat of switching from a DC alliance to the PCI. With 25.6 per cent of the vote, the electoral strength of the lay pole is now equal to that of the Communists.

The PCI in Search of a Strategy

Relegated to permanent opposition from 1947, the PCI soon abandoned the objective of a purely left-wing government, if it had ever seriously supported it. The Communists realised that, if they were to come to power, they would have to construct an alternative bloc of forces by breaking up that of the DC. Already in 1956 the party secretary, Togliatti, spoke of a 'new majority' that would include elements of the Catholic bloc as well as the PCI and PSI. Indeed, ever since the 1930s the Italian Communists had realised the crucial importance of the petty bourgeoisie (Amyot 1981:34-44). For Togliatti (1976) Fascism triumphed because the bourgeoisie, rather than the working class, was able to gain the support of this decisive stratum. From the VII Congress of the Comintern in 1935, the PCI has pursued a 'Popular Front' strategy aimed at winning over the middle strata and allying with the parties that represent them in order to ward off the fascist danger. In the postwar period, this implied the formation of a democratic coalition with the PSI, the minor lay parties, and/or progressive Catholics inside and outside the DC. However, there were different interpretations of this strategy within the PCI. In the mid-1960s, the Ingrao left emphasised the need to detach Catholic workers from the ruling party, while Amendola and the right regarded the small lay parties as the most natural allies. Berlinguer's proposal for an 'historic compromise' with the Catholics and the DC, advanced in 1972, was a version of the party's classic strategy designed for a situation in which neo-fascism was perceived as a real threat. However, the PCI's gains of 1975 and 1976 did not result primarily from the historic compromise strategy but rather from social movements which the party neither initiated nor promoted. Following the 1979 electoral losses, party secretary Berlinguer officially abandoned the historic compromise and replaced it with the demand for a 'democratic alternative', a government that would not include Christian Democrats.

However, the PCI, as a mass party, cannot shift its line 180 degrees from one day to the next. Traditions and habits of mind from previous eras survive like sedimented layers and constrain the leadership, which itself shares many of the same attitudes. By 1979, the majority of Communist cadres had been socialised during the period of the historic compromise: 68 per cent of party functionaries surveyed in 1979 had been hired by the PCI in the 1970s, and a full 43 per cent in 1975-79 (Sebastiani 1983: 166). This cohort enjoyed rapid promotion, in part because the party needed more functionaries to replace those assigned to local government posts after the elections of 1975. Imbued with the spirit of the historic compromise, they found it difficult to pursue the new line with total conviction. Moreover, the only credible alternative to an alliance with the DC was an accord with the PSI, which consistently rejected Communist overtures. In 1983, Craxi labelled the democratic alternative an 'Arabian phoenix'. Nevertheless, both the PCI left and the reform-oriented right represented by Napolitano began to promote the idea of a privileged link with the Socialists.

Other factors pushed the PCI toward change. The electoral defeat of 1979 was the most obvious; the decline in the party's fortunes continued in the European elections held shortly afterwards, in the 1980 regional and local elections, and in the partial local elections of 1981 and 1982. The fascist danger, the ostensible motive for the historic compromise, had abated, and the second oil shock of 1979 sharpened class conflict because real wages began to fall for the first time since 1968. Moreover, the crisis put an end to hopes of a 'Manchesterian' reforming alliance between workers, progressive capital, and the modern middle class. The intense struggle over mass layoffs at Fiat in 1980 symbolised the new tougher stance that many firms were adopting. Employers also began to demand the revision of the automatic cost-of-living escalator (*scala mobile*), which the unions regarded as a fundamental part of the workers' compensation package.

In addition, various new social movements, such as feminism, the peace movement, and the ecological movement gathered strength in the '70s and '80s. Both the PCI's party-political alliance strategies, the historic compromise and the democratic alternative, inhibited it from fully endorsing these movements: total support for the feminist movement would not sit well with potential Catholic allies, and the Communists' response to the peace movement was muted because of their desire to maintain links with the Socialists, who have held the defense portfolio for much of the 1980s. Nevertheless, especially after 1980, the PCI attempted to integrate these new movements. After the 1981 peace demonstrations revealed the issue's potential, the PCI became involved in the peace movement and was soon the dominant force within it. The PCI-sponsored Italian Recreational and Cultural Association (ARCI) founded the Lega Ambiente (Environment League) to appeal to the 'green' constituency. In a departure from the past, the party allowed considerable autonomy to groups like the Lega Ambiente. This enabled the PCI to approach the new movements without necessarily alienating other constituencies in the party that were hostile to their claims, such as the supporters of nuclear energy, in the case of the Lega Ambiente, or the supporters of the army who were offended by the anti-militarist tone of the Young Communists' agitation in the peace movement. In the 1983 election campaign, the Communists ran joint lists with the Party of Proletarian Unity (PdUP), formerly beyond the pale as part of the 'extra-parliamentary' left, and accepted many independent candidates, women, and even representatives of the gay movement on their lists.

This unprecedented openness to movements and groups outside the PCI and its sphere of control was accompanied by other significant changes in its line and practice. After the declaration of martial law in Poland, the PCI went further than ever before in its criticism of the USSR and the socialist bloc, and, in a famous pronouncement, stated that the October Revolution had 'exhausted its driving force' (Berlinguer 1982:16). Nonetheless, despite pressures to do so, the Italian Communists did not go so far as to declare that the USSR was no longer socialist, however much they considered the Soviet model inapplicable to Italy.

The discussion resulting from this *strappo* or rupture with the USSR, together with the insistent pressure of the party's left, forced the PCI leaders to allow a much more open debate than ever before during the preparation of the XVI Congress (1983). In many provincial federations, amendments to the Theses prepared by the Central

Committee were discussed and voted on. These called for the withdrawal of Italy from NATO, greater intra-party democracy, and a reaffirmation of links with the Soviet Union (proposed by Armando Cossutta, an executive member who opposed the break with the USSR), as well as other changes. In a few federations these opposition amendments were carried, but the national congress rejected them all. Nevertheless, the leadership had to make concessions: while the practice of democratic centralism was retained, Berlinguer promised to publicise the debates in the higher party organs in order to keep the rank and file informed. At the XVII Congress (April 1986), Berlinguer's successor, Alessandro Natta, presided over an even more open dialectic. Amendments to the leadership's texts were presented and debated in provincial and section congresses by Pietro Ingrao, the historic leader of the left, Cossutta, and opponents of Italy's alliance with the U.S.A. and of nuclear power plants. An amendment opposing the construction of nuclear plants was defeated by only 17 votes (out of 1091) at the National Congress.

At the same time, the question of wage indexation heightened tensions between the PCI and the Socialist-led government. The continuing negotiations over the *scala mobile* reached an impasse in February 1984 when the Communist-dominated union confederation, the CGIL, refused to accept a proposal to predetermine the number of indexation points the workers would be allowed in that year. The Craxi government, supported by the other two major confederations, decided to impose the change by a decree-law. The PCI, after obstructing the conversion of the decree into law in Parliament, decided to collect signatures for a referendum to abrogate the law. This marked a considerable shift in the party's stance from the time when it supported a temporary conversion of part of the indexation into bonds and the partial de-indexation of retirement bonuses (1977).

The referendum campaign was waged with considerable acrimony; in spite of the fact that it would have raised the monthly pay of every working Italian by 27,200 lire (gross), the Communist proposal obtained only 46 per cent of the vote in June 1985. The fact that the party was prepared to fight virtually alone on such an issue (with only the unwelcome company of the neo-fascists and the Proletarian Democracy group) demonstrates the degree to which the PCI was willing to go to consolidate its traditional base and, more importantly, obstruct the Craxi government, which was increasingly isolating the party.

Although the PCI reformed and modernised itself to some extent after 1980, this evolution was not decisive enough to win back the working-class and youth votes that had deserted it in 1979. In spite of major shifts in its positions, the PCI has changed less than the other two major parties since 1968. Moreover, the traditional working class, its principal constituency, has been shrinking since the mid-1970s. In 1983 the party barely held its own, losing 0.5 per cent of the popular vote, or 1.9 per cent if the PdUP's 1979 vote is also taken into account. The Communist share of the youth vote declined from some 42 per cent in 1976 to 34 per cent in 1979 (Amyot 1980) and only 27 per cent in 1983 (Ricolfi 1984). The 1987 results were little short of a disaster: the party fell to 26.6 per cent, a loss of 3.3 per cent. The Greens, running nationally for the first time, accounted for much of this loss.

For its part, the PCI has not been able to decide on a clear orientation after the abandonment of the historic compromise: the party is divided between those who seek an alliance with the Socialists and those who wish to keep the door open for possible agreements with the DC. The XVII Congress once again demonstrated the party's dilemma: isolated, it cannot elaborate a credible alliance strategy, and hence is open to the charge that its programme is vague. Natta's formula of a 'programmatic government' (*governo di programma*) - i.e. a government defined by its programme of reforms and open to all who support that programme, as opposed to one defined by its component parties - did not fully satisfy the PCI's right, which wanted an immediate 'alternative' (i.e. a coalition with the PSI). The PCI emerged from the Congress without a clear perspective, but with internal divisions accentuated by the strategic impasse.

New Movements and Old Parties

The relative backwardness of the Italian state and Italian society are closely related to the DC regime and its links to the petty bourgeoisie. This backwardness has given rise to very powerful social movements aimed at bringing Italy up to Northern European standards in such matters as environmental protection and women's rights; because of the magnitude of the problems, these movements often became quite radical. However, in contrast to other countries, the strength of the existing party system has made it difficult for truly autonomous social movements to form; all have had some kind of link to the traditional parties. In addition, the continued importance of the class cleavage, represented by the trade unions - a central point of reference for all progressive social forces in the 1970s - made the new movements less salient than in some other countries (Amyot 1987).

The new social issues which Inglehart (1977) has labelled

'post-materialist' were first championed by the Radical Party (PR), a small group of largely professional and white-collar activists (1984 membership 3335, as reported in *Partito Radicale* 1984). The party was founded in 1956 by Liberals and Republicans who were unable to accept their parties' governmental collaboration with the DC. Initially, its most distinctive plank was anti-clericalism. However, in 1967 the PR was revitalised under the leadership of Marco Pannella, and became the most vigorous supporter of all the new causes, from abortion to civil liberties to peace. The Radicals have enjoyed some striking electoral successes, winning 3.5 per cent of the popular vote and eighteen deputies in 1979, but unlike the Greens in Germany the party is unlikely to become the focus of the new movements. Of the new social movements, the feminists were partially co-opted by the passage of a series of reforms in the late 1970s, particularly the legalisation of abortion in 1978 (Ergas 1982). Divided by conflicting loyalties to parties and the extra-parliamentary left as well as opposition to 'male' modes of political activity, such as elections, feminists did not constitute a significant factor in the party system.

The peace movement was not truly autonomous from the existing parties. Nor is the ecological movement, in spite of the relative success of the Green Lists. In the May 1985 regional and local elections, when they obtained 1.7 per cent of the popular vote, these lists were presented by coalitions of various organisations, principally the Lega Ambiente, the Radicals, and independent environmentalist groups, or 'green greens'. Their creation was such a difficult process that in the end two competing lists were presented in Piedmont; in some other regions (e.g. Abruzzo) the lists were direct emanations of the Radical Party. In the 1987 national elections, the Green Lists obtained 2.5 per cent of the vote and 13 seats in the Chamber. In spite of encouraging electoral results, most green activists are opposed to the formation of a green party because they retain strong ties with existing parties. This contrasts sharply with West Germany, where the Greens could constitute a separate party because a large radical constituency had become totally disillusioned with the SPD during its years in power. In Italy, despite its erstwhile co-operation with the DC, the PCI was still able to play leading roles in both the peace and environmental movements. These ties between new social movements and established parties have thus far prevented the movements from altering the entrenched regime party system in any significant way. Instead, their inability to establish their autonomy makes them an important bridge between the established parties and sectors of opinion that would otherwise be politically alienated.

Conclusion

In spite of all the changes of the past twenty years, the DC regime persists, and it would be rash to predict its early demise. Nevertheless, the slow erosion of some of the party's traditional bases of support combined with long-term economic and social changes suggest that the regime, if not the party, cannot last indefinitely. Because its clientelistic factions are so strongly entrenched and it is organically linked to declining petty-bourgeois strata, the DC seems unable to transform itself. The PSI (and to a lesser degree the PRI and the PLI) is more flexible and more capable of becoming a 'catch-all' party with clientelistic appendages. Such a development might well be advantageous to Italian capital: although business must deal with the DC because only the DC can furnish it with a sufficient basis of consent, elements of capital regard the Socialists and the lay parties favourably because they would be freer to pursue the interests of business without demanding the costly pay-offs the DC regime requires. This might permit the construction of a 'post-Fordist' economic system in which the working class is again divided and excluded from political power (Davis 1984).

The PCI, on the other hand, can only hope that the gradual decline of the DC regime and the fading of the communist/anti-communist division will make voters mobile enough to vote for the opposition, allowing a two-bloc system to emerge. The PCI's best hope for this is an alliance with the PSI. Ingrao has even proposed abandoning pure proportional representation to encourage the formation of opposing coalitions before each election. The Socialists, however, are unlikely to agree to such an alliance unless they think that they can repeat Mitterrand's *coup* and compete with the Communists on an equal footing and eventually overtake them. Of course, the PCI might succeed in expanding its own appeal to youth, workers, and the new middle strata, reinforcing its role as the principal opposition force: the 1985 referendum showed it was capable of garnering support outside its usual electorate. If the PCI does not, however, the most interesting changes in the party system will take place within the governing coalition, as the DC regime slowly declines and is replaced by a new type of party system based on different social strata and a different form of consent. This is likely to occur: the DC regime has corroded and limited the salience of traditional cleavages. Moreover, a regime party system cannot exist for long without a petty-bourgeois base.

Notes

1. Sartori's framework is based upon the arbitrary (and incorrect) assignment of ideological positions to the various parties: the DC is seen as a 'centre' party, the PCI as an 'anti-system' one. In addition, the political instability which characterised Sartori's other cases of polarised pluralism contrasts strikingly with the stability, not to say immobilism, of the DC regime since 1945.

2. In a similar vein, Donolo (1979:165) called the DC a 'state party'. Alan Zuckerman (1979: ch. 8) first noted the similarities between these three parties, considering them examples of 'clientelistic factionalism.' Their symbiosis with the state is, however, their most important common characteristic, in my view, their *differentia specifica*.

3. The concept of a regime party system has some affinity with LaPalombara and Weiner's hegemonic political system, 'in which over an extended period of time the same party, or coalitions dominated by the same party, hold governmental power' (1966:35). However, I restrict the term to countries with a particular socio-economic structure, whereas LaPalombara and Weiner include the U.S.A. under the Democrats from 1932 to 1952 and Norway under Labour from 1935 to 1965 as hegemonic political systems. The socio-economic structure furthermore accounts for the possibility of a regime party.

4. The concept of Fordism as a 'regime of accumulation' has been popularised by the 'regulation school'. See Lipietz (1984).

5. 'Propaganda 2' (P2) was a secret Masonic lodge which was implicated in many maneuvers in the 1970s to destabilise the state and establish a more authoritarian regime. Many prominent public servants and politicians, including several Christian Democrats, were members.

6. The left wing of the PSI formed the Italian Socialist Party of Proletarian Unity (PSIUP) in January 1964; in 1968 the PSIUP captured 4.5 per cent of the popular vote, but in 1972 it fell to 1.9 per cent, failed to elect any deputies and dissolved itself. Most of its members entered the PCI.

References

Amyot, Grant (1980) 'Voto giovanile e voto differenziato nelle ultime elezioni italiane: una confutazione di alcune analisi,' *Rivista italiana di scienza politica*, X, 3, 471-83

Amyot, Grant (1981) *The Italian Communist Party: The Crisis of the Popular Front Strategy*, Croom Helm, London

Amyot, Grant (1987) 'Non-parliamentary Opposition in Italy: The New Social Movements' in Eva Kolinsky (ed.), *Opposition in Western Europe*, Croom Helm, London

Barbagli, Marzio, Piergiorgio Corbetta, Arturo Parisi, and Hans Schadee (1979) *Fluidita' elettorale e classi sociali in Italia*, Il Mulino, Bologna

Berger, Suzanne (1981a) 'Regime and Interest Representation: the French Traditional Middle Classes' in S. Berger (ed.), *Organizing Interests in Western Europe*, Cambridge University Press, Cambridge, 83-101

Berger, Suzanne (1981b) 'The Uses of the Traditional Sector in Italy: Why Declining Classes Survive' in Frank Bechhofer and Brian Elliott (eds.), *The Petite Bourgeoisie: Comparative Studies of the Uneasy Stratum*, Macmillan, London, 71-89

Berlinguer, Enrico (1982) Resolution of the Direzione of the PCI, 30 Dec. 1981, trans. in E. Berlinguer, *After Poland: Towards a New Internationalism*, Spokesman, Nottingham, 13-28

Caciagli, Mario (1985) 'Il resistibile declino della Democrazia cristiana' in Gianfranco Pasquino (ed.), *Il sistema politico italiano*, Laterza, Bari, 101-27

Cazzola, Franco (1985) 'Struttura e potere nel Partito socialista italiano' in Gianfranco Pasquino (ed.), *Il sistema politico italiano*, Laterza, Bari, 169-207

Corbetta, Piergiorgio (1979) 'Novita' e incertezze del voto del 3 giugno: analisi dei flussi elettorali,' *Il Mulino, 28*, 5, 715-48

Davis, Mike (1984) 'The Political Economy of Late-Imperial America,' *New Left Review*, no. 143, 6-38

Donolo, Carlo (1979) 'Social Change and Transformation of the State in Italy' in Richard Scase (ed.), *The State in Western Europe*, Croom Helm, London, 164-96

Downs, Anthony (1957) *An Economic Theory of Democracy*, Harper, New York

Ergas, Yasmine (1982) 'Allargamento della cittadinanza e governo del conflitto,' *Stato e mercato*, no. 6, 428-63

Golden, Miriam (1986) 'Interest Representation, Party Systems, and the State: Italy in Comparative Perspective,' *Comparative Politics, 18*, 3, 279-301

Gramsci, Antonio (1971) *Selections from the Prison Notebooks*, ed. Q. Hoare and G. Nowell Smith, Lawrence and Wishart, London

Inglehart, Ronald (1977) *The Silent Revolution*, Princeton University Press, Princeton

Italy, Ministero dell'Interno (1963) *Compendio dei risultati delle elezioni politiche dal 1848 al 1958*, Istituto Poligrafico dello Stato, Rome

Kirchheimer, Otto (1966) 'The Transformation of the Western European Party Systems' in Joseph LaPalombara and Myron Weiner (eds.), *Political Parties and Political Development*, Princeton University Press, Princeton, 177-200

LaPalombara, Joseph (1964) *Interest Groups in Italian Politics*, Princeton University Press, Princeton

LaPalmobara, Joseph and Myron Weiner (1966) 'The Origin and Development of Political Parties' in Joseph LaPalombara and Myron Weiner (eds.), *Political Parties and Political Development*, Princeton University Press, Princeton, 3-42

Lipietz, Alain (1984) *The Globalisation of the General Crisis of Fordism*, Programme of Studies in National and International Development Occasional Paper, Queen's University, Kingston, Ontario

Lipset, Seymour M. and Stein Rokkan (1967) 'Cleavage Structures, Party Systems, and Voter Alignments: An Introduction' in S.M. Lipset and S. Rokkan (eds.), *Party Systems and Voter Alignments*, The Free Press, New York, 1-64

Mancini, U. and Gianfranco Pasquino (1984) 'Moderati convinti e progressisti con riserve: il PSI tra craxiani e sinistra,' *Il Mulino, 33*, 1, 111-42

Martinelli, Alberto (1980) 'Organised Business and Italian Politics: Confindustria and the Christian Democrats in the Postwar Period' in Peter Lange and Sidney Tarrow (eds.) *Italy in Transition: Conflict and Consensus*, Frank Cass, London, 67-87

Parisi, Arturo (1979) 'Un partito di cattolici? L'appartenenza religiosa e il rapporto col mondo cattolico' in A. Parisi (ed.), *Democristiani*, Il Mulino, Bologna

Partito Radicale (1984) '30° Congresso del Partito Radicale, Relazione del Tesoriere Francesco Rutelli e Bilancio del P.R. 1983-84, Roma, 31 ottobre 1984'

Ricolfi, L. (1984) 'I giovani e la politica,' *Il Mulino, 33*, 3

Salvati, Michele (1972) 'The Impasse of Italian Capitalism,' *New Left Review*, no. 76, 3-33

Sartori, Giovanni (1966) 'European Political Parties: The Case of Polarized Pluralism' in Joseph LaPalombara and Myron Weiner (eds.), *Political Parties and Political Development*, Princeton University Press, Princeton

Sartori, Giovanni (1976) *Parties and Party Systems: A Framework for Analysis*, Cambridge University Press, Cambridge

Schumpeter, Joseph (1942) *Capitalism, Socialism, and Democracy*, Harper, New York and London

Sebastiani, Chiara (1983) 'I funzionari' in Aris Accornero, Renato Mannheimer, and C. Sebastiani (eds.), *L'identita' comunista: I militanti, la struttura, la cultura del Pci*, Editori Riuniti, Rome, 79-177

Sylos Labini, Paolo (1974) *Saggio sulle classi sociali*, Laterza, Bari

Therborn, Göran (1984) 'The Prospects of Labour and the Transformation of Advanced Capitalism,' *New Left Review*, no. 145, 5-38

Togliatti, Palmiro (1976) [1935] *Lectures on Fascism*, International Publishers, New York

Wertman, Douglas A. (1981) 'The Christian Democrats: Masters of Survival' in Howard Penniman (ed.), *Italy at the Polls, 1979*, American Enterprise Institute, Washington, D.C., 64-103

Zuckerman, Alan (1979) *The Politics of Faction: Christian Democratic Rule in Italy*, Yale University Press, New Haven

Chapter Four

Party System Transformations in the Federal Republic of Germany

William M. Chandler

The Federal Republic of Germany provides an unusual setting in which to study party system change. Students of party systems typically emphasise both the ways in which earlier cleavages are preserved in contemporary party systems and the gradual changes which result from broad social and economic changes. However, although one can readily explore both the roots of contemporary German parties and the impact of broad social changes such as industrialisation, secularisation, or urbanisation, it is impossible to understand the postwar German party system without considering the sharp breaks from the past. In the German case, domestic political violence and international conflict have combined to produce a history of discontinuities and ruptures unparalleled among modern democracies. A highly polarised and extremely fragmented multiparty system emerged under the imperial regime (*Kaiserreich*), and persisted in a modified form under the Weimar Republic. Following World War II, the combination of defeat, occupation, socio-economic, as well as constitutional and territorial, changes resulted in a moderate multiparty system dominated by two broadly based *Volksparteien*, or catch-all parties. The postwar party system is widely regarded as stable. Nevertheless, important changes in the social bases of parties, patterns of competition and coalition patterns have occurred, culminating in the recent entry of the Greens. This chapter will explore these changes in light of earlier transformations. However, in order to do so, it is useful to examine the circumstances in which German party politics emerged, particularly the relationship between party and state in Germany and the ways in which this shaped party politics.

Party and State in Germany

The prevailing dilemma for German parties has been the failure to reconcile party and state. From the beginning of the Bismarckian empire until the end of the Weimar experiment, the incompatibility between autocratic-bureaucratic traditions and representational bases of political legitimacy inhibited effective democracy. At issue was the centrality of political parties in the process of governing. In systems based on the British Westminster model political elites have long operated in a context of responsible party government. The reverse is true in the United States, where the separation of powers never incorporated a direct form of party control. Even in France, where regime crises have provided frequent shocks to the party system, a strong parliamentary tradition accords parties a central role in governing. This has been modified but hardly destroyed under the Fifth Republic.

In contrast, German political history has been far more erratic. Political parties developed under the *Kaiserreich* but lacked a firm constitutional or cultural basis for a direct role in government. Instead, parties developed a style of ideological conflict that ill-prepared them for sharing power (Smith 1979:24-5). Throughout the imperial and Weimar periods, parties and parliament suffered from a negative image. Terms of derision, like *Schwatzbude* (gossip chamber), were commonly used to describe the Reichstag (Lehmbruch 1979:147). On the discontinuity between perceptions of state and party, Dyson remarks:

> If parties embodied the fragmentation which was held to be characteristic of civil society, government was part of a wider, universal, and ethical community, the state, and acted with reference to the idea of a public interest which transcended the rivalries of groups...during the Weimar Republic *Parteienstaat* (party state) was primarily a pejorative term which offered an explanation of political crisis (1982:78).

Consistent with this negativism about parties is the view that parties, because they did not emerge and mature within a parliamentary tradition that accepted the basic principle of party government, came to behave as sectarian defenders of class or group interests (Smith 1979:9). When the Weimar Republic finally provided an opportunity for responsible party government in 1919, the parties remained the spokesmen for narrow class or group interests. Partisan behaviour reinforced perceptions of inherent irresponsibility. With the collapse of Weimar and the imposition of Nazi dictatorship, any possibility of gradual adjustment was aborted. However, the collapse of the Nazi regime and the subsequent occupation of Germany provided yet another opportunity for a reconciliation of party and state.

After 1945 a viable German version of party government took hold. This was made possible, in the first instance, by the removal and destruction of long-powerful elite groups. Newly established parties filled the temporary leadership vacuum and emerged as the only legitimate means of elite recruitment. This process was directly encouraged by the occupying powers through the licensing of democratic parties and was later embedded in Article 21 of the Basic Law so that parties became 'constitutionalised' (Johnson 1982:155). Reinforcing this changing relationship between party and state were shifts in public evaluations of parties that facilitated a gradual acceptance of party government (Pulzer 1982:9-37). In the postwar era, parties became the primary instruments for reinstating democracy. Through a complex process of partisan-bureaucratic interpenetration, a modern and legitimate *Parteienstaat* took hold (Dyson 1977). The postwar Bonn regime is unique in that parties have been accorded the centrality and prestige of governing free from an atmosphere of constant political crisis. The transformation of party politics in modern Germany must be viewed in the context of this dramatic break with the past.

Beyond this integration of party system and constitutional order, two dimensions of change are central to understanding the evolution of the party system. One involves changes internal to individual parties, resulting from changing social conditions. The other concerns changes in the electorate to which party elites have responded with new styles of competition. Both are intimately intertwined.

In the postwar era we observe the rise of a new type of party, the *Volkspartei*, of which the CDU was the prototype. A loose conservative coalition under a nonsecretarian Christian label, it stands in sharp contrast to its predecessor, the Centre Party (Zentrum). Christian Democratic success in the early years of the Federal Republic forced the electorally stagnant and ideologically rooted SPD to discard its *Klassenpartei* strategy for that of a *Volkspartei*.

This organisational trend has often been taken as evidence of an end of ideology. German developments in the 1950s and early 1960s provided the strongest single illustration of Kirchheimer's 'waning of opposition' thesis. Now with hindsight, it is easy to criticise this 'end of ideology' view. What is clear, however, is (1) that ideology did not end but was transformed (Smith 1982:63-4); (2) that the *Volksparteien* did make a lasting contribution to ideological convergence and to the restructuring of partisan cleavages; and, (3) that even with signs of new polarisation in the 1980s, these large, electorally oriented party organisations remain dominant *Staatsparteien* within the German *Parteienstaat*.

Continuity and Change in Party Competition

Among western systems in which democratic practice is based on a nineteenth or early twentieth century suffrage extension, one usually observes a core of partisan continuity rooted in this formative period. Ideological traditions, political families, and partisan labels often date back to the founding of democratic orders. This is true not only for relatively stable regimes like Great Britain, Canada and the United States, but also for nations that have experienced chronic regime instability like France and Italy. For Germany one could reasonably expect this general tendency to hold less well because of the discontinuities of war and dictatorship. Certainly the gaps between past and present patterns of party competition are greater than for most of Germany's neighbors, who at the end of World War II maintained or reconstituted pre-war party systems. In Germany the party system underwent a substantial transformation that constituted a sharp break with the past. Thus the Federal Republic can be viewed as a case of late but radical partisan restructuring.

Before discussing the extent and causes of these changes, several remarks are in order. First, this description of system change appears to be incompatible with the widely held view of postwar German democracy as a model of political moderation and stability. The paradox diminishes when we note that the period referred to corresponds to the rebuilding of a democratic polity. Changes in the 1940s and early 1950s provided the basis for a highly stable pattern of three-party competition that persisted through the next two decades. Second, the changes that did occur were a mixture of intended and unintended actions. As a divided and defeated nation, the rebuilding of civil authority in Germany was partly shaped by the goals and pressures of the occupying powers. These were felt initially through denazification and the licensing of parties in the immediate postwar years (Spencer 1984; Merkl 1963). This did not involve any systematic design for the future of the party system, but rather was an attempt to preclude any neo-nazi or authoritarian resurgence. Finally, although the dramatic changes that took place in the first years of the Federal Republic were succeeded by a period of relative calm, this does not imply that no changes occurred thereafter. In fact, as Kaltefleiter (1984:15-42) and Smith (1979:101-19) suggest, there was an evolutionary pattern of change over the next twenty years that is crucial to understanding West German politics.

In the immediate postwar years, many observers expected Germany to revert to older traditions. This implied either a revival of anti-democratic forces or a return to the polarised pluralism of Weimar. Attempts to mobilise authoritarian sympathies were constrained by allied licensing policies (and later by Article 21 of the Basic Law) and were pre-empted by the success of the democratic parties. Nevertheless, the first Bundestag election in 1949 re-established a complex multiparty pattern (twelve parties won representation), justifying its interpretation as the 'last election of the Weimar Republic' (Falter 1981:236).

The 1949 election did not provide an accurate prediction of postwar developments. By 1953 the number of parties in the Bundestag was reduced to six, with the three largest capturing 83.5 per cent of the popular vote. By 1961 only these three, with 94.3 per cent of the vote, retained parliamentary seats (Loewenberg 1978:8). Simplification and consolidation of support was rapid, thorough, and unanticipated. Two overriding features distinguish this period of consolidation: One is the elimination of all minor parties except the FDP. The other is the concentration of conservative forces within the CDU/CSU, whose popular vote jumped from 31 per cent in 1949, to 45.2 per cent in 1953 and 50.2 per cent by 1957, while the SPD stagnated at 30 per cent (see figure 4.1).

Among the factors accounting for the exit of the minor parties, two are most significant: the effect of the electoral system and Adenauer's strategy of absorbing the smaller middle-class, regional and special interest parties (Fisher 1974). The first was not felt in 1949 because the 5 per cent rule was applied only on a regional level. However, the 1949 election did permit Adenauer to become Chancellor and to initiate his strategy of building a broad coalition under the CDU/CSU umbrella. By 1953, with the 5 per cent barrier defined as a national minimum for a party to share in the proportional allocation of seats, the incentives for working with the Christian Democrats proved to be irresistible for formations like the German Party (Deutsche Partei) in Lower Saxony, the Bavarian Party (BP) and the League of Expellees and Those Deprived of Rights (Block der Heimatvertriebenen und Entrechteten (von Beyme 1983:26-9; Smith 1979:105)). While it is accurate to see these two factors as decisive, the transformation of the Christian Democratic alliance from its confessional roots in the Centre

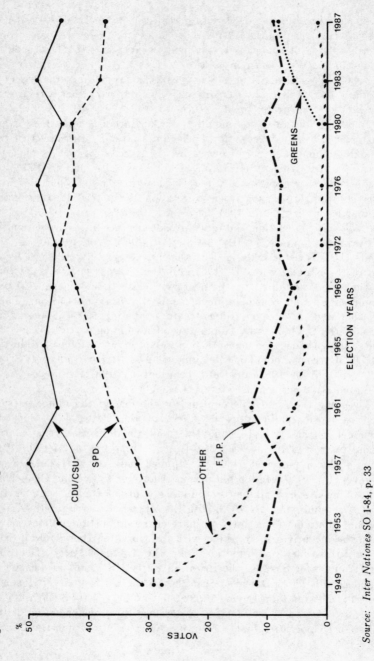

Figure 4.1 Elections to the Bundestag 1949-87

Source: *Inter Nationes* SO 1-84, p. 33

Party to a broad movement appealing to Catholics and Protestants alike was essential to this process of consolidation (Pridham 1978:332-9).

The elimination of anti-system extremism plus the amalgamation of the various minor/regional parties did not mean the immediate inception of consensus politics. Through the 1950s, policies diverged. The SPD was still formally committed to a socialist society and favoured the reunification of a neutral Germany. In contrast the CDU/CSU opted for a 'social-market' economy, a direct role in the western alliance, strident anti-communism and a policy of non-recognition (the Hallstein Doctrine) for dealing with East Germany and the Soviet bloc.

The 1960s and 1970s were an era of stability in terms of the number of parties, but these decades also saw the emergence of the SPD from its working-class milieu. The Bad Godesberg programme of 1959 marked a conscious transition to *Volkspartei* status and set in motion a concerted attempt to escape from a permanent minority role. This was significant because it confirmed the majoritarian vocation of both major parties, a development, like the demise of minor parties, unique in German party history. It is only with the post-Godesberg 1961 election that the Social Democrats were able to expand beyond their 'red' core. From 1961 through 1972 the SPD made gradual inroads especially among the new middle classes, finally achieving a new balance in the party system. During this period no new party was able to surpass the five per cent hurdle, although the neo-nazi NPD (Nationaldemokratische Partei Deutschlands) came very close in 1969.

Finally, the critical role of the Free Democratic Party must not be overlooked. The only minor party to survive the concentrating pressures of the 1950s, the FDP emerged as the Federal Republic's most durable governing force. A junior partner in both CDU/CSU- and SPD-led coalitions, the Free Democrats have often acted as a constraint on policy and as a guarantor against single-party excess. They also provided the pivot for both major partisan realignments of 1969 and 1982 and in the process have twice gone through their own crises of existence (Kaack 1977; Søe 1985).

By the early 1960s the trend towards catch-all parties had made Germany the most prominent case of convergence consistent with Kirchheimer's 'waning of opposition' (1957:128-56). Yet, by the next decade a revival of confrontation, political protest and fundamentalist critiques prompted speculation about a crisis of legitimacy within the party system (Kaltefleiter 1980; Offe 1979; Kaase 1979). This new phase, first seen in the extra-parliamentary protests of the late 1960s, became fully evident following the OPEC oil crisis of 1973-74. Competitive relationships in the 1970s increasingly reflected the erosion of prosperity-based consensus politics. These tensions were especially telling for the SPD, the major coalition partner during this era. They arose not only between government and opposition but, particularly after 1980, between the two coalition parties and, among the factions within the SPD itself (Braunthal 1982:72-7). Many activists within the SPD became disillusioned with the party establishment and especially with Chancellor Schmidt (whose disdain for the left-wing of his own party was undisguised) and began to channel their energies into new social movements like the *Bürgerinitiativen* and later the Greens. These developments are crucial to the emergence of a 'new politics' dimension in the German party system of the 1980s (Bürklin 1984).

Internal Partisan Adaptation

In the postwar era, we observe the erosion of traditional class cleavages through social and economic change. Mobility, secularisation and urbanisation created a society more differentiated and less compartmentalised than in the past and one in which class, ethnic and religious differences have become less important. In view of this, it is not surprising that parties have become more heterogeneous. For the SPD this meant a process of embourgeoisement, for the CDU/CSU, an increasingly inter-confessional base. Particularly since the catch-all strategy of *Volksparteien* has become the norm, complex coalitions of interests have developed within both major parties.

Complementing these changes in electoral strategies are changes in the social composition of party members and elites. Immediately after 1945 the CDU organisation was built on a Catholic membership base, drawn from the old Centre Party while the SPD resurfaced with its working-class tradition largely intact. Both have become more heterogeneous, but the similarity should not be overstated. The CDU consciously defined itself as an inter-confessional party with a catch-all vocation. In contrast, the SPD clung to its blue-collar heritage but unintentionally changed from the inside; over time, working-class members gradually gave way to better educated white-collar and civil servant activists. The extent of this long-term change is evident in table 4.1.

For the Christian Democrats, who in their pre-1933 incarnation, already constituted an inter-class party, the postwar diversification of membership primarily involved the realisation of its inter-confessional character. Over time it attracted an increasing proportion of

Table 4.1 The Changing Social Structure of Party Memberships (in %)

Occupation	SPD		CDU		CSU	FDP	
	1956-7	1977	1955	1977	1977	1965	1977
Workers	40	22	15	11	14	14	5
Employees	14	24	18	27	20	25	30
Civil Servants		13	9	12	12	15	14
Self-employed	7	5	34	26	32	31	19
Pensioners	25	18	7	5	6	11	12
Housewives	14	6	13	10	4	11	11
Those in training, education	-	5	-	6	4	9	

Sources: Kolinsky (1984) p. 76, Haungs (1983) pp. 35-6.

Table 4.2 Party Membership by Confession (in per cent)

| | Population | CDU | | | | SPD |
	(1974)	1967	1971	1977	1981	1977
Protestant	49.0	22.0	25.0	33.0	34.0	53.0
Catholic	44.6	77.0	73.0	61.0	60.0	28.0

Sources: Schmidt (1983) p. 648, Haungs (1983) pp. 33, 36.

Protestant members. However as table 4.2 demonstrates, this did not become pronounced until the 1970s when the CDU experienced an unprecedented influx of new members. Evidence on new members in the 1980s (47 per cent Catholic and 41 per cent Protestant) confirms the trend towards greater religious balance (Kolinsky 1984:137).

For both major parties the tendency has been toward increasingly heterogeneous group and class representation among party members and activists. In addition, all parties have tended to recruit activists and parliamentary candidates from among the better educated. This is equally apparent for the Greens and the FDP. All parties overrepresent public servants at the top of their organisational hierarchies, a phenomenon undoubtedly encouraged by the inter-penetration of bureaucratic and political careers. This inevitably reinforced the urban, highly educated characteristics of party elites, regardless of party label, and is without doubt related to elite consensus-building and party convergence. However, as Feist, Güllner and Liepelt (1978:172-5) have argued, the trend towards catch-all parties, measured by the social composition of membership and by the endurance of their traditional roots within core electorates, is far from complete. Neither CDU/CSU nor SPD is a perfect *Volkspartei*. Even so, the postwar trend toward catch-all strategies and political style of both major parties is beyond dispute.

Parties and Voters

Two countervailing themes for the analysis of partisan align-ments are a) that over time demographic and socio-economic characteristics of the electorate are subject to change but b) that party organisations tend to maintain loyal cores of support within distinctive class, religious or communal subgroups (Butler and Stokes 1971:1-12). Thus relationships among parties rest on a mix of stable and shifting components of popular support. Aggregate electoral trends provide a means of demonstrating the evolution of partisan alignments and explaining party system change.

Electoral analyses generate two competing hypotheses about shifting social bases of party support. One suggests relative stability. Fluctuations from election to election produce different winners and losers, but core support for major parties remains loyal (Pappi and Terwey 1982). The opposing view posits the erosion of traditional loyalties and realignment in response to changing social and economic conditions and changing political values. This implies long-term transformations within the electorate and changes at the elite level as well.

Prior to 1933 German parties represented particular interests and did not seek to build support beyond their own homogeneous class or confessional cores. The fate of each party depended heavily on the growth and mobilisation of its own social base. Parties rooted in declining social sectors would eventually decline. An expanding sector would gradually produce more votes and a stronger party. The growth of the industrial working class and the concomitant expansion of the SPD from a minor formation in 1871 to the largest single party in the Reich by 1912 typifies such a transformation (Ritter and Niehuss 1980).

Wartime destruction and defeat produced massive dislocations while postwar recovery and affluence generated new sources of change. As a consequence, the debate over partisan loyalties is now far more complex. Signs of dealignment and realignment of electorates in the postwar era have prompted an intriguing model of social change suggested by the 'coming of post-industrial society' (Bell 1973; Gustafsson 1978). This theory documents the expansion of the tertiary sector, particularly the rise of a new middle class made up of salaried employees, who are typically well educated, urban and secular. The growth of this sector is matched by the absolute or relative decline of farmers, blue-collar workers, and the old middle classes (artisans and the self-employed). The most important issue for the study of party systems is the extent to which changes in social structure have produced transformations in core support groups. In other words, to what extent has there been an erosion of traditional class/group partisan loyalties, and to what extent have new middle class voters allied themselves with existing parties or provided impetus for new political formations?

With regard to core support groups, one can observe certain basic continuities. The CDU/CSU has consistently attracted Catholics and practicing Protestants, farmers, white-collar workers and old middle class occupations. The SPD remains the primary party for blue-collar workers and especially for trade union families. The Free Democrats, despite a fragile core, continue to attract middle-class Protestants.

For the CDU/CSU the most basic continuity is in its confessional roots. However, its non-sectarian christian label and moderate conservatism has made it the natural party of large numbers of Protestants, especially in northern Germany. Christian Democrats have also attracted a significant minority of working-class voters, especially among non-unionised Catholics, while its market-oriented ideology has always appealed to a cross section of middle-class voters. As a result, no party better fits the catch-all model.

The SPD emerged from the war as a predominantly working-class party. After falling behind the Christian Democrats in the 1950s, it, too, sought a broader base and consciously appealed to new social groups. By the 1970s the SPD had achieved near balance with the CDU/CSU by appealing to young voters and to other social categories, such as women, white-collar employees, and the Catholic working class, where previously it had been weak (Conradt and Lambert 1974). The transformation of the SPD was far more dramatic than that of the CDU/CSU because the incorporation of middle-class members and voters increased the likelihood of conflict with the older working-class core. Educated, middle-class activists have tended to displace blue-collar party members (Feist *et al.* 1978:178-85). This combination brought the SPD closer to the catch-all model and accounted for its electoral gains, which peaked in 1972. However, with the onset of economic stagnation in the middle of the 1970s, these same changes produced built-in tensions and a strategic dilemma sharply accentuated by the emergence of the Greens on the left. The fundamental problem confronting the SPD, evident in the elections of 1983 and 1987, was that the party was attempting to appeal to two very different electorates at the same time.

In the early years of the Federal Republic, the FDP was an economically conservative element to the right of the CDU/CSU. Its roots were in the declining small town, old middle class of Protestant Germany. The need to find a new base of support within the growing, more progressive new middle classes was basic to the FDP's decision to ally itself with the SPD in the social-liberal coalition of 1969 (Kaack 1977).

Electoral Trends in the Social-Liberal Era

The electoral history of the Federal Republic includes the early ascendency of the CDU/CSU, the subsequent steady SPD gains over five election periods, a period of relative parity, and more recently, an erosion of Social Democratic support and, for the time being, a return to CDU/CSU ascendency. These trends suggest three critical turning points, 1953, 1969 and 1983.

The election of 1969 terminated twenty years of Christian Democratic hegemony. It confirmed the wisdom of both the SPD's Godesberg revisionism and its strategic alliance with the CDU/CSU during the period of the Grand Coalition. However, Social Democratic gains alone were insufficient. The conversion within the FDP in favour of a social-liberal coalition was critical to achieving the first fundamental *Machtwechsel* which, with Willy Brandt's election as

Chancellor, initiated an era of moderate reform. The transfer of power based on a new coalition was made possible by earlier social and economic successes and by gradual changes taking place within the German electorate (Klingemann and Pappi 1970a; Edinger 1970). The popularity of this change was confirmed in 1972; the Christian Democrats lost heavily where the SPD made its greatest gains. These losses were, however, partially offset by the gain of previous NPD voters. The erosion of Christian Democratic strength over the two elections emphasised the Catholic-rural core of its support (Conradt and Lambert 1974:74-5; Pappi 1973:191-213; Conradt 1972).

In 1969, the SPD had made impressive inroads into middle-class urban bases of CDU support. White-collar, salaried workers and especially Catholics within these categories were modal switchers as the SPD reached beyond its traditional working-class and Protestant core (Kaase 1973:157; Conradt 1972:33-8). Even though the SPD continued to gain strength, 1972 was not a simple reinforcement of 1969 changes. SPD advances were strong in both rural and industrial areas but not in metropolitan and middle-class areas. Working-class Catholics con-stituted the key group of switchers (Conradt and Lambert 1974:77-8). Because Brandt's appeal was also felt among younger voters, the reduction of the voting age to 18 following the 1969 election provided a substantial reservoir of strength for the SPD-FDP coalition.

For the Free Democrats, 1972 represented a great victory that raised them safely above the 5 per cent danger zone following the near disaster in 1969. The 1972 gains were most important in middle-class, urban areas. The FDP showed renewed strength especially among white-collar workers and the young, categories where the SPD had made its greatest gains in 1969. Part of the reason for the overlap in 1969 SPD support and 1972 FDP gains was due to the second ballot *Leihstimmen*, or loaned votes. In order to guarantee the survival of the minor coalition party, some SPD supporters split their vote and opted for the SPD on the first (constituency) ballot and the FDP on the second (party list) ballot.

Both 1969 and 1972 can be viewed as the culmination of realigning trends with 1972 signifying a high point for the SPD and a temporary 'ghettoisation' of the CDU/CSU. However, the years following this election tell a different story. Internally, the SPD faced increasing tensions and ideological infighting. These became par-ticularly acute when the more conservative Helmut Schmidt replaced Willy Brandt as Chancellor.

Despite the shock of the 1973 oil crisis and a subsequent period of relative economic stagnation, German party alignments throughout the 1970s gave a superficial appearance of relative stability: the SPD-FDP governing coalition won (1972 and 1980), or at least survived (1976), all three Bundestag elections over this time. However, beneath this calm were some systematic electoral shifts that set the stage for the erosion of the social-liberal majority and the collapse of the governing coalition.

Early in the 1970s the SPD began to suffer defeats in Land and municipal elections. Simultaneously, the CDU/CSU, which had experienced difficulty in adapting to its new role as opposition party, was entering a period of organisational rejuvenation and electoral revival (Feist *et al.* 1978:175-83). Out of power, the party could no longer operate merely as a supporting organisation (or *Kanzlerwahlverein*) as in the Adenauer era. The CDU began to recognise the need to attract new members and to rebuild at the grassroots (Barton 1984:196-209). During the mid 1970s there was a massive influx of new members - due primarily to a new climate of confrontation between government and opposition rather than to the conscious recruitment strategy of the CDU itself. By 1976 the CDU/CSU had made an impressive recovery, winning a near majority (48.6 per cent) of the party list vote. Helmut Kohl, often criticised for being an uninspiring leader, proved adept at recapturing traditional CDU/CSU loyalists.

While in 1969, and again in 1972, the SPD, and to a lesser extent the FDP, had made substantial gains among traditional CDU voters, in 1976 many prodigal switchers, typically both blue-collar and white-collar Catholics, returned to the fold. The CDU/CSU also gained 50 per cent of the first-time voters in the 18-22 age bracket. However, the 23-28 age group, i.e. first-time voters in 1972, who had previously voted heavily for Brandt, retained their preference for the SPD. Nevertheless, the new popularity of the CDU among German youth was a sign of future vitality.

For the CDU/CSU, the importance of 1976 lies in the reconstruction of its earlier electoral base. In West Germany as a whole, the shift in favour of the CDU/CSU was 3.7 per cent. But this was distributed unevenly across regions. The broadest generalisation concerns the so-called north-south split. The CDU/CSU did best in the south where it was already very strong and where some of its most conservative elements have their power bases. In North-Rhine Westphalia the CDU waged a hard campaign led by General Secretary Biedenkopf and came close to matching the party's national gains. But this regional gain of 3.5 per cent did not allow the CDU to crack the major SPD strongholds in the Ruhr, where SPD losses were often less than 2 per cent. In the Rhineland - where there is a higher proportion of Catholics and where the CDU has been traditionally strong, it made its greatest gains. But the religious factor appears in more limited aggregate breakdowns as well (Wildenmann 1976:4), and the impression emerging from this election is one of a return to normal (Converse 1967:9-39). In 1969 and 1972 Brandt captured a wave of new support which included many traditional CDU voters. In 1976 those same voters moved back to their traditional loyalties. From this perspective, the Brandt phenomenon of 1972 was a 'deviating' election and 1976 constituted a return to an earlier division, that is, a re-solidification of two dominant blocs, the bourgeois-christian on the one hand and the social-liberal on the other. This reinstating effect casts doubt on the extent of realigning trends within the German electorate and more generally on the convergence thesis (Verba 1965:131-54 and Conradt 1974:222-38).

The Bundestag election of 1980 provided a partial halt to the voting trends evident in 1976. Measured against other recent federal elections, the 1980 contest was characterised by the primacy of leadership images represented by the Chancellor and his challenger, and by the relative stability of the electorate as a whole. Although the confrontation between Helmut Schmidt and Franz Josef Strauss worked to the advantage of the governing coalition, it was primarily the Free Democrats who gained among middle-class anti-Strauss voters.

The 1980 election reinstated a governing majority equivalent in size to that of 1972, but beneath this superficial similarity there were sharp differences. The 1972 election was above all a victory for Brandt and the SPD; in 1980 the Social Democratic vote stagnated even though Strauss' candidacy provided an opportunity for substantial gains. The failure to win new votes resulted in SPD resentment against a Chancellor who had apparently solidified his own position but not that of his party. Paradoxically, in 1976 a narrow electoral advantage had produced a relatively cohesive and stable governing coalition; in 1980 an enlarged SPD-FDP majority produced unease, enmity and a difficult future for an aging SPD leadership (Feist and Liepelt 1981:34-58).

Because electoral defeat had been so widely foreseen, the CDU/CSU's worst performance in 30 years (44.5 per cent) did not have the negative impact one might have expected. The CDU/CSU remained the single largest bloc, but more importantly the election could be viewed as a crucial threshold which finally had been crossed. In contrast to the dissatisfaction in SPD ranks, the 1980 election opened up prospects for revitalisation. The election had not been the rout it might have been and the CDU/CSU alliance had been freed from the perennial, Strauss-inspired threat of schism.

The big winner in 1980 was the FDP. The Liberal surge to 10.6 per cent of the party list vote (its highest share since 1961) came as a surprise to many. In 1976 the Free Democrats had expected substantial gains but had not received them, and the cloud of a major Landtag election defeat in North-Rhine Westphalia hung over the party. Thus the FDP 'mini-landslide' justifiably can be seen as the most dramatic and unexpected facet of the 1980 election. Liberal gains came from both sides. Of more than a million new votes (compared to 1976) it is estimated that almost one half came from SPD deviators; a slightly smaller bloc came from the CDU/CSU camp with the remainder consisting of new voters and previous non-voters. The relatively poor showing of the Greens also helped the Liberals because the ecologist appeal was relatively strong among Free Democratic core voters. On the second ballot extensive ticket-splitting benefited the FDP, but unlike 1972 this does not appear to have been a 'loaned vote' phenomenon (Søe 1985:141-44).

An important consequence of Free Democratic electoral success was to increase its leverage within the social-liberal coalition. Although the new balance of power could work to the advantage of Chancellor Schmidt and the more conservative elements within the SPD, it would also have a less positive effect, aggravating left-right tensions within the SPD. As this happened, consensus within the coalition would erode, encouraging the FDP to think of an alternate Christian Democratic-Liberal coalition (Paterson and Smith 1981; Kaase and Klingemann 1983). By 1982 persisting economic stagnation and declining popularity had produced a deadlock resolved only by the collapse of the coalition and the election of Helmut Kohl as Chancellor (through a constructive vote of no-confidence).

The 1983 Bundestag elections, made possible by a contrived dissolution (as specified in Article 68 of the Basic Law), aroused a great deal of interest and emotion. Hailed by some as an election likely to shape German politics for the rest of the century, the 1983 election took on the characteristics of a high-stimulus election (Campbell 1967:44), characterised by a crisis atmosphere. This was rooted in political uncertainty and in the primacy of two issues, management of the economy and strategies for national security. Uncertainty about the future of the FDP and the Greens prompted many voters to express fears about ungovernability if - as had happened already in Hesse and Hamburg - no workable coalition could be found after the election. In view of the possibility of a major transformation in the German party system, a sense developed that the collapse of the SPD-FDP government and the subsequent elections were a fundamental turning point. This suggested an electorate under abnormally high pressure to re-evaluate standing political loyalties.

Indeed, 1983 provided critical victories for both the new coalition and the Greens. The success of the new Christian Democratic-Liberal alliance was not unexpected. Polls prior to the election had consistently shown the CDU/CSU leading the SPD by at least five percentage points. As the FDP became increasingly certain of gaining at least 5 per cent, the outcome appeared less and less in doubt. What was more surprising was the solidity of the victory and the resounding nature of the SPD defeat. The CDU/CSU won 48.8 per cent of the vote, while the SPD dropped to 38.2 per cent. At the same time, the Liberals won 7.0 per cent, and the Greens 5.6 per cent.

As the first new party to overcome the five per cent hurdle, the Greens jolted 'business as usual' politics. Since 1983 they have disrupted conventional parliamentary practices and broadened policy debates (Bürklin 1981:206-9; Fogt 1983). Regarded by some as a dangerous menace but by others as a refreshing stimulus, there can be little doubt that the Greens have altered coalition politics and electoral strategies. For the Social Democrats, the question of how to respond to the Green challenge has become a burning issue, highlighted by the establishment of the first red-green coalition in Hesse in 1985. For the Greens, electoral success in 1983 and again in 1987 accentuated the split between the coalition-oriented realists and the anti-system fundamentalists. Beyond these internal effects, the Green breakthrough fueled the larger debate over the extent and meaning of changes in party politics, in particular whether the Green phenomenon signifies a basic realignment of partisan support along a 'new politics' dimension (Dalton 1984; Bürklin 1985).

Whether 1983 marks a major realignment will remain a matter of controversy for some time to come. Beyond dispute, however, was the confirmation of a new conservative majority and the relegation of the SPD to opposition status. For the first time since the early sixties, a competitive imbalance (indicated by a 10 per cent spread in support between the two major parties) had been re-established. This prompted questions about the amount of electoral change compared to 1980. According to one survey research institute, 1983 produced the highest level of vote transfers in 25 years. The principal SPD losses were direct CDU gains (approximately 1.6 million). Among the most significant areas of Christian Democratic gains were the SPD

'Hochburgen' in North-Rhine Westphalia. For the past twenty years or more, the major industrial cities of the Ruhr had been stable Social Democratic strongholds, but this time many experienced substantial shifts away from the SPD. Here the CDU's stress on economic issues and governing competence paid off. Elsewhere, Social Democratic support was also depleted by the Greens who attracted about 750,000 ex-SPDers. The SPD recovered only a small number of voters from the FDP (Infas 1983:2).

The Greens ran strongest in Hamburg and Bremen and weakest in Bavaria and Rhineland-Palatinate, but the Green trend was national in character. In 1983 - as in previous and subsequent elections - the strength of the Greens was concentrated among the urban, well-educated and younger voters. Of the 21 districts where they captured 8 per cent or more of the vote, six included university towns. Green strength on the first ballot (4.1 per cent compared to the FDP's 2.8) suggested that the protest movement was more securely rooted than some observers were inclined to admit.

Although the 1983 results demonstrate substantial electoral movement (Berger *et al.* 1983:556-82; Feist and Liepelt 1983:287-310), this can be overstated because, to a considerable extent, these shifts signify a return of conservatives to the Christian Democratic fold. In 1980, the candidature of Franz Josef Strauss aroused misgivings among many voters, encouraging voting deviations. In 1983 the CDU made impressive gains in the same areas (Hamburg, Bremen, Lower Saxony and Schleswig-Holstein) where in 1980 the Schmidt-Genscher coalition had benefitted from anti-Strauss feelings among middle-class voters. It was also here that the FDP suffered its greatest setbacks. When one recalls that in 1983 Kohl as chancellor-candidate received almost exactly the same percentage of the vote as in 1976, it is certainly plausible to see CDU/CSU gains not so much as the winning of new voters but as the reconstitution of a conservative bloc that was previously imperfectly mobilised. From 1972 through 1980 the SPD benefitted from popular perceptions of leadership competence. This advantage passed to Kohl and the CDU as a result of Schmidt's withdrawal and of the CDU's own effective campaign. The absence of a 'chancellor effect' to bolster the SPD in March, 1983 allowed the real extent of Social Democratic weakness to surface (Güllner 1983:7; von Krockow 1983).

In contrast to 1983, when there was a significant CDU/CSU advance due to SPD losses, in 1987 both major parties lost ground. The CDU/CSU dropped 4.5 per cent, producing its worst showing since 1949. Suffering only limited losses (-1.2 percent), the SPD stabilised its electorate. The gap between the two *Volksparteien* was only marginally reduced. The 1987 vote produced very little transfer of support between right and left. Instead the prevailing shifts were from the CDU/CSU to the FDP or from the SPD to the Greens.

Although the ferocity of political debate within the Green party sometimes has tempted observers (including many Social Democrats) to underestimate the staying power of the Greens and even to predict their self-destruction, numerous land and local elections over the course of the 1980s have indicated how firmly established the Green electorate really is (Fogt and Uttitz 1984). Issues like nuclear energy, pollution, and peace have been effective and integral elements in attracting support for the Greens. The 1987 elections further confirmed the seriousness of the problems confronting the Social Democrats, who find themselves beleaguered and torn in different directions. Their disadvantage *vis-à-vis* the Christian Democrats is comparable to that of the early 1960s, and they must contend with a vigourous and credible challenge emanating from the Greens.

Four-party competition was further reinforced in 1987 by the significant advances made by the Free Democrats. In 1983 the FDP had paid a price for switching coalition partners, when many left-liberals either quit the party or switched to the SPD. Four years later national gains of 2.1 per cent (primarily at the expense of the Christian Democrats) demonstrated the renewed vitality of this crucial and pivotal party both within the electorate and as a coalition partner. FDP popularity was also evident in the several Landtag contests held in the months following the 1987 Bundestag election. However, while 1987 may be labeled the year of the Liberals, in the longer term the fate of the FDP remains an open question. Its loyal core remains dangerously small. Without second ballot 'loaned votes' from one of the other parties, the FDP is always in danger of falling below the five percent minimum required for parliamentary representation.

Conclusion: The Changing Shape of the German Party System

The literature on comparative parties suggests a continuum (figure 4.2) based on degrees of fragmentation ranging from polarised pluralism (Sartori 1966), where anti-system alternatives are strong, to consensus politics, where differences in partisan policy stances tend to dissolve under the pressures of convergence (Kirchheimer 1957).

The German party system has run the gamut of this dimension. Fragmentation developed under the *Kaiserreich* and persisted in the Weimar period, making Germany a classic case of extreme polarisation.

Figure 4.2 Varieties of Party Systems

Polarised,	Moderate	Centrist,	Convergence,
centrifugal	multipartyism	centripetal	consensus
pluralism		bipartism	politics

The characteristic features of the pre-1933 German party system included sectarian electoral cores and regionalised organisations. In 1912 only one party (the SPD) contested every constituency and had a coherent national organisation. Competition was fragmented and polarised, while the style of partisan debate was highly ideological and irresponsible (Smith 1979:9-25).

By comparison the immediate postwar era was one of moderate multipartyism in which the extremes were either truncated (Smith 1976) or marginalised. Licensing under the occupation authorities, followed by outlawing of the KPD and SRP under Article 21 of the Basic Law, provided immediate regulation of extremist formations. Less direct but equally important were the division of Germany, the Cold War and pervasive anti-communism that had already reduced the KPD to a fringe party well before it was declared illegal in 1956. Complementing this trend towards 'centrality' was the new dominance of *Volksparteien* whose catch-all tendencies made Germany the clearest demonstration of Kirchheimer's 'waning of opposition' thesis.

This resulted in a diversification of partisan electorates, a new stress on building majoritarian electoral blocs through broad appeals and flexible ideological positions. It also meant the erosion of sectarianism and of regionalism as bases for party competition. It did not produce a total convergence of major party electorates. Nor did competition for marginal voters in the centre of the political spectrum necessarily mean the dissipation of traditional partisan loyalties (Pappi and Terwey 1982:179-85). In this respect both CDU/CSU and SPD have remained only 'imperfect' *Volksparteien*. Each has maintained its electoral core, a Catholic base for the CDU/CSU and a trade union base for the SPD. Major party competition has then remained asymmetrically stable (Pappi 1977:206-9). The key targets for competition have been the urban, middle-class sectors which in recent elections have tended to divide rather evenly between Christian Democrats and Social Democrats and have been crucial both to the survival of the Free Democrats and to the success of the Greens. In general, the postwar transformation of the German party system suggests a non-linear evolution from early divergence through a consensus oriented convergence to patterns of party competition in the 1980s that reflect new strains towards polarisation superimposed on well-established catch-all parties.

References

Barton, T. (1984) 'Die CDU 1975-1983: Nach rechts rutschende Honoratiorenpartei? Zum Selbstverständnis von Parteitagsdelegierten', *Zeitschrift für Parlamentsfragen 15*, 196-209

Bell, D. (1973) *The Coming of Post-Industrial Society*, Basic Books, New York

Berger, M., W. Gibowski, D. Roth, and W. Schulte (1983) 'Regierungswechsel und politische Einstellungen. Eine Analyse der Bundestagswahl 1983', *Zeitschrift für Parlamentsfragen 14*, 556-582

Bürklin, W. (1985) 'The Greens: Ecology and the New Left', in H. Wallach and G. Romoser (eds.), *West German Politics in the Mid-Eighties*, Praeger, New York, 187-218

Bürklin, W. (1984) *Grüne Politik*, Westdeutscher Verlag, Opladen

Braunthal, G. (1982) *The West German Social Democrats 1969-1982, Profile of a Party in Power*, Westview, Boulder, Colorado

Butler, D. and D. Stokes (1974) *Political Change in Britain*, St. Martin's, New York

Campbell, A. (1967) 'Surge and Decline: A Study of Electoral Change', in A. Campbell, P. Converse, W. Miller and D. Stokes (eds.) *Elections and the Political Order*, Wiley, New York

Conradt, D. (1972) *The West German Party System: An Ecological Analysis of Social Structure and Voting Behavior, 1961-1969*, Sage, Beverly Hills

Conradt, D. (1974) 'West Germany: A Remade Political Culture? Some Evidence from Survey Archives', *Comparative Political Studies 7*, 222-238

Conradt, D. and D. Lambert (1974) 'Party System, Social Structure and Competitive Politics in West Germany: An Ecological Analysis of the 1972 Election', *Comparative Politics 7*, 61-86

Converse, P. (1967) 'The Concept of a Normal Vote', in A. Campbell, P. Converse, W. Miller and D. Stokes (eds.), *Elections and the Political Order*, Wiley, New York, 9-39

Dalton, R. (1984) 'The West German Party System between two Ages', in R. Dalton, S. Flanagan and P. Beck (eds.) *Electoral Change in Advanced Industrial Democracies*, Princeton University Press, Princeton, N.J. 104-133

Dyson, K. (1982) 'Party Government and Party State' in H. Döring and G. Smith (eds.), *Party Government and Political Culture in Western Germany*, St. Martin's Press, New York, 77-99

Germany

Dyson, K. (1977) *Party, State and Bureaucracy in Western Germany*, Sage, London

Edinger, L. (1970) 'Political Change in Germany, the Federal Republic after the 1969 Election', *Comparative Politics 2*, 549-578

Falter, J. (1981) 'Kontinuität und Neubeginn. Die Bundestagswahl 1949 zwischen Weimar und Bonn', *Politische Vierteljahresschrift, 22*, 236-63

Feist, U., M. Güllner, and K. Liepelt (1978) 'Structural Assimilation versus Ideological Polarization: On Changing Profiles of Political Parties in West Germany', in M. Kaase and K. von Beyme (eds.) *Elections and Parties*, Sage, London, 171-189

Feist, U., and K. Liepelt (1981) 'Stärkung und Gefährdung des sozialliberalen Koalition. Das Ergebnis der Bundestagswahl vom 5. Oktober 1980', *Zeitschrift für Parlamentsfragen*, 34-58

Feist, U. and K. Liepelt (1983) 'Die Wahl zum Machtwechsel: Neuformierung der Wählerschaft oder Wählerkoalition aus Hoffnung? Eine Analyse der Bundestagswahl vom 6. März 1983', *Journal für Sozialforschung, 23*, 287-310

Fisher, S. (1974) *The Minor Parties of the Federal Republic of Germany*, Martinus Nijhoff, The Hague

Fogt, H. (1983) 'Die Grünen in den Parlamenten der Bundesrepublik. Ein Soziogramm, *Zeitschrift für Parlamentsfragen, 14*, 500-516

Fogt, H. and P. Uttitz (1984) 'Die Wähler der Grünen 1980-1983: Systemkritischer neuer Mittelstand', *Zeitschrift für Parlamentsfragen, 15*, 210-225

Güllner, M. (1983) 'Bestätigung, kein Erdrutsch', *Die Zeit*, 18 March

Gustafsson, B. (1978) *Post-Industrial Society*, Croom Helm, London

Haungs, P. (1983) 'Die Christlich Demokratische Union Deutschlands (CDU) und die Christlich Soziale Union in Bayern (CSU)', in H.-J. Veen (ed.) *Christlich-demokratische und konservative Parteien in Westeuropa* I, Schöningh, Paderborn, 9-194

Infas, (1983) *Frankfurter Rundschau*, 8 March, 2

Johnson, N. (1982) 'Parties and the conditions of Political Leadership', in H. Döring and G. Smith (eds.) *Party Government Political Culture in Western Germany*, St. Martin's Press, New York, 154-173

Kaack, H. (1978) 'The FDP in the German Party System,' in K. Cerny (ed.), *Germany at the Polls, the Bundestag Election of 1976*, AEI, Washington, 77-110

Kaase, M. (1973) 'Die Bundestagswahl 1972: Probleme und Analysen,' *Politische Vierteljahresschrift, XIV*, 167

Kaase, M. (1979) 'Legitimitätskrise in westlichen demokratischen Industriegesellschaften: Mythos oder Realität?', in H. Klages and P. Kmieciak (eds.) *Wertwandel und Gesellschaftliche Wandel*, Campus, Frankfurt, 328-350

Kaase M. and H.D. Klingemann (eds.) (1983) *Wahlen und politisches System*, Westdeutscher Verlag, Opladen

Kaltefleiter, W. (1973) *Zwischen Konsens und Krise, Eine Analyse der Bundestagswahl 1972*, Carl Heymanns Verlag, Cologne

Kaltefleiter, W. (1980) 'A Legitimacy Crisis of the Germany Party System?' in P. Merkl (ed.) *West European Party Systems*, New York, Free Press, 597-608

Kaltefleiter W. (1984) *Parteien im Umbruch*, Econ Verlag, Düsseldorf

Kirchheimer, O. (1957) 'The Waning of Opposition in Parliamentary Regimes', *Social Research*, 128-156

Klingemann, H.D. and F.U. Pappi (1970a) 'Die Wählerbewegungen bei der

Bundestagswahl am 28. September 1969,' *Politische Vierteljahresschrift 11*, 111-138

Klingemann, H.D. and F.U. Pappi (1970b) 'The 1969 Bundestag Election in the Federal Republic of Germany: An Analysis of Voting Behavior', *Comparative Politics 2*

Kolinsky, E. (1984) *Parties, Opposition and Society in West Germany*, Croom Helm, London

Lehmbruch, G. (1976) *Parteienwettbewerb im Bundesstaat*, Kohlhammer, Stuttgart

Lehmbruch, G. (1979) 'Liberal Corporatism and Party Government' in P. Schmitter and G. Lehmbruch (eds.) *Trends Toward Corporatist Intermediation*, Sage, London, 147-84

Lipset, S.M. (1960) 'Party Systems and the Representation of Social Groups,' *European Journal of Sociology, 1*, 50-85

Lipset, S.M. and S. Rokkan (1967) eds. *Party Systems and Voter Alignments*, Free Press, New York

Loewenberg, G. (1978) 'The Development of the German Party System' in K. Cerny (ed.), *Germany at the Polls, the Bundestag Election of 1976*, AEI, Washington, 1-27

Merkl, P. (1963) *The Origin of the West German Republic*, Oxford, New York

Mintzel, A. (1984) *Die Volkspartei*, Westdeutscher Verlag, Opladen

Offe, C. (1979) 'Unregierbarkeit. Zur Renaissance Konservativen Krisentheorien', in J. Habermas (ed.), *Stichworte zur geistigen Situation der Zeit*, Suhrkamp, Frankfurt, 294-318

Pappi, F.U. (1973) 'Parteiensystem und Sozialstruktur in der Bundesrepublik', *Politische Vierteljahresschrift, 14*, 191-213

Pappi, F.U. (1977) 'Sozialstruktur, gesellschaftliche Wertorientierung und Wahlabschicht Ergebnisse eines Zeitvergleichs des deutschen Elektorats 1953 und 1976' *Politische Vierteljahresschrift, 18*, 195-229

Pappi, F.U. and M. Terwey (1982) 'The German electorate: Old Cleavages and New Political Conflicts' in H. Döring and G. Smith, (eds.) *Party Government and Political Culture in West Germany*, St. Martin's, New York, 174-96

Paterson, W. (1981) 'The Chancellor and His Party: Political Leadership in the Federal Republic', in W. Paterson and G. Smith, (eds.), *The West German Model, Perspectives on a Stable State*, Frank Cass, London, 3-17

Paterson, W. and G. Smith (1981) eds., *The West German Model, Perspectives on a Stable State*, Frank Cass, London

Pridham, G. (1978) *Christian Democracy in Western Germany: the CDU/CSU in Government and Opposition*, St. Martin's, New York

Pulzer, P. (1982) 'Responsible Party Government in the German Political System' in H. Döring and G. Smith (eds.) *Party Government and Political Culture in Western Germany*, St. Martin's, New York, 9-37

Ritter, G. with M. Niehuss (1980) *Wahlgeschichtliches Arbeitsbuch. Materialen zur Statistik des Kaiserreichs 1871-1918*, Beck, Munich

Rudzio, W. (1983) *Das politische System der Bundesrepublik Deutschland*, Leske, Opladen

Sartori, G. (1966) 'European Political Parties: the Case of Polarized Pluralism', *Political Parties and Political Development*, Princeton University Press, Princeton, 137-176

Schmidt, U. (1983) 'Die Christlich Demokratische Union Deutschlands', in R. Stöss (ed.), *Parteien-Handbuch I*, Westdeutscher Verlag, Opladen, 490-660

Smith, G. (1976) 'The Politics of Centrality in West Germany', *Government and Opposition 11*, 387-407

Smith, G. (1979) *Democracy in Western Germany*, Heinemann, London

Smith, G. (1982) 'The German *Volkspartei* and the Career of the Catch-all Concept' in H. Döring and G. Smith (eds.) *Party Government and Political Culture in Western Germany*, St. Martin's, New York, 59-76

Søe, C. (1985) 'The Free Democratic Party' in H. Wallach and G. Romoser (eds.), West German Politics in the Mid-Eighties, Praeger, New York, 112-186

Spencer, R. (1984) 'The Origins of the Federal Republic of Germany 1944-49' in C. Schweitzer (ed.), *Politics and Government in the Federal Republic of Germany, Basic Documents*, Berg, London, 1-23

Troitzsch, K. (1980) 'Mitgliederstrukturen der Bundestagsparteien' in H. Kaack and R. Roth (eds.), *Handbuch des deutschen Parteiensystems, I*, Leske, Opladen, 81-100

Verba, S. (1965) 'Germany: The Remaking of Political Culture' in W. Pye and S. Verba (eds.), *Political Culture and Political Development*, Princeton University Press, Princeton, 130-170

von Beyme, K. (1983) *The Political System of the Federal Republic of Germany*, St. Martin's, New York

von Krockow, Ch. Graf (1983) 'Kein Erdrutsch', *Die Zeit*, 25 March

Wildenmann, R. (1976) 'Warum sie so gewählt haben, eine Analyse des Wählerverhaltens 1976,' *Die Zeit*, 8 October, p. 4

Wilson, F. (1980) 'Sources of Party Transformation: the Case of France' in P. Merkl (ed.) *West European Party Systems*, Free Press, New York, 526-51

Chapter Five

The Austrian Party System: Continuity and Change

Frederick C. Engelmann

If these lines had been written about 1980, the Austrian party system would have been presented as second to none in stability. It is intriguing to approach the subject in 1987. If we consider only votes and seats, little has changed: the two mass parties founded about a century ago still come close to pre-empting Austria's vote at the federal and provincial levels. The election of 1986, however, strengthened the third party and brought a fourth party into the parliament. Together they won 14 per cent of the vote and seats in parliament. However, although Austria's two major parties may be weakening, nobody predicts their demise. At risk is their duopoly of eighty to ninety per cent - or more - of the vote. If further changes occur, these are less likely to result from the entry of new parties than the failure of the major parties to adapt to post-industrialism and the demands of the upwardly mobile sector of the population.

Certainly up to the time of writing, the Austrian party system has been more stable than other countries discussed in this volume. This chapter attempts to account for this stability, which is as old as mass participation in Austria, as well as for the factors that *may*, finally, bring about change.

Stability: Ninety-eight Years of Le Plus ça Change

On New Year's day in 1889, German Austria's Marxist and labour groups united to form the Social Democratic Labour Party. About the same time, but less formally, Catholic workers, craftsmen, and shopkeepers formed the Christian Social Party. On the two occasions when all adult males were entitled to vote for the imperial parliament, in 1907 and 1911, these two parties split the vote almost evenly with the German Nationalists, but most of the latter's vote was concentrated in areas now in Czechoslovakia and Yugoslavia. Nationalists continued to receive 15-20 per cent of the vote in the First Republic, but the rest was divided between Christian Socials ('blacks') and Social Democrats ('reds').

It would be mockery to speak of stability from 1933 to 1949: 1933 saw the closing of Parliament by the Christian Socials; 1934, the defeat of the Social Democrats in a brief civil war and the transformation of the Christian Socials into the Patriotic Front dictatorship; 1938, the *Anschluss* (annexation to Germany) with 99 per cent voting for the hitherto outlawed Nazis; 1945, the restoration of the republic with elections that excluded half a million lesser Nazis. When the latter were re-enfranchised in 1949 and given a party to vote for (then called the League of Independents) the pattern in table 5.1 emerged:

Table 5.1 Elections of 1930 and 1949 (Percentage of vote)

Parties (1930/1949 designation)	1930	1949
Catholic conservative (Christian Socials/ People's Party)	42	44
Socialist labour (Social Democrats/ Socialists)	41	39
German nationalists (Schober bloc/ Independents)	12	12

This picture is worth a thousand words. A vote shift of 2 per cent among 95 per cent of the voters is all that was brought on by the temporary eclipse of Austria, massive war casualties, the expulsion of Jews, and the four-power Allied occupation.

Clarity demands that the Austrian parties be described briefly at this point. The Austrian People's Party (Österreichische Volkspartei, ÖVP), the successor party of the Christian Socials, is the party of

Austrian business and agriculture, but it has a labour wing. It differs from some of Europe's Christian democratic parties in that there is no powerful capitalist group in Austria to lead it. It differs from the earlier Christian Socials in de-emphasising their clerical Catholic stance. The Socialist Party (Sozialistische Partei Österreichs, SPÖ) is a social democratic party, largely de-ideologised and thus quite different from its predecessor, the Marxist Social Democrats. The party of Austrian labour, it now has considerable white collar support. The Freedom Party (Freiheitliche Partei Österreichs, FPÖ) inherited former Nazis who were enfranchised in 1949, from its immediate predecessor, the League of Independents. Its recent gains are due to the victory of its charismatic and populist German nationalist leader, Jörg Haider, over its liberal wing. Compared to the major parties, it has a small membership and a limited vote potential.

Party positions derive from their original ideologies and their social bases. However, processes of de-ideologisation underway in the Second Republic have de-emphasised class struggle, as has the league structure of the People's Party (business, agriculture, workers and employees). While the SPÖ represents labour within the social partnership (discussed below) and the ÖVP agriculture and Austria's myriad of employers, the social partnership takes many issues (even such divisive ones as the reduction of the work week and the lengthening of minimum vacations) out of inter-party conflict. In contrast to the ideological battles of the First Republic, parties now compete principally for office.

Table 5.2 shows the vote share of Austria's two major parties and its only important minor party in all democratic elections held since 1919. As is apparent from the table, there has been very little change over time; although party ideologies and the style of political competition may have changed, party strengths have remained virtually the same as in the past. This amazing stability is adducible to initial stabilising factors, to factors established during the First Republic and to factors established during the Second Republic. What is equally amazing is that so far these factors have been reinforced, allowing all of them to operate in the Second Republic.

Initial Sources of Stability

The initial factors stabilising the party system in German Austria were party organisation and party support.

Organisation. It was the governmental impotence of the Austrian parties of the late nineteenth century which made them perfect organisations. Not all organisational features were constant

Table 5.2 Vote Share of Major Parties in Austria, 1919-1987 (Per cent; including German Nationalists and successors)

	1919	1920	1923	1927	1930	1945	1949	1953	1956	1959	1962	1966	1970	1971	1975	1979	1983	1987
Christian Socials (ÖVP)	36	42	45	49	42	50+	44	41	46	44	45	48	45	43	43	42	43	41
Social Democrats (SPÖ)	41	36	40	42	41	45+	39	42	43	45	44	43	48	50	51	51	48	43
Pan-Germans/ Independents (FPÖ)	18	17	13	6	12	-	12	11	7	8	7	5	6	6	5	6	5	10
Greens	-	-	-	-	-	-	-	-	-	-	-	-	-	-	-	-	3	5

Source: 1919-1962, F.C. Engelmann in R.A. Dahl (ed.), *Political Oppositions in Western Democracies* (Yale University Press, New Haven, 1966). p. 433; 1966-1983, *Die Nationalratswahl vom 24. April 1983* (Österreichische Staatsdruckerei, Vienna, 1984), p. 57.

throughout: para-military organisations were (fortunately) restricted to the First Republic, and the present functionally federal organisation of the People's Party is a phenomenon of the Second Republic.[1] However, the pervasive features of membership and ancillary organisations contributed to the stability of nearly one century in crucial ways.

We must remember that, for the average Austrian, it was legal to be a party member *before* it was legal to be a party voter. The Christian Social and Social Democratic parties became the political homes for many of the German Austrians - partially enfranchised in 1896, when they were allowed to vote for less than one-fifth of the parliamentary seats - and fully enfranchised in 1907. Both parties were vehicles of political education but, more important, they virtually monopolised the social life of their members. This they did in ancillary organisations with a veritable span from cradle to grave. The final point of activity has been portrayed with unique poignancy by Alfred Diamant (1958:134-5): the ultimate ambition of the active Christian Social was to lie in state in the domed church which housed the remains of Karl Lueger, as mayor of Vienna, the first successful Christian Social, in Vienna's central cemetery; the ultimate ambition of the active Social Democrat was to be cremated in Vienna's central crematorium, a few hundred meters to the north, facing the Lueger church in a final act of defiance.

The ancillary apparatus of the Social Democratic Party was impressive. There was a trade union wing, a youth movement, a women's movement and a full complement of cultural and avocational groups. The First Republic added a strong para-military organisation, the Republican Defense League (Republikanischer Schutzbund). During the interwar years, party membership averaged 700,000 (in a population of 6.5 million). While firmly anti-communist, the party preached a strong ideological line, Austro-Marxism, manifested in the Linz programme of 1926.

When Vienna was liberated, in April 1945, it took only days to revive what was now called the Socialist Party, though it had been outlawed for eleven years. At the same time, the trade unions of all parties united in the Trade Union Congress (Österreichischer Gewerkschaftsbund, ÖGB). Since the ÖGB maintained Socialist majorities, this move strengthened Socialist organisation. On the other hand, educational efforts lagged and the youth movement weakened, and there was no more para-military organisation. The party as a whole became more pragmatic, a phenomenon finally expressed in its Vienna Programme of 1958. While membership did not decline - it remains around 700,000 - its basis has become more instrumental; many people join in order to gain patronage positions and rights to public apartments, especially in Vienna. The ancillary organisations are weaker than in the First Republic, but most have survived.

Because Christian Socials could rely to some extent on organisations of the Catholic Church, the ancillary apparatus of the Christian Social Party was somewhat less developed than that of the Social Democrats. Originally, Christian Socials were a party of Catholic workers, tradesmen and small businessmen. The party widened its base considerably in 1907, when it amalgamated with the Conservative Party, a party of large landowners and peasants.

In the First Republic, the Christian Socials gained the support of much of Austria's industry and larger business. While the para-military organisations were less closely integrated than the Schutzbund was in the Social Democrats, the Home Guard (Heimatschutz or Heimwehr) did the bidding of the Christian Socials and later of the Patriotic Front (Vaterländische Front), as did the smaller Ostmark Storm Troops (Ostmärkische Sturmscharen).

True democrats among the Christian Socials were the first to work on the establishment of the successor to the Christian Social Party, the Austrian People's Party. In a break with the past, the People's Party was organised into three economic leagues (Bünde): Economic (Business); Peasants'; and Workers' and Employees'. The most important ancillary organisations (women, youth, senior citizens) are also organised in leagues. Individual (non-cumulative) membership in all leagues is in excess of 800,000. Many continue to belong because of their economic position. De-ideologisation has not been as formalised as with the Socialists; support for free enterprise and opposition to abortion remain pronounced.

In sum, about 30 per cent of Austria's voting age population belong to one of the two major parties. This unusual organisational density is an important factor in maintaining the stability of the party system. While parties are a bit less strongly organised where they are electorally weak (ÖVP in Carinthia, SPÖ in Tyrol and Vorarlberg), their organisations must be classified as strong everywhere in Austria.

Support. To a large extent, party support in Austria has been a function of party organisation. If we had public opinion data going back to the introduction of universal manhood suffrage in 1907, we would no doubt find considerable stability among the voters for both the Christian Socials/ÖVP and Social Democrats/SPÖ. The marriage of the Christian Socials and the Conservatives created a lasting social base for the Christian Socials: Catholic workers, tradesmen and small businessmen, and large landowners and peasants. The First Republic brought a firmer connection between Christian Socials and big business and industry. Social Democrats had already become the party of most workers (a comfortable majority of the labour force) who did not have a strong bond to the Catholic Church. In the case of both parties, these social bases were maintained by group ties to parties. In contrast, the German Nationalists (Pan-Germans, Agrarian League) spread across most social strata, but had strong representation from professionals and civil servants. The social bases of the major parties were stable throughout the democratic era of the First Republic (1918-33). After 1945, benefits such as patronage positions and public apartments reinforced their previous social bases.

In the all-zones election of 1945, which was miraculously (and foolishly) agreed to by the Soviet occupation authorities, all Austrians who had not been members of the NSDAP were permitted to vote. Fifty per cent went to the People's Party and 45 per cent to the Socialists, while the Communists were restricted to 5 per cent. In 1949, with the lesser Nazis now enfranchised and the just-licensed German nationalist League of Independents included, the election result, reported in table 5.1, mirrored the last free election nineteen years earlier, suggesting that the social bases of the two major parties had remained intact. Public opinion data from 1969 to 1983, reported in table 5.3, bear this out.

The classification for the 1983 data varies slightly from the others. SPÖ losses among white collar workers and lower public officials in 1983 may have been caused by the ending of the Kreisky era; losses among skilled workers in the same year may reflect improved economic position, making it less attractive to vote for the party of the working class. (The increase of SPÖ supporters among higher public servants - if valid - may be due to patronage.)

In general, table 5.3 shows that the basic socio-political division remains, though in a somewhat weakened form: labour continues to vote 'red'; business and agriculture, 'black'.[2] Fairly stable sociological support still contributes to the stability of the party system.

Stabilising Factors Since the First Republic

Electoral System.   The First Republic gave Austria a system of proportional representation which contributed to the stability of the party system. Since the last free federal election was held in 1930, we will never know how this system would have met the onslaught of the Nazis after 1931. Under this system, Austria was divided into 25

Table 5.3 Party Preference and Occupation in Austria, 1969, 1972,1977, 1983 (Per cent of Party Identifiers only)

	1969		1972		1977		1983	
	SPÖ	ÖVP	SPÖ	ÖVP	SPÖ	ÖVP	SPÖ	ÖVP
Skilled Workers	77	16	74	19	74	21	60	33
Other Workers	74	23	74	25	65	34	63	30
Higher Public Officials	67	28	13 ⎱	71	48	50	46	43
Other Public Officials[a]			62 ⎰	33	63	36	46	45
Business Owners	24	66	30	64	24	71	12	79
Higher White Collar	48	39	32 ⎱	63	36	57	34	56
Other White Collar			56 ⎰	36	54	44	41	46
Independent Farmers	10	88	7	90	9	88	6	89

Sources: 1969-77, P. Gerlich and H.C. Müller (eds), Österreichs Parteien seit 1945. Braumüller, Vienna, 1983, p. 149, data from IFES; 1983, S. Koren, K. Pisa and K. Waldheim (eds), Politik für die Zukunft. Bohlau, Vienna, 1984, p. 42, data from Dr. Fessel & GfK). Note: a. 1969 data include public blue collar workers.

districts, and the number of seats (if any) a party obtained in an electoral district was based on the quotient of the district's population divided by the seats allotted to the district. If the quotient was below one in all districts, the party obtained no seats at all. A party qualifying for a seat in any one of these districts under the Swiss Hagenbach-Bischoff formula would participate in the second round, when the remainders were distributed in four electoral regions under the d'Hondt formula (Steiner 1972). Unlike the Weimar system, there was a fixed number of seats (165); this furthered stability because it did not permit an increase of parliamentary seats to accommodate flash successes based on increased participation.

The Socialist Party under Bruno Kreisky formed a minority government in 1970. The price for the support of the liberal-national FPÖ was a modification of the electoral system, favouring minor parties of some strength. In the 1970 reform, the nine provinces became the electoral districts, the Hagenbach-Bischoff formula was eased, the number of electoral regions for the distribution of remainders under the d'Hondt system was reduced to two, and the number of seats increased to 183. Larger districts and employment of the Hare formula make it easier for third parties to obtain seats. Although the FPÖ vote had not increased, the electoral reform of 1970 gave it more seats. In fact, the Socialists obtained a majority of parliamentary seats in the first three elections held under the new system (1971, 1975, 1979). In 1983, with no party majority, the new electoral system helped the FPÖ substantially: its vote declined from 5.9 to 4.9 per cent, but its number of seats increased from 11 to 12.

Containment of German Nationalists. In the First Republic, the German Nationalists were weakened because most of the areas in which they had been strong became part of other successor states. Also, they split into the rural Agrarian League (Landbund) and the urban Pan-German Party (Grossdeutsche Partei). Together, they received about 15 per cent of the vote. A few provincial elections in 1932 showed the Nazis doubling this vote, with 15 per cent in Vienna, where they were weakest. The Patriotic Front dictatorship deprived us of any data about Nazi strength. Although it was over 99 per cent in the post-*Anschluss* plebiscite of 1938, one can only guess what it would have been in a free election; my guess is around 40 per cent. The loss of the war brought German Nationalists down to their former strength.

Not only was German nationalism thoroughly discredited in 1945, but all members of the NSDAP were barred from voting (Engelmann 1982). About 500,000, who had not been guilty of any crime, were restored to the voting lists in 1949. In anticipation of this, both major parties attempted to gain the votes of the lesser Nazis. The Socialists, feeling that they had less of a chance in this operation than the People's Party, were instrumental in persuading the Allies to recognise a new party, the League of Independents, which received just about as many votes as there were re-enfranchised Nazis; however, it did not make a dent in the major party vote (Engelmann 1982).

Changing the party from the League of Independents to the Freedom Party in 1955 hurt rather than helped its electoral fortunes. Although the Independents won 12 per cent in 1949 and 11 per cent in 1953, the FPÖ since then has won only 5-10 per cent of the vote. When the Socialists lost their parliamentary majority in 1983, they invited the FPÖ to become their coalition partner. Entry into government did not give the FPÖ any capability of destabilising the party system. However, as we shall see, the replacement of the young Viennese lawyer Norbert Steger by the German nationalist Jörg Haider may yet do so.

Stabilising Factors in the Second Republic

Political leaders. Although the record of the First Republic offered scant hope that Austria would ever bring forth effective leadership for a liberal democracy, from 1945 on, Austria had party leaders who stabilised not only their own parties and thus party alignment but also, because of elite interaction established by the Great Coalition of 1945-66, the political system as a whole. Pre-war Social Democrat Karl Renner, fortuitously found by Soviet troops and asked to head an anti-fascist concentration government, appointed Adolf Schärf, the First Republic caucus secretary, as leader of the reformed Socialist Party. Often called the '*Hofrat*' (assistant deputy minister would come closest) of the party, Schärf was capable of displaying both a small bureaucratic mind and real vision. Schärf insisted that radicals of First Republic vintage, no matter how meritorious, had no place in the party, and that the coalition regime with the People's Party was to be an *equal* partnership in which Socialists had as much right to veto People's Party policies as the ÖVP had to veto Socialist policies (Engelmann 1966).

Though he was always consigned to the Vice-Chancellor's position, by the time he was elevated to the federal presidency, Schärf had had twelve years to place his stamp on Second Republic governments. His successor, Bruno Pittermann, continued Schärf's policies. When Pittermann was replaced (against his will) by Bruno

Kreisky in 1967, the SPÖ gave Austria its most successful political figure. It took Kreisky only four years to turn the SPÖ into a majority party, a status maintained for twelve years, by building a societal consensus based on economic growth. In his later years, however, Kreisky had difficulty in inspiring young and upwardly mobile people. His struggle with the SPÖ's upwardly mobile scion, Hannes Androsch, placed a severe strain on the leadership stability which Kreisky himself had done so much to develop. His hand-picked successor, Fred Sinowatz, lost some popular support, but this is being rebuilt under the chancellorship of a 'red' banker, Franz Vranitzky.

Because the Christian Social 'strong man', Julius Raab, was vetoed by the Soviets, the inexperienced but very shrewd Leopold Figl became the first leader of the People's Party and chancellor of the Second Republic. Figl, a peasant leader, was most successful in dealing with the Soviets, and he held up his party's interests in the sometimes tense collaboration with the Socialists. The re-institution of Austrian capitalism, following Marshall Plan aid, led to the predominance of business and industry over agriculture in the ÖVP and to the replacement of Figl by Julius Raab as party leader and, in 1953, as Chancellor. In the election of 1956, following the State Treaty and lifting of the occupation, the ÖVP came close to a majority of parliamentary seats. Soon, however, Raab suffered a stroke. An impatient People's Party replaced him with Alfons Gorbach and soon thereafter with Josef Klaus. SPÖ leader Pittermann was no match for Klaus, and the SPÖ's first leadership crisis contributed to an ÖVP majority in the 1966 election. Although it looked as if the ÖVP had regained the stable leadership it had enjoyed under Figl and Raab, Kreisky beat Klaus in catching the imagination of young and upwardly mobile voters. The People's Party has suffered an almost permanent leadership crisis since 1970, but this has had little impact on the party system.

ÖVP problems of the last fifteen years and SPÖ problems since Kreisky's retirement in 1983 detract from the picture of leadership stability. Yet the image of the party leader created by Schärf and Kreisky, Raab and Klaus is still very much alive. However, if it is to continue, the image will have to be revitalised.

The Economic Regime. Corporatism in Austria is a time-honoured phenomenon, especially in the trades and crafts. Since 1850, these corporations have been anchored in law, and were later turned into sections of chambers of commerce. The short-lived coalition of Christian Socials and Social Democrats (1918-20) established corresponding chambers of labour, but the Dollfuss-

Schuschnigg regime turned both chambers of commerce and labour into authoritarian corporations, which did not survive the *Anschluss*. The Second Republic not only re-created strong, democratic Economic Chambers (formerly Chambers of Commerce) and Chambers of Labour, but also created a strong, united, supra-partisan Trade Union Congress.

Corporate economic organisation was bound to create social stability. It greatly reinforced partisan stability because partisan elections to the Economic Chamber and the Chambers of Agriculture always led to 'black' victories, and elections to the Chamber of Labour, 'red' ones. In addition, the Trade Union Congress and its member unions (with the exception of the public employees) are firmly 'red.' A threatening inflation in 1957 was headed off when Raab, and Klaus as president of the Economic Chamber, called on his personal friend Johann Böhm, the President of the Trade Union Congress, to join him in creating the Joint Commission on Wages and Prices. This Commission, with its economic advisory council, has now survived the Great Coalition of the two parties by two decades and forms the keystone of Austria's social partnership (*Sozialpartnerschaft*), which in turn has been instrumental in the management of the postwar economy (Pelinka 1981; Marin 1982).

Table 5.4 shows that the regime change from Great Coalition to government by the ÖVP and then by the SPÖ has had very little influence on the outcome of Chamber elections. There is one noticeable change over the years: the Workers' and Employees' League of the ÖVP gained in Chamber of Labour elections. Throughout the period, however, it is stability that stands out. The stable party make-up of the chambers - and the SPÖ domination of the Trade Union Congress - reinforces partisan stability in the Second Republic.

Stability: Summary and Conclusion

It is no wonder that the stability of Austria's party system has, thus far, survived the demise of the Habsburg monarchy in 1918, constitutional change (strengthening of the executive) in 1929, the eclipse of democracy in 1933-34, the *Anschluss* in 1938, the liberation in 1945, the institution of an elected presidency in 1951, the end of the Great Coalition in 1966, the coming of a Socialist government in 1970, the small coalition of SPÖ and FPÖ in 1983, and the re-establishment of the Great Coalition in 1987. Stability has had very much going for it: extensive party organisation and a stable support pattern for nearly a century, a rigid electoral system and the

Table 5.4 Partisan Outcomes of Chamber Elections in Austria (per cent)[a]

	1949		1959		1970		1979	
	SPÖ	ÖVP	SPÖ	ÖVP	SPÖ	ÖVP	SPÖ	ÖVP
Chamber of Labour	64	14	69	16	69	24	64	31
Chamber of Commerce	16[b]	77[b]	16[b]	79[b]	10	85	9	86
Chambers of Agriculture (provincial aggregates)	9	82	10	85	10	84	10	85

Sources: 1949 and 1959, F.C. Engelmann, in R.A. Dahl (ed.), *Political Oppositions in Western Democracies* (Yale University Press, New Haven, 1966), p. 434; 1970, K. Ucakar in H. Fischer (ed.), *Das Politische System Österreichs* (Europaverlag, Vienna, 1974), p. 414; 1979, A. Pelinka in K. Steiner (ed.), *Modern Austria* (SPOSS, Palo Alto, 1981), p. 236. *Notes*: a. Chamber elections occur in different years; data show the election preceding the year indicated. b. Figures are for contested elections only: total ÖVP vote share should be higher.

containment of the German nationalist 'third force' since the First Republic, and stable political leadership and a firm nexus of party and social partnership in the Second Republic. So much for stability. Change, until recently incipient, uncertain and difficult to detect, is now becoming more apparent.

Change: Semblance or Reality?

The regime change of 1966, from the Great Coalition to an ÖVP majority government, did not affect the party system. Neither did the change of government from ÖVP to SPÖ in 1970 or the change from an SPÖ majority government to the small coalition of the SPÖ-FPÖ in 1983. Paradoxically, the re-establishment of the Great Coalition in 1987 could do so.

Symptoms of Change

'Green' Events. Three potential harbingers of change occurred in 1973, 1978, and 1984. The first was not much noticed. The University of Vienna needed more space, and the Socialist city government was willing to provide it. Because of an incessant 'spare the trees' campaign on the part of the Vienna tabloids ('boulevard press'), the Conservative *Kurier* and the more sensationalist *Kronen-Zeitung* (partially dependent on the Trade Union Congress), the city decided to build an institute in a wealthy sector of town, where there was, if anything, a surfeit of trees. This did not placate the boulevard press, which pushed for a plebiscite. The Socialist city administration, used to winning municipal elections, agreed. They did not realise that the high Austrian voting turnouts were not easily transferable to plebiscites, and the environmentalist protesters won with 57 per cent of the vote.

The second event, five years later (1978), brought Austria its first national plebiscite. The energy crisis had led to an awareness of energy needs on the part of industry and the Trade Union Congress. The proposed solution was a nuclear power plant in Zwentendorf, near Vienna. Again, the boulevard press agitated for a plebiscite. Pressed by post-industrialists, Alois Mock, then the new leader of the People's Party, urged people to vote 'no.' With most of the press against the power plant, Anton Benya, president of the Trade Union Congress and First President of Parliament, led the fight for Zwentendorf. Just before the plebiscite, Chancellor Bruno Kreisky abandoned his neutral position and urged people to vote 'yes.' Despite this intervention, the faction of Greens, anti-nuclear people and the boulevard press defeated Zwentendorf by a vote of 51 per cent.

97

The third event (1984) concerned a plan of industry and the Trade Union Congress to construct a huge conventional power plant near the city of Hainburg, just above the Danube's outflow into Czechoslovakia. The goal was to alleviate Austria's trade deficit. It became obvious that plant construction, particularly cutting down old trees along still branches (*Auen*) of the Danube, would interfere with wildlife. Opponents of power plant acted in concert with Konrad Lorenz, Austria's Nobel Laureate animal behaviourist. Their activities were orchestrated by the boulevard press. When permits for construction by the Lower Austrian provincial government and the federal government were issued in December, 1984, articles and editorials in the boulevard press reached the fever pitch level, with the *Kronen-Zeitung* siding with what it perceived to be its reading public against its partial sponsor, the Trade Union Congress. Deforestation proceedings were to start on December 19, 1984. The area was experiencing its coldest winter since 1929. Despite this, hundreds of young people, mostly students, announced that they were going to camp out and 'lie in' in the frozen deforestation area. When the Trade Union Congress indicated that it would take direct action against the demonstrators, Chancellor Fred Sinowatz and Karl Blecha, the Minister of the Interior, (both Socialists) could keep trade unionists from direct action only by promising to have the area cleared by gendarmes. This happened on 19 December, and eleven demonstrators and eight gendarmes required medical attention. The boulevard press called it the darkest hour of the Second Republic. The government decided to halt the deforestation and the project now appears to be doomed.

Municipal Green Groups.　These events, unusual for Austrian politics, were not the only symptoms of change. Green groups also began appearing in municipal elections in the 1970s and 1980s. In an article on the municipal election in Innsbruck, the capital of Tyrol on 25 September 1983, Anton Pelinka, one of Austria's leading political scientists, wrote:

> Determining for the Austrian party system and for the electoral behaviour of Austrians were until recently - according to comparative political science - the following central characteristics: No other competitive party system in Europe showed as high a grade of concentration; the proportion of votes of Austria's two major parties was above any comparable value in Europe. Hardly another competitive European party system was characterised by an equally

stable electoral behaviour; Austria's proportion of floating voters was noticeably slight. In federal politics these characteristics are still valid... Things are different in municipal politics: for more than a decade, the party systems in Austrian cities have been in motion, and election returns show a markedly flexible electoral behaviour (Pelinka 1984:141).

Pelinka's observation certainly held until 1986. Salzburg had faced attempts of developers to jeopardise the beauty of the old part of the city. Environmentalists formed the Citizens' List (Bürgerliste) for the municipal election of 1977, which elected two members who gained much attention for bestowing 'sow's trunks' (Saurüssel) on the worst violators of the environment. In 1982, the Citizens' List obtained 17.7 per cent of the vote and seven of forty seats on City Council, outpolling the FPÖ and obtaining third place on the council. They did best in middle-class sections of the city. A survey showed their voters to be young (38 per cent below thirty) and well educated (27 per cent with at least secondary school matriculation, a high percentage for Austria); only 2 per cent were workers (Dachs 1983; 1984).

In Graz, Austria's second city, the Alternative List Graz fought its first election in 1983, received 7 per cent of the vote and gained four seats on City Council. As in Salzburg, it gained votes from all three major parties, but most of its voters were first voters either because of their age or because they had refused to vote before (Strobl 1984).

The Vienna election was held on the same day as the federal election of 1983. The Alternative List Vienna, formed just before the election, was poorly organised and polled 2.5 per cent of the vote, mostly from the middle-class inner-city districts (Bretschneider 1984). In Innsbruck, the Alternative List Innsbruck gained one member on City Council, polling close to 3 per cent of the vote (Pelinka 1984).

Federal Green Parties. The federal election of 1983 was contested by two Green parties: the United Greens of Austria (Vereinigte Grüne Österreichs, VGÖ) and the Alternative List Austria (Alternative Liste Österreich, ALÖ). The VGÖ received 93,798 votes (1.93 per cent), the ALO 65,816 votes (1.36 per cent). The failure of the Greens to obtain parliamentary representation can be ascribed to their organisational division. When I spent three weeks in Vienna in 1984, phone calls to a number of Green and Alternative numbers (personal and organisational) did not yield one single answer. If there had been one Green party, and if it had received every VGÖ and

ALÖ vote, seven Greens would have been elected in 1983 (Plasser and Ulram 1984:33).

The presidential election of 1986 - the election that made Kurt Waldheim federal president despite his revealed and belatedly admitted activity as Nazi intelligence officer in the Balkans - was to change the Greens' electoral fate. On the first ballot (Waldheim just missed a majority of votes, making a run-off necessary) the Green candidate, former Socialist Freda Meissner-Blau, received 5.5 per cent of the vote. Meissner-Blau's success in the presidential election enabled her to rally most of Austria's Greens behind a common banner. Organisational unity paid off in the November 1986 federal election: the Greens received 4.6 per cent of the vote and won eight seats.

In the 1986 presidential election, Meissner-Blau benefitted from the Chernobyl disaster. An analysis of the IFES Institute showed that only 29 per cent of the Meissner-Blau voters had supported the Greens in 1983; 33 per cent came from the ÖVP, 23 per cent from the SPÖ. Her best showing (ten per cent) was in Vorarlberg, where voters had given the Greens a record 13 per cent of the vote in provincial elections two years earlier. In the federal election, the Greens obtained above-average results in Vorarlberg (8.3 per cent), Vienna (6 per cent plus 0.7 per cent for a splinter group) and Tyrol and Salzburg (5.6 per cent each).

Unfortunately, public opinion data on the sources of the Green vote in 1986 are not yet available. However, the 1982 data presented in table 5.5 indicate that the Austrian Greens, like their counterparts elsewhere, were drawing disproportionate support from younger, more educated and more urban voters. Similarly, in 1983 the 'hard Green core' of the electorate (the three per cent which the VGÖ and the ALÖ received) was much greater among university students and graduates (15 per cent) and first voters (14 per cent), and noticeably greater among secondary school graduates (9 per cent) and voters below thirty (8 per cent). Support was lowest among workers, senior citizens, those with a common school education only, and in rural areas (Plasser and Ulram 1983:285).

Although younger, upwardly mobile professionals are probably doing more than any other group to destabilise the Austrian party system, support for the Greens cannot be attributed solely to post-materialism. The environmentalist movement has received considerable help from the boulevard press. It is doubtful that the Vienna referendum in 1973 could have defeated the city government without the strong involvement of the tabloids. Because of the close defeat of the nuclear power plant Zwentendorf in 1978, the role of the

Table 5.5 Probable Environmentalist Voters (Above average groups only; per cent)

	Municipal	Federal
Total	8	6
Below 30	11	8
30-49	9	6
High education	17	11
50,000 + population (without Vienna)	10	7
Vienna	13	9
FPÖ voters	15	12
No party preference	14	12

Source: F. Birk and K. Traar, 'Das Ende einer Ara,' in A. Khol and A. Stirnemann (eds.), *Österreichisches Jahrbuch für Politik 1983* (Verlag für Geschichte und Politik, Vienna, 1984), 56-57.

boulevard press there must be called pivotal. In Hainburg, without the boulevard press, deforestation would be in progress.

Finally, we should also consider the declining impact of parties. A 1981 study by the Fessel Institute showed that cynicism about party membership was highly correlated with youth. Only 14 per cent of those 50 years or older could imagine that one would join a party for *purely* egotistical motives, while 41 per cent of those below 25 years did so (Plasser and Ulram 1982). When I discussed the Austrian political scene with a number of politicians in 1984 and early 1986, a number of Socialists were concerned about the party's relation to yuppies and about party life in general. One mentioned that twelve years of complacency developed under majority government were to blame for the present laxity and sparseness of party activity. It must be remembered, in this connection, that a full party life on both sides - there is little reason to assume that it is now rich in the ÖVP - has been an essential element of Austrian party stability for nearly one century.

Other Evidence of Change. The Greens are not the only source of change in the Austrian party system. The FPÖ, after losing votes in every province except Carinthia in the 1983 elections, shot from their normal five per cent of the vote in 1983 to nearly ten per cent in 1986. The change in the FPÖ's fortunes reflects the shift in the party leadership from Norbert Steger, the party's first liberal rather than nationalist leader, to former Carinthian party chief Jörg Haider, whose stock in trade was advocating the repression of the Slovene minority in that province. Haider's elevation to FPÖ leadership triggered a break in the SPÖ-FPÖ coalition and precipitated the 1986 federal election. Haider's charismatic style suggests that the 9.7 per cent polled by the FPÖ in November 1986 was not a flash in the pan. In that election, the FPÖ achieved above-average results in Carinthia (20.1 per cent), Salzburg (15.9 per cent), Vorarlberg (12 per cent), Tyrol (11.2 per cent), Upper Austria (11 per cent) and Styria (9.9 per cent).

In addition to the entry of the Greens and the growth of the FPÖ, there is evidence of greater shifts between the two major parties. Austrian voting now shows a number of federal-provincial 'floaters'. In four 'black' provinces, containing 56.5 per cent of Austria's voters, we find the following 'red' pluralities (expressed in per cent SPÖ: per cent ÖVP) in federal elections: Styria, 1970 (48:46), 1971 (49:44), 1975 (50:44), 1979 (51:42), 1983 (49:42); Upper Austria, 1971 (48:45), 1975 (49:43), 1979 (50:42), 1983 (46:44); Salzburg, 1971 (45:43), 1975 (44:43), 1979 (45:43); and Lower Austria, 1979 (48:47). With two slight exceptions, *no* such incongruities of federal and provincial pluralities occurred from 1945 to 1966. Although such incongruities are often small, the total federal SPÖ plurality in four 'black' provinces in 1979 exceeded 150,000 votes. Another slight decline in habitual Austrian party stability occurred in Tyrol and Vorarlberg, where the Chamber of Labour now has 'black' majorities and presidents.

Outlook

Despite all this, it is foolish to overrate signs of change in the Austrian party system. Although the 96 per cent vote for the three traditional parties in 1983 is probably a thing of the past, the social partnership remains intact and the Socialists and the People's Party - once more in coalition with each other - continue to dominate not only electoral and parliamentary politics but also decision-making in general. However, a majority for either of the major parties seems unlikely in the foreseeable future: of the nine provinces, only Burgenland gave the major parties more than 90% in the 1986 elections. Moreover, if the major parties fail to adapt to new realities, and they have so far shown little capacity for dealing with post-materialist issues, Plasser and Ulram's prophecy might come true:

> The partisan mobility of Austrian voters could continue to increase and bring, in future elections, surprises which could change materially the historic 'ultra-stability' of the Austrian party system and lead to changing governmental majorities with small and often unpredictable arithmetic changes. After decades of transparent constancy, Austria's partisan landscape would become more fluctuating, and new government and electoral coalitions would form and in turn change in rapid succession (Plasser and Ulram 1984:42).

Meanwhile, however, Austria's passive political culture (Rosenmayr 1980; Barnes and Kaase 1979) may well maintain her underlying partisan stability for some time to come. The Great Coalition of 1987, however, may benefit the FPÖ and the Greens simply because they are in opposition.

Notes

1. For an overview of Austrian party life see Wandruska, 1984. The best English-language source for these and other facts about Austrian government is Steiner (1972).

2. The FPÖ is too weak for reliable data. It tends to be strongest among shopkeepers, artisans, and white collar employees.

References

Barnes, S. and M. Kaase, *et al.* (1979) *Political Action: Mass Participation in Five Western Democracies*, Sage, Beverly Hills.

Birk, F. and K. Traar (1984) 'Das Ende einer Ara,' in Khol and Stirnemann, *Österreichisches Jahrbuch für Politik, 1983* Verlag für Geschichte und Politik, Vienna, 45-62

Austria

Bretschneider, R. (1984) 'Die Wiener Gemeinderatswahl vom 24.4. - 1983,' in Khol and Stirnemann, *Österreichisches Jahrbuch für Politik, 1983* Verlag für Geschichte und Politik, Vienna, 113-31

Dachs, H. (1983) 'Eine Renaissance des mündigen Bürgers'? Uber den Aufstieg der Salzburger Bürgerliste, *Österreichische Zeitschrift für Politikwissenschaft, 12*, 311-30

Dachs, H. (1984) 'Das Modell Salzburg 2000' in Khol and Stirnemann, *Österreichisches Jahrbuch für Politik, 1983*, Verlag für Geschichte und Politik, Vienna, 319-32.

Diamant, Alfred (1958) 'The Group Basis of Austrian Politics,' *Journal of Central European Affairs, 18*, 134-55

Engelmann, F.C. (1966) 'Austria: the Pooling of Opposition,' in R.A. Dahl (ed.), *Political Oppositions in Western Democracies*, Yale University Press, New Haven, 260-83

Engelmann F.C. (1982) 'How Austria Has Coped with Two Dictatorial Legacies,' in J.H. Herz (ed.), *From Dictatorship to Democracy*, Greenwood Press, Westport, CT, 135-60

Khol, A. and A. Stirnemann, *Österreichisches Jahrbuch für Politik, 1983*, Verlag für Geschichte und Politik, Vienna

Marin, B. (1982) *Die Paritätische Kommission* Internationale Publikationen, Vienna

Pelinka, A. (1981) *Modellfall Österreich*, Braumüller, Vienna

Pelinka, A. (1984) 'Innsbruck: Zur Dekonzentration kommunaler Parteiensysteme,' in A. Khol and A. Stirnemann (eds.), *Österreichisches Jahrbuch für Politik, 1983* Verlag für Geschichte und Politik, Vienna, 141-56

Plasser, F. and P.A. Ulram (1982) *Unbehagen im Parteienstaat*, Böhlau, Vienna

Plasser F. and P.A. Ulram (1983) 'Wahlkampf und Wählerentscheidung 1983: Die Analyse einer "kritischen" Wahl, *Österreichische Zeitschrift für Politikwissenschaft, 12*, 277-92

Plasser, F. and P.A. Ulram (1984) 'Wahlkampf und Wählerverhalten - Analyse der Nationalratswahl 1983,' in Khol and Stirnemann, *Österreichisches Jahrbuch für Politik, 1983* Verlag für Geschichte und Politik, Vienna, 19-43

Rosenmayr, L., ed. (1980) *Politische Beteilung und Wertwandel in Österreich*, Oldenbourg, Munnich.

Steiner, K. (1972) *Politics in Austria*, Little Brown, Boston.

Strobl, H. (1984) 'Grazer Gemeinderatswahlen 1983,' in Khol und Stirnemann, *Österreichisches Jahrbuch für Politik, 1983*, Verlag für Geschichte und Politik, Vienna, 133-40

Wandruska, A. (1954) 'Österreichs politische Struktur,' in H. Benedikt (ed.), *Geschichte der Republik Österreich* Verlag für Geschichte und Politik, Vienna, 289-485

Chapter Six

Stability and Change in the Belgian Party System

Maureen Covell

On the surface, the life of the Belgian party system over the last twenty-five years has been turbulent. In 1960, the system was dominated by the three 'traditional' parties, Catholic, Socialist and Liberal, who had together received 95.4 per cent of the vote in the most recent (1958) election. The parties, in existence since the nineteenth century, had survived two foreign occupations and the thirties depression, and their relative positions in the system had not changed since the introduction of single vote manhood suffrage in 1919. Moreover, each party stood at the summit of a collection of associated organisations ranging from trade unions to football clubs; through this phenomenon of 'pillarisation', party affiliation provided the organising principle for many aspects of the population's existence.[1] The parties' ability to 'resolve' the conflicts 'arising' from this fragmented society was celebrated by indigenous and foreign analysts and had just been reconfirmed by the Schools Pact, an agreement on the financing of state and church school networks negotiated by the parties and dutifully ratified by the Belgian parliament.

Events since 1960 challenged the traditional parties' domination of state and society. The year 1960 ended with the 'Great Strike', an uprising that demonstrated that class relations were by no means pacified, exacerbated regional feelings, and put into question the degree

*
The research on which this article is based was made possible by the President's Research Grant Fund of Simon Fraser University, and a Leave Fellowship and Research Grant from the Social Sciences and Humanities Research Council of Canada.

105

of control which leaders of the country's parties and unions really possessed over their followers. Within the party system, the years 1960-1985 saw the drastic reorganisation of the Liberal Party, the entry in force of ethnically based community parties, and the division of the three traditional parties - once the defenders of Belgian unity - into separate Flemish and Walloon parties. A 1977 study of the Belgian party system listed 42 parties, and in the most recent election (1985) the six new versions of the traditional parties together gained only 78.6 per cent of the vote (Rowies 1977:30). Table 6.1, comparing the 1958 and the 1985 election results, demonstrates the contrasts between the pre-1960s party system and the present situation (See also figure 6.2).

On the electoral front, at least, these parties had undergone fragmentation and a loss of control over large numbers of their followers. Their monopoly over the process of governing was challenged in the last half of the 1970s when the 'community parties' joined governments and when parliamentary revolts against party leaders became an important source of government instability. By the end of the period, the unitary Belgian state, whose defense had legitimised the cartel-like behaviour of the traditional parties, had itself fragmented as the result of the constitutional revisions of 1970 and 1980.

Belgium was not the only European country to experience volatility and fragmentation in its party system during the 1960s and 1970s, and diverse theories were developed to explain the phenomenon and predict its future course. Some, such as the 'decline of ideology' school, focussed on developments that might be expected to loosen the attachments between voters and their habitual parties by diminishing the differences between those parties. The Belgian party system, organised as it was around class and religious cleavages, could be expected to change as the intensity of the cleavages waned (Rejai 1971). Other theories, such as those concerned with the rise of ethnonationalism and the development of 'post-industrial politics', focussed on the growing importance of issues that either divided existing parties or were outside their habitual range of discourse. Again, Belgium, with its 'uninstitutionalised' language conflict and advanced capitalist economic system was likely to be affected by this type of change (Urwin 1979). All the theories argued that the phenomena they discussed would lead to changes in the nature of existing parties, to the disappearance of some and the emergence of others, and to changes in the functions parties performed in the larger political system.

Table 6.1 Parties' Share of National Vote: 1958 and 1985

1958		1985	
Catholic Party	46.5%	Catholic Family	
		Christelijke Volkspartij (CVP)	21.3
		Parti Social Chretien (PSC)	8.0
			29.3
Socialist Party	37.3%	Socialist Family	
		Socialistische Partij (SP)	14.6
		Parti Socialiste (PS)	13.8
			28.4
Liberal Party	11.6%	Liberal Family	
		Partij voor Vrijheid en Vooruitgang (PVV)	10.7
		Parti des Reformes et de la Liberte (PRL)	10.2
			20.9
Others		Others	
Volksunie	2.0%	Volksunie	7.9
		FDF	1.2
		CP	1.2
Communist Party (PCB)	1.9%	UDRT-RAD	1.2
		PCB-KPB	1.2
		Agalev	3.7
		Ecolo	2.5

Sources: Luc Rowies, Les partis politiques en Belgique, Centre de Recherche et d'Information Socio-Politiques (CRISP), Dossier No. 10 (Brussels, 1977), Xavier Mabille & Evelyne Lentzen, 'Les elections legislatives du 13 Oct. 1985, CRISP Courrier Hebdomadaire Nos. 1095-6 (Nov. 1985). The Volksunie is the Flemish community party. The FDF, the Brussels community party, received 11.3 per cent of the national vote at its peak in 1971. The Rassemblement Wallon, which had 7.1 per cent of the national vote, or 20.5 per cent of the Walloon regional vote in 1971 had disappeared by 1985. The UDRT-RAD is a Francophone-Flemish party perhaps best described as poujadist. The Belgian communist party (PCB-KPB) lost its one seat in the Chamber in 1985. Ecolo (Francophone) and Agalev (Flemish, from Anders gaan leven) are the Belgian versions of 'Green' parties. Their share of the vote has been increasing, and in 1981 European elections, they received 3.9 and 4.3 per cent of the vote respectively.

Developments in the 1980s suggest that earlier theorists made the common error of assuming that what was happening in the present would go on happening in the future, only more so. Certainly the Belgian party system has not changed as drastically as the more apocalyptic predictions suggested it would. None of the major parties has disappeared, with one exception the community parties are no longer important, and parties stressing new issues such as ecology, while gaining support, have not yet generated even the transitory threat to the traditional parties that the community parties did. Organisational pillarisation remains an important feature of Belgian society, and the traditional parties dominate the new regional institutions established by the 1970 and 1980 constitutional revisions as they do those of the central state.

What accounts for the resilience of the Belgian party system? In addition to performing the functions of electoral mobilisation, agenda setting and government organisation, Belgian parties are related to the population and the state in other ways. These relationships did not change during the period under consideration, and provided the basis from which the parties were able to digest the changes of this period and to return to a version, however imperfect, of the pre-60s status quo.[2] However, since it is true that the party system has changed in some respects, I will also discuss the nature of the changes that did occur and the prospects for future, and possibly more basic, changes.

Origins of the System

Like many aspects of modern European political systems, parties are a nineteenth century invention. Their present shape is the result of their origins and historical experience as well as of present day conditions (See also Lijphart 1981). The divisions in the Belgian party system are usually traced to the successive emergence of three lines of cleavage, two of which gave rise to the system's first parties and one that was, until 1960s contained, although with difficulty, within the traditional party system. Groups based on conflict over the relationship between church and state already existed as philosophical tendencies when the country became independent in 1830, and by the late 1840s had given rise to a Catholic and a Liberal party. Class cleavages also existed at this time, but did not affect the party system until the 1880s when continued industrialisation and the mobilisation of the working class gave rise to the Belgian Workers' Party and drastically changed the nature of the Catholic party. The third cleavage, that based on the division of the country into Dutch and French speakers had made its way onto the political agenda by the mid nineteenth century, but in spite of the quarrels and occasional government crises it generated, its impact on the party system was not manifest until the late 1960s when parties campaigning on issues of community defense made rapid electoral gains and the three traditional parties split into separate Dutch and French organisations.

The development of the Belgian party system was influenced by three conditions. First, all three traditional parties, including the Socialist party, were in existence before the political mobilisation of the population; in proto-party form, Liberal and Catholic organisations pre-dated the foundation of the state and were able to shape its form. Secondly, while the philosophical differences among the parties created a classically fragmented polity and laid the bases for the pillars, or zuilen into which population and politics were organised, none of the parties opposed the existence or basic organisation of the Belgian state. Ostensibly irreconcilable philosophical differences proved quite amenable to resolution via judicious applications of money. Finally, for a whole series of reasons, the Belgian state was and still is, a weak state. The inability of the state to assert an autonomous existence allowed the parties to colonise it and assume many of its functions, thereby setting up the relationships on which their domination of the system is based (Zolberg 1977; Claeys and Loeb-Mayer 1984).

The coming to independence of Belgium was based on an alliance between the Liberal and Catholic tendencies into which the elite of the day was divided. As the name of their joint movement, 'the Union of the Oppositions' suggests, no overriding common vision pulled them together. Their feelings can be summarised by saying that although the Belgians were not sure that they wanted to be ruled by each other, they were quite sure that they did not want to be ruled by the Dutch. The latter sentiment led to the 1830 revolution, the former shaped the state that emerged from the revolution. First, neither Liberals nor Catholics wanted to create a state that would be stronger than civil society and in a position to shape it (Dyson 1980). Each group feared that such a state might be captured by the other side and used against it. Secondly, the bargain that made cooperation between the two groups possible exchanged Catholic acceptance of a civil state that was not explicitly Catholic in return for Liberal acceptance of the principle that that state should finance but not control the activities of the church, including charities and education. This is the beginning of the principle of subsidisation, the notion that the state should not try to reduce the fragments into which its society is divided, but rather should subsidise their organisational manifestations (Huyse 1984; Zolberg 1978). The roots of the zuilen system can easily be seen in this principle.

The 1832 constitution set up a parliamentary regime with a severely restricted suffrage: in 1830, only 46,100 were eligible to vote, approximately 2 per cent of the adult population; by 1892, the year before the introduction of manhood suffrage, the number of electors was still only 136,800, or approximately one of ten Belgian males (Luykx 1978). The lack of suffrage, however, did not prevent the founding of a socialist movement, centered at first on cooperatives and mutual help associations. The Belgian Workers' Party ('socialist' was deliberately omitted from the title) was founded in 1885, nine years before the first election under plural vote manhood suffrage. The socialists' organisational activities were parallelled, and sometimes preceded, by similar efforts on the part of the Catholic party, which recruited among rural as well as urban populations. The result was that by the election of 1894, much of the Belgian population was already enrolled in one or the other 'camp'. Under these circumstances, voting was less a choice among parties than an expression of organisational encadrement.

The 1894 election showed a fragmented polity, with Catholic domination exaggerated by the plural vote system under which property owners, degree holders and employers had two, and sometimes three votes. Although the number of eligible electors in 1894 was 1,015,360, the number of possible *votes* was 2,111,130 (Luykx 1978). However, in spite of the degree of fragmentation expressed in the election and very real differences in the philosophical and social bases of the parties, Belgian politics was not a war to the death among incompatible ideologies. The enfranchisement of 1894 occurred in response to socialist pressure and was based on a calculation by the Catholic party that it would profit more from the extension than the more narrowly based Liberals. However, Catholic and Liberal leaders had a common background (studies of the 19th century elites of the two parties can find almost no social differences: the distinguishing features are organisational affiliations such as membership in Freemasons Lodge and schooling). They also had a common interest in preventing the emergence of a strong Socialist party. When it appeared that the plural vote was not enough to rescue the Liberals from obliteration, the Catholic government of 1899 acceded to their demand for proportional representation. The price of saving the Liberals was the loss of over twenty Catholic seats, a price the Catholic leadership evidently found worth paying.

In spite of the Catholic and Liberal fear of the 'Socialist threat,' the Belgian Workers' Party was not dedicated to the overthrow of the system. The party had its more radical strains, but the most bellicose remark attributed to anyone with influence in the party was a threat by the founder of the socialist cooperative movement to 'bombard the bourgeoisie with buns and potatoes' (Chlepner 1972). The goals of the movement were above all to carve out a separate and autonomous world for the Belgian working class - hence the organisational effort. Later demands, however threatening they seemed to the Liberal and Catholic bourgeoisie, were not for the overthrow of the Belgian economic or political system, but for a place within it, via the legalisation of trade unions, the extension of the suffrage, and access to the resources of the state for the maintenance of the socialist organisational network. Continuing political pressure, and the fears inspired by the 1917 Bolshevik revolution and subsequent unrest elsewhere in Europe resulted in an invitation to join the wartime government in exile and the 1919 government of national unity, as well as the abolition of the plural vote in 1919. Since the 1919 election the Socialists have been the country's second largest party and a regular government participant. However, they have not been able to challenge the position of the Catholic party as the system's dominant political movement. Their perpetual minority position has meant that the Socialist parties do not see control of state power as the most important road to implementation of a socialist program and is one of the reasons for their support of the system of subsidisation with its emphasis on the defense of groups against state intervention.

Vast Clientelistic Ministates

If none of Belgium's parties seriously planned the overthrow of the Belgian state, none, except possibly the Liberals, identified with it or cared to strengthen its autonomous powers. The Socialists and Catholics were much more interested in using state resources and law-making authority to maintain and control their own organisational networks. Other social groups, most notably capital, found the existing state strong enough to perform the policing functions necessary to maintain their position in Belgium and, until 1960, in the Congo. Belgian capital organised itself at an early stage into gigantic holding companies which themselves resisted state initiative and intervention in their activities, although they encouraged state regulation of labour. The same lack of identification with the state existed with regard to Belgium's ethnic cleavage: both Flemings and Walloons considered the state a potentially hostile entity controlled by the other group. Citizens of Brussels, who came closest to identifying with 'Belgium', lacked the numbers to impose their point of view.

The results of this attitude toward the state can be seen in the relationship between state and parties. First, the parties have colonised the institutions of the state to an extraordinary degree. Domination by parties is expected in institutions such as the legislature and cabinet. In Belgium, however, party representation via quotas not only extends throughout the bureaucracy, including secretarial and janitorial functions, but also reaches beyond it to other institutions, such as courts and radio and television broadcasting, whose personnel are formally named by the government or parliament but actually designated by the parties. This colonisation also extends to many areas of expenditure. The Schools Pact is a party agreement regulating the division of state educational expenditure. A Cultural Pact, negotiated in 1973, establishes party quotas for expenditures in areas ranging from libraries to sports. Organisations must either declare their adherence to official ideological families, defined by the Pact as parties represented in parliament, or, if they wish to be defined as neutral, must give representation to the ideological families on their governing councils (Brassinne and Launier 1983). State expenditures in these broadly defined cultural areas are to be roughly proportional to party strength in Parliament. Not only does the pact remove the distribution of cultural expenditures from state control, it also makes it impossible for groups that want to operate outside the party-dominated system to get public financing.

The parties have also assumed a whole range of functions usually carried out by government agencies, via a series of party-connected organisations. These functions include the distribution of unemployment insurance, carried out by party-affiliated trade unions and the administration of medical insurance schemes, carried out by party-affiliated mutual assistance societies. In fact, most functions of the modern welfare state are carried out in Belgium by party-affiliated rather than government agencies. As a result, Belgian parties are highly complex institutions, or rather amalgamations of institutions. The organisational constellation that constitutes a 'party' includes not only elected officials and the party bureaucracy, but also unions and other groups, and the parties' voters constitute a clientele linked to the party via a multitude of other ties. A long-time observer of Belgian politics has characterised these conglomerates as 'vast clientelistic ministates' (Palmer 1983). They are not 'emanations' of Belgium's cleavages. In a sense, their relationship to the populations defined by the cleavages is not unlike that of Canadian provinces to their populations: the population is both power base and clientele for an institution with its own interests. By now, the existence of the institutional complex explains the perpetuation of the cleavages much more than the continued importance of the cleavage explains the existence of the institution.[3]

The pillars are not complete mirror images of each other. While the ideology and organisations of Freemasonry play an important role in the 'secular' Liberal and Socialist pillars they parallel but do not duplicate the public role played by the church in the Catholic pillar. In education, there is a separate Catholic system, while at the primary and secondary levels Liberals and Socialists use the state system. Only at the university level, are there private institutions (the two Free Universities of Brussels, Dutch and French) specifically identified with the secular pillar. The state education system is the object of periodic battles over the degree of representation it should give to Catholic interests in a country whose population is, statistically at least, overwhelmingly Catholic. Finally, two of the pillars, Catholic and Socialist, have geographical centres of gravity, Flanders and Wallonia respectively, which the Liberal pillar lacks.

In general, the Liberal party has the smallest organisational network and the greatest predominance of informal rather than formal ties with related groups. In part this is because most of its financial support comes from Liberals in Belgian business circles who do not need to be organised into unions or mutualities to be heard, and who prefer not to make their financial ties a matter of public knowledge. There is a small Liberal union movement, and Liberal mutualities do exist. Their relations with the party itself are sometimes tense - for example its 1961 'deconfessionalisation' was originally much resented - and in general looser than the relationships between Catholic and Socialist groups of organisations. The Socialist and Catholic networks are more elaborate, reflecting their historic function of mobilising and controlling a mass base. With its cross-class alliances and parallel education system, the Catholic pillar comes closest to reproducing a 'state within the state.' One of its main functions has been the prevention of the full emergence of class-based politics.

On the Catholic and Socialist side, the parties' most visible links are with the unions and the social welfare organisations. The Catholic 'family,' schematically represented in figure 6.1 also includes a large section of Belgian capital. The links between the parties and these organisations are both formal and informal. Each party has a formal organisation that groups the party and its affiliated institutions: 'Common Action' for the Socialists, the 'Agenda Committee' for the Catholics. More important, perhaps, are the less formal links. Representatives of affiliated groups sit officially on the Socialist Bureaus and less officially on the CVP and PSC's executive committees. Very often party bureaucrats and elected officials began their careers in one of the subsidiary organisations and still consider it

Figure 6.1 The Catholic 'Pillar'.[a]

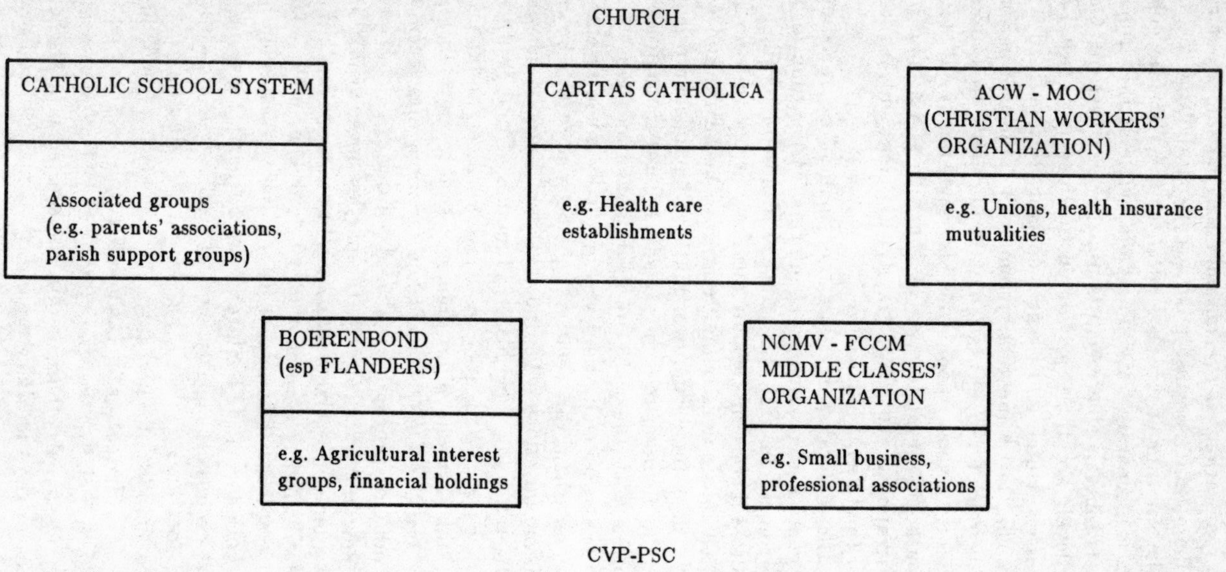

CHURCH

CATHOLIC SCHOOL SYSTEM	CARITAS CATHOLICA	ACW - MOC (CHRISTIAN WORKERS' ORGANIZATION)
Associated groups (e.g. parents' associations, parish support groups)	e.g. Health care establishments	e.g. Unions, health insurance mutualities

BOERENBOND (esp FLANDERS)	NCMV - FCCM MIDDLE CLASSES' ORGANIZATION
e.g. Agricultural interest groups, financial holdings	e.g. Small business, professional associations

CVP-PSC

The different 'cupola organizations' can best be conceived of as holding companies since each tops a large conglomerate of more specific purpose organizations.

Notes: a. Adapted from Mieke Van Haegendoren and Ludwig Vandenhove, 'Le monde catholique flamand (1)', CRISP, Courrier Hebdomadaire, 1.070, (February 1985), 34.

their 'base'. The organisations also have spokesmen in the parties' parliamentary wing, and lay claim to their share of ministerial posts and places in ministerial cabinets when the party is in government. While overlapping personnel are easy to trace, flows of money are not. Because programs such as unemployment insurance, pensions, and medical insurance are handled by these organisations, large sums of money must pass through their hands, but public accounting of its expenditure is non-existent. It is known that union movements finance much of the Socialist and left-wing Catholic press, but beyond that the financial links between the parties and affiliated organisations are as obscure as the links between parties and private capital (Van Haegendorn and Vandenhove 1985; Franssen and Martens 1984; Jenner 1982).

Elections, Governing and Agendas

In the Belgian system, changes in a party's share of the vote are important, if only because so much in the way of government expenditure and appointments is based on relative party strength. Furthermore, variations in party strength often, but not always, influence participation in government. However, since it is easier to vote against one's habitual party in Belgium than to leave it, variations in party vote are not variations in party strength. The fact that electoral and governing activities are not the whole of party functions in Belgium also means that changes in these areas do not necessarily imply changes in other parts of the party system.

The past twenty-five years have been a period of considerable volatility, if not change, in the electoral and governmental aspect of the party system. Since 1960, Belgium has had nine general elections and sixteen changes of government. The agenda of the period was, until 1980, dominated by issues revolving around community relations, a question that the elites of 1960 had tried to exclude from political debates, correctly fearing its impact on the cohesion of their parties. What caused these changes, and to what degree did they constitute real changes in this aspect of the party system?

As an examination of figure 6.2 shows, the changes in the behaviour of the Belgian electorate can be separated into three phenomena. The first is an over-all decline in the share of the vote going to the three 'traditional' parties, a decline that seems to have stabilised, although individual party fortunes fluctuate. The second is the rise of the community parties (VU, FDF, RW) and their subsequent decline. Finally, there is the recent appearance of the ideologically based non-traditional parties, Ecolo and Agalev.

Figure 6.2 Parliamentary Elections in Belgium, 1958-1985

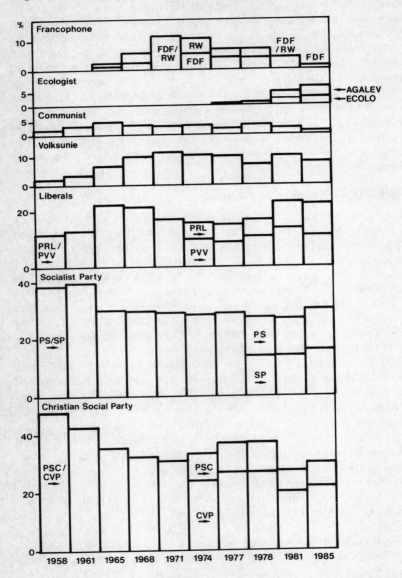

Source: Luc Rowies, *Les partis politiques en Belgique* and Thomas Mackie and Richard Rose, eds. *International Almanac of Election Statistics*, 2nd edition, 1983

The meanings of these changes would be easier to specify if we knew exactly who was doing the changing or even how many. The longitudinal studies necessary to determine whether we are dealing with a permanent pool of floating voters, or whether a majority of the Belgian electorate takes an occasional vacation from voting for its habitual party, are just beginning to be undertaken. They suggest that both phenomena exist, but that the latter may be more important. This impression is buttressed by studies of non-traditional voters in a single election. Overall they tend to be younger, either of higher or lower than average socio-economic status and more urban than the electorate in general.[4] However, the differences are often marginal, and in no case does the *majority* of a given category vote for a non-traditional party (Elchardus 1978; Delruelle-Vosswinkel *et al.* 1980, 1982). Voting is obviously less constrained by membership in a pillar than formerly but can hardly be said to have escaped its influence altogether.

There are several reasons for this loosening of the tie between membership in a pillar and party vote. First, the parties themselves have de-emphasised the act of voting as a defense of the pillar in favour of more 'modern' electoral propaganda. The Schools Pact of 1958, the subsequent withdrawal of the church from active intervention in politics and the deconfessionalisation of the Liberal Party, which opened itself to all 'neo-liberals' or conservatives in the early sixties have all contributed to lowering the importance of elections for the religious cleavage. The decline of religious practice: for example, weekly attendance at Mass declined from 42.9 per cent in 1967 to 30.2 per cent in 1976, must also be connected both with the drop in support for the Catholic parties and with the de-emphasis of religion in the parties' electoral propaganda (Van Haegendorn and Vandenhove 1985:9). Most recently the Flemish Socialist Party has attempted to attract members and votes from the Christian Left by opening its organisations to and running candidates identified with that group. This strategy appears to have had some electoral payoff but the party has not realised its ambition of replacing the CVP as the dominant party in Flanders, and there is considerable opposition within the SP to the movement of 'outsiders' into positions in party organisations (Govaert 1985). All parties, but most notably the Walloon Socialists, have emphasised the defense of regional interests in their electoral appeals.

Another root of electoral mobility can be found in social and economic changes that occurred in this period, including increased education, a more mobile population, and changes in the pattern of economic activity. These do not constitute a move towards post-industrial politics. First, the main issues of the period had a large economic content. The language laws of the early sixties were expected to have an impact on employment opportunities for Flemish and Francophones, while subsequent debates over regionalisation were very much debates over control of economic policy and over how much money would be spent in the regions and by whom. Even the new 'Green' parties, which stress what might be considered post-industrial issues, are strongest in places, such as Antwerp and Liège, that have a tradition of *industrial* working class radicalism (Mahoux and Moden 1984; Deschouwer and Stouthuysen 1984).[5] Finally, 'post-industrial' is too broad a description for the economic changes occurring in Belgium. Wallonia is de-industrialising, which is a quite different phenomenon, Flanders is trying to complete its process of industrialisation with technologically sophisticated industries and trying to cope with the decline of its older economic base, and Brussels, which was always dominated by the service sector, is trying to establish a new base now that its role as a financial centre has been diminished by the growing importance of international capital. The changes described above put people in situations in which adult socialisation does not reinforce childhood socialisation. That greater political mobility should follow is not surprising. The decline of the community parties and the failure of the Flemish socialists to achieve their electoral goals despite their strategy of espousing 'modern' issues such as nuclear disarmament, suggests that the changes have not yet created a permanent audience for 'post-industrial' political issues.[6]

Finally, the mobility of the past twenty-five years is also related to alienation resulting from the performance of the parties themselves. Although the dominant issues of the period, in terms of discourse and impact on governmental stability, were community issues, opinion polls consistently show that the electorate considered economic issues to be more important. Moreover, the period was one of considerable governmental instability. It is more probable that cabinet instability caused the traditional parties' loss of votes and the subsequent fragmentation of the party system than vice versa. Instability resulted because community issues split all parties into unitarists and federalists. It was exacerbated by the frequent need to assemble a government with a two-thirds rather than a simple majority in parliament for the purposes of constitutional revision. (This task was made even more difficult by the refusal of Liberals and Socialists to be in the same government. The 1980 coalition, which finally did put them together in a government with the Catholic parties, and did pass the regionalisation amendments was the first time the two parties had governed together since 1958. It lasted five months.) Opinion polls show that frequent collapses of government over issues that were often obscure to the voters increased alienation from the system. The number of spoiled ballots (voting is compulsory) increased. It would be surprising if some did not vote against their habitual party from the same motives (INUSOP reports, 1979).

The other major change in the party system was the division of each of the traditional parties along language lines. Parties first developed distinct and increasingly autonomous wings, and then divided into completely separate parties. The Catholic party split in 1968 over the issue of removing the Francophone section of the Catholic University of Louvain from its historic location in Flanders; the Liberals split in 1971, largely over the issue of whether or not the party should give more recognition to its linguistic wings; and the Socialists split in 1978, in part as a result of the strains of a decade spent debating community issues and in part because of growing ideological differences between the Flemish and Francophone wings of the party (Rayside 1978; Beaufays 1985). This fragmentation has complicated relations within governments but was not directly responsible for the government instability of the period. The two language groups of each ideological family continue to participate in government together, and, as table 6.2 shows, most governments fall because of disputes between ideologically different parties or because of a revolt within a single party, usually the CVP. Language and regional issues do divide Belgian governments, but usually with the dominant party in each region leading the attack and the smaller parties acting as peacemakers. Thus, in the Martens V government, quarrels over issues such as government aid to the Walloon steel industry pitted the Walloon Liberals against the Flemish Catholics. Their ideological partners, the Flemish Liberals and Walloon Social Christians, each of whom expected to lose votes in an early election, played a discrete mediating role.

Table 6.2 Belgian Governments, 1961-1985

Government (Composition) (Date of Installation)	Duration (Years:Months)	Reason for Fall
Lefevre - Spaak (Catholic - Socialist) (25 April 1961)	4:1	End of term
Harmel - Spinoy (Catholic - Socialist) (27 July 1965)	0:7	Interparty dispute
Vanden Boeynants - De Clerq (Catholic - Liberal) (19 March 1966)	1:11	Revolt of Flemish Social Christian Parliamentarians and ministers
Eyskens/Merlot - Cools (CVP/PSC - Socialist) (17 June 1968)	3:5	Interparty quarrels
Eyskens - Cools II (CVP/PSC - Socialist) (20 January 1972)	0:10	Interparty quarrels
Leburton - Tindemans - De Clerq (Socialist - CVP/PSC - PVV/PLP) (26 January 1973)	1:0	Interparty quarrels
Tindemans I (PSC/CVP - PVV/PLP) (25 April 1974)	0:2	Enlargement of majority
Tindemans II (PSC/CVP - PVV/PLP - RW) (11 June 1974)	2:9	Intraparty (RW) quarrel
Tindemans III (PSC/CVP - Socialist - FDF-VU) (3 June 1977)	1:4	Intraparty (CVP) revolt supported by Prime Minister
Vanden Boeynants (PSC/CVP - Socialist - FDF-VU) (20 October 1978)	0:2	Caretaker government
Martens I (PSC/CVP - BSP/PS - FDF) (3 April 1979)	0:10	Intraparty (CVP) and interparty quarrels

Table 6.2 (cont'd) Belgian Governments, 1961-1985

Government (Composition) (Date of Installation)	Duration (Years:Months)	Reason for Fall
Martens II (PSC/CVP - SP/PS) (23 January 1980)	0:2	Intraparty (CVP) quarrels
Martens III (CVP/PSC - PS/SP - PRL/PVV) (18 May 1980)	0:5	Interparty quarrels
Martens IV (PSC/CVP - SP/PS) (21 October 1980)	0:7	Interparty quarrels
Eyskens (CVP/PSC - PS/SP) (6 April 1981)	0:6	Interparty quarrels
Martens V (CVP/PSC - PVV/PRL) (17 December 1981)	3:10	Interparty quarrels

Sources: Theo Luykx, *Politieke Geschiedenis van België* (Brussels: Elsevier, 1978); Henri Lemaitre, *Les Gouvernements belges de 1968 à 1980* (Brussels: Editions J. Chauvenheid, 1982); Francis Delpérée, *Chroniques de crise, 1977 - 1982* (Brussels: CRISP, 1983).

The other major characteristic of the Belgian party system in its government role is the continuing dominance of the Catholic party, and particularly the Flemish CVP, which benefits from its position as the dominant party in the country's dominant region (Van Haegendorn and Vandenhove 1985). As table 6.3 shows, the CVP has had a near-monopoly on the prime ministership and the crucial economic ministries since 1961. Paradoxically, the declining importance of the religious cleavage has reinforced this dominance. Secularism was the only issue the Socialists and Liberals agreed on, and when the Liberals abandoned anticlericalism in favour of an emphasis on conservative economic policies, Socialist-Liberal governments became politically impossible. The cross-class nature of the Catholic parties allows them

Table 6.3 Party Occupation of Major Government Posts, 1961-1985 (years: months)

Party	CVP	PSC	SP	PS	PVV	PRL
Posts						
Prime Minister	19:0	2:7		1:0		
Interior	0:11	12:0	2:0	5:9	1:11	
Defense	9:11	7:5			3:0	2:4
Foreign Affairs	7:11	7:7		7:1		
Finance	9:10	3:5			7:11	2:4
Agriculture	10:4	11:5				
Middle Classes[a]	8:10	5:10				7:1
Social Security	13:7	1:10	1:0	5:6		
Public Health	17:10	1:4	3:5[b]			
Labour		13:5	6:8	2:6		
Justice	2:6	2:5	8:5	0:11	4:6	3:10
Economic Affairs	3:10	3:1	8:1	4:10		1:11
Public Works	8:1	1:0		6:7		
Total	112:6	73:4	28:1	35:7	16:5	24:5

Source: Adapted from Van Haegendoren and Vandenhove, 'Le monde catholique flamand'.

Note: a. The Ministry of the Middle Classes deals mainly with small business and independent and professional workers.

b. The Public Health Ministry was held as a dual portfolio by the SP and PS from 1968-71.

Totals are not the same for all ministries because of rearrangements of portfolios.

to ally with either Liberals or Socialists, although at the cost of some internal strains. As a result the CVP-PSC has been in power continuously since 1958.

Another change has been the strengthening of regional differences in party systems. As can be seen from table 6.4, Brussels is the most fragmented region, since the electorate divides along both party and language lines. In Flanders, the votes lost by the CVP have gone alternately to the right, to the PVV, or to the centre, to a 'modernised' Volksunie which now stresses effective management of the Flemish economy more than it does defense of Flemish cultural interests, or to a Flemish Socialist party that has largely abandoned pursuit of the class struggle. In Wallonia, some votes have gone to the Liberal party, but in general it is parties on the left who have gained. This, combined with the dominant position of the Socialist party gives the Walloon party system a centre of gravity distinctly to the left of the Flemish system. However, this is not so much a change in the Belgian party system as an extension of already existing tendencies.

Overall, the changes in Belgian voting behaviour in the last twenty-five years seem to combine a crisis partially overcome and a slower, less reversible change. The traditional parties have not recovered all the votes lost in the sixties and seventies, but they have managed to stop their losses to the community parties, largely by adopting their issues and becoming community parties themselves (Covell 1981). Only the Volksunie, the oldest of the ethnic-based parties and the only one to be able to add non-community issues to its appeal, survives in any strength. It is too soon to tell whether parties like Agalev and Ecolo constitute more fundamental challenges.

Parties and Pillars

The changing relationship between the parties as electoral-governmental-bureaucratic organisations and the other organisations that make up their pillars has followed the pattern of the relationship between the parties and their electorate: a gradual loosening but by no means a disintegration. The first step in this organisational decentralisation of the pillars occurred after the Second World War. Before the war both Socialist and Catholic parties had followed systems of indirect membership: one joined by being a member of an organisation directly affiliated to the party. Since the war individual membership is direct, and it is the organisations which are indirectly linked to the party. *Reported* membership in Belgian parties represents about one tenth of their electorate and has been stable or slightly declining since 1960.)

The postwar loosening of the connections between parties and affiliated groups was expected to continue. Considerations of organisational autonomy and the increased secularisation of both clerical and anti-clerical blocs would, it was thought, lead to the 'depillarisation' of the Belgian social and political systems. Some

Belgium

Table 6.4 Party Vote by Region, 1961 and 1985

Flanders	1961	1985	Wallonia	1961	1985
CVP	50.9	34.6	PSC	31.2	22.6
SP	29.7	23.7	PS	46.5	39.4
PVV	11.6	17.3	PL	11.6	24.2
KP	1.0	0.5	PC	6.3	2.5
VU	6.0	12.7	UDRT	-	1.6
Vlaams Blok	-	2.2	Ecolo	-	6.2
Agalev	-	6.1			

Brussels	1961	1985
PS	41.6	14.8
PSC	28.0	9.3
PL	11.6	26.0
PC	3.6	1.2
VU	1.6	3.4
FDF	-	10.9
CVP	-	8.0
Ecolo	-	5.5
UDRT	-	5.0
SP	-	5.0
PVV	-	4.6
Agalev	-	1.0

Source: X. Mabille and E. Lentzen, 'Les élections législatives du 13 octobre 1985'.

attempts were made to move in this direction. For example, experimental 'pluralist schools', which would be neither clerical nor secular - or rather, both - were proposed as a way of beginning the process. However, in spite of continuing tensions between the parties and their affiliated organisations, the expected disintegration of the pillars and reorganisation of the interest groups along functional lines has not taken place. There are several reasons for this (Huyse 1984; Billiet 1981). First, if it is difficult for an individual to leave a pillar, it is even more difficult for an organisation within a pillar to leave the constellation of groups of which it is a part. The organisational, personal and financial links among these groups create a strong tendency to inertia in the system. The organisational division of labour, in which the party defends the groups when money and positions are being allocated and programs are being drawn up in return for group support and acquiescence, constitutes a further link. Moreover, pillarisation creates a rivalry among groups that ostensibly have the same function: a socialist union is not likely to leave its pillar unless its catholic counterpart does the same thing at the same time.

The parties themselves can be expected to work for the preservation of the pillars. Particularly in view of the decline in reliable party vote, the affiliated organisations are seen as important lines of defense against further erosion of support. For a party in government the organisations provide an important means of social control. This can be seen most clearly in the area of relations with the unions. The Catholic-Liberal government of Wilfried Martens has been engaged in an austerity program that has reduced Belgians' real income by 15 to 20 per cent. Response to these policies has been crippled by the refusal of the Catholic federation of unions to join the Socialist unions' protests (Arcq 1984; De Feyt and Reman 1984). Even the Socialist unions have been restrained by the Socialist party's desire to preserve its position as a potential governing partner in the event of a Catholic-Liberal split.

Regionalisation and Parties

In addition to social and economic changes, Belgium has undergone a major alteration in its institutional arrangements. A series of laws and constitutional amendments passed in 1970 and 1980 created a new level of government with two sets of institutions. Some governmental functions in areas such as education and health care have been handed over to the two cultural communities, French and Dutch, while some economic powers have been given to the three regions, Flanders, Wallonia and Brussels; however, the transfer of powers to Brussels has not yet taken place because of disagreements on the exact status of the capital.

Communities and regions were given their own legislatures, formed of national parliamentarians from each community and region, their own executives, and their own bureaucracies, created by transfers from the central bureaucracy. The executives became autonomous at the beginning of 1982, and, once the Belgian Senate has been reformed, the regions and communities will have separately elected legislatures. Given the general domination of the parties, and the relative ages of the two different institutions, so far the parties have had more impact on the operation of the new institutions than vice versa.

The major effect that Belgian regionalisation could have been expected to have on the party system was already anticipated by the parties themselves, which split into separate regional organisations several years before the creation of the new institutions. If separate regional legislatures are created the parties might split further into units organised around national *or* regional politics, but the Belgian Senate has so far successfully resisted the changes necessary to bring these legislatures into existence. Practices such as party quotas in the administration and party deals over executive and parliamentary posts were immediately reproduced at the regional level. Posts in the regional executives have been assimilated to national posts in a single hierarchy. Ordinary positions are roughly equivalent to minor ministries or secretaryships of state in the national government and the presidency of the regional executive is regarded as equivalent to a major ministry at the national level. Unsatisfactory national ministers have been 'demoted' to a position at the regional level. After the 1985 election, the distribution of posts on the regional and community executives was discussed as part of the negotiations for the formation of the national government and approved at the same party congresses.[7] In other words, the parties, which controlled the regionalisation process, have also been able, so far, to control its impact on their organisation and styles of operation.

Conclusion: Prospects for Change

Although regionalisation itself has not yet changed the Belgian party system greatly, the continued importance of the regional element is likely to change the party system and the way national politics are conducted. One of the changes that has occurred is the development of different ideological balances in each region and of differences between the regional parties belonging to the same ideological family. Not only are politics in Flanders and Wallonia beginning to revolve around different issues, it means something different to be, for example, a Flemish or a Walloon Socialist. If these changes persist, they may lead to further disintegration at the national level. As an observer of Belgian politics once remarked: 'It is not dangerous for a system when parties oppose each other: what is dangerous is when they talk about different things, as if they were living in different systems' (Mabille 1976:148). So far the regional fragmentation of the party system has been muted by the fact that at the national level, the two branches of each family act in concert for the purposes of government formation. Differences in orientation already make subsequent governing difficult, further differentiation would make the whole process even more complicated.

There are also signs that groups interested in issues that are poorly articulated by the pillarisation system are increasingly moving out of party control. New parties such as Agalev and Ecolo, movements such as women's groups and revolts of workers against a union leadership too closely involved in the system all represent an increased rejection of the system itself. However, at the moment, they do not constitute an insurmountable challenge, and, given the past powers of recuperation of the system, any prediction that they will do so must be undertaken with caution. Belgium's parties and their associated zuilen have not proven to be 'pillars of sand', but rather of sandstone (Huyse 1984; Bakvis 1984). Sandstone does erode, and more quickly under modern conditions than in the past, but it has a discouraging tendency to outlast any individual observer.

Notes

1. For overviews of the Belgian political system, see Heisler 1974; Huyse 1980; Lorwin 1966; Zolberg 1978.

2. For a similar argument, see Huyse 1984.

3. An interesting, although not always convincing, extension of this argument can be found in Kieve 1981. See also Huyse 1984.

4. The figures are affected by the fact that one of the community parties, the FDF, recruits only in Brussels and its immediate suburbs.

5. Like the community parties, the Belgian 'Green' parties attract a certain number of generalised protest votes. Ecolo lost votes in 1985 in Liège, where it had participated in the municipal government coalition for the last three years.

6. Possible explanations for the decline of the community parties include the capture of their issues by the traditional parties and the related fact that the language dispute has become a traditional political issue, firmly identified with the present holders of political power.

7. See the accounts in *Brief uit België/Lettre de Belgique*, 1985, nos. 40, 41, 44, 45. I am grateful to the Belgian consulate for furnishing me with this weekly collection of excerpts from the Belgian press. For further discussion, see Delmartino, 1986.

Belgium

References

Arcq, E., (1984) 'Le C.S.C. et le programme gouvernemental de mars 1984,' Centre de Recherche et d'Information Socio-Politiques (CRISP) *Courrier Hebdomadaire 1032*

Bakvis, H. (1984) 'Toward a political economy of consociationalism,' *Comparative Politics 16*, 315-334

Beaufays, J. (1985) 'Le socialisme et les problèmes communautaires,' *1885-1985: Du Parti Ouvrier Belge au Parti Socialiste*, Institut Emile Vandervelde, Brussels

Billiet, J. (1981) 'Verzuiling als blokkade,' *De Nieuwe Maand 24*, 258-65

Brassinne, J., and Launier, P. (1983) 'Le Pacte culturel: 1973-1982, CRISP *Courrier Hebdomadaire* 986-7

Brief uit België / Lettre de Belgique, Various numbers

Chlepner, B.S. (1972) *Cent ans d'histoire sociale en Belgique*, Editions de l 'Université de Bruxelles, Brussels

Claeys, P.H., and Loeb-Mayer, N. (1984) 'Le 'parafédéralisme' belge: une tentative de conciliation par le cloisonnement,' *International Political Science Review, 5*, 473-90

Covell, M. (1981) 'Ethnic conflict and elite bargaining: the case of Belgium,' *West European Politics 4*, 197-218

De Feyt, P., and Reman, P. (1984) 'Les partis politiques face la réforme de la sécurité sociale,' CRISP *Courrier Hebdomadaire* 1041-2

Delmartino, F. (1986) 'Belgium: Between regionalism and federalism,' Paper presented to the Comparative Federalism Study Group (IPSA), Murten, Switzerland

Delruelle-Vosswinkel, N., and Frognier, A. (1980) 'L'opinion publique et les problèmes communautaires,' CRISP *Courrier Hebdomadaire* 880

Delruelle-Vosswinkel, N., Frognier, A., Dawance-Goossens, J., and Grodent, J. (1982) 'L'opinion publique et les problèmes communautaires,' CRISP *Courrier Hebdomadaire* 966

Deschouwer, K., and Stouthuysen, P. (1984) 'L'électorat d'Agalev,' CRISP *Courrier Hebdomadaire* 1061

Dyson, K. (1980) 'State and society in Western Europe: a model for comparative analysis,' *West European Politics 3*, 1

Elchardus, M. (1978) 'Bureaukratisch patronage en etnolinguisme,' *Res Publica 20*, 141-65

Franssen, P., and Martens, L. (1984) *L'argent du PSC-CVP*, Vie Ouvrière, Brussels

Govaert, S. (1985) 'Deux courants socialistes flamands: Doorbraak,' CRISP *Courrier Hebdomadaire* 1071

Heisler, M. (1974) 'Institutionalizing societal cleavages: the growing importance of the output side in Belgium,' in Martin Heisler, ed., *Politics in Europe: Structures and Processes in some Post-Industrial Democracies*, David McKay, New York

Huyse, L (1980) *De gewapende vrede*, Kritak, Leuven

Huyse, L (1984) 'Pillarization reconsidered, *Act Politica, 19*, 145-58

Institut Interuniversitaire de Sondage D'opinion (INUSOP), Various reports

Jenner, R. (1982) 'Le financement publique des partis politiques,' CRISP *Courrier Hebdomadaire* 973

Kieve, R. (1981) 'Pillars of sand: a Marxist critique of consociational democracy in the Netherlands,' *Comparative Politics 13*, 313-37

Lijphart, A., ed. (1981) *Conflict and Coexistence in Belgium: The Dynamics of a Culturally Divided Society*, Institute of International Studies, University of California, Berkeley

Lorwin, V. (1966) 'Belgium: religion, class and language in national politics,' in R. Dahl ed., *Political Opposition in Western Democracies*, Yale University Press, New Haven

Luykx, T. (1978) *Politieke Geschiedenis van België*, Elsevier, Brussels

Mabille, X.(1976) 'Adaptation ou éclatement du système de decision en Belgique,' *Recherches sociologiques, 7,* 11-49

Mahoux, P., and Moden, J. (1984) 'Le mouvement Ecolo,' CRISP *Courrier Hebdomadaire* 1045-6

Palmer, J. (1983) 'Saying goodbye to Brussels,' *Brussels Bulletin,* April 26

Rayside, D. (1978) 'The impact of the linguistic cleavage on the 'governing' parties of Belgium and Canada,' *Canadian Journal of Political Science 11* 61-97

Rejai, M., ed. (1971) *Decline of Ideology?* Aldine, New York

Rowies, L. (1977) *Les partis politiques en Belgique,* CRISP Dossier 10

Urwin, D. (1979) 'Social cleavages and political parties in Belgium,' *Political Studies 18,* 320-40

Van Haegendorn, M., and Vandenhove, L. (1985) 'Le monde catholique flamand,' CRISP *Courriers Hebdomadaires* 1070, 1080-1,1084-5

Zolberg, A. (1977) 'Splitting the difference: federalization without federalism in Belgium,' in M. Esman, ed., *Ethnic Conflict in the Western World,* Cornell University Press, Ithaca

Zolberg, A. (1978) 'Belgium,' in R. Grew, ed., *Crises of Political Development in Europe and the United States,* Princeton University Press, Princeton

Chapter Seven

The Netherlands: Continuity and Change in a Fragmented Party System[*]

Steven B. Wolinetz

The Dutch party system provides fertile ground for exploring party system change. Until recently, five parties dominated political life. However, in the late 1960s new parties and dissident factions emerged, demanding changes in the party system. Declining support and internal pressures forced political leaders to take demands seriously. Several parties began exploring alliances and mergers, and a special commission was set up to consider changes in the electoral law and the way in which the prime minister was designated.

By the 1980s a new party configuration was evident. The style and tone of party competition had changed and the party system was more polarised than before. Secular parties had gained at the expense of confessional parties. On the left, the Socialists (PvdA) had assumed a more radical posture. In the centre, the Catholic Peoples Party (KVP) and two Protestant parties, the Anti-Revolutionary Party (ARP) and the Christian Historical Union (CHU) had merged to form the Christian Democratic Appeal (CDA). On the right, the Liberal Party (VVD) had become more vocal and assertive. At the same time, Democrats '66, the party whose demands had inaugurated debate on

[*] This chapter extends research originally carried out for my PhD. dissertation (Wolinetz 1973) and updated at intervals throughout the 1970s and 1980s. The material derives from interviews with party officials and activists, conversations with informed observers, and a long-standing acquaintance with Dutch politics. The research has been supported by Fulbright Fellowships, a Canada Council post-doctoral fellowship, and Vice-Presidential and Social Science and Humanities Research Council General Funds from Memorial University of Newfoundland.

the party system, had become a permanent element of the party system. Though weakened, smaller parties survived on the right and the left.

The Changing Contours of the Party System

Through the 1960s, the predominant characteristics of the party system were its fragmentation, the stability of the party alignment, and the ways in which parties were rooted in a segmented or pillarised social structure. Reflecting previous mobilisation, Dutch society was divided into Calvinist, Catholic, and general subcultures or pillars. Each had its own schools, newspapers, interest associations, social and sports clubs. Five major parties and a host of minor parties represented divisions among and within subcultures. Socialists (PvdA) and Liberals (VVD) represented different strata within the general or neutral subculture, while the Catholic Peoples' Party (KVP) represented the Catholic pillar, which had been organised and orchestrated by the Dutch Church. Finally two Protestant parties, the Anti-Revolutionary Party (ARP), and the Christian Historical Union (CHU) drew support from different elements within the Calvinist subculture (Daalder 1966).

Parties represented distinct traditions. The Socialist Party (formally the Labour Party) had been established in 1946 in an attempt to broaden the base of Dutch Social Democracy. Located in the reformist traditions of Social Democracy, both the PvdA and its predecessor, the Social Democratic Workers Party (SDAP), found their access to power limited by confessional mobilisation. Early Socialists had hoped that the enfranchisement of the masses would produce a Socialist majority, but following the introduction of universal manhood suffrage in 1918, the SDAP leveled off at 20 to 22 per cent of the vote (see table 7.1). The reluctance of the larger Catholic party to ally with the Socialists confined the SDAP to the opposition until 1939.

The PvdA was established by the pre-war Social Democrats, Radical Democrats and Christian Democrats, as well as members of resistance groups, in an effort to rally Catholic and Protestant workers to the Socialist fold. PvdA founders argued that confessional parties were no longer necessary because they had secured state support for denominational schools. However, PvdA dreams of achieving an electoral breakthrough were thwarted by the re-emergence of the confessional parties. Although some Catholic and Protestant intellectuals rallied to the PvdA, few workers did. In the first postwar elections in 1946, the PvdA won only 28.3 per cent of the vote, less than the 1937 total of the three parties which had joined in its

Table 7.1 Parliamentary Election Results in The Netherlands, 1918-1937 (in percent of ballots cast)

	1918	1922	1925	1929	1933	1937
Major Parties or Tendencies:						
Anti-Revolutionary Party (ARP)	13.4	13.7	12.2	11.6	13.4	16.4
Christian Historical Union (CHU)	6.6	10.9	9.9	10.5	9.1	7.5
Roman Catholic Party (RKSP)[a]	30.0	29.9	28.6	29.6	27.9	28.8
Liberals:						
Liberal Party (LSP, 'De Vrijheidsbond')[b]	15.1	9.3	8.7	7.4	7.0	4.0
Radical Democratic League[c] (VDB)	5.3	4.6	6.1	6.2	5.1	5.9
Social Democratic Workers Party (SDAP)[c]	22.0	19.4	22.9	23.9	21.5	22.0
Minor Parties:						
Political Reformed Party (SGP)	0.4	0.9	2.0	2.3	2.5	1.9
Communists (CPH)	2.4	1.8	1.2	2.0	3.2	3.3
Christian Democratic Union[c] (CDU)	0.8	0.7	0.5	0.4	1.0	2.1
Other parties:						
with seats	2.8	2.5	3.6	3.2	5.4	4.2
without seats	1.3	6.3	4.3	2.9	3.9	3.9

Source: Centraal Bureau voor de Statistiek, Statistiek der Verkiezingen, 1971 (The Hague: Staatsuitgeverij, 1972), table 8, p. 22.
Notes: a) after 1945, the KVP, b) in 1918, Liberals under various labels, c) in 1946 the SDAP, VDB, and CDU (an interconfessional party) merged to form the PvdA or Labour party.

foundation (Wolinetz 1973; Manning 1968). Nevertheless, the PvdA emerged as a governing party and an important element in postwar coalitions.

A moderate and technocratically oriented party, the PvdA fit the end of ideology mold. Like the SPD in neighboring Germany, the PvdA had expunged remaining references to class struggle from its programme in 1959, and was committed to greater equality in the context of a mixed economy. Domestic policies were defined in terms of what was possible and what coalition partners would accept. In foreign policy the party was pro-NATO.

The centre of postwar spectrum was occupied by the three confessional parties. Established in 1879, the Anti-Revolutionary Party (ARP), had been the first mass party in the Netherlands. Organised to seek state support for religious schools, the ARP represented a militant Calvinism, but one bent less on converting the entire country than sheltering Orthodox Calvinists from a secular society. In the course of its struggle, the ARP began to define a separate subculture rooted in the Orthodox Reformed Churches. However, differences over suffrage extension led to a split in 1894, and the formation of the Christian Historical Union (CHU) in 1908 (Lipschits 1977). In contrast to the ARP, the CHU was less militant and more loosely organised. Although both were part of Calvinist subculture, the CHU drew its support from the Dutch Reformed Churches. Both represented the Protestant subculture. However, the ARP's militancy gave it a sharper definition. In the interwar period, the ARP was an arch-conservative force, committed to Sunday rest and opposed to any substantial government role in the economy. However, in the 1960s Anti-Revolutionaries began to extract a more radical message from the gospel and moved to the left. For its part, the Christian Historical Union was more oriented toward supporting governments. In the interwar period, Anti-Revolutionary strength ranged from 11 to 16 per cent of the vote and the Christian Historicals had 6 to 10 per cent (table 7.1). In the postwar period, fluctuations were less pronounced: the Anti-Revolutionaries usually had 9 to 10 per cent of the vote, the Christian Historical Union another 8 to 9 per cent.

The Catholic Peoples Party (KVP) was the exclusive representative of the sizable Catholic minority in the Netherlands. Supported by the Dutch hierarchy, the Catholic Party commanded the overwhelming support of Dutch Catholics. With 30 to 32 per cent of the vote, the Catholic party was the largest party in the parliament and an indispensable element in any coalition. However, this was not without its costs. Loosely organised, the KVP contained distinct labour and business wings, and functioned more like a holding company for Catholic organisations than a coherent political party. Reconciling different points of view meant that the party invariably ended up in the centre. Reorganisation of the interwar party, the Roman Catholic State Party (RKSP), in 1945 as the Catholic Peoples Party (KVP), a programmatic party open to anyone who agreed with its programmes, did little to alter this.

The fifth party in the postwar configuration was the Peoples Party for Freedom and Democracy (VVD), heir to Dutch liberal traditions. Instrumental in the development of parliamentary government, Liberals had been eclipsed by confessional and socialist mobilisation. Divisions over suffrage extension and other issues split the Liberals into two and sometimes three separate political parties. One of these, the Radical Democratic League (VDB) had joined in the establishment of the PvdA in 1946. Others rallied to the VVD when it was established in 1948. In postwar politics, the Liberals have been a right of centre but not necessarily a conservative force. Liberals accepted the welfare state and a managed economy. Drawing on the secular middle classes, Liberals commanded 10 to 12 per cent of the vote.

The Dutch system combined fragmentation with electoral stability. An extremely permissive system of proportional representation - one per cent of the national vote (two thirds of one per cent after the enlargement of the parliament in 1956) was sufficient to win a seat in parliament - facilitated the organisation and representation of a large number of political parties.[1] However, the segmentation of Dutch society meant that few votes were available for shifts in the party balance. Cradle-to-grave networks of religious or ideologically based organisations, initiated in the later portion of the nineteenth century and elaborated in the twentieth, proved to be ideal for the mobilisation of voters and the transmission of party loyalties. The services, ranging from the provision of education or insurance to the organization of clubs and leisure, which subcultural organizations provided were a source of loyalty and attachment. Within the Catholic pillar, the pressures of the church hierarchy, transmitted through periodic edicts and letters, as well as the activities of Dutch priests, produced steady support for the Catholic party (Bakvis 1981a). In the Calvinist pillar, Anti-Revolutionaries were able to inculcate deep and abiding loyalties to their party. For their part, Socialists could draw the support of the Socialist trade union movement and other affiliated organisations. Voters were unlikely to vote for parties identified with other subcultures. As a result, elections had a census-like quality (Houska 1985) and the principal movements were typically between parties identified with the same subculture. Neither smaller parties hoping to gain entry nor the Socialists, attempting to expand their base of support, could make substantial gains. Although fluctuations could occur - consider the vote for the ARP and the CHU in the interwar period - the party configuration remained the same.

Coalition patterns were not as rigid as the party aligment. Until World War II, the confessional parties constituted the right, Socialists and Liberals, the left (figure 7.1). Before 1918, common demands for state support for religious schools and the need to maximise their strength under a district system forced the three confessional parties into a durable electoral alliance, and confessional and Liberal cabinets alternated in office (Daalder 1966). In the interwar period, relations between the three confessional parties were strained, and their formal alliance was dissolved in 1925. However, cabinets typically included the three confessional parties, and one or more of the Liberal parties, while the Socialists were confined to the opposition. Antipathy to the Socialists and the absense of any alternative policy coalition facilitated the dominance of laissez-faire policies.

This changed after World War II. Distances among parties were reduced. Although the confessional parties rejected Socialist pleas for a breakthrough and a more fundamental reorganisation of the party system, Catholics, and later Christian Historicals and Anti-Revolutionaries, allied with the Socialists in a series of 'Red-Roman' cabinets. These laid the foundations for the postwar welfare state. This reflected the predominance of economic issues and the emergence of a new policy coalition agreed on the importance of full employment, the welfare state and a managed economy. In this altered configuration, the confessional parties constituted the centre and the Liberals the right (figure 7.1). Centre-left coalitions were in office from 1946 through 1958. However, once Socialists and Catholics had exhausted their initial agenda, centre-right coalitions predominated. (Daudt 1980)

The Unraveling of the Party System in the 1960s

The postwar configuration remained intact until 1966, when the party system came under siege from a variety of quarters. We can trace its demise to shifts in voting patterns, the emergence and success of minor parties, and the appearance of dissident factions in several parties. These developments took place against a background of social

Figure 7.1 The Changing Contours of the Dutch Party System

The interwar party system:

Communists	Socialists	Liberals	Confessionals
CPH	SDAP	VDB LSP	RKSP CHU ARP

left (secular)   right (confessional)

predominant
  coalition: --

The postwar party system (until 1967):

Communists/ other left	Socialists	Confessionals	Liberals	Religious right
CPN PSP	PvdA	KVP ARP CHU	VVD	GPV SGP

left   right

                                             1946-1958
predominant   ---------------------------------
  coalitions: 1959-67

The contemporary party system:

Communists/ other left	Socialists		Christian Democrats	Liberals	Religious right
CPN					RPF
PSP	PvdA	D'66	CDA	VVD	GPV
PPR					SGP

left   right

predominant
  coalition:
                                             1967-86
                                             ----

and economic change, including changing patterns of religious observance, the growth of the service sector, and the coming of age of a generation raised in relative affluence.[2]

Changes in previous patterns of mobilisation reflect the diminishing impact of pillarisation. Maintaining the previous party alignment depended on sustaining previous attachments. This could be done in a variety of ways: by inculcating deep party loyalties and ensuring their transmission to new generations; by exposing voters to the pressures of organisational networks; or failing that, by adapting party positions to the changing predilections of voters.[3] Segmentation facilitated the first two, but success depended on the maintenance of earlier fervor, the preservation of organisational networks, and the willingness of subcultural elites to continue them. A break in any of these processes could lead to more and more votes becoming available for changes in the party configuration.[4]

The three parties most directly rooted in pillarised social structures sustained themselves in different ways. Based in the Orthodox Reformed Churches and the smaller and more cohesive Calvinist subculture, the Anti-Revolutionaries relied on deep and abiding loyalties and close familial ties to sustain the party. In contrast, the larger Catholic subculture was far more loosely integrated and relied on organisational pressures to maintain support. Finally, the PvdA stressed its programmes and accomplishments, as well as its roots in the working class. Although all three subcultures were prone to some leakage, the way in which the Catholic pillar was orchestrated meant that the Catholic Party was particularly vulnerable to the changes in the Church which surfaced in the 1960s. As late as 1954, the Dutch Church was still issuing edicts stressing the importance of maintaining unity and the evils of joining either the Socialist Trade Union federation or the Dutch Society for Sexual Reform. However, the 1954 mandement was the last of its kind. Despite its outward posture, the Dutch Church had been divided between more orthodox Thomist factions and an existential current. By the 1960s, the orientation of the Dutch Church had changed. Previously loyal to the Vatican, the Dutch Church become caught up in the eucumenical movements of the 1960s and began to question basic dogmas such as the trinity. For their part, the faithful began to stray from the flock. Although Catholics remained loyal to their schools and other Catholic organisations, they began to desert the KVP (Thurlings 1971; Bakvis 1981a and 1981b). The initial effects of this were apparent in 1967, when the KVP dropped from its normal range of 30 to 32 per cent of the popular vote to 26.5 per cent (figure 7.2).

Figure 7.2 Parliamentary Elections in the Netherlands, 1946-1986 (in percentage of the popular vote)

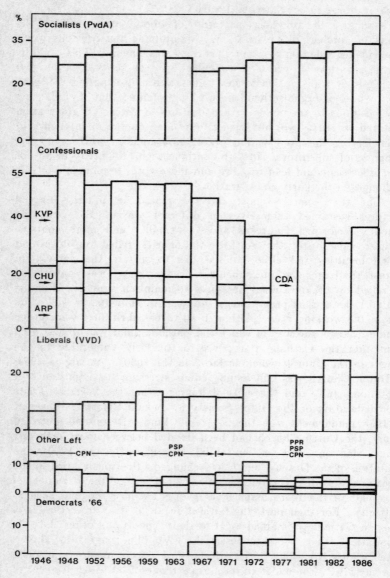

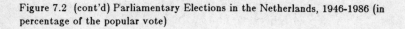

Figure 7.2 (cont'd) Parliamentary Elections in the Netherlands, 1946-1986 (in percentage of the popular vote)

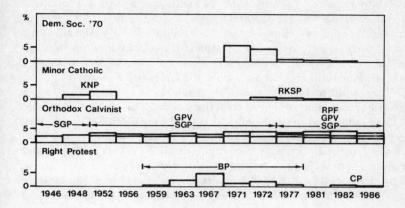

Source: Centraal Bureau voor de Statistiek, *Statistiek der Verkiezingen, 1977* (The Hague, Staatsuitgeverij, 1973), 27, *Keesings Historisch Archief*, 17 September 1982, p. 596 and 5 June 1986, p. 354.

This need not have signified either the demise of the KVP or the passing of the postwar party system. However, a younger, more impatient and more vocal generation was coming forward and changes were occurring elsewhere on the political spectrum. Socialists were also in decline, and minor parties were gaining support. The Farmers Party (BP), a Poujadist-style protest movement, founded in 1959, surged from 2.3 per cent in the 1963 parliamentary elections to 5.7 per cent in the June, 1966, municipal elections, while the Pacifist Socialists won 3.5 per cent. When early parliamentary elections were held in 1967, the Farmers Party won 4.7 per cent, and a new party, Democrats '66, organised with the explicit purpose of 'exploding' the existing party system and replacing it with a two-party system, won 4.5 per cent of the vote. At the same time, dissident groups appeared in several of the established parties.

The emergence of dissident groups is best understood in light of postwar coalition politics and the frustrations which it engendered. One significant difference between the pre-war and postwar party coalition patterns had been the inclusion of the Socialists. However, relations between the Socialists and Catholics were frequently strained.

The Red-Roman coalitions ended in 1958. After 1959, the confessional parties allied with the Liberals. The PvdA returned to government in 1965, when the confessional-Liberal Marijnen cabinet split over broadcasting policy. The new cabinet, consisting of Socialists, Anti-Revolutionaries, and Catholics, was to be the first in a series of centre-left coalitions. However, the Cals cabinet fell a year and a half later when the right wing of the Catholic Party withdrew its support. This led to an interim cabinet, early elections, and the formation of a new confessional-Liberal cabinet under the Catholic, de Jong.

The sudden fall of the Cals cabinet and the return to a centre-right formula produced reactions across the party spectrum. Socialists felt betrayed, and political activists were critical of the way in which cabinets had been made and unmade without recourse to elections. In the PvdA, a faction calling itself New Left emerged, and Christian Radical factions appeared in the three confessional parties. Finally, Democrats '66 gained support for its claims that the existing party system was undemocratic because voters had no say over who formed a government.

The emergence of newer parties and dissident factions under-mined the postwar party configuration. Previously, voters confronted a multiparty menu which contained a large number of alternatives, but few which they were likely to choose. The appearance of new parties such as D'66, untainted by a previous history or participation in government, offered voters - some of whom were already inclined to abandon earlier allegiances - a wider range of effective choice. D'66 provided a temporary stopping place for voters reluctant to support parties previously defined as enemies (Wolinetz 1973; Irwin and Dittrich 1984). D'66's success encouraged others to organise and increased the leverage of dissident groups in established parties. The latter occurred because of the distinct possibility that dissident factions might exit, form new parties and siphon off support.

The success of Democrats '66 and the clamor of dissident factions placed the question of party realignment on the agenda. D'66 argued that the existing parties were irrelevant and should be replaced by progressive and conservative alternatives. This was to be accomplished by changing the constitution in order to provide for direct election of the prime minister and replacing proportional representation with a district system. Confronted with demands for change, politicians responded by trying to absorb and channel them.

As a result, the Dutch ended up with an unusual debate on how their party system ought to be changed. Democrats '66, Christian Radicals, and New Left placed different proposals on the agenda. D'66 demanded a two-party system and suggested drastic means of achieving it: constitutional and electoral changes in order to force parties to regroup. The demands of New Left and the Christian Radical factions were different. Each wanted their parties to renew themselves, each demanded 'clarity' in the political system, and each wanted their parties to participate in a 'progressive concentration'. For the Christian Radicals, this meant a durable alliance with the PvdA. For New Left, it meant cooperation with parties to the left (the Pacifist Socialists and, later, the Radical Political Party (PPR)), but, for moderates in the PvdA, it meant alliance with Democrats '66.

These proposals were eventually distilled into three alternatives: (1) constitutional reforms, taken up by a special all-party commission; (2) attempts by the Socialists (PvdA) to enlist Democrats '66 and the Radical Political Party (PPR) in an electoral alliance and the possible formation of a more broadly based party; and (3) an effort to amalgamate the Catholic People's Party, the Anti-Revolutionary Party and the Christian Historical Union into a single party. The first failed because of insufficient support and was overtaken by the second and the third.[5] In subsequent sections, we will consider the ways in which these gambits reshaped the party system.

The PvdA and the Reshaping of the Dutch Left

Changes on the left reflect the way in which the PvdA responded to electoral decline, the demands of its New Left faction and the challenge presented by Democrats '66. As we noted earlier, Dutch Socialists had hoped to rally a broad following but found their aspirations thwarted by confessional mobilisation and their access to power restricted by the predilections of the Catholic party. Consensus on postwar reconstruction and the desirability of full employment, a managed economy and the welfare state enabled the Socialists to govern in the 1940s and 1950s, but the PvdA found itself in a less comfortable position in the 1960s.

Once the PvdA and the KVP exhausted their initial areas of agreement, cooperation between the two parties became increasingly difficult. Socialists went in opposition in 1958, returned to the government in 1965, but found themselves excluded again in 1966. Their frustrations were compounded by electoral decline. Socialists had advanced to 32.7 per cent in 1956, but declined to 30.3 per cent in 1959, 28.0 per cent in 1963, and 23.5 per cent in 1967. Electoral alignments were becoming more fluid, the Catholic party was losing support, and many of the votes which the PvdA had sought were increasingly available. However, these were moving not to the PvdA, but rather to newer parties such as D'66. The left, originally populated by only the PvdA and the Communists, but later shared with the smaller Pacifist Socialists, was becoming increasingly crowded. If that were not enough, Democrats '66 was demanding that existing political forces be regrouped into broadly based progressive and conservative alternatives. The former, of course, was what the PvdA thought itself to be.

The success of D'66 gave the PvdA strong reasons for considering alliance and even merger with the new party. However, coping with D'66 was not the only problem confronting the PvdA. The party also had to deal with New Left, a dissident faction which blamed the PvdA's problems on its moderation and willingness to join cabinets. New Left argued that the PvdA was in decline because it had abandoned socialist principles and been too willing to compromise. Rejuvenation required changes in leadership and democratisation of the party organisation. Joint memberships on the party executive and the parliamentary caucus were to be eliminated and the executive was to assume greater control over elected representatives. Renewal of socialist commitments implied not a return to nationalisation or class struggle, but rather a 'cultural policy' to ensure greater mobility of workers, democratisation of social and political organisations, and a foreign policy less oriented to NATO. Finally, the PvdA was not to enter cabinet coalitions with the KVP (van den Berg and Molleman 1974).

In contrast to previous dissident groups, New Left launched a public attack on the party leadership. New Left organised events throughout the country, became involved in party sections, and took advantage of the positions and skills of its activists to present its case through the media. Under ordinary circumstances, New Left would have been instructed to cease its activities or leave the party. However, New Left represented a youthful element whose support the PvdA needed if it was to recover. Rather than expelling New Left - and running a risking that they might form a new party - PvdA leaders tried to integrate them into the party.

New Left had been gaining influence at the base by being more active than others and by expressing the frustrations and resentments of many party members (Boivin et al. 1978). The reluctance of PvdA leaders to oppose them directly facilitated further penetration. By 1972, New Left held a majority of the executive, ten seats on the caucus, and, as a result of a compromise, the chairmanship of the party. In addition, New Left's activities had provoked a split and the formation of a right-wing socialist party, Democratic Socialists '70 (DS'70).

142

New Left penetration influenced the PvdA's response to Democrats '66. Frustrated by its exclusion from the cabinet, the PvdA endorsed demands for greater popular influence over the designation of the prime minister (but not direct election as D'66 had originally proposed) and supported limited changes in the electoral law. However, rather than endorsing the fundamental regrouping which D'66 proposed, the PvdA promoted the idea of a progressive concentration. Initially, this was to bring the PvdA, D'66, and progressive elements within the confessional parties together in a new political formation. Later, the Radical Party (formed by dissident Catholic Radicals) became a key element in the strategy. However, many New Left adherents wanted to include the Pacifist Socialists (PSP) as well.

The idea of a progressive concentration never got beyond the stage of electoral alliances. Discussions to form a progressive accord (PAK) among members of the PvdA, D'66, the PPR, and the PSP began in 1969, but the PSP quickly withdrew. The PAK discussions continued, but when proposals for a new entity were floated in 1971, they found little support among the parties they were to bring together. There were two difficulties: the PAK discussions had been discussions among party members rather than the parties themselves. Second, Democrats '66 was reluctant to tarnish itself by associating with the PvdA.

Because parties felt bound to indicate with whom they preferred to govern, electoral alliances materialised in 1971 and 1972. In 1971, the PvdA, the PPR, and D'66 designated a 'shadow cabinet' which was to assume office if three parties secured a majority. In 1972, the PvdA, the PPR and D'66 again formed an electoral alliance. However, the shadow cabinet was dropped in favor of an elaborate common programme, *Turning Point*, which was to form the basis of a future cabinet. In the protracted cabinet formation which followed, the 'progressive three', who had won 36.3 per cent of the vote - vs. 31.3 per cent for the three confessional parties - insisted on the primacy of their programme and demanded that they be allowed to form a government. Eventually, a five-party cabinet of PvdA, PPR, D'66, KVP and ARP, took office under Socialist leader den Uyl.

After the 1972 elections, the idea of a progressive concentration disappeared from the political agenda. Democrats '66 leader van Mierlo wanted to proceed with formation of a new party, but the PvdA and the PPR had lost interest. This reflected the changing perspectives of the parties involved. The PvdA had been most interested when it was in decline. However, in 1971, the PvdA won

24.7 per cent despite a split to the right. When new elections were held in 1972, the PvdA accelerated to 27.3 per cent. However, D'66, which had reaped 6.8 per cent in 1971, slid to 4.2 per cent, while the PPR advanced from 1.8 per cent in 1971 (its first electoral outing) to a surprising 4.8 per cent in 1972.

In addition, the PvdA, under the influence of New Left, had little inclination to join in the formation of the more pragmatically oriented party which D'66 favoured. For its part, the PPR had evolved from a party of Catholic radicals, organised as a temporary way station en route to a progressive concentration, to a more radical party; PPR leaders were now more interested in using their position to prod the PvdA to the left.

By 1977, the present shape of the Dutch left was largely determined. The idea of electoral alliances resurfaced but was dropped. Democrats' 66 had declined precipitously in the 1974 provincial and municipal elections and nearly disbanded in 1975. However, the party was resurrected in 1976 under a new leader, Jan Terlouw. Terlouw argued that D'66 was a progressively oriented liberal party and took care to maintain some distance from the PvdA. The PvdA and the PPR broached an alliance for the 1977 parliamentary elections, and laid down conditions for entry into a cabinet, including the number of ministers they would demand. However, the two parties split prior to the elections, and little effort was made to heal the rift. The PPR had become an increasingly independent member of the den Uyl coalition, and the PvdA was willing to compete without them.

For its part, the PvdA had emerged as a more radical and populistic party. Electorally, the party was stronger than before. Competing alone in 1977, it told voters that they had to support the PvdA if they wanted a continuation of the den Uyl cabinet. The ploy worked and the PvdA won 33.8 per cent, gaining ten seats, largely at the expense of smaller parties to its left. The PvdA now appealed to a younger, more middle class electorate, and was drawing support not only from the secular working classes and non-practicing Protestants, but also from Catholics (*De Nederlandse Kiezer 1977*).

Previous divisions within the party had healed and new ones were emerging. New Left disbanded in 1971, but former New Left activists and individuals who had joined the party since the 1960s occupied influential positions within the party. With the exception of party leader den Uyl, the older generation had retired, and the party had a younger and more radical style. However, the changing of the guard did not mean an end to internal conflict. Party congresses and meetings of the party council were lively, 'democratised' affairs in which delegates debated inordinately large numbers of resolutions and called leaders to account. At the same time, the party executive sparred with PvdA cabinet ministers and the parliamentary caucus and expressed its solidarity with a variety of causes. Reflecting the openness of the party, not even New Left was in control. When Wim Meijer, a former New Left activist and junior minister in the den Uyl cabinet ran for the party chairmanship, he was attacked as the candidate of the 'Hague establishment' and defeated by an 'outsider', Max van den Berg, a party activist and alderman from the city of Groningen.

Although the party was further to the left, changes in foreign policy were more pronounced than changes in domestic policies. Edging toward an anti-NATO stance, the PvdA argued that Dutch membership in NATO should be measured against the ability of the alliance to defuse east-west tensions. At home, the PvdA embellished longstanding commitments to the welfare state and greater equality with endorsement of political activism, pleas for codetermination, support for feminism, opposition to nuclear energy, and defense of the environment. However, party positions were often not as radical as the ways in which they were packaged and advocated. Once taken, positions were often asserted rigidly and used as a yardstick to measure the performance of party leaders and the suitability of coalition partners. Equally characteristic was the variety of the causes which might be endorsed and the ways in which party activists tried to tie the hands of party leaders. As in the past, the PvdA insisted on the primacy of its demands. However, in contrast to 1972, when the PvdA's tenacity resulted in the formation of a left of centre cabinet, in the 1977 cabinet formation, the PvdA gave its leaders insufficient room to bargain and ended up in opposition despite winning ten seats.

By the 1980s, the contour of the Dutch left had changed considerably. Electoral alliances and the idea a progressive concentration had been forgotten. D'66 survived, but defined itself as a progressively oriented liberal party - a 'reasonable' alternative to the PvdA. The left remained divided between the PvdA and smaller parties on its flanks. However, the PvdA had been transformed into a radical and populist party prone to flaunting socialist symbols and defending a potpourri of causes. The PvdA was still willing to join coalitions, but the party was now more demanding, with the result that it often ended up in opposition.

The KVP and Christian Unity

Efforts to amalgamate the three confessional parties into a single party were also rooted in declining support. However, in contrast to the ill-fated attempts to establish a progressive concentration, efforts to establish an interconfessional party resulted in the formation of the Christian Democratic Appeal.

We can trace the origins of the CDA to the changes in the Catholic subculture. Prior to 1967, the KVP regularly mobilised 30-32 per cent of the popular vote, but the KVP declined to 26.5 per cent in 1967, 21.9 per cent in 1971, and 17.7 per cent in 1972. The initial decline was sufficient to place the future of the KVP on the political agenda. The position of the KVP within the confessional bloc drew the ARP and the CHU into the discussion.

In order to understand why relatively small electoral changes could call the future of a large and stable political party into question, it is useful to recall the relationships among the Catholic Church, the Catholic Party, and the Catholic subculture. Both the Catholic Party and the Catholic pillar had been created not only to seek state support for denominational schools, but also to promote the 'emancipation' of Dutch Catholics. The Dutch Church had been involved not only in the initial development of Catholic social and political organisation but also in the blossoming of the Catholic subculture in the 1920s and the 1930s and the postwar reorganisation of the Catholic Party.

In many respects, the Catholic Party was an extension of the Catholic subculture. Pressures from the Church brought disparate elements together in one party. However, the Catholic Party was loosely integrated; political unity was maintained by balancing off different wings and planting the party in the centre of the spectrum. The advancement of Catholic interests provided the party with its raison d'être. However, this made the party vulnerable to the changes in the Dutch Church which we described earlier. KVP support was closely tied to religiosity. But, by the late 1960s, church attendance was declining and the clergy were no longer actively mobilising support for the party.

When electoral decline became apparent in 1967, the KVP was ill-prepared to cope with it. Little thought had been given to the future of the party, or how it might respond to changes in the Church (Bakvis 1981a). Without change further decline appeared inevitable.

Debate on the future of the party began in 1967. Christian Radicals demanded alliances to the left, another group wanted the KVP to become a secular party, and yet another preferred remaining a

Catholic party. However, the predominant view, endorsed by party leaders, was that the KVP should merge with its Protestant counterparts. Intellectually, the maintenance of a Catholic Party made little sense in an eucumenical era, and electorally, Christian unity seemed to be a logical step. The KVP could not broaden its base of support because few non-Catholics would rally to an explicitly Catholic Party. In contrast, an interconfessional party would have a wider appeal. Finally, an interconfessional party would be broader version of the Catholic Party: integrating different elements, it too would be a party of the centre (Wolinetz 1973).

The principal difficulty with this was that it relied on the cooperation of the ARP and the CHU. Anti-Revolutionaries and the Christian Historicals had mixed views on the formation of an interconfessional party. Both were willing to talk with the KVP, and a top level forum, the Group of Eighteen, was quickly established. However, neither was willing to proceed with the formation of a new party. Anti-Revolutionaries preferred a federative relationship in which they preserved their own autonomy and insisted that any new entity be a 'consequent' Christian party in which the inspiration of the gospel was evident. Christian Historicals were more favourable to an interconfessional party in which Catholics would serve as a counter-weight to the ARP, but they preferred federation to merger.

Anti-Revolutionary and Christian Historical points of view reflected a mixture of concerns. Although both were vulnerable to deconfessionalisation, neither were as immediately or directly threatened by it as the KVP. To some extent, both had suffered its effects in the past, but neither party attempted to rally or represent an entire religious group. Moreover, the Anti-Revolutionaries retained a loyal core of supporters within the Orthodox Reformed Churches. The Christian Historicals were less secure, but electoral decline (particularly evident when the party slipped to 4.8 per cent in 1972) was only one of several considerations. Both parties feared reactions to any premature embrace of the KVP. The CHU had to deal with lingering anti-papism among its ranks. Anti-Revolutionary leaders wanted to retain the support of more conservative followers as well as their radical faction.

Nevertheless, both the ARP and the CHU had important reasons for engaging the KVP. Deconfessionalisation could well be a problem in the future. Moreover, both parties depended on Catholic numbers to exert influence within the political system. The erosion of the confessional centre threatened to undermine their position.

Differences among the three parties meant that the pace of negotiations could be dictated by the most reluctant partner. The

Christian Democratic Appeal emerged from a process of merger by slow degrees. The Group of Eighteen was established as a forum for discussion in 1968. However, few tangible steps occurred until 1971, when the three parties announced their intent to govern or oppose together. A year later, the Christian Democratic Appeal was established as an organisation coupling the three parties. Individuals could either remain members of the three confessional parties or become direct members of the CDA. However, Anti-Revolutionaries and Catholics continued to argue about positions and principles; at times the Christian Historicals balked as well. After considerable debate, there was sufficient agreement to establish a common caucus in 1976 and submit a joint list of candidates for the 1977 parliamentary elections. The marriage of the three parties was completed in 1980, when the ARP, the CHU, and the KVP agreed on a constitution, merged their organisations, and formally dissolved themselves.

Although the Anti-Revolutionaries were able to delay the merger by insisting that their followers needed more time to adjust or that principles required further clarification, events and circumstances moved the process farther along. At different stages, impending elections provided an incentive to reach agreement. The ability of the PvdA and its allies to divide the three confessional parties during the 1972-73 cabinet formation demonstrated that a loose federative accord was insufficient to preserve the strength of the confessional centre. In addition, the possibility, in the mid-1970s, that the KVP might pursue other alternatives (becoming a secular party was considered) provided an incentive for resolving differences.

Ultimately, the process developed a momentum of its own. Competing with a joint list in 1977, the CDA won 31.9 per cent of the vote and managed to arrest the decline of the confessional centre. In the cabinet formation which followed, the CDA, under the leadership of Andreas van Agt (Minister of Justice in the den Uyl cabinet and a Catholic), stood its ground against Socialist demands, and ended up in a cabinet not with the Socialists, but with the Liberals. Van Agt's leadership, and in particular, his almost Calvinistic way of reflecting on moral issues, helped to solidify the CDA. Although some Anti-Revolutionaries continued to protest, others had become used to the CDA and, along with Catholics, were impatient with delays.

Finally unified in 1980, the Christian Democratic Appeal has proved to be more cohesive than its slow and tortuous formation would have suggested. The CDA is neither the bland catch-all party that many had feared, nor the evangelical party that some Anti-Revolutionaries preferred. Neither internal divisions nor dialogue are the same as before. Initially, party offices and positions on lists of candidates were balanced in proportion to previous party strengths, but protocols assigning positions to different 'blood groups' during the first four years were eliminated in 1984. Although former party affiliations remain apparent, the principal divisions have been between dissidents on the left and a broader mainstream, increasingly inclined to the right. Former Anti-Revolutionaries are prominent on the left. However, most dissenters have remained loyal to the CDA even when they did not get their way.

In many respects, the profile of the CDA has been determined by its leaders. Both van Agt and his successor, Ruud Lubbers aligned the CDA with the Liberals. When the CDA and the PvdA were unable to agree on the distribution of portfolios in a second den Uyl cabinet in 1977, van Agt formed a coalition with the VVD. In 1981, when the CDA and the VVD ended up one seat short of a majority, the CDA allied with the PvdA and D'66. However, the new cabinet had barely assumed office when disputes on employment policies caused a crisis. Although the differences were repaired, the cabinet lasted less than a year. The coalition was hamstrung by disagreements on economic policy and personal differences between Prime Minister van Agt and Vice Premier den Uyl. New elections in 1982 paved the way for a renewed centre-right coalition under Ruud Lubbers, who succeeded van Agt during the 1982 cabinet formation.

Under Lubbers, the CDA has moved to the right. Determined to cut government spending, the Lubbers cabinet curtailed public sector wages and social welfare benefits. After considerable delay, the Lubbers cabinet also agreed to the deployment of cruise missiles. Despite protests from its left, the CDA caucus has endorsed government policies. This reflects changing economic circumstances and the fact that alliances with the PvdA were tried but proved unworkable. New economic orthodoxies - the need to cut public sector spending in order to facilitate market-led recovery - and the unavailability of alliances to the left have weakened radical elements in the CDA. Paradoxically, by insisting on primacy for its policies, the PvdA encouraged not only the unification but the integration of its rival, the CDA.

The Party System in the 1980s

In examining the PvdA's journey to the left, the formation of the CDA, and the gap between these two parties, we have directed our attention to the more visible arguments and conflicts. However, this is only part of the story.

Change has also occurred on the right. Less divided and less directly affected by declining support, Liberals remained aloof from debate on the party system but nevertheless benefitted from the process. Before 1971, the VVD was a small party with barely 10 per cent of the vote. Since then, the VVD has grown considerably: 14.4 per cent in 1972, 17.9 per cent in 1977, 17.4 per cent in 1981 and a peak of 23.1 per cent in 1982 before dropping back to 17.4 per cent in 1986. Liberal growth reflects the contraction of the confessional centre, and the VVD's decision, early in the 1970s, to bring forward a younger leader, Hans Wiegel, who gave the party a more definite profile. Under Wiegel and his successor, Ed Nijpels, the VVD has been a magnet for younger middle classes who favoured less taxation and government spending, policies more oriented to business, and a pro-Western foreign policy. This is reflected in the party's membership, which has grown tremendously since the 1960s.[6]

Liberal growth, however, is not the only phenomenon which we must consider. Smaller parties have also rooted themselves on the extremes of the party spectrum. On the right, there are now three smaller Calvinistic parties representing different religious groups and styles of opinion. The oldest, the Political Reformed Party (SGP), was established in 1918 and has consistently won two to three seats in the Dutch parliament. The second, the Reformed Political League (GPV) was founded in 1948 and has held one or two seats. The third, the Reformed Political Federation (RPF) was established in 1975 and gained strength as a result of the formation of the CDA and the latter's willingness to tolerate abortion under certain circumstances. More dynamic and less sectarian than its earlier counterparts, the RPF won two seats in 1981 and 1982 elections, but only one in 1986. Together, the three parties control five to six seats. The narrow base of CDA-VVD cabinets provides 'small right' with marginally greater leverage than before; in the event of divisions within the CDA - the case on the cruise missile deployment - small right can make up the difference.

At the opposite end of the spectrum, the Communists (CPN), the Pacifist Socialists (PSP) and the Radical Party (PPR) are less securely ensconced. Until recently, each held about 2 per cent of the vote and two to three seats in parliament. However, in the 1986 elections, the three parties declined from 5.8 per cent to 3.4 per cent of the vote. The Communists, continually represented since 1918, fell from 1.8 per cent to 0.6 per cent and lost their three seats. Pacifist Socialists dropped from three seats to one. Only the Radicals managed to hold their two mandates. The strength of the three parties has been sapped by internal divisions, the sharper polarisation of the party system and the positions which the PvdA has taken on key issues such as nuclear power or deployment of the cruise missile. Both the Pacifist Socialists and the Communists have been internally divided, and the Communists in particular, have been in state of change: an aging old guard, Stalinist in character, is being pushed aside by younger radical feminists.

In the centre, Democrats '66 has led an up and down existence. Burned by drawing too close to the Socialists, D'66 nearly disbanded in the mid 1970s, but by 1976 had re-established itself as a progressively oriented party. D'66 won 5.4 per cent of the vote in 1977, 11.1 per cent in 1981, but only 4.3 per cent in 1982. However, with the return of its first leader, Hans van Mierlo, D'66 climbed to 6.1 per cent in the 1986 elections. Surveys indicate that rather than establishing a permanent base of support D'66 has served as a temporary resting place for voters changing parties (Irwin and Dittrich 1984, *Keesings Historisch Archief*, 5 July 1984, 360-61). Nevertheless, the party survives by filling a gap in centre-left of the political spectrum.

Though smaller parties persist and in some circumstances could provide crucial support for a cabinet, with the exception of Democrats '66, their activities have been eclipsed by the contest among the larger parties. The clash between the centre-right Lubbers coalition and the opposition PvdA dominated the 1986 parliamentary elections. Despite disagreements on euthanasia (a secular majority, which included the Liberals, favoured legalisation while Christian Democrats were opposed) Liberals and Christian Democrats let it be known that they would continue their coalition if they retained a majority, while Socialists hoped to unseat the government. Opinion polls indicated that this might well occur: surveys in the fall of 1985 showed the CDA and VVD in decline and the PvdA winning as much as 40 per cent of the vote and ten additional seats (*Keesings Historisch Archief*, 5 June 1986:360). Nevertheless, when the votes were counted, the elections were a clear victory for the Christian Democrats and Prime Minister Lubbers. The CDA advanced from 29.3 per cent to 34.6 per cent and gained nine seats. Although the Liberals dropped to 17.4 per cent, CDA gains offset VVD losses, leaving the narrow centre-right majority (81 of 150 seats) intact. The Socialists won 33.3 per cent and gained five seats. However, these gains, which came from the smaller parties to its left, were regarded as a defeat (*NRC Handelsblad, Weekeditie Voor het Buitenland*, 27 May 1986, *Keesings Historisch Archief*, 5 June 1986). The election returns left little doubt about the subsequent cabinet formation: within two months a second CDA-VVD cabinet under Ruud Lubbers was in office.

By the late 1980s, the Dutch party system had changed from the 1960s. A stable five-party configuration had given way to a more volatile system dominated by three parties, but still populated by several others. Although in some respects, the party alternatives in the 1980s resembled those of the 1960s, the content and the format of party competition had changed. Instead of relying on fixed clienteles, parties had to bid for the support of a more volatile electorate. In the process, party profiles had become more diverse: Liberals and Socialists had penetrated Catholic regions in the South. At the same time, Christian Democrats demonstrated some potential to expand beyond the aging base of practicing Catholics and Protestants on whom the party had relied in the early 1980s. Moreover, the PvdA's drift to the left, and the CDA's move to the right had given the party system a sharper definition. Elections were no longer a census weighing the strength of different groups, but rather a contest about who would govern. Reflecting the PvdA's growth, the left was stronger than before, but, the PvdA was in no position to govern alone. The Liberals had also grown and a centre-right coalition was securely ensconced. Despite all that had changed, the confessional bloc, reorganized as a single Christian Democratic party, retained its pivotal position.

The Dutch Case Further Considered:

Let us retrace our steps. Several factors have been central to our analysis. These include the ways in which parties have responded to changes in the electorate, the moves and gambits of other parties, the frustrations of the left, and the open-endedness of the process which we have been considering.

We can illustrate this by reconsidering the 1960s. Relatively small electoral changes led to extensive changes in the ways in which parties presented and defined themselves. Party elites reacted to the pressures of political activists and the emergence of new parties and apparent changes in public values and demands. In doing so, they triggered off further changes in the party system. However, none of this was predetermined. Had PvdA leaders expelled New Left, or KVP leaders not abandoned their party but cultivated an alternate rationale for it, then the party sytem would have evolved differently.

If there is one central theme which has led to changes in the party system, it is the repeated efforts of the Socialists to escape the confessional stranglehold. Although the 'breakthrough' at the end of World War II failed to broaden the base of Dutch Socialism, it facilitated the crystallisation of a new policy coalition and resulted in the full incorporation of the Socialists in the political system. Because the PvdA continued to be incorporated in the 1960s, the party was poorly positioned to channel discontents fueled in part because the PvdA had been excluded from the cabinet. As a result, PvdA had to adapt in order to ensure its position as a party of reform. In the process, the party was transformed by the middle class activists who gained control over its organisation. Unable to participate in cabinets with the KVP on terms which it found acceptable, the PvdA sought alternate routes to power. Throughout the 1970s, Socialists attempted to build alternate policy coalitions around which they could rally a majority. However, although the PvdA was able to broaden its base of support, its efforts helped to solidify its rival, the Christian Democratic Appeal. Competition between the two blocs, each trying to maintain or expand its base of support among a volatile electorate, resulted in further changes in the party system.

Paradoxically, the way in which parties responded in the 1960s made the Dutch party system more resilient in the 1970s and 1980s. Countries such as Denmark were rocked by the emergence of parties protesting the size and scope of the welfare state in the 1970s. More recently, green parties have appeared in a number of countries, expressing a melange of environmental and anti-nuclear concerns, as well as reactions against the established parties. However, the Dutch have been largely immune from both phenomena. By assuming a more vocal posture in the 1970s, Dutch Liberals were able to absorb and channel protests against the welfare state. Equally, although green lists have recently appeared in the Netherlands, they have had little success; the PvdA and D'66, as well as the three parties to their left (who contested the 1984 European elections as the 'Green Progressive Alliance'), already anticipated many of the themes articulated by green parties elsewhere.[7] In effect, earlier changes and greater scope for minor parties precluded the tremors which shook the party system in West Germany.

But what of the future of the Dutch party system? At the moment, the party system is dominated by the battle between the predominant confessional-liberal coalition on the right and the socialists on the left. Despite the absense of the constitutional and electoral reforms which D'66 sought, elections have become a more clearcut struggle for power between sharply defined alternatives, and smaller parties, except for Democrats '66, have lost significance. In 1986, the three largest parties won 85.3 per cent of the vote and 133 of the 150 seats in the lower house. If we add D'66 (the only other party likely to participate in a cabinet) to this club, then the larger parties commanded 91.4 per cent of the vote and 142 of the 150 seats, a share of the vote equivalent to that of the five major parties before the party system began to change in the 1960s.

Whether this will last or not is another matter. The electoral system has not been changed and the Dutch electorate remains sufficiently volatile to permit a variety of further changes, including the resurgence of the smaller parties. Even so, despite occasional incursions, party competition is likely to remain dominated by the larger parties. Over the years, these have become more resilient and more adept at presenting themselves in the media, which focusses its attention on them. Moreover, as several observers (including a number of small left activists) have noted, clearcut contests for power, the case in both 1977 and 1986, tend to divert support from the minor parties (*Keesings Historisch Archief*, 5 June 1986, 362).

However, the outcome of the major party battle remains more difficult to predict. In the 1986 elections, the Christian Democrats demonstrated that with a popular and highly regarded leader at the helm, the CDA could expand beyond the aging base of support inherited from its three predecessors. Whether Socialists and Liberals will permit this is another matter. Much to their chagrin Socialists have discovered that recent electoral gains have landed them in the opposition. In the future, Socialist efforts to gain power, either by seeking some kind of compromise with the CDA or the VVD or, more remotely, by trying to rally support on the left, could lead to further changes in the party system. So too could rivalries between the Liberals and the Christian Democrats, always present beneath the surface. All in all, in view of the diminishing scope and impact of pillarisation and the weakening of fixed clienteles, the safest prediction is that electoral volatility and shifts among the three major parties and Democrats '66 will persist.

Notes

1. The Dutch use the de Hondt or highest averages system of proportional representation. The country is divided into 18 electoral districts, but the ability to link lists in separate districts means that the country, for all intents and purposes, is one national constituency. In order to win a seat, a party must win at least the electoral divisor (the number of votes divided by the number of seats). Parties must submit a small deposit (1000 guilders per district) forfeited only if the party fails to

gain three fourths the electoral divisor. The number of parties submitting lists and winning seats has always been high: between 1913 and 1933 the number of parties submitting lists ranged 32 to 54, the number winning seats from 10 to 17. The introduction of deposit requirements and other changes in the electoral law reduced the number of parties submitting lists to 20 in 1937, of which ten won seats (Irwin 1980). From 1946 to 1959, the number of parties submitting lists ranged from 10 to 13, the number winning seats from seven to eight. However, the number of lists submitting and the number winning seats began to increase as early as 1963. Since 1967, ten, and in some instances (1971 and 1972) as many as fourteen, parties have been represented in parliament. For details on the electoral law and the number of parties, see Irwin 1980, Daalder 1965-66 and Wolinetz 1973.

2. For a discussion on the extent and impact of social changes, see Andeweg (1982) 79-120.

3. There has been some debate about the extent to which voters were deeply attached to or identified with political parties. Using data from a three-wave panel study carried out in 1970, 1971 and 1972, Thomassen (1976) discovered that party identifications changed as rapidly as voters' preferences and suggested that voting decisions reflected the close relationships between parties and the segmented social structure rather than any psychological attachment or deep-seated loyalty to political parties. However, Thomassen did not consider the possibility that different processes and mechanisms of attachment may have operated in each pillar. Moreover, his argument was based on data from a period in which change was already underway. Whatever the case, there is considerable evidence that pillarisation influenced voting behaviour. Using aggregate data, Houska (1985) discovered a strong relationship between the consistency of party support, political orthodoxy (support for the appropriate subculturally based party) and the strength of subcultural organization in different regions between 1948 and 1972. Focusing on the Catholic subculture, Bakvis (1981) discovered similar relationships. Successive surveys have demonstrated a strong relationship between religiosity, measured by the regularity of church attendance, and support for the confessional parties, and a weaker relationship, among secular voters, between social class and party preference. There is also a relationship between support for pillarised or segmented social organizations and voting (Andeweg 1982). For summaries and analyses see Wolinetz 1973; Lijphart, 1974; *De Nederlandse Kiezer '72*; *De Nederlandse Kiezer '73*; *De Nederlandse Kiezer '77*; and especially Bakvis, 1981a and Andeweg, 1982.

4. Changes in voting behaviour have variously been attributed to deconfessionalization and changing patterns of religiosity, generational turnover and the entry of a baby boom generation, changes in mass values, as well as the activities of political elites. Andeweg (1982) examined the principal explanations of electoral change and found that none could be sustained by the available survey data. Although declining support for the confessional parties could be traced to changing patterns of religiosity, there were no clearcut relationships between changes in voting

behaviour and the broader phenomenon of deconfessionalisation, social mobility, and changes in class structure, generational change or the impact of events. As a result, Andeweg argued that the considerable changes in Dutch voting patterns from the 1960s onward may well have reflected changing fashions, or 'winds of change' among the electorate. This is an interesting but not wholly satisfying explanation. Andeweg's findings may reflect the quality of earlier data and difficulty of accounting for a complex series of changes through the analysis of survey data. There were few systematic surveys before 1966 and those carried out in 1966 and 1967 were not explicitly designed to trace value changes or changing patterns of identification or attachment. The more extensive survey data accumulated from 1970 onward shows an electorate, if not entirely adrift (older voters often retained earlier loyalties) then certainly loose from previous moorings (see Irwin and Dittrich 1984). However, these data do not provide any firm baseline from which to assess subsequent changes. Moreover, both the format of the party system and the ways in which parties positioned and defined themselves changed considerably after 1967. The changing array of parties and party alternatives probably intensified the 'winds of change' and voters' propensity to switch parties. However, such effects would not readily be detected by survey research, which typically assumes that party alternatives are constant.

5. A bare majority of the Cals-Donner Commission on Constitutional and Electoral Reform recommended changes in the electoral law (proportional representation within twelve large districts) and that voters be allowed to designate a cabinet formateur who, if he gained the confidence of the parliament, would become the prime minister. However, there was no majority for the entire package. Socialists and their allies favoured both changes but did not make them a top priority when they were in office from 1973 to 1977. The confessional parties favoured the switch to proportional representation within districts but not the election of the cabinet formateur. The Socialists were unwilling to support the former without the latter.

6. VVD membership had grown from approximately 23,000-30,000 in the 1950s to 38,000 in 1969. Membership figures between 1983 and 1984 ranged between 91,000 and 101,000. In comparison, the PvdA, (which had some 111,000 members in 1969) ranged between 105,000 members in 1982 and 100,000 in 1984, and the CDA between 153,000 in 1982 and 132,000 in 1984. Earlier data, drawn from Wolinetz 1973, were supplied by party officials, while the later data were provided by the Documentation Center for Dutch Political Parties from data from party officials and the *NRC Handelsblad*, 25 September 1984.

. 7. A Green list contested the 1984 European elections and won 1.3 per cent, considerably less than the 5.6 per cent won by the 'Green Progressive Alliance'. In the 1986 parliamentary elections, the Greens won only 0.2 per cent. (*Keesings Historisch Archief*, 5 July 1984, 5 June 1986)

The Netherlands

References

Andeweg, Rudy B.(1982) *Dutch Voters Adrift: On Explanations of Electoral Change 1963-1967*, Department of Political Science, University of Leiden

Bakvis, Herman (1981a) *Catholic Power in the Netherlands*, McGill-Queens University Press, Kingston and Montreal

Bakvis, Herman (1981b) 'Electoral Stability and Electoral Change: The Case of Dutch Catholics,' *Canadian Journal of Political Science, 14,* 519-55

Boivin, Bertus, Herman Hazelhoff, Bert Middel and Bob Molenaar (1978) *Een Verjongingskuur voor de Partij van de Arbeid,* Kluwer, Deventer

Daalder, Hans (1965-66) 'De kleine politieke partijen - een voorlopige poging tot inventarisatie,' *Acta Politica, 1,* 172-96

Daalder, Hans (1966) 'The Netherlands: Opposition in a Segmented Society' in Robert Dahl, ed., *Political Oppositions in Western Democracies,* Yale University Press, New Haven, 188-236

Daudt, H (1980) 'De ontwikkeling van de politieke machtsverhoudingen Nederland sinds 1945' in H.B.G. Casimer, ed., *Nederland na 1945: Beschouwingen over ontwikkeling en beleid,* van Loghum Slaterus B.V., Deventer, 178-98

De Nederlandse Kiezer '72 (1973) Samson Uitgeverij, Alphen aan den Rijn

De Nederlandse Kiezer '73 (1973) Samson Uitgeverij, Alphen aan den Rijn

De Nederlandse Kiezer '77 (1978) VAM, Voorschoten

Houska, Joseph J. (1985) *Influencing Mass Political Behavior: Elites and Political Subcultures in the Netherlands and Austria,* Institute of International Studies, University of California, Berkeley

Irwin, Galen (1980) 'Patterns of Voting Behaviour in the Netherlands' in Richard T. Griffiths, ed., *The Economy and Politics of the Netherlands,* Martinus Nijhof, The Hague, 199-222

Irwin, Galen and Karl Dittrich (1984) 'And the Walls Came Tumbling Down: Party Dealignment in the Netherlands' in Russell J. Dalton, Scott C. Flanagan, and Paul Allen Beck, eds., *Electoral Change in Advanced Industrial Democracies: Realignment or Dealignment?* Princeton University Press, 267-97

Lijphart, Arend (1968, 1975) *The Politics of Accommodation: Pluralism and Democracy in the Netherlands* (2nd edition), University of California Press, Berkeley

Lijphart, Arend (1974) 'The Netherlands: Continuity and Change in Electoral Behavior' in Richard Rose, ed., *Electoral Behavior: A Comparative Handbook,* Free Press, New York, 227-70

Lipschits, I. (1977) *De protestants-christelijke stroming tot 1940,* Kluwer, Deventer

Manning, A.F. (1968) 'Geen doorbraak van de oude structuren: de confessionele partijen na 1945' in L.W.G. Scholten, *et al., De Confessionelen,* Amboboeken, Utrecht, 61-88

Thomassen, Jacques (1976) 'Party Identification as a Cross-National Concept: Its Meaning in the Netherlands' in Ian Budge, Ivor Crewe, and Dennis Farlie, eds., *Party Identification and Beyond,* John Wiley and Sons, London, 63-80

Thurlings, J.M.G. (1971) *De Wankele Zuil: Nederlandse Katholieken tussen assimilatie en pluralisme,* Katholieke Documentatie Centrum, Nijmegen

van den Berg, J. Th. and H.A.A. Molleman (1974) *Crisis in de Nederlandse Politieke,* Samson, Alphen a/d Rijn

van Welderen Rengers, W.J. (1955) *Schets eener Parlementaire Geschiedenis van*

Nederland, vierde deel, Nederland 1914-1918 (vierde bijgewerkte uitgave door C.W. de Vries).

Wolinetz, Steven B. (1973) *Party Realignment in the Netherlands*, PhD. diss., Yale University

Chapter Eight

Continuity and Change in the Scandinavian Party Systems

Eric S. Einhorn and John Logue

Denmark, Norway, and Sweden provide an unusual laboratory in which to examine continuity and change in party alignments. All three countries have multiparty systems in which parties have been closely tied to economic interest groups, and all three, for the last half century, have been dominated by Social Democrats. The stability of Scandinavian party systems in the 1950s and 1960s set them apart. However, the elections of 1973 in Denmark and Norway demonstrated that landslides could occur even in Scandinavia. Overnight, the number of parties in the Danish parliament doubled from five to ten, and extensive changes occurred in Norway as well. More recently, both party systems have stabilised, but in ways which differ from before. As a result, the three party systems diverge much more than in the past. The Danish party system remains highly fragmented, and minority governments (sometimes narrowly based) are the rule. In Norway, a bipolar party system has developed: the Conservatives now dominate the bourgeois parties in the same way that the Social Democrats dominate the left. Only in Sweden is the earlier five-party configuration intact. Nevertheless, even in Sweden, there have been significant changes in social bases of individual parties.

Although Danes, Norwegians, and Swedes emphasise their differences, the similarities in their political development and party systems are striking. Parties emerged under comparable circumstances in the last quarter of the 19th century when the establishment of parliamentary democracy was at issue, and changes in one country sometimes spilled over into the others. The same basic three-party system - Liberals, Conservatives, and Social Democrats - had developed by the turn of the century; the division of the liberals into urban (Liberal) and rural (Agrarian) parties and the split between Social Democrats and Communists prior to 1920 added two more parties.[1] Competition today takes place under similar electoral laws in all three countries and parties continue to be sufficiently similar to permit common classification.

But things have changed in the 1970s and 1980s; that is the focus of this essay. We will begin by reviewing the historical development of the three party systems in the first section. The next section examines the Social Democrats and other parties with bases in the labour movement. Similarities among Social Democratic parties permit broad, but reasonably accurate generalisations about common patterns in all three countries. In the last two decades, the Social Democratic dominance of government that began in the 1930s has been called into question: their monolithic base in the working class has eroded, new competition has appeared on the left, and on the right their bourgeois opponents have - at least for short periods - overcome their differences. The development and collapse of bourgeois unity is the subject of the section that follows; here national patterns have diverged sharply, particularly in the 1970s, and many generalisations require national qualifications. The final section considers changing coalition patterns.

The Development of the Scandinavian Party Systems

Multipartism has been the norm in Scandinavia throughout the twentieth century. Most parties were born in the struggle for parliamentary democracy between 1870 and 1920. During this period of severe (though generally nonviolent) political struggle, parties strengthened their ties to specific socio-economic interests, such as farmers and workers. Echoes of these struggles reverberated in Scandinavian politics. As Lipset and Rokkan (1967) suggest, parties' current ideologies, programs, and tactics were often influenced by distant historical experience.

Though we may think of the Scandinavian countries as model democracies today, the development of parliamentary democracy there lagged behind the rest of Europe and was not completed until the end of World War I. While the Swedish parliament (*Riksdag*) claimed a lineage dating to 1435, it remained an Estates General with four separate estates until the reforms of 1866 created a bicameral parliament. However, the new upper house was elected by a restricted suffrage that gave multiple votes to the well-to-do. Not until 1917, in the shadow of war and revolution, did the Swedish conservatives and the king accept parliamentary democracy; universal, equal suffrage was attained by 1921.

The Norwegian parliament (*Storting*) was established in 1814, during Norway's brief period of independence between Danish and Swedish rule. Reluctantly accepting union under the Swedish crown in the same year, Norway retained constitutional autonomy, and, in 1884, the Swedish king accepted the supremacy of the Norwegian parliament in domestic affairs. Universal manhood suffrage followed in 1898. In 1905, the union was peacefully dissolved, and the Norwegian parliament acquired full sovereignty.

Denmark was the last to establish a parliament, but leaped from absolutism to liberal constitutionalism when a bicameral parliament (*Rigsdag*) was established in 1849. However, the loss of Schleswig and Holstein after the war with Austria and Prussia in 1864 resulted in an 1866 reaction which turned the upper house into a bastion of privilege. The battle for the supremacy of the popularly elected lower chamber - *Folketinget* - was not concluded until 1901. Universal suffrage was achieved in 1915.

By 1920, the basic five-party system that would survive until the 1970s was in place. In each country the Liberals and the Conservatives had been the great antagonists of the 19th century. The Liberals supported parliamentary supremacy and an expanded suffrage while the Conservatives resisted. The Social Democrats grew with the urban working class and served as the Liberals' junior partners in the struggle for political democracy. With the expansion of the suffrage, Social Democratic parliamentary representation grew rapidly, especially in the decade before the First World War. Following the establishment of parliamentary democracy, the liberal movement divided into urban liberal and rural agrarian wings; this phenomenon began in Denmark in 1905 when the Liberals split into a left liberal party, *det Radikale Venstre* (the Radical Liberals), with strong support among progressive urban intellectuals and small family farmers and the more traditional, agrarian-based moderate Liberals (*Venstre*) and concluded with the formation of farmers parties in Sweden between 1913 and 1921 and Norway in 1920. The Communists, emerging from the split in the international socialist movement which followed the Russian Revolution, were the last to join the five-party constellation.

Proportional representation (PR) was introduced in Sweden in 1909, Denmark in 1915, and Norway in 1921. The Scandinavian variants of PR have gradually been made more proportional, but minimum vote requirements still keep the smallest parties out of parliament. Parties must reach modest thresholds of 2 per cent in

Denmark and 4 per cent in Sweden before accurate proportional representation occurs. Lacking supplementary seats, the Norwegian electoral system overrepresents large and underrepresents small parties; the dividing line is around 10-12 per cent of the vote. The Norwegian system easily yields anomalous results: The Labour Party's parliamentary majorities from 1945 to 1961 were won with 41 to 48 per cent of the popular vote, and in the six elections since 1965, the parties winning the parliamentary majority have won a majority of the popular vote on only one occasion.[2]

The Interwar Years

The attainment of universal suffrage and parliamentary supremacy removed the issue of political democracy from the political agenda and increased the salience of economic, cultural, and regional cleavages. Norway was a partial exception in that parliamentary supremacy (1884) predated independence; there the national question (i.e. relations with Sweden) moderated internal divisions. But following the dissolution of the union in 1905, Norwegians turned to domestic issues: economic, cultural, and regional. The existing Norwegian parties detailed positions on these questions which, to a significant extent, continue to characterise them today. These issues split the liberal movement. In addition to the Agrarian Party, created in 1920 to defend the interests of Norwegian farmers, the Christian People's Party was organised in 1933 to promote the religious and cultural values strongly held in southwestern Norway. The long period of Labour Party hegemony that began in 1935 was based not only on the partial reconciliation of its own factions, but the continuing division among the bourgeois parties.

In Denmark regional and cultural issues were less salient. Its party system was stable after 1920, when the peaceful resolution of the so-called 'Easter Crisis' confirmed the acceptance of parliamentary democracy by all of the major political parties. Still, the establishment of the Justice Party (Danmarks Retsforbund) in 1919, created to promote the political ideas of the American reformer Henry George, demonstrated the opportunities open to idiosyncratic splinter parties under an electoral law requiring only 2 per cent of the vote in order to win representation; by the end of the 1930s, the Danish parliamentary spectrum stretched from the Communists to the Nazis. Yet despite some fragmentation, Denmark enjoyed effective majority coalition government from 1929 until the German occupation in 1940. The coalition of Radical Liberals and Social Democrats, led by Social Democratic Prime Minister Thorvald Stauning, reduced the significance of the socialist/non-socialist division in Danish politics.

Especially for the Radical Liberals, the 1930s provided a model of broad political cooperation across class lines; however, the agrarian Liberals also provided key support for several social and economic reforms.

In Sweden the political agenda also shifted to economic and cultural issues. The 1920s - the period of 'minority parliamentarianism' - were remarkable for cabinet instability: there were nine different governments between 1920 and 1933. Because the dominant Liberals split over prohibition in 1924, the Conservatives, with 25-30 per cent of the vote, were the largest non-socialist party. Rural and religious factions controlled the Prohibitionist Liberals (*Frisinnade*) while the remaining rump was in the hands of more radical urban groups. In 1934 the two factions reunited under the current Liberal label (*Folkpartiet* - literally, 'the People's Party'), but the period of Liberal dominance was past. The new Agrarian Party (*Bondeförbundet*), which competed for the Liberals' rural constituency after 1913, played only a minor role in the 1920s, but following the 1932 Social Democratic election victory, the Agrarians found a new opportunity for influence. In 1933 Prime Minister Per Albin Hansson struck a deal with the Agrarians. In return for price supports on agricultural products, the Agrarians supported the economic crisis package of the government. This ' Red-Green' alliance, similar to the Danish compromise of the same year, was a major step in loosening the previous left-right rigidity of Swedish politics. At first, the collaboration was informal. During the summer of 1936 the Agrarians formed their own minority government following a parliamentary defeat of the Social Democrats on the defense issue. When the Social Democrats again won a large victory in the September 1936 elections, a formal coalition between the Social Democrats and Agrarians was formed. This continued until 1940. A national coalition government was formed during the war.

Models of the Party System

The post-1920 consensus on constitutional and parliamentary democracy and the homogeneity of Scandinavian society allowed the class and economic bases of Scandinavian politics to predominate. Hence it is not surprising that Scandinavian parties can be arranged on a single left-right continuum. This emphasises the economic issues which predominate except during periods of peak international tension, such as 1939-45 and 1948-53. Even the new parties of the 1970s can easily be placed on the same continuum. The one real exception to this is the urban-rural dimension which bifurcates the centre-right of the political spectrum, separating the largely urban liberals and the overwhelming rural agrarians. The cultural cleavage expressed in the development of the Christian parties lies along that dimension as well.

It is common to divide the major parties into two camps, with the Conservative, Liberal, and Agrarian parties comprising the 'non-socialist' or 'bourgeois' bloc and the Social Democratic (or Labour) and Communist (or radical socialist) parties comprising the 'socialist' bloc. (Cf. Berglund and Lindström, 1978:16ff.) Although this reflects the historical and ideological roots of the parties and unquestionably corresponds to the way many voters perceive the party system, it is an oversimplification of political history and of party tactics. In fact, parliamentary alliances *within* these two blocs have occurred only since the mid-1960s. Prior to this, coalitions cut across bloc lines - something which has happened frequently during the last twenty years as well.

The stable party systems in place since the 1920s in Norway and Denmark collapsed in the 1973 elections when the number of parties represented in parliament jumped from five to eight in the former and five to eight in the latter in the aftermath of highly divisive referenda on Common Market membership in 1972. This explosion in the number of parties stimulated the development of new analytic models.[3]

The changes of the 1970s require the modification of the traditional five-party model to include the new parties of the left, centre (where most of the new groups are to be found) and right (see table 8.1). The left has fragmented. There is a significant radical socialist presence in parliament, particularly in Denmark, but it bears no loyalty to Moscow. The remaining Moscow loyalists have little more electoral influence than the Maoist and Trotskyist parties which sporadically contest elections. Although they lack parliamentary significance, the parties of the sectarian left colour street demonstrations and the politics of a few unions.

The centre is the scene of maximum parliamentary fragmentation: Christian parties have taken seats in both the Danish and Swedish parliaments and the Centre Democrats have joined other centrist groups in Denmark. In addition, both the anti-Common Market Georgists in Denmark and pro-Common Market liberals in Norway briefly held seats in the 1970s. On the right, significant right-wing protest movements won representation in Norway and Denmark in 1973, and continue to hold seats. Though voters may circulate freely between the traditional, system-sustaining Conservatives and the 'Progress' parties on the right, the chasm between these two parties is deep.

Note that the bulk of the parties in this categorisation share the

Table 8.1 Parties Contesting the 1984-85 Elections in Scandinavia

	Denmark	Norway	Sweden
The left sectarian fringe	Marxist-Leninist Parti[a] Inter.-Soc. Arbejderparti[a] Danmarks kommunistiske Parti[a]	Rød Valgallianse[a] Norges kommunistiske parti[a]	Socialistiska partiet[a]
Radical socialist	Socialistisk Folkeparti Venstresocialisterne	Sosialistisk Venstreparti	Vänsterpartiet kommunisterna
Social Democratic	Socialdemokratiet	Det norske Arbeiderparti	Sveriges Socialdemokratiska Arbetarepartiet
Centre parties:			
Rural			
Agrarians	Venstre	Senterpartiet	Centerpartiet
Christian Democratic	Kristeligt Folkeparti	Kristelig Folkeparti	Kristen Demokratisk Samling[b]
Idiosyncratic	Retsforbundet[a]		
Urban			
Liberal	Det radikale Venstre	Venstre (anti EEC)[a] Det liberale Folkeparti (pro EEC)[a]	Folkpartiet
Personalist	Centrum-Demokraterne		
Environmentalist			Miljöpartiet
Conservatives	Det konservative Folkeparti	Høyre	Moderata Samlingspartiet
Right protest	Fremskridtspartiet	Fremskrittspartiet	

Notes: a. Did not win parliamentary seats in the 1984-85 elections. b. The KDS and Centre ran a common slate in the 1985 elections leading to the election of the first KDS member of parliament.

centre of the spectrum where part - but only part - of the fragmentation reflects the urban-rural cleavage. The lines between socialist and bourgeois blocs that play such a major role in voters' perceptions and Scandinavian political debate are thoroughly blurred because of the fragmentation of the centre. As our model would suggest, the lines of division on policy issues and coalition-building need not be drawn between socialist and non-socialist alternatives. In fact, the norm from the 1930s through 1950s was a Social Democratic alliance with one or more of the parties of the centre. As we shall see later on, the alternation of socialist and bourgeois coalitions has been an innovation of the last two decades.

The relative electoral strength of the major parties since World War II is charted in figures 8.1-8.3. Note three common patterns throughout the period: (1) the socialists and non-socialists have been almost evenly balanced with about 50 per cent of the electorate each; (2) while the Social Democrats have rarely held majorities, they have almost always won more votes than the next two parties combined; and (3) the division of votes within the socialist bloc has been stable, but the division of strength between the major non-socialist parties has varied sharply from one election to the next.

What is not clear from the election results is the one political constant which really set Scandinavian party politics apart from that in the rest of Europe: the hegemony enjoyed by the Social Democratic Party since the Depression.

Social Democrats and Radical Socialists

The Social Democratic labour movement in Scandinavia has transformed society in the half century since it came to power during the depths of the Depression. Elsewhere in Europe, the capitalist crisis long predicted by Social Democratic theoreticians brought anything but socialist government. The litany of disasters from the collapse of Hermann Müller's Social Democratic government in Berlin in 1930 to the final destruction of the Spanish Republic in 1939 is overwhelming. Only in Scandinavia did the Social Democrats take and hold power.

In office, the Scandinavian Social Democrats undertook a series of reforms which proved so successful that the Social Democrats dominated the political scene for the next half-century: the Danish Social Democrats held power for 42 of 58 years between 1929 and 1987; the Swedish Social Democrats, 49 of 55 years since 1932; and the Norwegian Labour Party, 36 of 52 years since it took power in 1935. Moreover, the German occupation accounted for five of the years they were out of power in Norway and two in Denmark. Five factors account for this remarkable success.

Figure 8.1 Parliamentary Elections in Sweden, 1948-1985

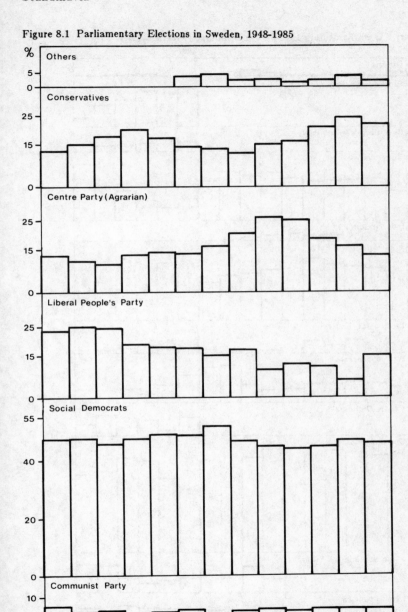

Figure 8.2 Parliamentary Elections in Denmark, 1947-1984

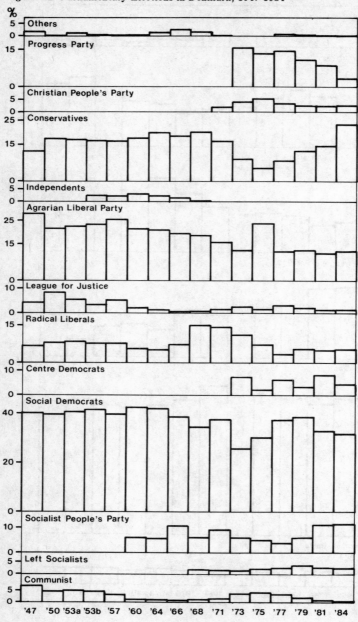

Figure 8.3 Parliamentary Elections in Norway, 1949-1985

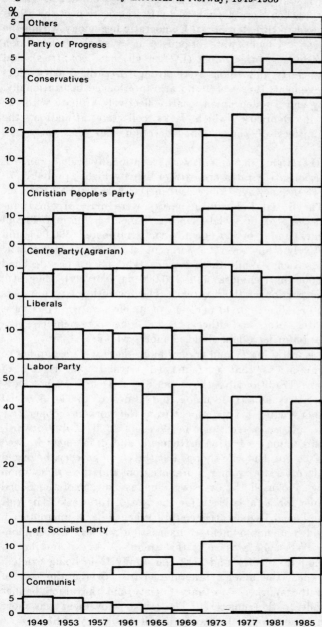

First, the labour movement was unified. The Communist parties of Norway and Sweden were decimated by Bolshevisation in the 1920s and quickly ceased to threaten Social Democratic hegemony within the labour movement. Unions were organised in a single trade union centre (called *Landsorganisationen* (LO) in all three countries), and the ties between party and unions were strong. Described as two legs of the same movement, they were (and are) interlocked institutionally. In both Norway and Sweden union locals collectively affiliate with the party,[4] while in Denmark, which lacks collective affiliation, the executive committees of the union federation and the party are intertwined.

Second, the labour movement was exceptionally well organised. Trade union organisation rates are extraordinarily high: probably 70 per cent or more in Norway, 75 per cent in Denmark, and 80 per cent in Sweden. The Social Democratic parties were mass organisations themselves. At the peak of Social Democratic membership in 1948 and 1949 in Denmark and Norway, membership numbered 300,000 and 200,000 respectively; thus, over 25 per cent of all Social Democratic voters were organised. While these organisations have since declined (to about 120,000 in Denmark and 160,000 in Norway), they still organise a large portion of their voters. The Swedish party numbers over 1 million, or more than 40 per cent of its electorate. Thus most Social Democratic voters are either party members or members of a labour organisation or have household members who are.

In addition to the party and trade union, there were a number of subsidiary organisations that encompassed virtually all aspects of members' lives. Traditionally, the good Social Democrat not only belonged to his party and trade union, but also read the local Social Democratic paper, rented his apartment from the workers' cooperative housing society, played soccer for the Workers' Ball Club Forward, vacationed at his union's vacation settlement, and drank beer brewed by the workers' co-op. His wife shopped at the co-op grocery, belonged to the Social Democratic women's organisation and the trade union ladies' auxiliary, and used the oversized Sunday edition of the Social Democratic paper for a table cloth for the rest of the week. His kids belonged to the Social Democratic scouts. When he was unemployed, his union provided unemployment compensation and ran the employment service. When he was sick, the union's sickness and health benefit fund paid the doctor and kept the family from being evicted. And when he died, the union's funeral benefits covered the cost of burial through the Workers Mortuary Society and the union banner followed his body to the cemetery. The labour movement was more than an economic and political organisation; it was a way of life.

This helped to create and maintain the third factor, a culture inside the labour movement characterised by the principle of solidarity. 'You rise with your class,' the Swedish phrase has it, 'not out of it.' The sense of solidarity - of collective responsibility - was deeply rooted in the practice of trade union locals. But it was also a product of the very rapid conversion of traditional societies into modern ones that carried forward the cohesion of peasant communities into a modern group identification. This was most pronounced in Sweden and Norway which, on the eve of World War I, were still rural societies. The new industrial workers moved easily from the solidarity of the village to that of working-class organisations.

The unity and solidarity of the labour movement - our fourth point - stood in stark contrast to the division of its opposition. The non-socialists were divided into three camps: the conservatives, who particularly in Denmark and Sweden had opposed parliamentary democracy; the liberals, who advocated its extension; and the agrarians, who represented the farmers' movement. Before World War II, neither the liberals nor the agrarians trusted the conservatives; instead, at key junctures, they cooperated with the Social Democrats.

Fifth, the Scandinavian Social Democrats undertook an implicit but fundamental compromise in the 1930s with the parties of the centre, the agrarians and liberals, which left the existing distribution of income and wealth intact in return for the centre parties' agreement to improve the economic situation of the weakest members of society through public sector programs. Scandinavian Social Democrats put socialisation of the means of production on the back burner, and the centre parties accepted state efforts to manage the economy and the use of the public sector for redistributive purposes. Here was the basis for the welfare state consensus which, along with economic growth, transformed the Scandinavian countries from poor, backward societies - a famous Social Democratic tract of 1913 characterised Sweden accurately in its title as 'the fortified poorhouse' (Höglund, et al., 1913) - into rich and egalitarian societies. As the Swedish Social Democratic and iconoclastic economist Gunnar Adler-Karlsson put it,

in Sweden all the participants in the economic process have reached the insight that the most important task in economic life is to make the common cake bigger, so that everyone will have a greater chance to satisfy their appetites with a bigger bite... We have kept the goals of socialism, but have chosen other means to achieve them than by socialising the means of production. (1967, 1973 translated:37)[5]

Socialism in Scandinavia had once been a millennial mass movement; now the public sector became its church, its institutionalised expression. The 'other means' of which Adler-Karlsson spoke involved expanding governmental tasks through (1) the creation of an interventionist state managing the economy to insure full employment and economic growth, and (2) the use of the public sector to improve the conditions of those worst off by providing economic security against involuntary declines in income from sickness, disability, unemployment and old age, raising the incomes of those with small market incomes and large needs, and providing some goods and services, like health care, outside the market, on the basis of need. Redistributive policies provoked less political conflict in Scandinavia than elsewhere because what was being redistributed was the 'growth dividend.' For a generation rapid economic growth permitted a simultaneous increase in private consumption and redistribution through the public sector.

In the late 1960s and early 1970s, the welfare state was redesigned for a full employment economy. The old transfer programs, which had been designed to provide minimally adequate standards, were supplemented so that transfer payments almost replace the loss of market income. Social services like day care and home assistance for the elderly were extended to villages and rural areas, and newer social services for children and the elderly were developed apace, expanding the sphere of state activity. In short, the welfare state did for all the people, in a more lavish fashion, what the various benefit societies of the labour movement had sought to do at a rudimentary level for the working class.

Is There a Crisis of Social Democracy?

There are many reasons why the Scandinavian Social Democratic model has been particularly successful. The homogeneity of population, small size of the nations, and policy consistency during a half century of predominantly Social Democratic government are frequently cited. But the cultural value of solidarity also played an important role.

Solidarity, as one turn-of-the-century Danish trade union tract put it, meant 'common responsibility or reciprocal obligation' (Anonymous [C.M. Olsen] 1911). Reciprocal obligation was the foundation for the trade union benefit societies and farmers' cooperatives that sprang up in the half century before the First World War. But solidarity to the Scandinavian popular movements was more than an instrumental value: it had a moral status that gave the working class movement claim to higher ethical standards than the self-seeking individualism of bourgeois society.

There is a great deal of evidence that the solidaristic values of reciprocal obligation and responsibility were generation specific. In the early period these values were fostered in the atmosphere of small group cohesion; they were reinforced and extended through the resistance (cf. Heckscher 1984:41-52; Samuelsson 1968:288-99). Institutionalised in the welfare state programs, they were bureaucratised and professionalised and, ultimately, diminished.

A growing egotism seems to be taking their place. There is evidence of a marked generational shift in utilisation of welfare state benefits that has increased take-up rates (and costs) without any appreciable improvement in welfare (Logue 1985b; see also Andersen 1984a, 1984b). The political expression of this egotism has focused on taxes. Its most obvious manifestation is the appeal of the tax protest parties: the Progress parties of Denmark and Norway and the Danish Centre Democrats. These parties have had more success in appealing to the Social Democratic constituency than traditional bourgeois parties; at least as long as they were perceived principally as protest movements, they attracted substantial support from young, male workers (Borre, *et al.* 1976:69-87; Statistisk Sentralbyrå 1974: Tables 14-17). The Conservative parties, which exploited the tax reduction issue in all three countries, have had little success in appealing to working-class voters. However, their use of the tax issue has attracted votes from the other bourgeois parties, limiting possible coalitions for minority Social Democratic governments.

As a consequence, the once monolithic Social Democratic support in the working class has eroded. According to detailed survey data, workers drifted away from the socialist parties between the 1950s and 1970s. This trend was greatest in Norway and least in Sweden (cf. Borre 1984:352-54). Figures 8.4 and 8.5 show the declining cohesion of the Danish and Swedish working-class vote. Figure 8.4 charts the declining solidity of the Danish manual workers' vote for labour parties. In 1961, labour parties polled roughly 90 per cent of the vote from blue-collar households; the Social Democrats polled the lion's share, or roughly 80 per cent of the blue-collar vote. By 1971, the non-socialist parties had raised their share from one vote in ten to one in six, and it continued to grow to about one vote in four in 1981. Although the sample size for 1981 is too small to permit excessive confidence, the erosion of class cohesion has been greatest among the unskilled; one in three in unskilled families voted bourgeois in that

173

year.[6] Most of the movement across bloc lines seems to have been toward tax protest parties, especially Mogens Glistrup's Progress Party. The Swedish figures in figure 8.5 reflect the same tendency, though at a lower level; the traditional bourgeois parties have a limited appeal to working-class voters, though the agrarian Centre Party has, to some extent, escaped that stigma.

Figure 8.4 Declining Working-Class Cohesion

Party preference in blue collar households in Denmark, 1961-1981 (in percentages)

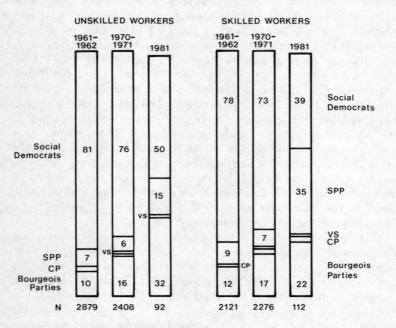

Source: Data from Gallup Markedsanalyse

But if the bourgeois parties have been the beneficiaries of a diminished working-class cohesion, middle-class voters in increasing numbers have turned left in Denmark and Sweden (Norway is an exception to this generalisation (cf. Borre 1984:352-54)). The evidence is clearest among younger, well-educated white-collar employees. Figure 8.6 illustrates the changing party preference among Danish

Figure 8.5 Maintaining Working-Class Cohesion

Party preference in blue collar households in Sweden, 1946-1979 (in percentages)

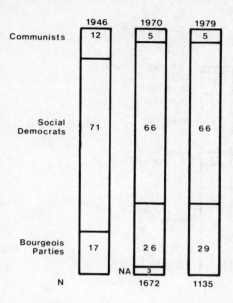

Sources: 1946: Hans Ingulfson and Rolf Hagman, 'De svenska partiernas sociala och andra grundvalar' in Elis Håstad (ed.) *'Gallup' och den svenska väljarkåren* (Uppsala, Hugo Gebers Förlag, 1950), 158.   1970:   Statistiska Centralbyrån, *Allmänna valen 1970* (Stockholm: SCB, 1973), 99. 1979: Sören Holmberg, *Svenska väljare* (Stockholm: Liber, 1981), 300.

voters with more than thirteen years of schooling over the past two decades. Though their political predilections were solidly bourgeois (80 per cent) in the early 1960s, by the early 1980s, the socialist vote had doubled, with all the gains going to parties to the left of the Social Democrats.   Student voting patterns are even more dramatic: bourgeois support fell from 62 per cent in 1961-62 to 27 per cent in 1977 (Ns = 606 and 813, respectively), and here the vote for parties to the left of the Social Democrats jumped from 4 per cent to 52 per cent (Logue 1982:175).   A substantial portion of this change reflects the salience of new issues, such as nuclear power, feminism, and environmental questions, in these well-educated strata.

The decline in class cohesion in voting among manual workers

Figure 8.6   The Educated Become Less Bourgeois

Party preference among voters with thirteen or more years of schooling
in Denmark, 1963-1981 (in percentages)

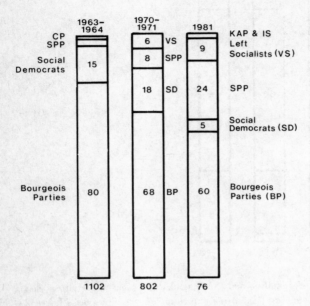

Source: Data from Gallup Markedsanalyse

and among the well-educated new middle class produced offsetting
flows of voters between the labour and bourgeois blocs. This meant
little in tallying the votes but a great deal in judging the nature of
parties. Declining class cohesion had only positive consequences for
bourgeois parties which deemphasised organisation and rejected class
as a principle of political organisation: it gave them the claim to
represent all the people. The consequences for the Social Democrats,
on the other hand, were negative. Declining working-class cohesion
undercut the unity of the labour movement - it was preserved at the
top but diminished at the bottom - and eroded the once-homogeneous
class culture that supported it. Moreover, the Social Democrats also
faced a new threat from the left.

The Resurgence of Radical Socialism

All three countries have witnessed the rise of a different sort of radical socialist party from the dogmatic, pro-Moscow Communists who had, by the end of the 1950s, ceased to be more than a minor irritant on the Social Democrats' left flank. Between 1958 and 1964, the traditional Communist Parties in all three countries either lost their position to home-grown radical socialist groups or were taken over by similar factions.

This process started in Denmark, where the Danish Communist Party expelled Aksel Larsen, who had chaired the CP for 26 years, for his purported Titoism after the party's 1958 congress. Old political warhorse that he was, Larsen did not retire but continued to lead a dissident faction. The Socialist People's Party (SPP - *Socialistisk Folkeparti*), which was founded formally in February 1959 by Larsen's faction, proved to have substantially greater popular appeal than the CP. In the 1960 elections, the SPP polled twice the vote that the CP had in 1957 and replaced the CP in parliament. The SPP's electoral success had repercussions to the north. A left-wing faction of the Norwegian Labour Party organised a similarly named Socialist People's Party in time for the 1961 elections; it repeated the Danish SPP's success by replacing the CP in parliament. Confronted by the likely formation of a Swedish equivalent, the old leadership of the Swedish Communist Party relinquished the chairmanship of the party in 1964 to what we would now call the Eurocommunist wing under economist C. H. Hermansson. This change in course was reflected symbolically by changing the party name to *Vänsterpartiet Kommunisterna* (VpK - Left Party-Communists) in 1967. While the Moscow loyalists initially accepted Hermansson as a compromise choice, the new leadership's 'detached and somewhat indulgent indifference to the Soviet bloc' (Tarschys 1974) led the pro-Soviet faction to organise a separate party - Arbetarpartiet Kommunisterna (ApK) -in 1977.

By the time that ApK separated itself from VpK, the Moscow loyalists in Sweden had been reduced to a tiny sect without electoral importance; recognizing its position, ApK did not contest the 1985 election. The Norwegian CP underwent a similar evolution after its Eurocommunist elements, including party chairman Reidar Larsen, elected to remain within the Socialist Left Party, which had developed out of the alliance between the Norwegian SPP, CP, non-affiliated trade unionists, and left Labourites in opposition to Norwegian membership in the Common Market in the 1972 referendum and 1973 parliamentary election. Of the three Communist Parties, only the Danish CP enjoyed any electoral success after 1973, but even that proved fleeting; by 1979 they retained only a handful of city council seats.

Though Scandinavian radical socialists have much in common with Eurocommunists (the Danish SPP members of the European Parliament participate in the Communist group) and have fraternal relations with the Italian CP, the fact that they were premature Eurocommunists influenced their development. This was particularly true of the Danish SPP, whose leaders were excommunicated from the international movement as 'Titoist revisionists;' the SPP developed an independent stance which ultimately enabled it to incorporate (with considerable strain) feminists and greens in a working-class party (cf. figures 8.4 and 8.6). The Norwegian SPP and the Socialist Left Party, which subsequently emerged from the anti-Common Market campaign, and the Swedish VpK have struggled with this same problem with more strain and less success. Even so, in all three countries similar radical socialist groups have emerged as viable alternatives for younger Social Democratic voters.

This has been a mixed blessing for the Social Democrats. While the Danish Social Democrats initially continued the practice pursued successfully against the CP and refused to consider passing legislation for which the SPP would provide the margin of victory, they changed their attitude when the SPP proved to be a permanent parliamentary fixture and the Social Democrats' traditional coalition partner, the Radical Liberals, moved right under Hilmar Baunsgaard in 1965-66. It was difficult to maintain a Cold War-style mobilisation against the SPP in the unions, where the party pushed the campaign for a labour majority to enact the policies the Social Democrats advocated. Since 1966, when SPP gains created an SD-SPP majority (the first parliamentary labour majority in Danish history), Social Democratic cabinets have regularly turned to the SPP for support. While the Norwegian SPP and, more recently, Socialist Left Party and the Swedish VpK have had less bargaining power, Social Democratic governments have frequently used their parliamentary seats in assembling majorities.

While the Swedish Social Democrats retained a rhetorical radicalism on foreign policy issues during the Vietnam era, the Danish and Norwegian Social Democratic leadership found themselves compromised by the demands of NATO diplomacy. In addition, Common Market membership in both countries became a focus for a range of discontents which enabled the left to recruit widely in the core Social Democratic labour constituency. This was particularly true in Norway where the Labour Party made a costly effort to maintain party discipline on the question. As a result an entire generation in Denmark and Norway matured in an atmosphere in which the Social Democrats were no longer seen as the natural home for all but sectarian leftists.

The End of the Social Democratic Era?

The consequences of the fragmentation of the labour movement and the decline of class cohesion cannot be read out of the figures on seats in parliament. Political scientists like to point at the indices of class voting - the labour parties' proportion of the blue-collar vote has declined from about 85 per cent in the early 1960s to about 75 per cent today - but the change is far deeper than these figures suggest. What has happened is that the 'working class' has increasingly been reduced to an economic concept, not a cultural one.

This has profound consequences for party organisational life. Party membership has declined. This is most notable in Denmark, which lacks the pattern of collective affiliation of trade union locals to the Social Democratic Party that is common to Sweden and Norway; Danish Social Democratic Party membership has fallen from the peak of 300,000 in 1947 to about 120,000 today, or from more than 40 per cent of voters to about 15 per cent of voters. Norwegian Labour Party membership has declined from 200,000 at its peak in 1949 to about 160,000 or from about 30 per cent to 20 per cent of its voters. However, Swedish Social Democratic membership has grown from about 550,000 in 1946 to more than a million today, or from 38 per cent of its vote to 42 per cent; the growth is a consequence of increased collective affiliation.

Membership figures say little about parties' internal life. Here the situation looks bleaker. While there are few reliable statistics on meeting attendance, the general perception is that the numbers attending meetings have declined. Many subsidiary Social Democratic organisations - clubs, papers, cooperatives, etc. - have folded; others, like sports clubs, survive but have lost their political tie. Moreover, in organisations which are expanding, such as trade unions, the amateur officials of the past have been replaced by professionals. The bureaucratisation of the movement has become pronounced.

The elan of the movement has diminished. A variety of reasons can be cited. The anti-communist mobilisation declined with the demise of the pro-Moscow CPs as a credible force inside the labour movement. The anti-capitalist mobilisation declined more slowly but, seemingly, inexorably with growing affluence. Only the Swedish Social Democrats are an exception to this; they have attempted since the 1960s to maintain class mobilisation both in election campaigns and in their use of the massed union flags, the Internationale and other symbols of the past.

But the principal cause of demobilisation was success. The malaise of the Social Democratic labour movement is related to economic success and the means by which it has been achieved, not to failure. The completion of the welfare state cost Social Democrats their clarity of purpose. Reforms continued, but they were generally marginal improvements of existing programs. But the political support generated by raising unemployment compensation from 80 per cent to 90 per cent of wages or adding dental care to the national health system pales beside the enthusiasm generated by establishing a minimal system of unemployment compensation or national health insurance to begin with.

The creation of the welfare state helped undermine the basis for the separate working-class culture which had been part of the basis for Social Democratic strength. Affluence, of course, played a role; the possessions previously reserved to the bourgeoisie were now within reach of the Social Democratic constituency. Social Democratic housing policy moved a good portion of the blue-collar working class out of the densely populated urban neighborhoods where the party and its organisations had been a way of life; those customs did not move easily to suburbia. Moreover, the centralised mechanisms of the welfare state eliminated the need for solidarity, which had been a crucial characteristic of the labour movement. Previously, solidarity had provided the welfare infrastructure for the working class - trade union benefit societies covering sickness, unemployment, old age and death; housing cooperatives, and the like - but now the need for solidarity and schooling in it were attenuated.

Because of their identification with the existing public sector, the Social Democrats were unable to capture the growing enthusiasm for participatory democracy evident since the 1960s. For Social Democrats, centralisation and bureaucratisation were the means to an admirable end, not grounds for protest. The issue of Common Market membership placed discontent with distant and bureaucratic government on the ballot, and the referenda campaigns transformed a vague sense of ill ease into concrete political protest. (It is no coincidence that the great electoral explosions of 1973 in Denmark and Norway, which sent voters rushing to protest parties of the left, right, and centre, followed on the heels of the Common Market referenda. Sweden faced neither.) In part what was underway was a generational shift. For the older generation which had known poverty and periodic unemployment, the benefits of the welfare state were worth almost any cost in bureaucratisation. But for the younger generation which had grown up with full employment and relative affluence, the mechanisms that made the welfare state work became the target for protest.

At the same time, the role of the unions *vis-à-vis* the party is undergoing transformation. The line between the political and economic legs of the labour movement is disappearing. The political wing - the party - has become increasingly involved in setting wages and other matters traditionally in the trade union sphere. But the unions have moved into politics as well in the last decade, taking political stands independent of the party. Some Danish unions, including the Transport and General Workers' Union (Specialarbejder-forbundet), have endorsed pluralism in the movement by providing financial support for all working-class parties in parliament. The unions forced the Danish Social Democratic government into opposition in 1982, and in Sweden the unions imposed the recently enacted wage earner fund proposal on a reluctant party.

For half a century Social Democratic political hegemony rested not only on the party's strength and its absolute dominance of the labour movement, but also the disunity of the bourgeois parties. The most immediate cause for the end of Social Democratic dominance was the end of bourgeois division.

The Bourgeois Parties

The term 'bourgeois' does not sound so quaintly Marxist in its Scandinavian form (*borgerlig*); rather it describes the non-socialist parties' common historical and ideological roots. But it is a misnomer in many ways. If middle-class values have become predominant among many Social Democrats in the last forty years, the bourgeois parties have also accepted collectivist policies. There had always been support for educational and social policy innovation among these parties, and some early welfare legislation was introduced by bourgeois governments. While abstract collectivist issues (such as the nationalisation of finance and industry) were divisive in Scandinavian public policy debates in the 1940s (Lewin 1967), the development of welfare state programs and of the use of fiscal policy to manage the economy directed the debate about collective measures into channels where grand ideological premises seemed less important. The orientation toward performance and pragmatism has served the interests of the non-socialist parties well.

Only in Denmark did the bourgeois parties appear to be a viable governing alternative to the Social Democrats between 1945 and 1965, and that was principally in the immediate aftermath of the war.

During most of this period the non-socialists had only two tactics: collaborate with the Social Democrats to protect special (generally agrarian) interests or project an image of offering a 'realistic alternative' to Social Democratic collectivism. Collaboration, well established in the 1930s, was always an option for centrist parties while the role of loyal opposition (permanently) awaiting power appealed to the Conservatives.

The increased power of the non-socialist parties as a bloc since 1965 has been the result of socio-economic and political changes in Scandinavia. First, increased affluence achieved under Social Democratic rule made possible a vastly expanded welfare state collectively financed by wage earners. In practice, most welfare state policies proved acceptable to the bourgeois parties. Second, as noted above, the Social Democrats abandoned their orthodox socialist goals in favour of pragmatic economic and social policies. This convergence permitted the bourgeois parties to offer voters an alternative which was comfortably similar to existing policies. (Ironically, it was only when radical students challenged this consensus after 1968 that the bourgeois parties again sought a more distinctive profile.) The trend appeared first in Norway with the formation in 1963 of the first non-socialist government in a generation; that government lasted only a matter of weeks, but it set the stage for a bourgeois election victory and majority government in 1965. Denmark followed in 1968-1971 with a bourgeois majority coalition, the country's last majority government. Not until 1976 would the cautious Swedes fall for the 'discreet charm of the (political) bourgeoisie'.

The political role of the non-socialist parties has been transformed in the postwar period. The bourgeois parties changed from being parties that variously served as a permanent 'loyal opposition' or Social Democratic coalition partners (1945-65) to being parties of alternative government (since 1965). Centrist parties abandoned their periodic coalitions with the Social Democratic or Labour parties. Instead, the non-socialist parties fashioned a competing vision of the welfare state that emphasised individual opportunity and enterprise as well as a more cautious fiscal policy. Such an alternative rested on a belief that social policy was limited by resources and that real social gains depended upon growth and not primarily redistribution. Nevertheless, the numerous non-socialist parties have continually faced a dilemma: to present a credible alternative to the socialists, they must subsume their pluralism in a common governing program. Historical, organisational, and often tactical reasons, however, simultaneously encourage them to maintain distinct individual party profiles.[7] They must do so in an environment in which their traditional socio-economic basis of appeal is eroding but at the same time their scope for political maneuver has increased.

Although socio-economic status is still an important factor in Scandinavian bourgeois politics, its role has declined. One may identify bourgeois parties by their ties to business and finance or farmers, but their programs no longer focus on such specific interests. Though the powerful economic interest organisations remain aligned with specific parties, they are now more effective in delivering resources than votes. The most narrowly defined parties, the Agrarians in Norway and Sweden, have taken the more ecumenical Centre Party label in order to appeal to urban voters.[8] In Denmark, the agrarian Liberals, who in any case were never exclusively rural in name or program, have attracted an urban vote (primarily in Jutland) after two decades of energetic effort.

The reason is two-fold. First, farmers and small business - the traditional occupational bases of the Agrarian and Liberal parties - have been in numerical decline for the better part of this century. Farmers vote overwhelmingly for the Agrarian parties (the agrarian movement was as much a way of life for farmers as the labour movement was for workers), but even when the vote can be delivered, limiting a party's appeal restricts its influence. Second, voters find it increasingly difficult to fit easily into political categories which are a century old. An industrial worker may spend most of his day seated at a sleek control desk with computer terminals taking the place of the foreman. He commutes to work in his own automobile, in part so he can get home in time to potter around the garden of his suburban house. Conversely a university graduate may find her professional activities constrained by hierarchical bureaucracies, her salary dependent upon legislative action, and having chosen an urban residence, she may find herself a regular consumer of public transportation and cultural facilities. What is her 'class interest'? Her problem is typical of the growing white-collar strata. Much of this 'new middle class' has as little autonomy as the traditional industrial working class but is far more differentiated. It lacks the organisational infrastructure that characterised the farmers' and the labour movements. Not surprisingly, party identification is weakest and voter mobility greatest among white-collar employees.

While our model of the Scandinavian party system (see table 8.1) emphasises the economic dimension, it also includes a traditional geographic component which should not be discounted. Regional interests remain strong, especially in Norway. Moreover, some post-industrial or 'post-affluence' issues (Inglehart 1981) have revived divisions in both the non-socialist and socialist blocs. The nuclear power issue has had that effect in Sweden, and the EEC referenda in Norway (1972) and Denmark (1972 and 1986) have increased the salience of regionalism and the urban-rural cleavage.

Among the non-socialist parties - which have all sought to broaden their appeal beyond their traditional constituencies - the strength of party identification has declined dramatically. Voters respond to mass media images, leading political personalities, and especially credible performance. Environmental concerns, nuclear power, women's issues and other questions that defy clear links to the old definitions of parties in economic terms have come to the fore. Ideology has not disappeared, but its connection to occupation has diminished.

As a consequence, voter mobility has increased. In all three countries, mobility between the socialist and bourgeois blocs pales by comparison with the substantial circulation of voters among the bourgeois parties (see Borre *et al.* 1976:13-37 and Borre *et al.* 1979:10-11 on Denmark; on Sweden, Petersson 1977:149-95; see Borre 1984:339-41 for comparative data). Both surveys and election results clearly demonstrate sharp increases in voter mobility among parties of the centre and right since 1970. Minimum estimates based on net movements between elections suggest that voter mobility in the bourgeois bloc has doubled in Sweden, tripled in Norway, and quadrupled in Denmark in relation to the stable voter allegiances of the 1950s. An increasing portion of the bourgeois voters identify less with an individual party than with a general area of the political spectrum. These floating bourgeois voters are the cause of the growing volatility in elections and their fickleness complicates the task of bourgeois politicians in their effort to form stable parliamentary coalitions.

Coalition politics shape the environment within which individual bourgeois parties pursue their increasingly mobile potential voters. The complexities of the Danish pattern demand review before we examine the current state of the bourgeois parties.

The war produced two significant changes *vis-à-vis* pre-war party patterns. As noted above, Communist strength surged in 1944-45, but with the onset of the Cold War fell almost as quickly as it had risen. Of lasting importance, however, was what happened on the right: the Conservative parties emerged from the war strengthened by their patriotic role and by the disappearance of other right-wing competition. The parties of the centre - Liberals and Agrarians - found the Conservatives to be loyal democrats and potential allies. This ended the Conservatives' political isolation, which had precluded a serious non-socialist governing alternative during the 1930s.

Initial postwar Communist strength weakened the Social Democrats throughout Scandinavia, but only in Denmark were the non-socialist parties able to capitalise upon this. When desultory negotiations failed to produce a basis for collaboration on the left, the agrarian Liberals stepped into the breach with Radical Liberal and Conservative support. But their two year minority government was undistinguished and internally fractious, and the Social Democrats regained power in time to enjoy the benefits of the Marshall Plan. The Social Democrats' commitment to the North Atlantic Treaty in 1949 impeded ties to their pre-war coalition partners, the Radical Liberals, whose traditional anti-militarism survived the war and occupation intact (Einhorn 1975). Domestic economic problems overwhelmed the Social Democrats in 1950, and the agrarian Liberals, now in formal coalition with the Conservatives, returned to power. The coalition enjoyed three years of political 'armistice' as all significant parties united behind a major constitutional reform. In 1953 the Social Democrats again returned to power with a minority government. Security and foreign policy differences with the Radical Liberals hampered a formal coalition - the Radicals opposed Danish membership in NATO - but the two were able to cooperate informally on domestic issues. In 1957, without fully conceding their foreign policy objections, the Radicals entered a Social Democratic-led coalition that also included the Georgists (the Justice Party) until that party lost its parliamentary seats in 1960 (Einhorn 1975:61-79). The Social Democratic-Radical Liberal coalition retained its majority only by the deft maneuver of inviting one of the two Greenland members of parliament - who had heretofore remained outside the parliamentary blocs - to join the cabinet as Minister for Greenland. The Social Democratic-Radical Liberal coalition was ended by mutual consent in 1964.

In Sweden the Agrarians joined the Socialists between 1951 and 1957. The coalition ultimately failed as both parties found the costs in policy too high. As in Denmark, the junior partner lost votes. In 1957 the Socialists sought what was then seen as a radical new collectivist measure - the comprehensive general pension scheme - which the Agrarians refused to accept. They went into opposition instead.

Links across the centre did not disappear after these two attempts. But they generally proceeded pragmatically, issue by issue, rather than through formal coalitions. In the 1960s, all three countries faced new political issues. The Social Democrats were pressured by the appearance of new left-wing parties far less doctrinaire than the Communists. The non-socialist parties recognised that their only route to power was through increased cooperation. In Norway the four bourgeois parties took advantage of an unexpected opportunity to form a short-lived coalition in 1963. In 1965 the electorate allowed them to renew the experiment, which lasted until 1971, when it collapsed over the divisive Common Market (EEC) issue. Denmark followed suit with a non-socialist majority coalition government led by the Radicals' Hilmar Baunsgaard in 1968, but that government lost the 1971 election to the Social Democrats. Sweden was the last to experience shifting coalitions. Not until 1976 were the bourgeois parties successful in wresting power from the Socialists.

In the last two decades, the bourgeois parties have experienced both the delights and costs of power. The latter has been a principal cause of increased volatility in electoral behaviour and a degree of cabinet instability unknown since the 1920s. The most notable occurrence was the electoral shock of 1973, when one Danish voter in three cast a ballot for a party not represented in the previous parliament; in Norway, one voter in five did the same. Protest parties appeared to the right of the Conservatives: the Progress party organised by Mogens Glistrup in Denmark and the Anders Lange's Party for the Substantial Reduction of [Income] Taxes, Excise Duties, and Government Intervention, in Norway. (Following Lange's death in 1975, the party changed its name to the Progress Party.) In Denmark the new Christian People's Party, patterned after the Norwegian example, entered parliament as did a splinter from the Social Democrats, the Centre Democrats; the Georgists returned as well. The number of parties represented in parliament doubled from five to ten in Denmark and grew from five to eight in Norway (Pedersen 1981:12-39). The voter revolt reflected the effects of the previous years' Common Market referenda in both countries and the dissatisfaction felt by many bourgeois voters with their traditional parties' performance in government.

In Sweden the fireworks were limited to the government itself. The bourgeois parties squandered the parliamentary majority that they won in 1976 by running through four different governments in six years, as disagreement over atomic power and taxation tore successive bourgeois majority cabinets apart (Elder *et al.* 1982:76-99). But perhaps it was this demonstration of disunity that spared the Swedish bourgeois parties the loss of votes to protest parties that their Danish and Norwegian equivalents experienced.

Current Status of the Bourgeois Parties

Since the late 1960s, the bourgeois parties in the three countries have developed in very different directions. As can be seen in figures 8.1-8.3, the agrarian parties enjoyed a renaissance among voters in Denmark and Sweden in the early 1970s, but not in Norway. The Liberals waxed and waned in Denmark and Sweden but underwent a secular decline in Norway that eliminated them from parliament in 1985. Protest parties on the right have become a fixture of political life in Denmark and Norway, but not in Sweden. These developments require a country-by-country survey.

Denmark. With its numerous parties, the bourgeois bloc in Denmark is the most difficult to define. As noted, there have been five periods of non-socialist government since 1945. A distinct bourgeois profile failed to appear during either the 1945-47 or the 1950-53 terms. Indeed, the latter minority coalition of the agrarian Liberals and Conservatives reflected agreement on the proposed constitutional reforms as well as the new broad foreign and security policy consensus (excepting the Radical Liberals). Moreover, the Social Democrats had failed to define how their postwar program could be enacted in view of the country's still severe economic constraints.

The 1968-71 majority non-socialist government capitalised upon the failure of Denmark's first 'opening to the left': the informal coalition between the Social Democrats and the Socialist People's Party in 1966-67. Never was the Social Democratic hegemony clearer (at least to bourgeois voters) than during the agrarian Liberal-Conservative-Radical Liberal government of Hilmar Baunsgaard. Economic problems were not confronted, while social spending and public taxation soared. The bourgeois voters punished the coalition in 1971, when especially the Conservatives lost votes. The wave of protest was only starting. From nowhere came Mogens Glistrup, former tax law scholar and current tax law evader. In the December 1973 election, his newly established Progress Party received 16 per cent of the vote on its first try and became the second largest parliamentary party, winning more seats than any other non-socialist party. Glistrup's message was a mixture of rightist formulas, populist anger, and political caricature. Although Glistrup's party drew support from across the political spectrum, among the non-socialist bloc the Conservatives again suffered most.

The protest also unhinged the *de facto* Danish 'opening to the left' of the Social Democratic-Socialist People's Party collaboration. Erhard Jakobsen, a Social Democratic MP and mayor of a Copenhagen suburb, encouraged and exploited the dissatisfaction in the Social

Democratic right wing to undermine the government's tax reform plans and fight the party's leftist leadership. Jakobsen also produced an 'instant' political party - the Centre Democrats - on the eve of the 1973 elections; non-socialist and pragmatic in program, the Centre Democrats won 7.8 per cent of the vote in 1973.

Other elements of the political counterculture gained from voter discontent in 1972-73. In 1971 the five traditional parties had collectively received 93 per cent of the vote. In December 1973, their share declined to only 64 per cent. The number of parties represented in parliament doubled from five to ten, including the Christian People's Party, Justice Party (Georgists), and Communists, as well as the Progress Party and Centre Democrats; the Left Socialists recovered their parliamentary representation in 1975. All of the established parties suffered, but the losses were especially severe for the Social Democrats and the Conservatives, and it took several elections for them to recover their strength (See table 8.2). The 1973 elections produced unprecedented political volatility precisely at the moment when international economic conditions called for stability and cooperation.

The 1974-75 agrarian Liberal government, resting upon only 22 of the Folketing's 179 seats, resulted from the 1973 election shock. From 1975 to 1982 the Social Democrats returned to power and attempted to weave their way through the economic crisis by obtaining broad agreements across the centre for successive economic emergency legislation. The unusual 1978-1979 coalition between the Social Democrats and the agrarian Liberals reflected the new direction. By 1982 the Social Democrats had exhausted their options and resigned.

The rejuvenated Conservatives, who now had 14.5 per cent of the vote (up from 5.5 per cent in 1975) seized the political initiative as Poul Schlüter formed a minority government with the Liberals, Centre Democrats, and Christian People's Party. The prospects for the new bourgeois government did not seem bright. Parliamentary success would require the support of the weakened Radical Liberals and tolerance from the disintegrating Progress party. The new government confronted the fiscal and economic problems directly. Social programs were cut. Public spending was contained. And, above all else, taxes on corporations and capital accumulation were raised. Forced to call an election in January 1984, Schlüter emerged with the Conservative party greatly strengthened (23.4 per cent) and his allies intact. Although its working majority remained only a vote or two, Schlüter's government surprised observers with its pragmatism and parliamentary successes. Its greatest political achievement was a broadly based tax

Table 8.2: The Danish Electoral Earthquake of 1973

Party	% of Vote 1971	% of Vote 1973	Change
Social Democrats	37.3	25.6	-11.7
Radical Liberals	14.4	11.2	- 3.1
Conservatives	16.7	9.2	- 7.5
Agrarian Liberals	15.6	12.3	- 3.3
Socialist People's	9.1	6.0	- 3.1
Communists	1.4[a]	3.6	+ 2.2
Christian People's	1.9[a]	4.0	+ 2.1
Justice	1.7[a]	2.9	+ 1.2
Centre Democrats	--[a]	7.8	+ 7.8
Progress	--[a]	15.9	+15.9

Note: a. Not represented in Folketinget in 1971.

reform (the Social Democrats and Radical Liberals joined the four government parties) which greatly reduced the ability of high income groups to avoid high taxes. This progressive measure was closer to the previously rejected Social Democratic goals than to the original Conservative proposals. Its enactment reflected the declining political threat posed to the Conservatives by Glistrup's Progress Party which, by 1984, held only one quarter of its 1973 vote.

In just over ten years - from December 1973 to January 1984 - Denmark experienced unprecedented political turmoil and dealignment: six parliamentary elections, the rise and decline of protest parties, and six major or minor cabinet shuffles. What emerged? It is important to remember that the balance between the two blocs in postwar Danish politics has always been narrow. Schlüter and his allies have convinced Danish voters that they have alternative policies that at least ought to be tried. They have capped the welfare state but not rolled it back. Some programs have been reduced: unemployment compensation has

been trimmed and sick pay for the initial day of illness has been eliminated. Wage indexation has been ended. In practice the bourgeois government has acted with moderation, despite some occasional rhetorical flourishes. Danes want their welfare state, but they have come to recognise that it must have a sound economic basis.
Norway. Across the Skagerrak the large off-shore oil reserves insulated Norway from the cruel economic realities of the past decade. However, these economic differences surprisingly are not reflected in major political differences from the other Scandinavian and European countries. The pattern first visible in the mid 1960s with the establishment of a non-socialist government under Conservative leadership has continued. In the non-socialist bloc, the pattern noted by Borre, Valen, and others has continued; there has been flux within the bloc, but little change between the two blocs. The destabilising influence of the Common Market issue between 1971 and 1973 was severe, but temporally limited. Nevertheless, the initial political shock was substantial. In 1973, the Labour Party lost substantially while the new leftist faction - the Socialist Alliance for the Election, which soon became the Socialist Left Party - soared. In the non-socialist bloc the Liberals split (over the EEC issue) into two weak factions portending the demise of the country's oldest political party. No Liberals were elected in the 1985 election despite the tactic of pledging to support a Labour government after the election. On the right, the Anders Lange/Progress Party provided a Norwegian equivalent to Mogens Glistrup. Although not as strong, the Norwegian Progress Party posed a new threat to a decade of bourgeois cooperation, already weakened by the divisive Common Market issue.

In Norway the storm blew over. Soaring oil prices, the *coup de grace* of the politics of the 'golden sixties' in other western democracies, were a windfall to Norway. Exploitation of her offshore oil wealth became immensely profitable and served as collateral for deficit financing to maintain high employment, social services, and stable taxes. The non-socialists remained true to the 'lesson of 1963-65'; politically the whole is greater than the sum of the parts. The Common Market issue was closed, and the Progress Party was kept in the cold. The emergence of Conservative Party dominance over the bourgeois bloc probably reflects factors similar to the Danish case: effective leadership and a revival of public support for economic growth even at the temporary expense of social policy. Norway has even less 'rollback' than Denmark, although curtailment of popular public programs (health and education) has been controversial. Taxes and spending have been capped by the non-socialists in the 1980s. The

Conservatives' smaller coalition partners, the agrarian Centre and the Christian People's Party (which joined the minority Conservative government in 1982) are too parochial to challenge the distribution of the non-socialist voters.

The 1985 elections demonstrated the even balance between blocs in Norway and the failure of the 'new right' (in the form of the Progress Party) to make headway, though it retained just enough parliamentary strength to bring down the Conservative coalition and bring back Labour in 1986. Four years of Conservative-dominated bourgeois rule had undermined the appeal of a frontal attack on the welfare state. If the rise of anti-tax rightist parties in Denmark and Norway reflected the protest of voters disappointed with earlier non-socialist rule, the decline of the Progress parties in both countries suggests that the traditional bourgeois parties have regained this group's confidence.

Sweden. Sweden remains the most solid Scandinavian bastion of Social Democratic hegemony, though no longer with boring predictability. The non-socialist electoral victories of 1976 and 1979 were a political sensation in a country that had seen more than forty years of Social Democratic rule. But the achievements of the bourgeois governments between 1976 and 1982 were modest. The three parties disagreed on many basic policies. Although nuclear power resulted in the most spectacular conflict, the coalition partners also differed on spending priorities and tax policies. The Centre Party broke up the first bourgeois coalition in 1978; the Conservatives the second in 1981. Thus the bourgeois parties seemed as willing to fight among themselves as to demonstrate what their alternative to Social Democratic policies would be. This was reminiscent of their failure to achieve a credible non-socialist alliance in the 1950s. The failure of the coalition to attract significant support from previous Social Democratic voters meant that each party sought to maintain a distinct profile in order to hold their traditional voters and win votes from their allies.

Tactically, the Swedish Conservatives have managed the best. Their withdrawal from the vacillating bourgeois coalition preserved their image as a party with untried alternatives. Whether they are remains to be seen. Their electoral gains in 1976, 1979 and 1982 did not alter the fact that they cannot govern without their weaker sisters (Berglund and Lindström 1982:72-78). Sensing a chance for a major advance in 1985, the new Conservative leader, Ulf Adelsohn, ran a militant and protracted campaign which called for a 'system change' in the 'Swedish model.' Voters responded by dealing the Conservatives a setback in the September 1985 election: their vote declined from 23.6

to 21.3 per cent, they lost ten seats, and the non-socialist bloc failed to win a majority.

The Liberals (Folkpartiet) suffered significant erosion of their electoral strength through the 1970s, despite ruling alone in 1978-79. Despite the party's reversal of its precipitous electoral decline in the 1985 election, the Swedish Liberals have yet to prove whether the ideological message of liberalism can still appeal to a meaningful group of voters. The Liberals' remarkable gains (from 5.9 to 14.3 per cent and 30 seats) came in spite of the party's traditional and vague election platform. Much of the credit goes to Bengt Westerberg, the party's new leader, who is more 'libertarian' and less collectivist than his predecessors. His moderate and conciliatory style, as well as the reduced credibility of the other bourgeois party leaders, made Westerberg's party the choice of 'floating' bourgeois voters, and gave the Swedish Liberals yet another opportunity to try to lead the non-socialist bloc.

The Centre Party has found new issues beyond its traditional concern for Swedish agriculture. Imaginative leaders seized the initiative on 'green' (ecological) issues in the early 1970s. In doing so, the Swedish Centre revived the 'rural-urban' political dimension in a form quite different from the traditional issues of farm and rural subsidies. But environmental concerns have become common elements in several parties, and the experience of negligible economic growth during most of the past decade has made the 'small is beautiful' alternative less attractive. However, the Centre Party is the only non-socialist party currently capable of attracting significant numbers of voters from socialist ranks and no non-socialist government is possible without Centre's support. The party's decline in the past two elections has hurt non-socialist chances to form an alternative government. In 1985, this decline accelerated despite (or perhaps because of) its electoral alliance with the smaller Christian Democrats, which for two decades have sought to break into national politics with their typically Scandinavian blend of social liberalism and cultural conservatism.[9] Even with the alliance, the Centre's share of the vote fell from 15.5 to 12.5 per cent.

Missing from Sweden's political spectrum is a rightist anti-tax protest party analogous to the Danish and Norwegian Progress parties. It is, of course, almost impossible to explain why a political phenomenon does not occur, but plausible explanations for Sweden's exception include the growth of social policies (and accompanying taxes) at a more gradual pace in Sweden when compared to the two other states, deliberate appeals by the Conservatives to those opposed to high taxes, a sense that the Conservatives have not yet really had a chance to change the system, and the effect of the 4 per cent threshold in deterring the formation of new parties. It might not be amiss to suggest that the political and organisational strength of the Social Democrats have given critics of the welfare state and postwar collectivism less opportunity to attack disappointing policies (see Wilensky 1976 and Rehn 1984: esp. 163-8).

Summary

Although Lipset and Rokkan's (1967) thesis about 'frozen party structures' was quite appropriate for Scandinavia at the time, this turned out to be the twilight of a historical period. The ensuing two decades saw more partisan change than the previous fifty years. What occurred was not a revolution but rather a more normal oscillation of power between two increasingly dynamic and complex blocs. The bourgeois parties moved from permanent opposition or junior partnership with the hegemonic Social Democrats to more or less effective collaboration within their own camp. In Denmark and Norway, the non-socialists sold their alternative to the voters, but became the frustrated administrators of a largely Social Democratic polity. In Sweden, the non-socialists finally achieved office but failed to demonstrate coherence or vision. It was less a new era of bourgeois hegemony than the end of Social Democratic hegemony. In each case the period commenced with the socialists losing power rather than the non-socialists winning power. No matter - the bourgeois parties got their opportunity. In partisan struggles, that counts for a lot.

The Transformation of Scandinavian Coalition Patterns

In contrast to other countries with multiparty systems where single party parliamentary majorities are rare, the Scandinavian countries have been examples of exceptional stability in government and policy consistency throughout most of the last half century *even though minority governments have been more common than majority coalitions.* The reasons basically are four: (1) Social Democratic dominance of a divided opposition; (2) the focus of Scandinavian politics on issues where compromise is possible; (3) an unusual practice of seeking broad legislative coalitions, rather than narrow majorities, to pass major reforms; and (4) the nature of internal organisation and norms in Scandinavian parties.[10]

Social Democratic dominance has been a fact of political life in Scandinavia since the 1920s. In terms of election support, the Social Democrats became the largest party in Sweden in 1917, Denmark in

1924, and Norway in 1927. They have held power alone or in coalition for two-thirds or more of the years since 1929 in Denmark, 1932 in Sweden, and 1935 in Norway. In both Denmark and Sweden, the non-socialist parties were divided by the bitterness left by the struggle between Liberals and Conservatives over establishing political democracy. The hostility that remained rendered a united non-socialist coalition government impossible between the wars. Similar animosity between Social Democrats and Communists excluded the latter from coalitions until the end of the 1950s; the only exception was the summer of 1945 when the Communists participated in Danish and Norwegian liberation cabinets.

For both Liberals and Agrarians, formal government participation or informal agreements to support the Social Democratic minority governments was preferable to collaboration with the Conservatives. At crucial junctures in all three countries in the 1930s, agreements between the Social Democrats and the Agrarians or Liberals provided broad support for important reforms. The Social Democratic-Agrarian alliance was a feature of life in Sweden from 1936 to 1957 and led to Agrarian participation in Social Democratic governments in 1936-39 and 1951-57. In Denmark, the Radical Liberal Party, which drew much of its vote then from family farmers, played the same role, cooperating formally or informally in governments with the Social Democrats between 1929 and 1964. Similar coalitions were less important in Norway, because the electoral system generally produced Labour majorities in parliament; however, a similar pattern of compromise was maintained. The pattern of coalitions across the centre of the political spectrum, diagramed in figure 8.7, persisted from the 1930s through the end of the 1950s in Sweden and the mid 1960s in Denmark.

Since then, this pattern has broken down. On the right, the residue of bitterness between Conservatives on the one hand and the Liberals and Agrarians on the other disappeared. The increased acceptability of the Conservatives as coalition partners for the non-socialists of the centre after World War II gradually made the idea of a non-socialist majority coalition a politically viable alternative. There had, after all, been non-socialist majorities in the Danish parliament throughout the entire period of Social Democratic government, and non-socialist majorities in Sweden had been common as well in the 1930s and 1950s. The real breakthrough came in Norway in 1963 when Jon Lyng, the Conservative leader, pieced together a minority coalition of all the non-socialist parties for the few weeks when the Socialist People's Party forced the Labour minority

Figure 8.7 Scandinavian Party Coalitions from the 1930s to the 1950s

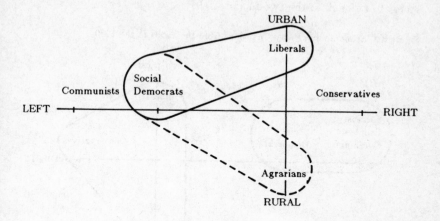

government from office over the government's failure to take safety precautions for the Kings Bay miners. On the left, the replacement of the pro-Moscow Communists by the Socialist People's Party in Denmark's parliament in 1960 and the 1964 victory of similar 'Eurocommunists' within the Swedish party provided the Social Democrats with more congenial partners than the Communists had previously been.

As a result, a two-bloc model increasingly emerged as an alternative to the coalitions of Social Democrats and Liberals or Agrarians of the previous period. In both Norway and Sweden, Social Democratic minority cabinets began to depend regularly on the parliamentary backing of the SPP (later the Socialist Left Party) and the Communists, respectively, but without making formal agreements; in Denmark in 1966-67 and again in 1973, Social Democrats made formal agreements on common policies with the Social People's Party but without the SPP taking cabinet posts. This pattern of alternative coalitions is presented in Figure 8.8. While this pattern has continued in Sweden and, to a lesser extent, in Norway in the 1970s and 1980s, it broke down in Denmark after the 1973 election. Between 1973 and 1982, there was a succession of minority governments, principally led by Social Democrat Anker Jørgensen (prime minister from 1975-82), which sought support across the centre of the political spectrum. These included a brief minority coalition government with the

Agrarian Liberals in 1978-79. But since Poul Schlüter's Conservative-led minority coalition was established in 1982, the trend seems to be back to the two-bloc model.

Figure 8.8 Scandinavian Party Coalitions from the 1960s to the 1980s

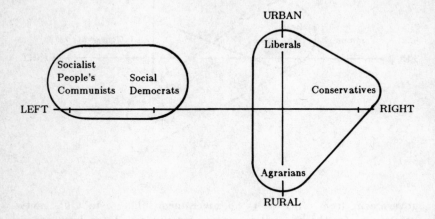

Scandinavian party coalitions proved relatively durable, we suspect, principally because of long periods of Social Democratic dominance. Fear of Social Democratic dominance lent stability to bourgeois coalitions as well. Coalition stability was increased because the principal issues were social and economic rather than the racial, religious, ethnic, and cultural conflicts which proved to be so intractable in many other countries. A good portion of the consensus and compromise which characterise Scandinavian politics stems from the fact that socio-economic issues are susceptible to compromise.

Non-negotiable issues in Scandinavian politics have been rare. One exception in the 1950s was the Swedish supplemental pension program, which led the Agrarians to leave the government. Such issues have become somewhat more common in the 1970s: Per Borten's non-socialist majority coalition in Norway collapsed in 1971 over Norwegian membership in the European Community, and Thorbjörn Fälldin's first cabinet - the first non-socialist government in Sweden since 1936 - collapsed after two years in office in 1978 over commissioning new atomic power plants. Still such issues are rare enough to be easily counted.

Moreover, coalition stability is increased by the practice of seeking broader coalitions than the minimum necessary to pass legislation. Even majority governments often seek the support of one or more opposition parties for major legislative initiatives, even if this means weakening proposals in order to get broader support. This attitude is reflected in Anker Jørgensen's comment that passing 'major reforms by narrow majorities is a cause for misgivings'. The obvious consequence of the practice is that reforms, put in place with broader support, are not likely to be repealed should the opposition come to power. A less obvious result is to reduce the inter-bloc animosities and divide the opposition by giving one or more opposition parties some influence, lessening the vigour of their attack on governmental policy.

Finally, party discipline plays a role. Although almost all Scandinavian parties contain considerable divergence of views, their cohesion is impressive. Parliamentary discipline is strong enough that compromises almost always hold. Individuals who break with their party on principle are seen as eccentric, not heroic. There was no tradition in Scandinavia of 'personal parties' like those of Pierre Poujade or General De Gaulle in France which periodically confounded the party system of the Fourth Republic until the leader-centered parties of Mogens Glistrup (the Progress Party) and Erhard Jakobsen (Centre Democrats) in Denmark and Anders Lange (Anders Lange's Party) in Norway appeared in 1973. However, this occurred after the 1972 Common Market referenda in both countries had confounded traditional voter allegiances; no personal parties have appeared since then.

A New Realignment?

Developments of the last twenty years suggest the possibility of yet another realignment of Scandinavian coalition patterns. The two-bloc pattern, with the coherent governmental alternatives that it entails, is in disarray. The most obvious cause is the demonstrated instability of non-socialist majority coalitions. The growing mobility of voters within the non-socialist bloc has forced the bourgeois parties to emphasize their differences even if it ruptures their alliances. In both Denmark and Norway the non-socialist majority coalitions of the late 1960s could not be reconstructed immediately after the defeat of the Social Democrats in the early 1980s. In Norway, Kaare Willoch initially took office after the 1981 election with a Conservative minority government, though he subsequently broadened it in June 1983 to a narrow majority by including the agrarian Centre and Christian People's Party. That majority was lost in the 1985 election, but the Willoch government continued with the tacit support of the Progress Party. Despite a non-socialist majority, Danish Prime

Minister Poul Schlüter has led a minority Conservative coalition since 1982. In neither Norway nor Denmark is a coalition of all the non-socialist parties politically plausible today, in no small measure because of the divisive role of the Progress Party in each country. In fact, Schlüter was forced to call new elections in 1983 by the 'un-Scandinavian' combination of the various labour and socialist parties on his left and Glistrup's Progress Party on his right; a similar coalition ousted Willoch in 1986. In Sweden, the non-socialists demonstrated similar disunity in power (1976-82), running through four cabinets in six years in office. The first Fälldin government collapsed over the nuclear power question in 1978, and the second Fälldin government, a majority cabinet, lost its Conservative coalition partner as a result of the 1981 tax compromise between the Centre and Liberals in government and the Social Democrats in opposition. All-party non-socialist governments are a less viable alternative to Social Democratic minority cabinets because of the obvious disunity within bourgeois ranks.

The second factor, related to the first, is the emergence of the Conservative Party in each of the countries as the principal non-socialist party. In the confusion and disunity of non-socialist ranks, the relatively hard ideological line of the Conservatives offers a clear profile that non-socialist voters have found attractive, not least because of the political competence of Schlüter in Denmark and Willoch in Norway and Gösta Bohman and his successor Ulf Adelsohn at the helm of the conservative Moderate Unity Party in Sweden. It is easy to overestimate the importance of swings among non-socialist parties - in the early 1970s there were convincing shifts to the agrarian parties under Thorbjörn Fälldin in Sweden and Poul Hartling in Denmark - but if the swing to the Conservatives should prove long term, it is possible to imagine them dominating the right of the political spectrum in the fashion that the Social Democrats have dominated the left. Journalists often do. But we suspect that the increasing fickleness of non-socialist voters demonstrated in recent election studies is a weak basis for long term political dominance. Nor does the attraction that the Reagan-Thatcher policy model exerts on some Scandinavian conservatives bode well for their long term prospects, unless, of course, these policies ultimately prove correct. However, the fragmentation of the centre in Denmark and Norway offers no obvious alternative to the Conservatives comparable to that provided by the Liberals or the Centre Party in Sweden.

Last, but probably most important, is the decline of Social Democratic hegemony. From the 1930s through the early 1970s, the

Social Democrats appeared to be the natural party of government in all three countries. Flush with confidence, they proceeded to transform society, constructing what are probably the best developed welfare states in the world. The late 1960s and early 1970s saw the final stages of that construction. To a significant extent, subsequent Social Democratic governments in Denmark and (to lesser extent) Norway, weakened by defections to the left over foreign policy and Common Market membership, have served more as caretakers than architects of the edifice that their predecessors had erected. The sense of solidarity that supported the Social Democratic policies has declined, and the monolithic working class support for the party has eroded. Only in Sweden have the Social Democrats managed to enact major reforms and to project their vision of the Sweden of the future, but their support among voters stems less from the popularity of their most recent reform, the wage-earner fund (cf. Hancock and Logue 1984), than from voters' perception that they are the most competent administrators of the state.

If this analysis is correct and (1) the demonstrated lack of bourgeois party cohesion makes stable, long-term non-socialist coalitions improbable; (2) the current ascendence of the Conservatives proves transitory and they fail to establish a permanent dominance of their side of the political spectrum comparable to that which the Social Democrats have enjoyed; and (3) Social Democratic programmatic, though not organisational, hegemony is a thing of the past, then what does the future hold?

The answer, we fear, is not very satisfying. The most likely prospect is a situation like the 1920s, when shifting coalitions predominated. The most likely patterns are Social Democratic minority cabinets and those led by the Conservatives, as long as they remain ascendent in the bourgeois bloc. Our crystal ball suggests no dramatic departures in policy but a good bit of tampering at the margins of existing policies. Decreased coherence in policy will mean less forward motion than sideways drift. This is the way most nations handle their politics, of course, but it will frustrate Scandinavian specialists who are used to a more orderly and purposeful pattern in politics.

If the half century of Social Democratic hegemony and the stability of coalitions that this engendered really is at an end, should we not lament its demise? Perhaps. Nostalgia has its appeal, even to political scientists. But why not rather praise its longevity? As former British Prime Minister Harold Wilson noted in a slightly different context, 'a week is a long time in politics.'

Notes

1. We use the term *Social Democrats* to include the Social Democratic Parties of Denmark and Sweden and the Norwegian Labour Party; *Liberal* to include Det radikale Venstre (Radical Liberals) in Denmark, Venstre in Norway, and Folkpartiet in Sweden; *Conservative* to include Det konservative Folkeparti in Denmark, Høyre in Norway, and Det moderata Samlingspartiet in Sweden; *Agrarians* to include Venstre in Denmark, Senterpartiet in Norway, and Centerpartiet in Sweden; and *Radical Socialists* to refer to Socialistisk Folkeparti and Venstresocialisterne in Denmark, Sosialistisk Venstreparti in Norway, and Vänsterpartiet-kommunisterna in Sweden. In general we have used the English labels in the left hand column of table 8.1 to designate the Scandinavian parties named in the three columns to the right.

2. The technical characteristics of the electoral system clearly have affected the party systems. The temptation to split and seek representation as a new party is far greater in Denmark than in Norway.

3. Olof Petersson, for instance, has developed an eight bloc system to capture the developments and the schisms of the past generation: Communist and Left Socialist, Social Democrats, Centre and Agrarian, Liberal, Other Centrist, Conservative, Protest, and 'Environmentalist and Women's (Miljö och Kvinnopartier).' All except the last fit the standard left to right dimension. (Petersson 1984:51). The other notable innovation is Ole Borre's two-camp, four bloc-scheme, which he uses to analyze electoral outcomes since World War II. Borre makes the conventional distinction between socialist and bourgeois 'camps,' divides the socialists into 'left-wing' and 'social democratic,' and the bourgeois parties into 'liberal centre' and 'conservative.' Borre subdivides the last group into the traditional moderate conservatives and the protest 'populist' right-wing parties, principally the Progress parties of Denmark and Norway that appeared on the scene in 1973. Borre's less detailed scheme suggests that both the data and the policy consequences of recent Scandinavian politics do not demand detailed analysis of every party contesting parliamentary elections. He notes that, despite the greater instability of partisan support in the elections of the 1970s, the 'normal support levels' for both the bourgeois and socialist camps are basically unchanged. (Borre 1984:330-1, 362).

4. Collective affiliation by local union branches produces substantial union involvement in and influence on municipal government. This precludes the bloc voting that union affiliation at the national level encourages in the British Labour Party.

5. Gunnar Adler-Karlsson, *Funktionssocialism* (Stockholm: Prisma, 1967). The quotation is translated from the Danish version, *Funktionssocialisme* (Copenhagen: Fremad, 1973), p. 37.

6. The data for the Danish figures in this section are from Gallup Markedsanalyse and are answers to the question 'Hviklet parti ville De stemme på, hvis der var folketingsvalg i morgen?' in 1961 to 1971 and to the question 'Stemte De ved folketingsvalget den 8. december 1981? - På hvilke parti?' in 1981. They

were derived from the following sources: 1961-62, Roper Public Opinion Research Center; 1963-64, Ingemar Glans, *Tabellsamling I: Stratifieringsvariabler och partipreferenser* (Lund: mimeographed, n.d.); 1970-71, Gallup Markedsanalyse and Berlingske Tidende; 1981, 'Valgundersøgelsen 1981,' carried out by Gallup Markedsanalyse for Valgforskningsgruppen (Ole Borre, Hans Jørgen Nielsen, Steen Sauerberg and Torben Worre), Jørgen Goul Andersen and Ingemar Glans and made available through Dansk Data Arkiv (DDA arkivnummer 529). Our thanks to these individuals and institutions for making these data available.

7. Throughout the postwar period there has been discussion of the virtues of merging various bourgeois parties. Periodic proposals to merge the Swedish Liberal and Centre parties and Danish agrarian Liberal and Conservative parties foundered on organisational egotism. The place where merger would make greatest sense - in the centre - is also the place of greatest fragmentation today.

8. As politicians have become even more conscious of modern advertising and public relations techniques, they have sought to find labels that attract rather than distinguish. Not only have the Norwegian and Swedish 'Farmers' have become 'Centrists,' the Swedish Conservatives went them one better by changing their name in 1969 from 'Högerpartiet' - the Right - to Moderata Samlingsparti, or, Moderate Unity Party. While hardly truth in advertising, this change caught the mood of the times. Mogens Glistrup's seizure of the term 'Fremskridt' - Progress - to designate his party which sought to turn the clock back in practically every area of public policy is yet another misnomer.

9. The Swedish Christian Democrats had consistently polled about 2 per cent of the vote but had been kept out of parliament by the 4 per cent threshold. This 'wasted' vote would have been worth about 7 seats if the Christian party had gotten over the electoral hurdle. The common list with the agrarian Centre was designed to do just that.

10. This section draws in part on Logue (1985a).

References

Adler-Karlsson, Gunnar (1967) *Funktionssocialism*, Prisma, Stockholm

Andersen, Bent Rold (1984a) *Kan Vi Bevare Velfaerdsstaten?*, AKF, Copenhagen

Andersen, Bent Rold (1984b) 'Rationality and Irrationality of the Nordic Welfare State', *Daedalus, 113*, 109-139

Anonymous [C. M. Olsen] (1911) *Ned med de Samvirkende Fagforbund! Et Par Ord af en Fagforeningsmand*, Bording, Copenhagen

Berglund, Sten and Ulf Lindström (1978) *The Scandinavian Party System(s)*, Studentlitteratur, Lund

Berglund, Sten and Ulf Lindström (1982) 'The Conservative Dilemma: Ideology and Vote Maximisation in Sweden', in Zig Layton-Henry (ed.) *Conservative Politics in Western Europe*, St. Martin's, New York

Borre, Ole (1984) 'Critical Electoral Change in Scandinavia', in Dalton, R. J., S. C. Flanagan and P. A. Beck *Electoral Change in Advanced Industrial Democracies: Realignment or Dealignment?* Princeton University Press, Princeton, 330-364

Borre, Ole, Hans Jørgen Nielsen, Steen Sauerberg and Torben Worre (1979) *Folketingsvalget 1977*, Akademisk Forlag, Copenhagen

Borre, Ole, Hans Jørgen Nielsen, Steen Sauerberg and Torben Worre (1976) *Vaelgere i 70'erne: Resultater fra Interviewundersøgelser ved Folketingsvalgene i 1971, 1973 og 1975*, Akademisk Forlag, Copenhagen

Einhorn, Eric S. (1975) *National Security and Domestic Politics in Post-War Denmark. Some Principal Issues, 1945-1961*, Odense University Studies in History and Social Sciences, 27, Odense

Elder, Neil, A.H. Thomas and D. Arter (1982) *The Consensual Democracies?*, Martin Robinson, Oxford

Glans, Ingemar. (n.d.) *Tabellsamling I: Stratifieringsvariabler och Partipreferenser*, mimeographed, Lund

Hancock, M. Donald, and John Logue (1984) 'Sweden: The Quest for Economic Democracy', *Polity, 17*, 248-270

Heckscher, Gunnar (1984) *The Welfare State and Beyond*, University of Minnesota Press, Minneapolis

Höglund, Z., Hannes Sköld and Fredr. Ström (1913) *Det Befästa Fattighuset*, Frams Fölag, Stockholm

Inglehart, Ronald (1981) *The Silent Revolution: Changing Values and Political Style among Western Publics*, Princeton University Press, Princeton

Lewin, Leif (1967) *Planhushallningsdebatten*, Almqvist & Wiksell, Stockholm

Lipset, Seymour M. and Stein Rokkan (1967) 'Cleavage Structures, Party Systems and Voter Alignments: An Introduction', in Lipset, Seymour M. and Stein Rokkan (1967) *Party Systems and Voter Alignments: Cross-National Perspectives*, Free Press, New York, 1-64

Logue, John (1982) *Socialism and Abundance: Radical Socialism in the Danish Welfare State*, University of Minnesota Press, Minneapolis

Logue, John (1985a) 'Stable Democracy Without Majorities? Scandinavian Parliamentary Government Today,' *Scandinavian Review 73*, (Autumn), 39-47.

Logue, John (1985b) 'Will Success Spoil the Welfare State? Solidarity and Egotism in Scandinavia', *Dissent,32* , 96-104

Pedersen, Mogens N (1981) *Denmark: The Breakdown of a Working Multiparty System?*', Institut for Samfundsvidenskab Working papers, Odense University

Petersson, Olof (1977) *Valundersökningar. Rapport 2. Väljarna och Valet 1976*, Statistiska centralbyran, Stockholm

Petersson, Olof (1984) *Folkstyrelse och Statsmakt i Norden*, Diskurs, Uppsala

Rehn, Gösta (1984) 'The Wages of Success', *Daedalus, 113*, 137-168

Samuelsson, Kurt (1968) *From Great Power to Welfare State*, Allen and Unwin, London

Statistisk Sentralbyrå (1974) *Stortingsvalget 1973*, 2, Statistisk Sentralbyrå, Oslo

Tarschys, Daniel (1974) 'Cultural vs. Institutional Power: The Role of the Swedish CP in National Politics', mimeographed, Stockholm

Wilensky, Harold J (1976) *The 'New Corporatism', Centralization, and the Welfare State*, Sage, London

Chapter Nine

Continuity and Change in Britain

George Breckenridge

The British party system is in a state of flux. Both the Social Democratic Party (SDP) and the revived Liberal Party, competing together as the Social Democratic-Liberal Alliance, have been challenging the predominant position which Labour and the Conservatives have occupied throughout the postwar period. Three party competition is not unprecedented in British politics but it is unusual. Unlike most Western European systems, the predominant pattern since the development of modern parties in the 1870s has been two-party competition. The Liberal and Conservative Parties dominated politics from 1869 to 1918, while the Labour and Conservative parties were the only serious contenders for power between 1931 and 1981.

The impetus towards a two-party system has been greatly reinforced by a tradition of one-party government and the electoral system. Although minor parties have occasionally been able to deprive the principal parties of a majority in the House of Commons, single party governments have been the rule; coalition governments have been formed only in times of crisis. The use of single member districts and a plurality decision rule has worked to the disadvantage of third parties. Unless they are able to rely on regional pockets of support (the case of the Ulster Unionists and the Liberals after their decline) third parties have experienced difficulty commanding sufficient resources and credibility to survive (Bogdanov and Butler 1983).

Forced to compete nationally and present themselves as an alternate government, British parties have needed broad, moderate appeals to be successful. A. Lawrence Lowell, writing at the beginning of this century, contrasted the typical continental European party 'of fixed political creed' with the 'opportunist' Liberal and Conservative Parties of Britain, which he characterised as 'instruments of government, representing general political tendencies...(whose) proximate aim (is) to get into power' (Lowell 1914:97). Such parties have of necessity been coalitions of interests and ideological tendencies and the maintenance of party unity is always a major preoccupation for them. One of the strengths of the Conservative Party has been its ability to minimise internal struggles even when, for example since 1975, it has been badly divided over policy. Both the Liberal and Labour parties, on the other hand, have at times been greatly weakened by internal warfare. Nevertheless, because of the electoral system, the splitting off of significant groups from the major parties has been rare and has only occurred when an alternative electoral alliance was available, for example, when the Liberal Unionists moved to the Conservatives after 1868 or, more recently, when discontented Labour politicians formed the Social Democratic Party (SDP) which allied with the Liberals in 1981.

Although the principal focus of this chapter is the contemporary British party system, the longer sweep of British electoral politics provides an opportunity to examine continuity and change over time. Recent changes in the party system will be examined in the light of the demise of the nineteenth century Liberal-Conservative system and the rise of the class-based Labour-Conservative system in the twentieth century.

The Liberal-Conservative System, 1869-1918

The formative period for modern party politics followed the second extension of the franchise in 1867. This eliminated the remaining patron controlled seats in the House of Commons and forced the parliamentary elites to develop national organisations in order to appeal to the electorate on the basis of party loyalty. The characteristic British party structures date from this period: a central party headquarters, a national organisation of constituency supporters, and an annual party conference at which the leaders rally the party faithful (McKenzie 1963).

In the election of 1869, the loose coalition of Whigs, Radicals and Peelites, which had composed most governments since 1846, came together as the Liberal Party under Gladstone's leadership, behind a banner of carefully modulated reformism and opposition to privilege and oppression (Vincent 1966). At the same time, Disraeli created the modern Conservative Party by broadening the Tory base of the rural gentry and Anglican clergy. He appealed to segments of the working class by defending traditional institutions, glorifying the Empire, and advertising a paternalistic concern for the 'condition of the people' (Blake 1970). Disraeli's 1874 victory confirmed the new system of two broadly-based moderate parties, a development unique in Europe.

The basis of the division was religion; not Protestant-Catholic since Britain was overwhelmingly Protestant, nor religious-secular since religious observance was still widespread, but rather between the non-conformist churches, to whom the Liberals appealed, and the established and socially dominant Anglican church. The reformist and conservative appeals of the parties fitted the contrasting historical experience and world views of the two religious camps, perpetuated, in England at least, through the predominance of church schools until the beginning of the twentieth century (Wald 1983).

Table 9.1 MPs Elected at General Elections By Party, 1868-1910

	Liberal	Conservative	Liberal Unionist	Labour	Irish Nationalist
1868	387	271	-	-	-
1874	302	350	-	-	-
1880	416	236	-	-	-
1885	319	249	-	-	86
1886	191	316	77	-	86
1892	271	268	46	-	81
1895	177	340	71	-	82
1900	183	334	68	2	82
1906	399	132	24	29	83
1910J	274	240	32	40	82
1910D	271	236	36	42	84

Sources: F.W.S. Craig, (1977) *British Parliamentary Results, 1832-1885*, Macmillan, London. F.W.S. Craig, (1976) *British Electoral Facts 1885-1975*, Macmillan, London.

Initially, the Liberals were the dominant party (table 9.1). However, following the doubling of the electorate in 1885 to include most working class males, the Conservatives were able to shake loose several of the elements of the Liberal coalition and become the dominant party. Nationalism had been growing in Ireland and the enlargement of the electorate enabled the Irish Nationalist Party to take most of the Irish seats away from the Liberals. Gladstone's subsequent decision to support Irish Home Rule in turn resulted in many former Whigs and businessmen joining the Liberal Unionists. This was essentially a middle-class revolt against an excess of reform (James 1978). The Liberal Unionists concluded an electoral compact with the Conservatives and eventually merged with them. The extension of the franchise also set off a thirty year struggle between the Liberals and advocates of independent labour representation for the allegiance of the working class. The Independent Labour Party, a socialist organisation, was established in 1892, but it was not until some of the trade unions were persuaded to set up the Labour Representation Committee (which became the Labour Party) in 1900 that any headway was made (Pelling 1965). The new party remained in a weak position because socialists and trade unionists could not agree on a distinctive agenda and because of wide working class support for the Liberals' reform agenda. The Liberals swept back into power in 1906. However an informal electoral pact between the two parties allowed Labour to win a limited number of seats in the elections of 1906 and 1910.

In spite of the increasing importance of class issues after 1885, religious culture remained the principal basis of the party system until the First World War. It was the war that brought the first modern British two-party system to an end (Wald 1983).

The Labour-Conservative System, 1918-1940

By the end of the 1920s class had replaced religion as the basis of political competition, and collectivist values had replaced the individual values of the Victorian era (Beer 1969). The Liberal Party was well on its way to political marginality and had been 'replaced' by the Labour Party which had finally broken through to major party status.

The war demoralised the Liberal elites and divided them into two factions based on loyalty to Lloyd George or Asquith. The Liberals' agenda of institutional reform was completed with the creation of the Irish Free State in 1920 and new ideas such as legislative devolution and proportional representation aroused little interest. By prolonging his coalition with the Conservatives after the war Lloyd George precluded the possibility of appealing to the working class with interventionist policies. The innovative 'new deal' proposals of 1929 came too late.

At the same time, trade union enthusiasm for the Labour Party had grown steadily and an increase in union membership which started before the war gave the unions a new confidence and aggressiveness

Table 9.2 MPs and Share General Election Vote by Party, 1918-1935

| | Conservative | | Labour | | Liberal | |
	MPs	% Vote	MPs	% Vote	MPs	% Vote
1918	382	38.6	57	20.8	163	25.6
1922	344	38.5	142	29.7	115	28.8
1923	258	38.0	191	30.7	158	29.7
1924	412	46.8	151	33.3	40	17.8
1929	260	38.1	287	37.1	59	23.6
1931	522	60.7	52	30.8	36	7.0
1935	429	53.3	154	38.1	21	6.8

Sources: F.W.S. Craig (1978) *British Electoral Facts, 1885-1975*, Macmillan, London.

which galvanised the party (McKibbin 1974). The party structure was reorganised to allow for individual membership in addition to the mass affiliation of their members by the trade unions. This opened the party to those who were neither socialists nor trade unionists but did not change the party's collectivist model of internal democracy by which delegates to the annual conference cast the block votes of their union or local party organisations. In its 1918 constitution the Labour Party committed itself for the first time to socialism, 'the common ownership of the means of production, distribution and exchange'. The socialist commitment separated Labour from the Liberals and set an idealistic but imprecise goal which united the disparate elements in the party such as socialists, trade unionists and the disillusioned radicals who had left the Liberals during the war. At the same time, the Labour Party believed deeply in democracy and shared the general British confidence in the parliamentary system. The Labour Party's sense of how socialism would be achieved was not derived from Marx but from the Victorian faith of its founders in the inevitability of moral progress.

It was, in fact, the Conservative Party which benefitted most from the class polarisation of the electorate. The emergence of the 'socialist threat' enabled it to position itself as the defender of traditional values and manager of the status quo. By the end of the 1920s it had attracted most of the Liberal vote (Butler and Stokes 1971:108) consolidating the bulk of the middle class behind it while retaining a minority of the working-class vote.

The realignment of the 1920s was based on working-class hopes and middle-class fears, not on an actual programme for change. In spite of the prolonged depression of the interwar years, the Conservatives were able to wield power for all but three years between 1922 and 1940 by promising nothing more than the status quo. Labour improved its share of the vote at each election in the 1920s, becoming the largest party in 1929. Its advance was halted, however, by the revelation during its second minority government (1929-1931) that Labour had developed no alternative to the rigid economic orthodoxy of the times.

Faced with international depression, the Labour Government rejected both the programme of intervention and nationalisation put forward by the affiliated ILP (Skidelsky 1975) and the new deal proposals of the Liberals. In the end, its orthodox deflationary policy came into direct conflict with the interests of its supporters and the government fell apart over the international banks' requirement that unemployment benefits be cut (Skidelsky 1967; Marquand 1977). The party chose the defense of the working class over power and only a handful of ministers followed Prime Minister MacDonald into the Conservative-dominated National Government. In spite of its failure in office, Labour retained the loyalty of much of the working class, holding 30% of the vote at the election in 1931. The Liberal Party had reunited behind Lloyd George's new programme in 1929 but failed to increase its seats significantly. With the formation of the National Government the Liberals split again, leaving Labour with an effective monopoly of opposition.

The passivity of politics in Britain throughout the 1930s is testimony to popular faith in the parliamentary system and strength of the party loyalties forged in the 1920s. The Depression produced neither the policy innovations of the American New Dealers or the Scandinavian Social Democrats, nor the social turmoil of other European nations. Fascist and Communist attempts to mobilise the unemployed drew little support in Britain. Trade union expectations that change could be brought about by industrial confrontation had died with the general strike in 1926.

For the Conservatives the period was one of increasing rigidity and staleness. The leaders who had taken charge of the party in 1922 continued to rule without effective challenge. For Labour, it was a time of reappraisal. In defeat, the party reaffirmed its commitment to achieving a socialist society by parliamentary means and rejected the strategy of a 'national front' against the Conservatives (Pimlott 1979). As a generation of leaders with new intellectual expertise and municipal experience took control, an interventionist Labour programme began to take shape (Addison 1975). Labour's decision to lay aside its pacifist tradition in the face of fascism and its support for British rearmament after 1937 paved the way for its return to office in the wartime coalition government (Cowling 1975).

The interwar period had seen the emergence of a new two-party system based on class identification but the policies of the two parties were still largely based on the ideas of the pre-World War I era. The wartime coalition provided a transition to a new policy agenda which both parties adopted and twenty years of two-party competition. Ironically, although Liberal intellectuals such as Beveridge and Keynes played key roles, their ideas were appropriated by the Labour and Conservative Parties, while the Liberal Party was reduced to a handful of rural seats in Wales and Scotland.

The Building of the Postwar Consensus, 1940-1964

The Coalition Government had a particular importance for the Labour Party. It provided the new generation of leaders with experience in office, and planning for postwar reconstruction fleshed out Labour's key policy aspirations. The Beveridge Report provided a plan for universal social insurance while the new Keynesian economics, the most important product of the interwar stagnation, removed the stigma from government intervention, legitimised government management of the economy and made a full-fledged welfare state possible (Winch 1969; Harris 1977). As a result, Labour faced the postwar electorate with experienced leaders and policies attuned to the general desire for change, while the Conservatives, relying on Churchill and pre-war fears of socialism, equivocated about policy. Labour increased its middle class support and swept to power with a majority.

In power from 1945 to 1951, Labour implemented its manifesto. It maintained full employment, established a comprehensive welfare system, and granted full recognition to the trade unions for the first time. It created a 'mixed' economy through its major programme of nationalisation. The widespread pre-war belief that full employment would only be possible in a planned economy had been demolished by Keynes in 1936, and the Labour Government's intent to retain the comprehensive system of wartime economic controls gave way to pressures for their removal. The alternative was Keynesian fiscal management and it was Hugh Gaitskell in 1950 who was 'the first consciously Keynesian Chancellor' (Winch 1969:280).

The existence of non-socialist legitimation for most of Labour's accomplishments and the popularity of the welfare state made it

Table 9.3 MPs and Share of General Election Vote by Party, 1945-1987

	Conservative MPs	Conservative % Vote	Labour MPs	Labour % Vote	Liberal[a] MPs	Liberal[a] %Vote	Nationalists MPs	Nationalists % Vote
1945	210	39.6	393	48.0	12	9.0	-	-
1950	298	43.5	315	46.1	9	9.1	-	-
1951	321	48.0	295	48.8	6	2.6	-	-
1955	345	49.7	277	46.4	6	2.7	-	-
1959	365	49.3	258	43.9	6	5.9	-	-
1964	304	43.4	317	44.1	9	11.2	-	-
1966	253	41.9	364	48.1	12	8.5	-	-
1970	330	46.4	288	43.1	6	7.5	1	1.7
1974F	297	37.9	301	37.2	14	19.3	9	2.6
1974O	277	35.8	319	39.2	13	18.3	14	3.5
1979	339	43.9	269	37.0	11	13.8	4	2.0
1983	397	42.4	209	27.6	23	25.4	4	1.5
1987	375	42.3	229	30.8	22	22.6	6	1.7

Sources: F.W.S. Craig (1976) *British Electoral Facts, 1885-1975*, Macmillan, London. D. Butler and D. Kavanagh (1980) *The British General Election 1979*, Macmillan, London. D. Butler and D. Kavanagh (1984) *The British General Election 1983*, Macmillan, London. *Manchester Guardian Weekly*, June 21, 1987.

Note: a. Liberal - SDP Alliance in 1983 and 1987.

possible for the Conservative Party to accept them. In foreign policy, Labour's embrace of the American alliance, which had led to the development of British nuclear weapons and rearmament at the time of the Korean war, posed no problems for the Conservatives. The Conservatives' acceptance of the new status quo and middle-class weariness with austerity brought them back to power in 1951, in time to benefit from the world investment boom, which brought unprecedented economic growth to Britain and enabled them to stay in power for the next thirteen years.

The policies of the two parties thus converged on a new consensus on the primacy of full employment, the mixed economy, and the welfare state. In foreign policy both sides supported NATO and the American alliance and the dissolution of the Empire. While each party retained a distinctive class base and cluster of associated interest groups and continued to clash sharply in style and rhetoric, neither proposed to amend the consensus in any major way. As table 9.3 indicates, the major parties were able to mobilise almost universal support for the new consensus. The two-party share of the vote soared from 90 percent in 1931 to over 96 percent in the 1950s, a period in which voter turnout and party and union membership reached new peaks.

The postwar consensus had a major impact on the ideologies and internal balance of both parties. Conservative acceptance of the consensus was confirmed by the prosperity and political successes of the fifties. An attempt by some ministers in 1958 to make inflation control rather than the maintenance of full employment the focus of economic policy led to their resignations.

The Labour Party was proud of its achievements in office. It had radically improved the conditions and opportunities for working-class people, which had always been the principal component of its vision of socialism. For the trade unions, their enhanced status, along with full employment and a benevolently neutral role for government, had created the ideal conditions in which to exercise their rights of 'free collective bargaining'. Nevertheless, the fifties were a time of turmoil and transition for the party.

From 1950 to 1955 a group of left-wing MPs around Aneurin Bevan fought bitterly but in vain to commit the party to a further programme of nationalisation and a more neutral foreign policy. The Bevanites were supported by many of the local activists, but the party conference and its National Executive Committee remained firmly controlled by an alliance between the parliamentary leaders and the principal trade union leaders. In 1955, Hugh Gaitskell, with solid union support, easily defeated Bevan's bid for the party leadership.

Gaitskell wanted to bring Labour thinking in line with the changes in the role of government and in the functioning of capitalism, which the party had helped to bring about. In an argument best laid out in Anthony Crosland's *The Future of Socialism* in 1956, socialism in an affluent society was no longer about the ownership of the means of production but about creating equality. The urgency of the task was increased by Labour's third, successively worse defeat by the Conservatives in 1959. At a time when prosperity seemed assured and class and ideology increasingly irrelevant, the effective demise of the Labour Party was widely predicted (Abrams *et al.* 1960). Gaitskell's attempt to remove Clause Four, the commitment to socialism, from the party constitution was rebuffed by the unions, but a revised list of policy objectives was adopted in which nationalisation was downgraded.

The most serious challenge to the policy consensus and to Gaitskell's leadership came not over domestic policy but over the party's continued support for British nuclear weapons. At the 1960 conference the established policy was defeated when several unions deserted the leadership. The defeat also foreshadowed the rise of a 'new left' opposition within the party. Bevan had accepted the nuclear weapons policy for the sake of party unity before his death in 1960 and the anti-nuclear campaign was led by the extra-parliamentary Campaign for Nuclear Disarmament (CND) which had been founded in 1958. It required all of Gaitskell's influence with the unions and an organised campaign within the party by his social democratic supporters to reverse the defeat in 1961 and save his leadership.

Faltering economic growth enabled Labour to return to power. With the end of the investment boom, renewed pressure on the British balance of payments led the Conservatives into the first of a series of unsuccessful attempts by both parties to reduce inflationary pressures by limiting the rate of growth of wages, breaking the postwar truce with the unions. Harold Wilson, who became leader on the premature death of Gaitskell in 1963, presented Labour as a modern meritocratic party capable of restarting economic growth through national indicative planning and the encouragement of new technology. In 1964 the Labour Party slipped past the Conservatives. Labour substantially increased its margin in 1966. Thus the Labour Party was finally installed as the manager of the system whose foundations it had laid twenty years before but at a time when the problems built into the Keynesian system were becoming increasingly apparent.

The Two-Party System Under Pressure, 1964-1983

The defeat of the Conservatives in 1964 and 1966 did not mark, as Wilson expected, the long term replacement of the Conservatives by Labour as the normal governing party in Britain. Rather it marked the beginning of a series of alternating one-term cabinets in which successive governments were defeated for failing to restore the prosperity and social harmony of the fifties.

There were in fact two periods. In the first, the pendulum continued to swing between the two parties. During the elections of 1964, 1966, and 1970, party loyalties remained strong and the revival of the Liberal Party and the stirrings of the Nationalists in Scotland and Wales remained limited. Between 1970 and 1974, however, the strength of party loyalties declined (Sarlvik and Crewe 1983:333-8). The resulting volatility not only opened the political arena to third parties but opened up serious internal divisions in each party. In the

Conservative Party, insurgents captured the leadership in 1975. In the Labour Party a guerilla war erupted and eventually led to the establishment of the SDP in 1981.

The dealignment of the electorate can be explained by two sets of factors: the failure to solve economic problems and changes in the political culture. The primary factor was the failure of governments to produce the stable economic growth which voters expected and the parties promised. The largest drop in the strength of party identification occurred between 1970 and 1974. The problem was how to dampen the inflationary pressures accompanying full employment without creating unemployment. The Keynesians in each party adopted the same strategy. Both parties sought to reach agreement with the union movement on wage limitation and failed (Dorfman 1973). Then each attempted to coerce the unions and was blocked by their resistance.

The second set of factors was a change in attitudes. Although there was no 'collapse of the civic culture' as Samuel Beer (1982) has argued, the generation which began entering politics in the 1960s had little reverence for the achievements of their elders and considerable impatience with the institutions which had produced them. The 1960s were marked by increased extra-parliamentary agitation, including CND marches at the beginning and student turmoil at the end, as well as increased strike activity, mostly initiated from the shop floor.

Ideology was also reinjected into politics. The focus of debate shifted from the achievements of the Keynesian consensus to the compromises it involved. Neo-liberals attacked Keynsianism for conceding too much to socialism, while neo-marxists attacked it for falling short of socialism. Neo-liberals in the Conservative Party drew their intellectual authority from Milton Friedman's monetarist critique of Keynes and from a rediscovery of Friedrich Hayek. The emergence of Marxist ideas as a significant force in the Labour Party for the first time reflected the flowering of Marxist scholarship after its release from its Stalinist straightjacket.

The Labour Party, 1964 to 1970

Soon after 1966, the Wilson government was faced with an economic crisis. In a lengthy, losing struggle to avoid devaluing the pound, the government abandoned its national economic plan and cut back social spending, dropping policies which had helped unite the party. Equally serious was a sharp deterioration in the government's relations with the unions.

The relationship between the party and the unions had long been governed by an informal but rigorous demarcation between their respective political and industrial roles. Since the 1920s a working alliance between the leaders of the largest unions and the parliamentary leaders had enabled the latter to use the unions' block votes at the party conference to control the party organisation. In 1948, when a Labour Government had asked the unions to limit wage increases, the unions had reluctantly come to the aid of the government. However, by the 1960s, things had changed. The group of right-wing leaders of the largest unions who had controlled the political voice of the union movement since the 1920s had dissolved. The personal influence that union leaders like Ernest Bevin had wielded in the 1930s and 1940s had exaggerated the degree of political unity among the unions (Minkin 1978) and disguised the weakness of the Trade Union Congress. In the 1960s increased militancy by local activists not only made it more difficult for union leaders to accede to government request's for wage restraint but was also producing a new breed of militant leaders in some of the largest unions (Panitch 1976).

The Wilson government was increasingly concerned about the impact of strikes on the economy and on Labour's popularity. To demonstrate their willingness to discipline the unions, Wilson and his Secretary for Employment, Barbara Castle, a Bevanite, tried in 1969 to impose a new legal code on the unions (Dorfman 1979), but this was blocked by a revolt in cabinet and parliament.

These developments had a major impact on the Labour Party. Faced with opposition to its economic policies from the unions as well as from the left, the Labour leadership suffered an unprecedented series of defeats at the party conference. The government's refusal to change course shattered the myth that policy was determined by the party. The end of the alliance with the union leaders deprived the parliamentary leadership of its control of the party. The party conference became a battleground between an increasingly aggressive left and an increasingly defensive right. By 1973 a loose alliance of constituency representatives and union leaders, opposed to the leadership of the caucus, were in control of the National Executive Committee (NEC).

The Conservative Party, 1964 to 1979

Defeat in 1964, after thirteen years in office, triggered changes in the Conservative Party. Edward Heath succeeded Alec Douglas-Home in 1965. Re-thinking their policies, but motivated less by ideology than by technocratic pragmatism, Conservatives began to rely more on market forces and move away from intervention in the economy. The union problem was to be solved by a comprehensive legal framework for industrial relations.

In office from 1970 to 1974, the Conservatives faced deteriorating trade relations and soaring oil prices several years before North Sea oil became available. Unwillingness to risk rising unemployment drove the government back to interventionist economic policies, a move later scorned by neo-liberals as a pusillanimous U-turn. The unions responded to the Industrial Relations Act in 1972 with a combination of resistance and confrontation which undercut the government efforts to restrain wages and opened up the prospect of legal and industrial chaos. A strike over wages by the National Union of Mineworkers in the winter of 1973-74 tempted Heath to appeal to the electorate in February 1974 for support against the unions.

Heath's defeats in February and October 1974 doomed his leadership. His decision however to defend his government's record by seeking re-election as leader strengthened the neo-liberal challenge mounted by Margaret Thatcher and helped her to vault into the leadership. Thatcher's repudiation of the party's postwar Keynesian policies, together with her aggressive 'politics of conviction' have been divisive. However, the Conservative instinct for power and obsession with party unity have stifled overt opposition and compelled Mrs. Thatcher to work with her opponents. The electoral successes in 1979, 1983 and 1987 along with the Conservative tradition of conceding great personal authority to a successful leader, have kept the initiative in her hands.

The Labour Party, 1970 to 1983

The vulnerability of the parliamentary leadership to the ideological changes in the party became evident after Labour's defeat in 1970. The left used its growing strength on the NEC and at the party conference to attempt to dictate the policy of the next Labour government. Proposals for a new industrial strategy involving more public ownership and increased government control over private investment were approved (Hatfield 1978). Meanwhile parliamentary and trade union leaders scrambled to renegotiate their relationship. The former needed to bolster their control of the party machinery and restore the credibility of their economic policies, while the latter needed support against Conservative attempts to regulate the union movement. The result was the 'Social Contract', concluded by party and trade union leaders in 1974. Trade unions agreed to try to limit wage increases in exchange for specific legislative commitments, an arrangement which drew the union leaders more deeply into policy determination than at any time in the party's history.

The increasing power of the left in early 1970s also divided the right. Foreshadowing the disagreements which finally split the party in 1981, parliamentary leaders disagreed about making concessions to the left in order to maintain party unity, as Wilson wanted, or standing and fighting on principle, as Gaitskell had done in 1960. The immediate issue was British entry into the European Economic Community. Abandoning his previous government's endorsement of EEC membership, Wilson opposed the terms of entry and promised the left that a national referendum (the first in British history) would be held on EEC membership.

Labour emerged as the marginal victor in the elections of 1974 but both major parties lost substantial ground to third parties. In spite of the shift to the left reflected in Labour's election manifesto, the tradition of renominating sitting MPs meant that there was less change in the composition of the parliamentary party and almost none in the composition of the Labour Government. To the frustration of the left, whose policies were either watered down or abandoned, there was substantial continuity in government policy. This time, however, there was close consultation between the cabinet and the principal union leaders, which protected the government from the party conference. The only change in policy was the proposal for elected assemblies in Scotland and Wales. Fearing the loss of seventy Labour seats to Scottish or Welsh nationalists, the government tried to hold a reluctant party behind the scheme. However, this radical constitutional change was defeated in a referendum in Wales and supported by an insufficient majority in Scotland.

The social contract with the unions came under increasing strain as inflation kept rising and the government demanded lower wage increases. Although the government and the unions managed to agree on wage restraint between 1975 and 1978, the agreement with the unions gave way to a series of strikes during the winter of 1978-79. James Callaghan, who had succeeded Wilson in 1976, negotiated a pact with the Liberals in 1977-78 in order to retain a majority. Callaghan also delayed elections to the last minute, but Labour lost the 1979 election. In the process, the rise of the Liberal Party was halted and the Nationalists lost most of the ground they had gained in 1974.

Defeat in 1979 exposed the Labour right to the anger and organisational skills of the left. Since the initial success of the left in the early 1970s, the Labour Party had become a magnet for a variety of Trotskyite groups. The 1973 abolition of the proscribed list of organisations in which membership had been ruled incompatible with membership of the Labour Party facilitated an influx of new activists (McCormick 1980). Although the party had always patrolled its left flank to avoid association with non-democratic politics, after 1973 the boundary was open. There were now 'no enemies on the left'. In many constituencies where party membership and activity had declined (Whiteley 1983) it was relatively easy for activists to take control.

The main goal of the left was to amend the party constitution to give the party organisation greater control over the parliamentary party and Labour governments. The 1980 party conference passed amendments which required the reselection of MPs between elections and removed the election of the party leader from the parliamentary party to an electoral college in which trade unions had forty per cent of the votes and the parliamentary party and the constituency parties each had thirty per cent. In November 1980 (the last leadership election under the old system) the designation of Michael Foot, a popular survivor of the old Bevanite left, over Dennis Healey, whose appeal to voters was much stronger but whose deflationary policies had angered the unions, signalled the surrender of the parliamentary right to the new balance of power in the party. This, along with the prospect of an electoral alliance with the Liberals finally brought about a formal split in the Labour Party. Three of Callaghan's former ministers, David Owen, Shirley Williams, and William Rodgers, formed the Social Democratic Party in March 1981, along with Roy Jenkins who was returning to British politics after four years as president of the EEC Commission. They were joined by more than twenty Labour MPs and one Conservative MP.

Elections in the 1980s

The Conservative Government of 1979 was the first government dedicated to abandoning major facets of the postwar consensus and determined to engineer a shift in the balance of political forces and in British political values. The central change in policy was a willingness to deflate the economy to squeeze out inflation and enforce business efficiency without regard to the level of unemployment. Allowing unemployment to rise ran counter to the established wisdom of the postwar period and the sagging popularity of the government in 1981 underlined the risk it was taking. However British success in the Falklands war in 1982 put Mrs. Thatcher's position in the party beyond challenge and enabled her to replace cabinet skeptics, ruling out another Conservative U-turn. The big Conservative majority in the election of 1983 vindicated the neo-liberal strategy, but the decline in the Conservative vote indicated that the state of the Labour Party was a major factor in the Conservative's success.

The 1983 election was a disaster for Labour. Divided by a decade of ideological struggle, with its leadership and policies dictated by party militants rather than electoral needs, it won its lowest share of the vote since 1918. Labour's share of the working-class vote, which had already fallen substantially since 1966, plummeted to 38%, only five points above the Conservative share (Crewe 1983). Further, with the arrival of the Social Democratic-Liberal Alliance, Labour had lost its monopoly of opposition to the Conservatives.

The Alliance had a qualified success. It did considerably better than the Liberals had done on their own, but since it drew very evenly across class and regional divisions (McAllister and Rose 1984), and therefore across constituencies, its twenty-three seats were grossly disproportionate to its 25.4 per cent of vote (table 9.3).

Between 1983 and 1987 the Conservatives pursued the same mix of policies. Unemployment remained high and disproportionately concentrated in northern and peripheral areas. The Conservatives' low point in the polls came in early 1986 when mishandling of a dispute over military contracts led to the resignations of two prominent ministers.

After the debacle in 1983, Neil Kinnock, from the 'soft left', replaced Foot as leader of the Labour Party. Building an alliance with the right, he was able to control the NEC and the parliamentary party. Kinnock's strategy was to isolate the 'hard left' (several prominent members of the Trotskyist Militant Tendency were expelled from the party), play down nationalisation, and concentrate on unemployment and the social services. The price for maintaining party unity was retaining an anti-nuclear defense policy. This unified the left and was close to Kinnock's heart, but it was also the issue on which the party was most out of step with the electorate.

In the Alliance, David Owen (who replaced Jenkins as the leader of the SDP) resisted efforts to merge the two parties. The Alliance made gains in local government elections and won by-elections from both the Conservatives and Labour. However, interparty coordination on defense proved to be difficult because important elements in the Liberal Party supported an anti-nuclear position.

Despite considerable fluidity in opinion polls and by-elections, the 1987 General Election results were close to those of 1983. Conservatives won a third term in office, something which no party had accomplished under the same leader since the early nineteenth century. Despite predictions of a greatly reduced majority, the Conservatives secured 42.3 per cent of the vote (a loss of .1 per cent) and won 375 seats, 100 more than the collective total of the opposition parties. Under Kinnock, Labour ran a highly professional campaign and struggled to disassociate itself from the confrontational politics of its hard left. However, it was handicapped by its policy of unilateral nuclear disarmament. Labour won 30.8 per cent of the vote (an increase of 3.3 per cent) but only gained an additional 21 seats, mainly in northern cities and Scotland, for a total of 229.

The biggest losers in the 1987 election were the Social Democrats and Liberals. In the face of strong campaigns by the other parties, the Alliance was unable to break out of the third party trap. Despite its leaders' hopes, the Alliance declined from 25.4 per cent in 1983 to 22.6 per cent in 1987, ending up with only 22 seats (17 Liberals and 5 Social Democrats), five fewer than the 27 which they held at dissolution. Although the Alliance's problems were blamed on its dual leadership, the poor showing reflected the difficulties of competing in a polarised election campaign under a single member district system. Encouraged to vote for or against a continuation of the Thatcher government, many potential Alliance supporters rejected the centre.

Thus, by the end of the 1980s, in spite of Conservative dominance in the House of Commons, the future of the British party system remained uncertain. The failure of the Alliance to advance in 1987 seemed to reaffirm two-party competition. Yet, the failure of the Conservatives and particularly the Labour Party to regain the levels of support attained in the 1950s and 1960s continued to provide substantial opportunities for a third party. Divided opposition and the single member district system had contributed greatly to the Conservatives' successes in the 1980s. Because neither are likely to change in the immediate future, continued Conservative government in the 1990s remains the most likely prospect.

Conclusion

The first modern British party system, based on religious loyalty, broke up after the First World War when the Liberal Party was no longer able to contain the hopes of the fully enfranchised working class. The emergence of the Labour Party forced a realignment of loyalties in the 1920s, producing a new two-party system based on class identification. The process of integrating the working class into the British parliamentary system was taken a step further when Labour came to power after the Second World War and executed a major policy shift which the Conservatives accepted, consolidating the two-party system around consensus on the welfare state and the maintenance of full employment by Keynesian economic management.

By the late 1960s, the expectation of prosperity and social harmony was no longer being fulfilled by either party, accelerating the erosion of the class loyalties on which the two-party system was based and opening the door to third party competition. Electoral failure led to a successful ideological revolt against the Keynesian consensus within both major parties, the course of which was shaped by the structure and ethos of each party. The resulting increase in ideological influence on party policy at a time when the need to persuade the electorate had increased, allowed the Social Democratic-Liberal Alliance to draw support evenly across classes and make inroads into the support of both major parties in 1983. Although the Alliance was less successful in 1987, the absence of any stable electoral realignment indicated that electoral volatility and three-party competition were likely to continue for some time to come.

References

Abrams, M., R.Rose and R. Hinden (1960) *Must Labour Lose?* Penguin, London

Addison, P. (1975) *The Road to 1945*, Jonathan Cape, London

Beer, S.F. (1969) *British Politics in the Collectivist Age*, Vintage, New York

Beer, S.F. (1982) *Britain Against Itself*, Norton, New York

Blake, R. (1970) *The Conservative Party from Peel to Churchill*, Eyre and Spottiswoode, London

Bogdanov, V. and D. Butler (1983) *Democracy and Elections: Electoral Systems and Their Consequences*, Cambridge University Press, Cambridge

Butler, D. and D. Stokes (1971) *Political Change in Britain*, College Edition, St. Martin's, New York

Cowling, M. (1975) *The Impact of Hitler: British Politics and British Policy 1933-1940*, Cambridge University Press, Cambridge

Crewe, I. (1983) 'The Electorate: Partisan Dealignment Ten Years On', *West European Politics*, 6:183-215

Dorfman, G. (1973) *Wage Politics in Britain 1945-1967*, Iowa State University Press, Ames, Iowa

Dorfman, G. (1979) *Government versus Trade Unionism in British Politics since 1968*, Macmillan, London

Harris, J. (1977) *William Beveridge*, Clarendon, Oxford

Hatfield, M. (1978) *The House the Left Built: Inside Labour Policy Making 1970-1975*, Gollancz, London

James, R.R. (1978) *The British Revolution: British Politics 1880-1939*; Methuen, London

Lowell, A.L. (1914) *The Government of England, Vol. 2*, Macmillan, New York

Marquand, D. (1977) *Ramsay MacDonald*, Jonathan Cape, London

McAllister, I. and R. Rose (1984) *The National Competition for Votes: The British General Election 1983*, Frances Pinter, London

McCormick, P. (1980) 'The Labour Party: Three Unnoticed Changes,' *British Journal of Political Science, 10*, 381-388

McKenzie, R. T. (1963) *British Political Parties*, Mercury, London

McKibbin, R. (1974) *The Evolution of the Labour Party, 1910-1924*, Oxford University Press, Oxford

Minkin, L. (1978) *The Labour Party Conference: A Study in the Politics of Intra-Party Democracy*, Lane, London

Panitch, L. (1976) *Social Democracy and Industrial Militancy*, Cambridge University Press, Cambridge

Pelling, H. (1965) *The Origins of the Labour Party, 1880-1900*, Clarendon, Oxford

Pimlott, B. (1979) *Labour and the Left in the 1930s*, Cambridge University Press, Cambridge

Sarlvik, B. and I. Crewe (1983) *Decade of Dealignment*, Cambridge University Press, Cambridge

Skidelsky, R. (1967) *The Politicians and the Slump: the Labour Government of 1929-1931*, Macmillan, London

Skidelsky, R. (1975) *Oswald Mosely*, Macmillan, London

Vincent, J. (1966) *The Formation of the British Liberal Party, 1857-1868*, Penguin, London

Wald, K. (1983) *Crosses on the Ballot: Patterns of British Voter Alignment Since 1889*, Princeton University Press, Princeton, New Jersey

Whiteley, P. (1983) *The Labour Party in Crisis*, Methuen, London

Winch, D. (1969) *Economics and Politics: A Historical Study*, Hodder and Stoughton, London

Chapter Ten

Ireland: From Predominance to Competition

R.K. Carty

The 1980s opened in Ireland amid unprecedented political turmoil. Three general elections within eighteen months each produced a change in government. Two of those elections were precipitated when the usually subservient Dail (lower house) surprised itself by successively defeating the only two governments available. Fianna Fail, the governing party, whose electoral successes were universally believed to be rooted in its superior organisation, was locked in a bitter internal conflict; Fine Gael, traditionally a lethargic second party, was undergoing major organisational changes and rapid electoral growth; the Labour party seemed unable to make up its mind about whether to engage in coalition politics, while circumstances forced it to fight four consecutive elections with new leaders.

Yet for all this apparent change observers remained ambivalent about its significance. Gallagher (1981:281) argued that 'by any criteria, the continuities in Irish politics between 1960 and 1981 were far greater than the changes,' while I claimed that 'the dramatic electoral and governmental turnovers of 1981 and 1982 conspire to emphasise the profound stability of the Irish party system' (Carty 1983:ix). Such competing images of continuity and change reflect differing interpretations of the same reality. This essay examines the changes that are beginning to modify Irish parties and transform the party system. Paradoxically, this requires beginning with those things that are not changing.

At first glance the Irish party system appears stagnant. The same three parties that institutionalised electoral competition after independence not only persist, but also command the same degree of support that they had half-a-century ago. The structure of competitive relationships amongst the parties, and the substance of the differences that separate them, have changed little. To an unexpected degree stability rather than volatility characterises Irish electoral behaviour (Marsh 1985). The parochial, personalistic, and conservative dynamics of the system render it an ineffective mechanism for either political recruitment or public choice (Carty 1981a:ch 7).

Despite this, the party system is beginning to change in ways that will reshape Irish electoral competition. Though these changes are set within the parties themselves, their impact is most obvious at the level of the party system which is evolving from a predominant party system to one that is genuinely competitive. In Gordon Smith's (1978) terms this will transform the system from one that is 'indecisive' to one that is 'decisive', giving Irish elections new meanings. Although, Ireland is undergoing socio-economic change at a rate unmatched in any other West European state, the incipient reordering of party competition is unrelated to those changes. Instead it reflects the decisions and behaviours of politicians, thus confirming the 'autonomy of the political' that has characterised so much of past Irish experience (Mair 1979).

The Predominant Party System

Contemporary Irish party politics began with independence from Britain in 1922. In its aftermath new political conflicts between factions of the nationalist Sinn Fein movement led first to civil war and then to the creation of new parties. Despite considerable political confusion and volatility, by 1932 a new party system had been institutionalised. That system was interrupted by two flash parties in the 1940s but the basic alignment was not shaken. Thus, unlike many other European systems, we need look back only a generation (the founders survived into the 1960s) to discover the divisions that structure party competition.

A Political Cleavage

The Irish invented the European mass-based political party. For a century before independence a succession of parties mobilised the bulk of the population in opposition to British control. The Sinn Fein elite who won independence split over the symbolic and constitutional dimensions of the settlement with London. This politically inspired conflict, which did not correspond to any socio-economic cleavages, rippled down from the top, polarising the movement and the country, and establishing the division that structured party-building once the war ended.

Although by the early 1930s they had combined with other parliamentary notables to form Fine Gael, the moderates, in office for the first decade of state-building, paid little attention to the imperatives of political organisation (Moss 1933:ch 3). Their cautious, conservative policies had a bourgeois cast that denied the nationalist excitement which had long been the stuff of Irish politics. Fianna Fail was built by the more militant republicans. Seeing itself as the carrier of the race's historic claims, it concentrated on creating an organisation capable of mobilising the nation.

The two major parties were thus separated by a political cleavage whose substantive manifestation (the role of the British crown and empire) declined in salience over time. The cleavage persisted because the parties very existence institutionalised it, and the irredentism stimulated by Northern Ireland fueled its symbolic meaning. The two parties were not mere reflections of one another. Their origins, in government and opposition, distinguished them: Fine Gael was dull and underorganised while Fianna Fail was aggressively nationalistic and committed to nurturing a disciplined mass base and winning elections.

Labour was the third party in a bipolar system. Tied to the trade union movement it argued that class, not nationalism, was the proper basis for electoral competition. As a working class and nominally socialist party it had no natural appeal to the traditional Catholic peasantry that dominated the Irish electorate. Nationalism suffocated socialism, and Labour was condemned to a marginal role in the party system. Labour has been further weakened by its inability, in most elections, to contest every constituency (Carty 1981a:34, 54-5).

The 1932 general election, the first after it became clear Fianna Fail would play by constitutional rules, marked the institutionalisation of this new party system. These three parties are the only ones to have contested every election, attracting almost 90 per cent of the vote (table 10.1). The uneven pattern of support levels are typical of what Blondel (1968) describes as a 'two-and-a-half party system'. With half the vote Fianna Fail support has been stable for half-a-century; it has consistently outpolled Fine Gael by an average of 15 percentage points. When support for these parties slipped it went either to independents or the minor groups that sporadically appeared rather than to Labour which has managed to win but one voter in ten. This pattern persists because familial socialisation reproduces strongly held partisan allegiances in succeeding generations (Carty 1981a:81-3). Party loyalties, as measured by electoral behaviour, are strongest among Fianna Fail supporters, weakest among Labour voters. The result has

Table 10.1 Party Vote Shares 1932-1987 (in percentages)

	Fianna Fail	Fine Gael	Labour	Others[a]
1932	44.5	35.3	7.7	12.5
1933	49.7	30.5	5.7	14.1
1937	45.2	34.8	10.3	9.7
1938	51.9	33.3	10.0	4.8
1943	41.9	23.1	15.7	19.3
1944	48.9	20.5	11.5	19.1
1948	41.9	19.8	11.3	27.0
1951	46.3	25.7	11.4	16.6
1954	43.4	32.0	12.0	12.6
1957	48.6	26.6	9.1	15.7
1961	43.8	32.0	11.6	12.6
1965	47.8	33.9	15.4	2.9
1969	45.7	34.1	17.0	3.2
1973	46.2	35.1	13.7	5.0
1977	50.6	30.5	11.6	7.2
1981	45.3	36.5	9.9	8.3
1982 f	47.3	37.3	9.1	6.3
1982 n	45.2	39.2	9.4	6.3
1987	44.1	27.1	6.5	12.0
mean	46.2	30.9	11.0	11.3

Note: a. Includes minor parties and Independents and in 1987 the Progressive Democrats. The 1940s saw the rise of two flash parties.

been a set of party alignments as frozen as any of Lipset and Rokkan's (1967) social cleavage based systems.

The Parties

This is the prototypic catch-all system. Whatever their initial differences, there is now little to distinguish the parties' basic policies or appeal. Both Fianna Fail and Fine Gael claim to be centrist parties best able to provide sound economic management. Though their leadership and style has varied over the years,.compared to parties elsewhere they look remarkably alike. Labour seeks to stand apart by offering a socialist alternative but it is a fairly conventional social democratic party. It removed the concept of a 'workers republic' from its constitution in the 1930s to appease the country's conservative clergy, and only once (in 1969) did it depart from a mildly reformist

posture to run on a socialist platform (Gallagher 1982). Labour's place
in the system is reflected in its deeds rather than its words. On five
occasions since World War II it has entered Fine Gael governments
without making any significant impact on them. In general, the
policies and programmes of Irish Parties are more likely to agree than
to differ, and the clash of ideologies is almost inaudible.

Catch-all parties have heterogeneous clienteles. The social
profiles of the Irish parties not only mirror the electorate but resemble
each other (Carty 1981a:71-5). The only exception to this is the
regional character of Labour's small base: the party has never done
well in the northern or western parts of the state. However it is hardly
the party of the Dublin working class; Fianna Fail commands greater
support among every segment of the electorate, including workers.
But these differences pale in comparison to those in other nations; the
Irish case, in which none of the parties has a socially distinctive base, is
unique in western Europe.

Labour has intimate relationships with the trade unions, a few of
which are affiliated to it, but the heterogeneous cast of the parties has
meant that the other parties are not systematically tied to distinctive
interests or organisations. While governments have engaged in the
negotiation of 'national understandings' with peak business and labour
groups over the last decades, the parties themselves have played no
part in these discussions. As catch-all parties they are reluctant to
advocate any particular interest. With no links to Irish society beyond
those provided by individual politicians the parties are detached from
the policy-making process. Their concerns are electioneering,
administration and policy outcomes as they affect their voters.

Irish party organisations are shaped by their social and political
environment. The homogeneous political culture, though mediated
through British institutions, still bears the imprint of its peasant
heritage (Chubb 1982:ch. 1). Conservative, nationalistic and
anti-intellectual attitudes thrive in a society dominated by an
authoritarian Catholicism. Discipline and loyalty are held to be among
the highest political virtues, political relationships are defined in
parochial and personalistic terms, and politics and government are seen
as essentially distributive. These attitudes govern the electoral
practices of politicians and the competitive behaviours of their parties.

The electoral system - the single transferable vote in multi-
member constituencies - has been no less important. Its proportional
character (O'Leary 1979) has increased both the stability and
predictability of electoral outcomes. Previous outcomes led most to
expect elections to produce Fianna Fail governments (Carty 1981a:79).

Equally important, the transferable ballot puts running mates in direct competition with one another for the higher preferences of party voters. The result is a complex pattern of intra-party and inter-party competition in which many of the competitive turnovers take place between sitting members (TDs) and their running mates (Carty 1980, 1981b; Marsh 1985:196). In this circumstance electoral competition within parties becomes almost as important as that between them, and the coherence of constituency parties is problematic.

The basic units in Irish parties are local branches, ideally centred on the parish, and tied together in constituency associations. It is at these two levels that most organisational activities - recruiting members, raising funds, nominating candidates, and conducting campaigns - take place. An annual conference is generally held but, in the two larger parties, this is more of a partisan outing than an effective decision-making affair. Party membership is modest and the central offices are small, poor, and not capable of much more than general encouragement and nominal supervision of the local organisations.

Policy and strategy are the business of the parliamentary parties. With the exception of Labour, Irish partisans seem content to give their elected representatives wide discretion in these matters. Neither of the major parties has the capacity to develop and discuss policy or programme in any detailed way, nor is there much internal demand that they do so. In the same way the selection and removal of party leaders is exclusively in the hands of the parliamentarians.

Around this framework there is a vast system of individual networks that constitutes the working party. The key figures are the professional politicians that make up the parliamentary parties. Each of them has a chain of associates, friends and supporters reaching down to the voters. These are highly personal machines, held together by transactional bonds and particularistic expectations. Wherever possible, these informal networks are integrated into the formal party apparatus, but the electoral system guarantees that most constituency parties will have several such organisations competing with one another. National officials and leaders normally stay out of constituency affairs, not only because their intervention would be resented by the locals, but also because they have limited capacity to affect change at that level. This leaves the machine politicians as the principal link between the grass roots and the centre, and the Irish parties as little more than coteries of parochial notables.

Electoral Competition

This system perpetuates an extraordinarily conservative politics.

At the local level politicians compete in terms of individual service to maximise personal not party interests. TDs try to suppress talent and in extreme cases even maneuver to have their party lose by-elections in their own constituency. The system is notorious for its limited capacity to provide for political recruitment and inheritance has become the surest path into the political class. As a result there has been little elite circulation and the system has remained relatively closed.

Inter-party competition has had a simple bipolar structure: Fianna Fail versus the others (Chubb 1979). This division replicates the civil war polarisation and is animated by Fianna Fail's we-they conception of politics. Because they commanded nearly half the vote, the only alternative to a Fianna Fail government was one composed of all its opponents. The consequence was long periods of Fianna Fail government. In the half-century since 1932 the party held power three-quarters of the time. Opposition coalitions managed to hold office only for short periods, and most of them ended with some discontented members.

Thus Ireland had a predominant party system. Fianna Fail thought and behaved as if it was the natural governing party: the other parties seemed to acquiesce and appeared uncertain whether they could hold power. Voters knew that elections could change governments, but they didn't expect them to do so. Two factors underlay continuing predominance: the strength of the Fianna Fail 'moral community', and the fragmented character of the opposition.

Fianna Fail believes that it is a national movement, not merely an ordinary political party, and thinks of itself as morally superior to its opponents. This sense of identity and purpose has provided the basis for superior organisational strength and solidarity; Fianna Fail's members are the most committed and disciplined in the Irish electorate. The party has operated in a tradition of unquestioning loyalty to the leader, and a belief that discipline is the primary political virtue. As a community of partisans it goes into elections more determined, better prepared and working harder than its opponents.

The other half of the system has always been divided. The fragmentation of the opposition increased in the 1940s when Labour temporarily split and two flash parties appeared in an atmosphere soured by the opposition's impotence (Carty 1981a:48, 57-8). The first inter-party government (five parties plus some independents) collapsed in the early 1950s amid mutual recrimination, but from that point on the opposition began to consolidate. By the mid-seventies Fine Gael and Labour had regained most of the non-Fianna Fail vote, but as long as they were divided Fianna Fail easily dominated.

With no fundamental issues separating the parties, national elections centre around the two themes that articulated the structural basis of Fianna Fail predominance: nationalism and the ability to govern (Mair 1981). The existence of Northern Ireland ensured that nationalism thrived as a political force in the Republic (Cox 1985). As the obvious beneficiary of latent (and not so latent) nationalist sentiment Fianna Fail was best placed to play the nationalist card. This powerful emotion is dangerous for the party as government, for it then must struggle with terrorists/patriots while at the same time ensuring law and order. However, for the party as electoral machine, nationalism has always been the greatest source of both its internal coherence and external appeal.

The second theme that Fianna Fail developed was governance. It argued that voters had a choice of Fianna Fail or chaos, for the opposition could never be united by anything more than a desire to put them out. Coalitions, they proclaimed, were inherently divisive, incoherent, and unstable. There is some evidence that this argument evoked a positive response from voters. When the opposition first managed to oust Fianna Fail they carefully called themselves an inter-party government to avoid the negative connotations that had been attached to the very idea of a coalition. And when in 1973 Fine Gael and Labour finally ran on a common platform they adopted the slogan 'There is an Alternative' and went on to win the election with it!

Very little of this portrait has changed. But a number of developments within the parties have begun to erode the two conditions that have long sustained Fianna Fail predominance. Before considering those changes we should note the forces that are rapidly transforming the social and economic context of Irish politics.

A Changing Ireland

Traditional values and practices survived longer in Ireland than in other parts of northern Europe. But the last decade has seen changes that are not only generating new issues and challenging the traditional political agenda, but are reshaping the social structure of the society and the cultural values that have sustained it.

Demographic trends are central to this transformation. In the mid-sixties the country's population began to grow, reversing a century's steady decline. During the 1970s it actually expanded by 13 per cent. Such a dramatic shift created new political pressures.

Ireland ceased to be one of the oldest societies in Europe and quickly became the youngest. Education and employment have become enormous problems.

In the past emigration provided a safety valve. However the countries that were the traditional destinations of migrants now have restrictive policies; emigration can remain a significant feature only if the Irish are willing to go to Europe. Those that'do not go abroad are moving to the cities, especially Dublin. The sprawling capital now contains about 30 per cent of the country's population. Rapid urbanisation has not only made the provision of infrastructure difficult, but also has disrupted traditional social patterns. As a consequence 'nearly every indicator of social disorganisation seems to have made a quantum leap in recent years' (Shade 1979:32).

Irish governments face equally serious economic challenges. Demographic changes include a general decline in the role of agriculture which now accounts for just 17 per cent of civilian employment, down from over a third only two decades earlier. Despite growth, other sectors have not been able to absorb an increasing population and the shift from the land. There has been a steady rise in structural unemployment and a corresponding drain on the social services.

Ireland is, aside from Portugal and Greece, the poorest country in western Europe. Its economic strategies have depended on export led growth and their success has relied on world trade and Irish competitiveness. Both have deteriorated in recent years. The country was particularly hurt by the oil crises of the 1970s. Instead of making internal adjustments, Irish governments sought to ride out the storm with foreign borrowings. The result was to marry growing unemployment to high rates of inflation, incur an external debt larger (as a percentage of GDP) than any other OECD country's, and create excessively large public borrowing requirements. Comparatively high levels of unionisation kept wage levels from falling, but at the expense of competitiveness.

Compounding these difficulties has been a growing rural-urban tension. This was to be expected given the rapid changes taking place, but it has been aggravated by the effects of the Common Agricultural Policy. When Ireland joined the EEC in 1973 its high price food policy provided an immediate stimulus to the Irish countryside. As farmers paid relatively low or no income taxes, this generated widespread resentment among urban dwellers and trade unionists. When the terms of trade turned against the farmers they in turn felt betrayed. Now neither section of the community believes that income or tax burdens are being shared fairly. Both have carried their views into the streets in protest against the conventional posturing of the Irish parties.

Most observers suggest that the political culture is in a state of flux. In general these shifts are in the direction of 'a general slackening of authoritarianism' (Shade 1979:31), and a movement towards a more pluralistic value system. Changes have been greater among the young rather than the old, and among urban middle classes rather than country folk. But the changes only look significant when Ireland is compared with its past. If weekly mass attendance levels have fallen to 82 per cent leading some to ask 'Is Irish Catholicism Dying?' (Kirby 1984), others respond that in some respects Ireland remains 'the antithesis of a secular society' (Chubb 1982:34). The political impact of any of this is not obvious. In the early eighties a constitutional referendum opposing abortion was successfully promoted by both major parties. Whether this is a measure of the old order, or a harbinger of the new remains to be seen.

All this change has yet to spill into the party system in any systematic fashion. Individual politicians have taken up particular issues or problems, but the catch-all parties are unable to offer the electorate any patterned choices on the principal questions of public policy in the 1980s.

The Party System Unstuck

The electoral and governmental turnovers of 1981 and 1982 gave dramatic evidence of increased political uncertainty and competition. Yet they were a natural extension of the events of the seventies. In 1973 Fine Gael and Labour had formed (for the first time) a pre-election coalition, campaigned on a common platform (Gallagher 1982:190) and, despite an increase in the Fianna Fail vote share, won. Capitalising on the new government's economic difficulties, and its own rebuilt organisation, Fianna Fail then swept back to office in 1977 with the largest landslide in the state's history (Farrell 1977; Penniman 1978). But only two years later the European elections provided Fianna Fail with a major set-back (Carty 1981c), and set the stage for three close elections in which power would shift between both sides of the system (Beamish 1983; Busteed 1982; Mair 1982; O'Leary 1982; O'Malley 1983).

Each of the last five elections has produced a change in government with Fianna Fail and Fine Gael-Labour administrations alternating in office. This marks a shift from predominance to bipolar competition. Though the substance and practice of Irish party politics seems much the same, the way in which the system works has been transformed. This reflects changes in both the Fianna Fail and opposition halves of the system whose origins can be traced to the break down of normal politics across the border in Northern Ireland.

Politicians in the Republic could not ignore the escalating violence in the North. It posed particularly difficult problems for Fianna Fail which had long lived off Irish nationalism and a commitment to reunification. In 1970, the government was rocked by the 'Arms Crisis' which saw the prime minister dismiss senior members of the party and government accused of illegally importing guns (for use in the North) into the country. No convictions were obtained but the political fallout was enormous.

Several Fianna Fail TDs left the caucus, while the disgraced Minister of Finance, Charles Haughey, languished on the backbenches. Touching as it did on the party's self-identity as a nationalist movement the rift was potentially very damaging. If some believed they were defending the integrity of the state, others feared the party was abandoning its *raison d'être*. While the former predominated among the leadership, the latter believed themselves the real heart of the party. These unprecedented events confirmed the fears of many Fine Gael and Labour politicians. They worried that Fianna Fail republicans might drag the country into the violent conflict. Realising that only a united opposition could defeat Fianna Fail, they began moving towards coalition politics. As these developments rippled through the parties they began to alter the system's dynamics.

Fianna Fail

'No other ruling party in western Europe derives its electoral support from such a broad cross-section of the voting population' (T. Gallagher 1981:60), and this diverse nationalist constituency has long been held together by the disciplined loyalty of an intensely leader-focused party. Fianna Fail voters continue to exhibit high levels of party solidarity; it is the behaviour of the politicians in the caucus that has changed and is altering the party.

The parliamentary party's major function has been to provide support for its leadership and, when necessary, to choose a new leader. Until the mid-sixties this was not at issue; the leadership rested with the founding generation. When two rivals (George Colley and Charles Haughey) clashed over the leadership in 1966 the caucus opted for Jack Lynch as a compromise, and the other two became senior members of his governments until the arms crisis. During the seventies Haughey nursed his grievances and watched Colley emerge as the party establishment's candidate for the succession.

Fianna Fail tradition let the leader decide the timing of his retirement so it was a major shock when, in the aftermath of a series of electoral setbacks in 1979, sufficient backbench pressure was mounted to force Lynch's resignation. The ensuing contest pitted Colley against Haughey, with the latter winning by the narrow margin of 44 to 38. At the heart of this division were two factions that had been developing over the decade. The factor that most distinguished their core groups was frontbench membership: that group heavily supported Colley. Haughey owed his victory to the party's rank and file; the characters Garvin (1981:119) aptly describes as 'the classic clientelist Fianna Fail backbencher, beloved of political anthropologists'. He notes that their 'network of localist connections' is the 'central motor' of the party, so that 'Haughey's accession represents the assertion of the organisation over the establishment of the parliamentary party'.

The establishment was bitter. Some had deep personal animosities that reached back to the arms crisis, but many genuinely distrusted Haughey's latent republicanism, were suspicious about his presidential leadership style, and disapproved of his blatantly tactical approach to politics. More important, they saw the Haughey putsch as a fundamental revision of the most important norms in Fianna Fail. They believed these events 'legitimised the withholding of loyalty to, and support for, the elected leader' (Garvin 1981:121). Leadership was now apparently to be conditional on electoral success.

Yet even electoral success has not stilled the faction fighting in the caucus. Following the party's election victory of February 1982 Haughey faced an unprecedented challenge to his leadership, and a few months later twenty-two TDs actually voted no confidence in their leader and prime minister. Within weeks of losing the November 1982 election the struggle broke out anew. A majority demanded a meeting to review the leadership, though in the end Haughey survived by a handful of votes (Joyce and Murtagh 1983).

For half-a-decade the Fianna Fail caucus was divided over the party leadership. Because the series of votes forced all members to choose sides, the division became deeper and wider. Moreover, the prospect of new elections with attendant changes in the composition of the caucus gave the faction leaders an incentive to push the faction fight down into the constituencies. There, by influencing the party's nominations and the local intra-party electoral contests, they could strengthen their position in succeeding Dala. Of the twenty-two TDs who opposed Haughey in October 1982, six lost their seats the following month, but only one lost to an opposition candidate; the other five were lost to Fianna Fail running mates. It would appear that Haughey supporters were actively working to shift votes away from TDs who had opposed their boss (O'Malley 1983).

These developments suggest that the institutionalisation of factionalism in Fianna Fail is underway. One of Ireland's major political directories now reports the factional affiliation of every Fianna Fail TD in their biographical portraits (Magill 1984). These data show that factionalism has reached into most local parties. Just 29 per cent of the constituencies return only Haughey deputies, all the others send TDs who are either divided among themselves or opposed to the leader.

The persona of Charles Haughey has been central to this nascent factionalism. However the division goes beyond personality and represents the two distinct strains within Fianna Fail. Haughey's faction combines traditional nationalist appeals and parish pump politics. His opponents represent a newer breed of centrist politicians concerned with the problems of directing a modern state apparatus.

It is not clear whether this conflict, which ultimately concerns the kind of party Fianna Fail will be, can be contained within the parliamentary party. No matter how representative the TDs are of their people, there may be considerable pressure to expand the debate to a wider forum. One way in which this could occur is for a faction to appeal a leadership decision to a party conference. Given its more populist nature, the Haughey group might be more likely to push the party in that direction (Joyce and Murtagh 1983:338-40), but whatever the source, any such development would crystalise a new pattern of party organisation in Ireland.

Though the ascendancy of the Haughey camp provided a respite for the party, the long term consequences of these changes remain uncertain. On the one hand, severe internal conflicts might sap morale and weaken organisational solidarity, reducing the party's competitive capacity. On the other, it can be argued that intra-party conflict has always been a part of Irish party politics, often stimulating campaign efforts that improve a party's performance (Carty 1980:564). The data from the 1982 elections indicate that factionalism has yet to hurt the party at the polls. The party's vote share oscillated, as it has for fifty years, about its historic mean, and intra-party vote transfers were as high as ever.

Local organisations in Irish parties have always been honeycombed with small personal factions. These new factional groups are national in scope and are being organised at the center and from the top down. The future of the party, and the character of party competition, will depend on how these two forms interact. It seems likely that the national factions, by enlisting TDs, will seek to absorb local machines, but the local machines will try to exploit the resources of national factional leaders in their parochial struggles. In some locales the two imperatives may mesh smoothly but in others they will clash. In either event this is bound to add a layer of complexity to the patterns of clientelism that drive the system.

The Opposition

During the 1960s the anti-Fianna Fail vote was coalescing behind Fine Gael and Labour but they seemed permanently stuck in opposition. Fine Gael looked and acted like a party tailor-made to lose elections, while Labour would not consider a partnership with it. Both of those conditions changed in the 1970s.

Fine Gael's electoral record in the past decade hints at considerable internal change. Its vote share grew slowly over the sixties, but the 1977 general election was disastrous. Its vote dropped by 5 percentage points, and the caucus shrank by 20 per cent (table 10.2). Then in the three elections of 1981-82 the vote rapidly climbed to almost 40 per cent, making the caucus almost as large as Fianna Fail's. This was the direct consequence of deliberate efforts to reconstruct the party and its place in the system.

After the debacle of 1977, the new party leader, Garret FitzGerald, set about modernising the party organisation. He recognised that while Fine Gael had fewer hard core supporters than Fianna Fail it had also been much less effective at mobilising them. This meant that a new party machine had to be built, new tactics and campaign practices developed, and large numbers of attractive new candidates recruited.

The party's sitting TDs, anxious to avoid disruptions that might threaten their seats, had to be circumvented. To do so the new party managers appointed professional organisers for each constituency. Selected independently of the TDs, they were responsible for stimulating and directing partisan activity in the constituency. This gave the leadership a window into each constituency, and a mechanism to draw new people into Fine Gael. This important new coterie of activists has given the party machine a depth it never had before.

FitzGerald appointed individuals with backgrounds in advertising, public relations, and broadcasting to the party's national headquarters. He realised that the party had neglected to do any opinion polling in 1977 and was determined to 'encourage all concerned to take these polls more seriously in the future' (Meagher 1983:123), as the basis for regular election planning. That activity was matched with increased attention to the party's television face.

235

Table 10.2 Irish Parliamentary Parties 1948-1987: caucus size

	Fianna Fail	Fine Gael	Labour	Progressive Democrats
1948	68	31	19	-
1951	69	40	16	-
1954	65	50	19	-
1957	78	40	12	-
1961	70	47	16	-
1965	72	47	22	-
1969	75	50	18	-
1973	69	54	19	-
1977	84	43	17	-
1981	78	65	15	-
1982 f	81	63	15	-
1982 n	75	70	16	-
1987	81	51	12	14

Both the slaughter of 1977, vacating many of the party's seats, and a 12% increase in the size of the Dail eased the recruitment of new candidates.   Thus, while Fianna Fail was 'full-up' because of its landslide victory in 1977, Fine Gael was able to offer new opportunities to aspiring young politicians.

These changes, plus the appeal of FitzGerald who appeared to have the most realistic grasp of the country's economic problems, produced the electoral outcomes of 1981 and 1982.   The growing sophistication and effectiveness of the party's electoral tactics and machinery can be seen in the proportion of the party's candidates elected.   It was greater than 50 per cent in all three contests, and for the first time surpassed Fianna Fail's (60.9 vs. 56.8) in November 1982. Internal transfer rates also increased, evidence of a solidifying party vote (Magill 1982:11).   The long standing inferiority of the Fine Gael machine seems a thing of the past; the party now has the 'most professional team ever to direct general election campaigns in Ireland' (Magill 1983:6).

As Fine Gael's caucus grew it was remade. Over half of its TDs first entered the Dail in 1981 or later. This new caucus is, on average, younger, better educated and more female than those of the other parties (Gallagher 1984). This transfusion of talent into the parliamentary party, unprecedented in the history of the state, so transformed the party's elite that FitzGerald's 1982 cabinet contained only two of his party colleagues from the 1973-77 coalition. Thus Fine Gael has pried open the sclerotic recruitment channels of the Irish party system to the kinds of politicians that are likely to represent Ireland's future, rather than its past.

But for this new Fine Gael to become a party of government the Labour party had to join it in coalition. The question of whether or not it should do so has preoccupied Labour for a quarter-century (Gallagher 1982). This tactical issue inevitably forces Labour to consider what sort of party it wants to be.

The arguments for and against coalition politics are clear. By opting in Labour chooses power: the opportunity to implement some of its policies and programmes, while, at the same time, keeping Fianna Fail out of office. And as long as Haughey leads Fianna Fail, the distrust he evokes reinforces Labour's incentive to pursue a coalition with Fine Gael.

Two reasons are advanced by those who oppose coalition. The first is pragmatic. Each time Labour has participated in a coalition its vote has fallen in the subsequent election, indicating that the party is punished, not rewarded, by the voters for its involvement. At a minimum, participation in Fine Gael governments robs Labour of its distinctive identity. The loss of 44 per cent of its vote since 1969 indicates the electorate has indeed been hard on the party. Moreover, Labour could run just 41 candidates for 166 seats in the post-coalition election of February 1982, the lowest number it had mustered since 1961.

A second argument against coalition comes from the party's left. They claim that membership in a bourgeois coalition inhibits Labour from developing a radical socialist alternative. Avoiding coalition politics is a necessary part of politicising the Irish Labour movement and moving the party to the left. Labour must provide an alternative to the two catch-all parties and then be prepared to wait in opposition until the electorate responds to its analysis and appeal.

This ideological dimension to the coalition issue parallels some of the structural fault lines in the party. Labour's militants have always been more opposed to coalition politics than its parliamentary notables (Gallagher 1982:184-5, 245): 9 of 15 caucus members got some 'pay-off' from the 1981 coalition. At party conventions, delegates from Dublin and the trade unions are disproportionately anti-coalition, while those from the rural constituencies are much more in favour. Labour voters' propensity to transfer preferences to Fine Gael candidates suggests they generally endorse the coalition strategy.

As the Labour vote has declined the internal conflict has increased, hardening factional lines. To cope, the party now avoids any formal pre-election commitment entering into negotiations only after the electoral outcome is known. Then a specially called conference decides whether or not the party should enter a government. This strategy has only increased uncertainty: recent elections have seen the party chairman and other Administrative Council members publicly contradicting their leading candidates (O'Leary 1982:368). These episodes have increased the frustration of Labour TDs trying to hold their seats. It was this feeling of being undermined by extraparliamentary officials that finally provoked Labour's leader, Michael O'Leary, into quitting the party weeks before the second 1982 general election. While a major break between the parliamentary party and the larger organisation has not occurred, the potential for a serious crisis exists. Whether the party could survive such a rift is debatable.

A Competitive Irish Party System

Irish elections have always been competitive and featured a syndrome of intra-party competition in catch-all parties that produced a conservative politics. Even in the most recent turbulent general elections half of the TDs who lost their seats did so to a running mate (Mair 1982:89).

When I recently asked one of the new Fine Gael Deputies, long a professional observer of Irish politics, what surprised him most about being a TD he replied: 'How difficult it is going to be to hold my seat. I expected it would be difficult to win the first time, but keeping it is going to be just as hard.' As a result he is now spending much of his time nurturing the grass roots, and working to thwart fellow partisans who have their eye on his seat. All this perpetuates the localism that is endemic to Irish party activity. And if anything, Gallagher's (1984) evidence suggests that a local base 'is becoming more important', and that inheritance remains an important channel to public office.

In the past intra-party competition led to a stagnant electoral cycle. Developments in Fianna Fail indicate the party may be harnessing that dynamic to some new form of factional politics, while in Fine Gael party leaders must find some way to counter it if they do not wish to see their recent changes come to naught. But in either case intra-party competition will now exist in an environment of more intense inter-party competition.

Incipient factionalism may be straining Fianna Fail's moral community blunting any special competitive edge over its opponents. The party knows it no longer enjoys the luxury of a completely divided opposition and must now hold together and win elections on its own. With the largest base it remains well placed to do so. Certainly deeply fractionalised parties have maintained their preeminence in other systems, and Fianna Fail might bear comparison with the Italian Christian Democrats, or the Japanese Liberal Democrats. Like those parties, the relations among the factions, and between factions and other parties and interests, will be central to Fianna Fail's competitive posture in the next decade.

More important from the perspective of party system change has been the growth of Fine Gael, and its ability to work with Labour. Fine Gael's expansion has largely been at the expense of other anti-Fianna Fail interests, and the two large parties now monopolise Irish politics to a greater extent than ever. In 1982 they commanded 84 per cent of the vote, leaving Labour and other minor groups as marginal electoral competitors. Paradoxically, because they hold the balance of power these groups now have more influence in the Dail. The electorate has begun to sense this heightened competitiveness and vote intentions have become volatile, 'a seemingly new phenomenon in Irish political life' (Meagher 1983:125).

By the early sixties the combined Fine Gael-Labour vote matched, or exceeded, Fianna Fail's. But Fianna Fail predominance persisted because those two parties preferred going it alone. Their 1973 decision to combine produced a balanced bipolar party system. Since then, the side that won the largest vote share has formed the government. Elections have become 'decisive' events, and inter-party competition central to Irish politics. Indeed, each of the last five elections has produced a change of government.

This new party system developed because a small group of leading politicians in Fine Gael and Labour wished it to. Should they change their minds and political tactics, as one Labour faction seeks, then the system might revert to predominance. But other possibilities exist. An implicit coalition has existed for a decade now, and if Labour formally abandoned it the party might find some of its rural voters (and perhaps TDs as well) deserting to Fine Gael. The distance between the two is hardly very great.

Another possibility is more intriguing. If Fine Gael can maintain its recent gains, then Labour could be in a position to determine which of the two major parties could form a government. That would allow Labour to play a role not unlike the German Free Democrats, and give the party some real leverage to shape the system's agenda. Rather than being pulled towards the two large parties, Labour might, on some issues, be able to pull them towards its preferred space. This might well be facilitated by Fianna Fail factionalism: competition between faction leaders might give some of them incentives to establish links with Labour politicians in areas of mutual interest. Such developments could enable the party system to offer voters substantive policy choices.

It is striking how little of this party system change is connected to the rapid social, demographic, and economic changes going on in Ireland. Catch-all parties, detached from social cleavages, are apparently less affected by such environmental change than socially homogeneous parties. An entire system of catch-all parties, like Ireland's, thus seems more immune to exogenous forces than any other - it cannot be 'unfrozen' - and so it is potentially the most stable of all systems. Change, when it comes, is politically inspired, and depends upon the decisions of politicians acting in what they conceive to be their best interest. In this sense catch-all parties represent a genuine autonomy of the political.

Does Any of This Make a Difference?

If we accept that the Irish party system has changed in the dramatic fashion suggested by the title of this essay then it seems reasonable to conclude by asking what difference all this is going to make. Conventional assessments of the Irish party system suggest that it has traditionally performed most functions rather badly, so one might hope any changes to be for the better.

Recruitment has been one of the party system's greatest failures. It has kept the political elite closed and narrowly based, and it has drawn into politics men (and a few female relatives) more concerned for the parish pump than for policy-making. Despite the influx of new people into Fine Gael, there is not a lot of reason to believe the intra-party dynamics that govern the process have changed. If anything, internal party factionalism may aggravate the problem. Increased inter-party competition, by heightening electoral uncertainty, may stimulate more intra-party conflict and could make the recruitment of policy oriented politicians even more difficult than it is now.

Irish parties have never bothered themselves with *policy-making*. That has been left to parliamentary leaders and, when in office, their civil service advisors. None of the changes in the parties have increased their capacity as organisations to formulate policy alternatives that they might present to the electorate. The economic realities facing the country can no longer be ignored, but the widespread agreement that the only real option available is a prudential fiscal policy means that elections are focused on the personal qualities of the leaders. This is perhaps inevitable in a catch-all party system in which the only choice available is between people, not policies or ideas.

With the passing of the predominant party system voters now have a *choice* of governments. This will deprive Fianna Fail of its 'strong stable government' issue and force it to develop a new language of electoral politics. In the short-run the party may be tempted to resort to its other traditional appeal - nationalism - but its own internal divisions, and Haughey's record, make that a risky strategy. Because the two sides of the system reflect the ideologically homogeneous cast of the society they cannot provide Irish voters with clear policy alternatives. What the choice does provide is *accountability*. Irish voters can now hold governments accountable because the party system finally assures them that elections can be used to remove unpopular governments. In view of the regularity with which voters have employed this new power in the past decade, Irish parties and politicians, have had to learn new meanings for the concept of responsible government.

The party system now makes it possible for the Irish to choose their governments, and then to hold them accountable. These features are central to our notions of liberal democracy. Thus, the *democratic* character of the Irish political system has been enhanced as the party system has shifted from predominance to competition.

And Back to Predominance? The 1987 General Election

Events since 1984 make this assessment of the Irish system look more dated than most essays on continuity and change should! But while the scenario played out was unanticipated, it reflected a mix of all the tensions driving the party system over two decades.

Fianna Fail returned to power (with just 81 of 166 seats) after a February election forced by the collapse of the Fine Gael-Labour coalition. This sixth successive change of government followed an election in which Fianna Fail was able, at least temporarily, to reassert the predominant position which it previously enjoyed. Fianna Fail won 44.1% of the vote (close to its historic mean), but both coalition partners lost 31% of their 1982 supporters leaving Fine Gael with 27.1% (its lowest vote in three decades) and Labour with a mere 6.5%. The slack was taken up by the Progressive Democrats (PD) a new party that captured 12% of the vote to become the third largest in the country and the Dail. Whether the PD will fade, as two flash parties in the 1940s did, will depend as much on the response of the old parties as on anything it does itself.

The emergence of the Progressive Democrats was stimulated by changes in both sides of the party system. The PD orginated in Fianna Fail faction fighting: it was created by two anti-Haughey TDs expelled for not towing the leader's line. They were soon joined by two other well known caucus dissidents. There were some differences over policy (the PD is the first serious Irish party to advocate abandoning the constitutional claim to the North) but the new party is basically rooted in personal animosity. Before the Dail was dissolved a discontented Fine Gael TD had also crossed the floor, and the new party had signed up more members than Labour. But the PDs do not seem to have attracted significant numbers of Fianna Fail voters: the aggregate results suggest it has simply fragmented the opposition half of the system.

Though PD politicians came from Fianna Fail, it was Fine Gael and Labour that paid most of the electoral price. That is measure not only of continuing Fianna Fail solidarity but also of the fragility of their opponents. Fine Gael failed to consolidate its rapid gains of the previous decade. FitzGerald's attempt to move the party towards pluralist policies upset traditional supporters (prompting one TD to quit, claiming the coalition was 'anti-Catholic') and then floundered with the defeat of a referendum to provide for divorce. Labour finally resolved its internal conflicts by deciding not to enter into any further coalition, a signal to voters that the party did not want to be in power. The PD breakthrough (14 seats) left Fine Gael with only 51 TDs, Labour with only 12.

Like the changes described above, these new twists in the party system have all been wrought by politicians redefining the shape and organisation of political competition: more evidence of the 'autonomy of the political' in Irish politics. As if to confirm that, the 1987 election, fought principally on economic issues, saw the parties differing mainly on style, emphasis and leadership, not substance. Whether this new constellation will persist remains to be seen. If the Progressive Democrats survive, then real competition (allowing voters a chance to choose governments) will require new alliances and new patterns of coalition politics. Otherwise Ireland may revert to the all too familiar pattern of Fianna Fail predominance.

References

Beamish, B. (1983) 'The Irish Election of November 1982', *West European Politics 6*, 271-76

Blondel, J. (1968) 'Party Systems and Patterns of Government in Western Democracies', *Canadian Journal of Political Science 1*, 180-203

Busteed, M.A. (1982) 'The 1981 Irish General Election', *Parliamentary Affairs 35*, 39-58

Carty, R.K. (1980) 'Politicians and Electoral Laws: An Anthropology of Electoral Competition in Ireland', *Political Studies 28*, 550-566

Carty, R.K. (1981a) *Party and Parish Pump: Electoral Politics in Ireland*, Wilfrid Laurier University Press, Waterloo, Ontario

Carty, R.K. (1981b) 'Brokerage and Partisanship: Politicians, Parties and Elections in Ireland', *Canadian Journal of Political Science 14*, 53-81

Carty, R.K. (1981c) 'Towards a European Politics: The Lessons of the European Parliament Election in Ireland', *Journal of European Integration 4*, 211-241

Carty, R.K. (1983) *Electoral Politics in Ireland*, Brandon Books, Dingle, Ireland [a 2nd ed. of Carty, 1981a]

Chubb, B. (1979) 'Ireland' in S. Hening (ed.), *Political Parties in the European Community*, Allen & Unwin, London

Chubb, B. (1982) *The Government and Politics of Ireland* 2nd ed. Stanford University Press, Stanford

Cox, V.H. (1985) 'The Politics of Irish Unification in the Irish Republic', *Parliamentary Affairs, 38*, 437-454

Farrell, B. (1977) 'The Irish General Election, 1977', *Parliamentary Affairs, 31*, 22-36

Gallagher, M. (1981) 'Social Change and Party Adaptation in the Republic of Ireland, 1960-1981', *European Journal of Political Research, 9*, 269-85

Gallagher, M. (1982) *The Irish Labour Party in Transition 1957-82*, Manchester University Press, Manchester

Gallagher, M. (1984) '166 Who Rule: The Dail Deputies of November 1982', *Economic and Social Review, 15*, 241-64

Gallagher, T. (1981) 'The Dimensions of Fianna Fail Rule in Ireland', *West European Politics, 4*, 54-68

Garvin, T. (1981) 'The Growth of Faction in the Fianna Fail Party, 1966-1980', *Parliamentary Affairs, 34*, 110-23

Joyce, J. and P. Murtagh (1983) *The Boss: Charles J. Haughey in Government*, Poolbeg Press, Swords, Ireland

Kirby, P. (1984) *Is Irish Catholicism Dying?*, Mercier, Dublin

Lipset, S.M. and S. Rokkan (1967) 'Cleavage Structures, Party Systems and Voter Alignments: An Introduction', in their *Party Systems and Voter Alignments*, Free Press, New York

Magill (1982) *Election '82*, Magill, Dublin

Magill (1983) *Book of Irish Politics 1983*, Magill, Dublin

Magill (1984) *Book of Irish Politics 1984*, Magill, Dublin

Mair, P. (1979) 'The Autonomy of the Political: The Development of the Irish Party System', *Comparative Politics, 11*, 445-65

Mair, P. (1981) 'Towards an Available Electorate? Parties, Party Loyalty and Patterns of Opposition in Post-War Ireland', (unpublished paper)

Mair, P. (1982) 'Muffling the Swing: STV and the Irish General Election of 1981', *West European Politics, 5*, 75-90

Marsh, M.A. (1985) 'Ireland' in I. Crewe and D. Denver (eds.), *Electoral Change in Western Democracies: Patterns and Sources of Electoral Volatility*, Croom Helm, London

Meagher, J.F. (1983) 'Political Opinion Polling in the Republic of Ireland', in R.M. Worcester (ed.), *Political Opinion Polling*, Macmillan, London

Moss, W. (1933) *Political Parties in the Irish Free State*, Columbia University Press, New York

O'Leary, C. (1979) *Irish Elections 1918-77*, Gill and Macmillan, Dublin

O'Leary, C. (1982) 'The Irish General Elections of 1981 and 1982', *Electoral Studies, 1*, 363-80

O'Malley, J, (1983) 'The Election', in T. Nealon and S. Brennan (eds.), *Nealon's Guide 24th Dail and Seanad*, Platform Press, Dublin

Penniman, H.R. (ed.) (1978) *Ireland at the Polls: The Dail Election of 1977*, American Enterprise Institute, Washington, D.C.

Shade, W.G. (1979) 'Strains of Modernisation: The Republic of Ireland Under Lemass and Lynch', *Eire-Ireland, 14*, 26- 46

Smith, G. (1978) 'Trends in Western European Party Systems?', *Parliamentary Affairs, 31*, 37-51

Chapter Eleven

The Canadian Paradox: Party System Stability in the Face of a Weakly Aligned Electorate

Herman Bakvis

The Canadian party system represents a quintessential paradox. It enjoys relative stability and continuity, despite the fact that the majority of voters lack strong attachments to political parties. It constitutes a state of affairs that Lawrence LeDuc (1984) has termed 'stable dealignment', and, if one accepts the available evidence, it has been a feature of Canadian political life for many years. The Liberals were in power almost continuously from 1921 through 1984, their dominance broken only occasionally by brief periods of Conservative rule. And although the New Democratic Party has established a solid foothold in the parliamentary arena as a third party, neither this nor other minor parties have succeeded in mobilizing weakly aligned or non-aligned voters over a sustained period.

This chapter examines factors that might account for the paradox of system stability and weak alignment: the social underpinnings of the party system; institutional considerations such as the electoral system; and the behaviour of parties and party leaders. However, there are no ready answers; indeed my examination of these factors yields more puzzles than resolutions, and ultimately points back to some basic characteristics of the electorate that are not necessarily visible or readily elucidated through survey evidence.

The Canadian Party System: Past and Present

The Canadian party system does not fit easily into categories commonly used in the comparative study of parties. It qualifies neither as a two-party nor as a multiparty system. Its apparent stability is anchored neither in distinct subcultures nor in widely held party identifications within the electorate. And although one can speak of major electoral shifts in given elections, it is questionable whether such shifts constitute genuine realignments or critical elections, or even whether they occur on a national scale.

A number of features are either unique to the Canadian system or regarded as more important than elsewhere: (1) the concept of 'one-party dominance' which denotes the phenomenon of a single party dominating the system over long periods of time; (2) the 'brokerage theory' in which the two major parties are seen as practitioners of catch-all strategies with emphasis on the role of the leader; (3) the simultaneous existence of different federal and provincial party systems - for example, Social Credit and the Parti Quebecois hold or have held power at the provincial level but are of no significance at the federal level; and (4) a pronounced but not overwhelming link between religion and voting - Catholics tend to vote Liberal while Protestants tend to support the Progressive Conservatives - even though the parties lack any ostensible religious identification and religion rarely becomes an issue in election campaigns (Meisel 1973). Voting patterns also tend to be strongly regionalized. Even though there are no specific regional parties as such, region can be used as a predictor of vote and, secondly, a shift or realignment in one region does not necessarily occur in other regions (Blake 1972, 1979). In addition, any generalization concerning parties or voting behaviour is bound to be contradicted in at least one of the regions.

The present party system stands in contrast with the one that prevailed prior to the first world war. From 1867 to 1914 the Conservatives enjoyed national office for 28 years and the Liberals for 19. On the eve of World War I, it was felt that a stable two-party system had been successfully implanted on Canadian soil. However, this assessment was premature. The war proved to be divisive: military conscription, introduced by the Conservative government in 1917 but bitterly opposed in Quebec, split the Liberals. Many pro-conscription Liberal MPs joined with the Conservatives to form the coalition 'Unionist' party for the 1917 election. The Unionists won 57 per cent of the popular vote but obtained only 24 per cent in Quebec. Yet it was the Conservatives rather than the Liberals who were hurt by this alliance. What followed was a departure from the two-party model and a long period of Liberal dominance.

In the 1921 election the Conservatives suffered heavy losses, not only in Quebec but also in western Canada. As figure 11.1 shows, the prime beneficiary was a new party, the Progressives, which swept the prairie provinces on a platform of agrarian populism. While receiving only 23 per cent of the national vote, it nevertheless obtained 27 per cent of the seats in the House of Commons. In contrast, the Conservatives won 30 per cent of the vote but only 21 per cent of the seats. The Liberals under Mackenzie King received 49.4 per cent of the seats, and subsequently formed a minority government. The party system was in disarray: the Conservatives were now in third place in parliament and no party held a majority. Both Liberals and Conservatives had done poorly in western Canada, indicating that the two-party system had failed to take root in an important area of the country. Thus, while the basic structure of most European party systems was beginning to congeal (Lipset and Rokkan 1967), the Canadian system was coming unstuck.

The Progressive successes proved less durable than the third party phenomenon they helped to introduce. In 1925 the Conservatives reversed their fortunes, obtaining roughly 47 per cent of seats and votes. In the election the following year the Liberals gained the majority of seats and succeeded in reducing the Progressives to a splinter party with less than 10 per cent of seats and a little over 5 per cent of the vote. The Liberals absorbed a good portion of Progressive support and membership while the Conservatives, sometime later, inherited the title. In 1942 the Progressive premier of Manitoba, John Bracken, assumed the Conservative leadership; virtually the sole legacy of his brief stewardship was his renaming the party the Progressive Conservative party (PC). The phenomenon of third parties did not disappear, however. In 1933, the Co-operative Commonwealth Federation (CCF) consolidated left-wing elements of the Progressive movement and various socialist groupings and gained a small but significant foothold in parliament in the 1935 election. In 1961, the CCF became the New Democratic Party (NDP).

At the provincial level the third party phenomenon was much more pronounced. Progressive governments were elected in Ontario in 1919 and in Alberta and Manitoba a few years later. In 1935 the Alberta progressive government (the United Farmers of Alberta) was replaced by a more radical movement, the Social Credit party, which promised to expand the money supply and extend credit. In Quebec the provincial Conservative party was effectively displaced by the Union Nationale, which took power in 1935. When the CCF took power in Saskatchewan in 1944, it was the first time that a Socialist government had been elected in North America (Lipset 1968). Since then, the CCF-NDP, the perennial third party at the federal level, has governed for long periods in Saskatchewan and Manitoba and a briefer interval in British Columbia, where it has usually been the official

Figure 11.1 Parliamentary Elections in Canada, 1878-1984 (in percentages)

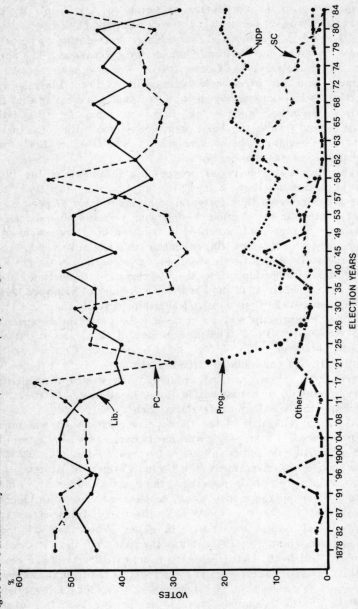

Source: (J.M. Beck, *Pendulum of Power* (Prentice Hall, Scarborough, 1968) and Hugh Thorburn (ed.) *Party Politics in Canada*, 5th edition (Prentice Hall, Scarborough, 1985)

opposition.[1] It is important to note that the actual acquisition of government office by third parties has been restricted to the provincial level. As can be seen in figure 11.1, except for the rapid waxing and waning of the Progressives in the 1920s and the brief rise of the Creditistes (the Quebec wing of the federal Social Credit party) in the 1960s, the party system at the federal level has revolved around two major parties, the Liberals and the Conservatives, and one minor party, the CCF-NDP. The last has never held power in Ottawa. Moreover, despite the change and turmoil during the decade following the First World War, the Liberals have been in office for 53 of the 66 years between 1920 and 1986. This has led Reg Whitaker (1977) to characterize the Liberal party as the 'government party' and underscores the continuing relevance of the term 'one-party dominance' (Smiley 1958).

Some qualification of 'one-party dominance', as normally applied, is required in light of the past three decades. Change, when it occurs, does not necessarily lead to long-term dominance by a new party. Rather the pattern since 1920 has been relatively long periods of liberal rule interspersed by much briefer periods of Conservative rule. Only the Liberals, it seems, have been able to settle in for the long haul. Second, Liberal party dominance has been tenuous at times: from 1963 to 1968 and from 1972 to 1974, the Liberals formed minority governments, with the result that major issues were often resolved between parties in parliament rather than within the dominant party. One-party dominance often rests on a more fragile basis than might be inferred from the longevity of governments.

The Unanchored Electorate

This fragility of party support is evident on a variety of levels. In a classic article J.A.A. Lovink (1973) pointed out that the rate of turnover in seats in any given election, even when it did not involve a change in government, is markedly higher in Canada than in either the U.S. or the U.K. In textbooks the volatility of the Canadian electorate figures prominently in discussions of parties and elections (e.g. Dawson and Ward 1970; Corry and Hodgetts 1965). This volatility, it is argued, results from the major parties rendering themselves virtually indistinguishable on policy issues, largely because they see it as their goal to act as vehicles for the accommodation of diverse religious, linguistic and regional interests. This stress on brokerage has elevated the importance of leadership in that stress on personality helps gloss over actual differences between the parties. Further, it is claimed, the loyalties of both party workers and voters tend to be to the leader, not the party. When the leader disappears, so too will support for the party. This transitory loyalty would also account for the apparent sudden shifts in electoral support after long incumbency by one party. However, multiple shifts on the part of voters need not spell major changes at the aggregate level. Or, to put it differently, stability in the overall electoral outcome can mask considerable change and turmoil in individual voting behaviour.

The claim of volatility and lack of voter loyalty to parties has come under close scrutiny. One set of critics has argued that Canada compares quite favourably to both the U.K. and the U.S. (Sniderman *et al.* 1974). They note that the average fluctuation in the distribution of the vote in Canada over the period 1926-72 for the Liberals and Conservatives was lower than that for the Democrats and Republicans in the U.S. and only slightly higher than for the Conservatives, Liberals and Labour in the U.K. over roughly similar time periods. On the individual level, they note that turnover in Canada (i.e. people who voted for different parties as a percentage of all who voted for the same party twice) is only slightly higher than in Britain and a fair bit lower than in the U.S., in spite of the much higher turnover rate in seats in Canada. They also note that partisan stability among those who identify with a political party is only slightly lower in Canada than in the U.S. (75 per cent versus 80 per cent). On the other hand their findings, based on election surveys from the three countries, indicate that British and American respondents were 50 per cent more likely to be stable in both vote and partisanship than their Canadian counterparts. Canadians were also twice as likely to vary in both partisanship and vote, at a minimum suggesting that partisanship in Canada differs both in meaning and in consequences from that in the U.S. The possibility remained, therefore, that supporters of political parties in Canada are more likely to abandon those loyalties or switch votes than their U.S counterparts.

This supposition is corroborated by evidence and analyses from other sources. Relying on aggregate data, Donald Blake (1979) points out that the summary statistics used by Sniderman *et al.* (1974) to characterize the 1926-72 period disguise instances both of highly volatile elections as well as subperiods when volatility generally was higher than the overall average. As well, the researchers responsible for the 1974, 1979 and 1980 election surveys (Sniderman *et al.* relied mainly on the 1965 and 1968 surveys) found that throughout the 1970s the majority of the electorate had either unstable, weak or inconsistent partisan attachments, in spite of a relatively high level of aggregate electoral stability (Clarke *et al.* 1984). This led Lawrence LeDuc

(1984) to coin the term 'stable dealignment' to describe this paradox, a concept that appears to fit well with the basic evidence.

According to LeDuc 'stable dealignment' is a longstanding phenomenon in Canada, even if it might be a relatively new arrival in countries like the United States. LeDuc (1985) has provided cross-national survey evidence over the past two decades indicating that the proportion of strong identifiers was, until the late 1970s, much higher in the U.S. and the U.K. (see figure 11.2). But at the same time these data indicate that partisanship in Canada certainly was not absent. It might be better, therefore, to speak of 'weak' alignment rather than dealignment. Furthermore it has been noted that the present distribution of partisan attachments does favour one party, the Liberals (Clarke *et al.* 1984:74; Johnston 1985). At the same time long periods of stability in party rule tend to be punctuated by sudden change, as was the case in 1958 when the Conservatives under Diefenbaker swept the country and more recently in 1984 when the Conservatives under Brian Mulroney repeated the feat.

'Weak' alignment implies the possibility of realignment, however fragile such new configurations might be. Blake (1979) has demonstrated that the notion of critical elections and realignment is applicable, but only in restricted circumstances and in certain regions. Thus he notes that in the 1958 Diefenbaker sweep the enormous gains in votes and the mobilization of the electorate as a whole largely disappeared in the elections of 1962 and 1963. The 1958 election was a limited critical election because realignment was restricted to specific regionally based electorates. In the West the Conservatives were able to overcome enmities dating from World War I and the depression and displace the Liberals. In the West, the Conservatives were unable to sustain their 1958 gains. Moreover, their popular vote in Quebec dropped from a high of 49.6 per cent in 1958 (their highest vote share since 1887) to 29.6 per cent and 19.5 per cent in the elections of 1962 and 1963 respectively. However, these shifts in Quebec cannot be put under the heading of 'deviating election' since the votes lost by the Conservatives did not easily revert back to the Liberals. Instead the Quebec wing of the federal Social Credit party, the Creditistes (Raillement Creditiste), scooped up many of these votes in the depressed rural areas of eastern Quebec, obtaining 26.0 and 27.3 per cent of the Quebec vote in the 1962 and 1963 elections. Neither the previous dominant party, the Liberals, nor the Conservatives, were considered adequate to the voters in question (Pinard 1971). In the 1968 election the Liberals regained a number of these seats, but the Creditistes were not eliminated until the election of 1980.

Figure 11.2 Percentage of British, Canadian, and U.S. National Samples Reporting a 'Strong' Identification with a Political Party, 1963-80

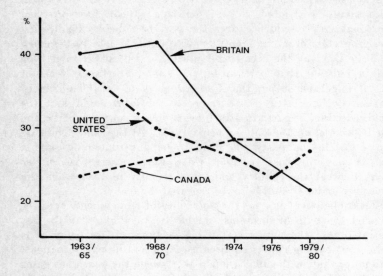

Source: Reprinted from L. Leduc, 'Partisan Change and Dealignment in Canada, Great Britain, and the United States,' *Comparative Politics, 17* (1985), 318.

Blake's discussion of the election of 1896, which saw the defeat of the Conservatives and the onset of 15 years of Liberal government under Wilfrid Laurier, underscores a similar point. On the surface it can be considered a realigning election par excellence: historically the election is considered an important turning point, the juncture at which the link between the Catholic hierarchy and the Conservative party in Quebec began breaking down and the Liberals came to be identified with the protection of Catholic and francophone interests across Canada. However, genuine change occurred only in one province, Quebec, and movement was underway well before 1896 with changes evident in 1887. The process of realignment culminated in the 1896 election, indicating the existence of a transitional period rather than a single critical election. In Ontario and Manitoba above average change occurred in 1896 and 1900, and in both cases the second election merely corrected shifts in the previous election, suggesting deviation rather than realignment.

Blake's analysis, therefore, indicates that in specific regions, as opposed to the country as a whole, major shifts have taken place and that in some instances these shifts have been sustained over several decades. In some instances there have been major landslide victories on a national scale, but for the most part these typically constitute deviating rather than realigning elections (e.g. the elections of 1917 and 1958, both involving the Conservatives). While based on aggregate data, Blake's evidence is nevertheless consistent with the notion of stable yet weak alignment.

Reference should also be made to the separation of provincial and federal party systems.[2] The existence of these 'two worlds' (Blake 1985) is seen by some as contributing to weak partisanship (Clarke *et al.* 1979, 1984). In brief, all provinces have fully formed party systems, and these systems often differ considerably from the federal system. Voters are often seen as being pulled in two different directions, or, alternatively, failing to find reinforcement for their federal party identification at the provincial level. The most extreme example involves British Columbia where one of the two main protagonists, the NDP, is present at the federal level only as a third party, and the other, Social Credit, is currently non-existent at the federal level.

Only in the Atlantic provinces, and possibly Ontario, is there a rough congruence between federal and provincial party systems. Even so the same party is not necessarily in power at both levels. Voters, assuming they are so inclined, are frequently required to develop separate federal and provincial party identifications; in British Columbia an adherent of the federal Conservative party is quite likely to identify with Social Credit provincially. While Clarke *et al.* (1984) feel that these split or inconsistent identifications contribute to the overall weakness of partisanship in Canada, Blake contends that this is not necessarily the case, at least as far as British Columbians are concerned. Survey evidence from that province shows that voters are fully capable of developing and maintaining separate party identifications and that 'split partisans were no more likely than consistent partisans to switch votes within levels once intensity of partisanship is taken into account' (Blake 1982:710). At the same time Blake notes that the existence of two worlds may lead to fewer strong identifiers, although there is no firm evidence on this point.

Assessing the impact of social structure on Canadian voting behaviour is also problematic. Region and religion tend to be the best predictors of vote (Blake 1972): western Canadians are more likely to vote Conservative, particularly since the 1958 Diefenbaker sweep, while those in Quebec are more likely to vote Liberal. Religion remains the strongest single predictor of vote, but its effects are somewhat mysterious. Catholics are much more likely to support the Liberals, while Protestants are more prone to vote Conservative. For example, in the 1974 election 68 per cent of all Catholics voted Liberal versus 40 per cent of Protestants, while only 15 per cent of Catholics voted Conservative versus 45 per cent of Protestants. Although the overall level varies, these differences between the main religious groups holds regardless of region with the exception of Newfoundland where the relationship is reversed.[3] Class is a relatively poor predictor of the vote. Although blue collar workers are somewhat more likely to support the NDP than clerical and managerial/professional categories the differences are minor. In 1974, for example, 14 per cent of blue collar workers voted NDP versus 11 per cent of those in the other two occupational categories. Even so, class is not absent in Canadian politics. At the provincial level, particularly in British Columbia, class is much more in evidence.[4]

The alignment of religious differences with political parties reflects readily identifiable historical legacies. The Liberals, since the days of Laurier, have been seen as protectors of Catholic and francophone rights and, prior to the second world war, provincial rights as well. The Conservatives, in turn, became identified at an early stage with Protestantism, as symbolized by the now long dormant Orange Lodge, and even today are still seen as placing a somewhat higher value on the Crown and the British connection generally. What remains a puzzle, however, is the manner through which these legacies are kept alive. Religion is rarely a political issue, and in the last several decades the parties have generally made sure that it does not become one by refraining from raising it, through collusion if necessary.[5] The current leaders of both major parties are Catholic, as were their immediate predecessors.

Within the electorate itself it is very difficult to discern an active religious agent. In most West European countries there is typically a strong relationship between strength of religious adherence, as measured by frequency of Church attendance, and vote. Yet in Canada such a link is barely discernable and then only among Protestants (Meisel 1973). Canadian Catholics who attend mass regularly are no more likely to vote Liberal than those who rarely or never attend mass. Almost by default the family appears to be the primary transmitter and reinforcer of the historical link between religion and vote (Irvine 1974; Irvine and Gold 1980).

Extra-familial agents, however, cannot be completely ignored. Richard Johnston (1985) points to higher transmission rates for Liberal

Catholic families compared to Conservative Catholics. If familial socialization is key then why the difference? Johnston suggests that the Catholic community is in many ways self-contained by virtue of separate school systems and other institutions, which have important consequences for mate selection and family formation. Secondly, although Catholicism is not a direct surrogate for ethnic identity, Johnston notes that in all likelihood the ethnic centre of gravity of the Catholic community differs from that of the non-Catholic community. All this points to a more generalized ethos outside the immediate family which helps to reinforce the basic Liberal-cum-Catholic identity acquired within the family. Although certainly not on the same level as the highly organized spiritual subcultures found in Western Europe (Lorwin 1971), particularly the smaller European countries, or even the more loosely defined 'familles politique' (Deutsch *et al.* 1965) found in France, there quite likely still are informal subcultural networks which influence, albeit indirectly, voting and intergenerational transmission of partisanship. Thus there do exist indirect support bases for Canadian parties; but they are not strong, especially as far as the Conservatives are concerned.

In sum, there appears to be a certain amount of anchoring of the electorate, both through party identification and social structure, most specifically religion, although it is not strong and can be overridden. At the same time, when major shifts do occur, whether nationally or more likely regionally, they revolve around the two major parties. This is clearly evident in figure 11.1. Regional movements such as the Progressives in the 1920s and the Creditistes in the 1960s do arise, but they tend to be deviations and rarely become permanently entrenched in the party system. The NDP, in contrast, has become a durable feature of the Canadian party system, but when major shifts occur they are equally likely to be losers as beneficiaries.[6] Other than the CCF-NDP, small parties lacking a specific regional basis have enjoyed no success at the national level whatsoever. In short while the Canadian party system may be potentially volatile, there is little danger of fragmentation. But this does not provide us with an explanation of why this should be so. Should we attribute this state of affairs to the astute behaviour of parties and political leaders? Or is the basic anchoring of the system to be found in the formal rules governing the electoral process? Let us turn to the latter question.

The Electoral System

The Anglo-American first-past-the-post plurality system based on single or dual member electoral districts is generally considered to be restrictive. Thus one common belief has been that the Canadian electoral system, like the British on which it is based, helps to create majorities in the House of Commons when there are only pluralities in terms of votes. As well, the electoral system is alleged to help promote a national and accommodative posture on the part of the major parties. This blissful image, however, was altered significantly by Alan Cairns' (1968) piece challenging prevailing assumptions about the alleged benefits. While not denying that the electoral system can help create artificial parliamentary majorities, Cairns pointed out that these majorities have been far less frequent than generally thought. Contrary to then prevailing beliefs, he noted that the electoral system has an inherent bias favouring regional or sectional appeals. Simply put, if the party is weak in certain areas of the country, it is no use wasting valuable electioneering resources on voters in those areas. Any votes so gained are likely to be wasted votes. Further, he argued that the Canadian electoral system facilitates the entry of smaller parties *whose support is regionally concentrated.*

Cairns provides evidence of electioneering behaviour, fostered by the electoral system, which runs directly counter to the national accommodative politics model. For example, he notes the blatantly sectional appeals by the Liberals in Quebec prior to the First World War and, further, points to the success of the so-called Churchill strategy of 1957. The Conservatives, at the suggestion of Gordon Churchill, a party stalwart and later cabinet minister, deliberately ignored Quebec in their campaigning, calculating that they might obtain enough seats in English Canada to come close to forming a majority, thereby at least displacing the Liberals. They were indeed successful and duly formed a minority government. Less than a year later they called an election and altered their strategy, appealing to Quebec voters not to be left out of the federal cabinet (Beck 1968). They duly obtained 50 of the 75 seats in Quebec (versus nine seats in 1957) and won in a national landslide. The stage for this enormous victory, however, was set in 1957.

A recent example of sectional politics can be found in the 1980 Liberal election campaign. The major issue was domestic energy pricing; and the Liberals explicitly favoured the energy consuming and more populous eastern half of the country at the expense of the energy producing Western half. The result was a Liberal parliamentary majority, which had only two seats west of Ontario and none west of

Manitoba. It underscored two unfortunate effects of the electoral system: the efficacy of sectional appeals and the exaggeration of the regional character of the party system by simultaneously over- and under-representing the different regions in all three parties. For example, while the Liberals in 1980 obtained over 22 per cent of the vote in the three western most provinces they received no seats; and while the Conservatives in the same election obtained 13 per cent of the Quebec vote they received but one seat in that province.

An additional feature of the electoral system is that third parties whose electoral support tends to be concentrated in specific regions tend to do much better than third parties whose support is dispersed. In the 1960s the Creditistes, concentrated in a specific region of Quebec, were ideally situated to benefit from this aspect of the electoral system. The NDP, whose limited support has generally stretched across the country, has been hurt by the system.

However, the electoral system does not require parties and party leaders to make sectional appeals; it only provides some advantages in doing so. There are many instances of parties and leaders adhering to the adages found in the older textbooks, that is attempting to appease groups in as many regions as possible and devising compromise platforms to appeal to both anglophone and francophone voters. The Conservative campaigns under Robert Stanfield and Joe Clark in the late 1960s and 1970s clearly fall into this category, even though they failed to make much headway in Quebec. Moreover, given the inherent bias of the electoral system towards regionally based parties, it is surprising that there have not been more region specific third parties along the lines of the Creditistes. In short, we cannot depend upon explanations invoking the special properties of the electoral system to resolve the paradox of relative stability in the face of a weakly anchored electorate. This suggests either that there may be something within the electorate itself militating against the success of regional third parties, in spite of the absence of strong links favouring the present parties, or that the leadership of the major parties has been unusually adept in mobilizing what voter loyalties do exist.

Party Organization, Leadership and Strategies

As noted earlier the two major parties are thought to practice 'brokerage politics', appealing to and bridging the needs of a wide variety of groups and individuals and in the process obscuring rather than clarifying policy stances. Mackenzie King, leader of the Liberal party from 1921 to 1948 and Prime Minister for 22 of those 27 years, is generally considered to have been past master in the art of 'brokering'.

Those well disposed towards the practice see in it national conciliation and the accommodation of the needs of the two primary language groups. For example, Mackenzie King defused to some extent the highly divisive issue of compulsory military conscription during World War II, favoured by English Canadians but largely opposed by the French Canadian community, by using the slogan, 'conscription if necessary but not necessarily conscription'. Critics of the practice see it as a deliberate and often successful effort to draw attention away from class issues (Brodie and Jenson 1980; Porter 1965). Regardless, all agree that King succeeded remarkably well in capturing the political centre on behalf of the Liberal party.

But, as suggested earlier, not all parties and leaders always practice brokerage politics all of the time. And it is also evident that in recent years old fashioned brokering has been transformed into something which transcends rather than merely obscures regional and ethnic differences.

Before discussing current strategies, I should note the basic structural and organizational obstacles that leaders need to overcome. First, the phenomenon of 'two worlds' discussed earlier is also evident at the level of party organization. In the past, party organizations had more of a confederal form, that is the provincial party also constituted the federal wing of the party. However, these arrangements began to change more than two decades ago. The Liberals, for example, created separate federal organizations in most of the provinces. It has also been suggested that in earlier eras, specifically during the period of Mackenzie King, the links between federal and provincial leaders were much stronger, acting as an integrative force (Smiley 1980). For example, Jimmy Gardiner, Liberal premier of Saskatchewan in the 1930s and later federal minister of agriculture under Mackenzie King, maintained close links with the provincial party while in the federal cabinet. This sort of mobility is now very rare, and federal and provincial wings of the same party are frequently at odds with each other, sometimes in highly visible fashion. There have been important differences between federal and provincial Liberals in Quebec, and it has been suggested that in 1979 the Conservative premier of Alberta deliberately undercut the position of the Conservative prime minister, Joe Clark, over the energy issue, contributing to Clark's defeat in 1980 (Simpson 1980). At a minimum, federal party leaders cannot always depend on their provincial counterparts to help mobilize the vote. Provincial leaders, especially premiers, are sensitive to the needs and perceptions of their provincial populations and often do not want to be seen to be too close to Ottawa.

Federal party organizations are also limited in size and scope. Overall, with the possible exception of the NDP, party organizations are weak, coming alive only at election time when frequently there is a mad scramble by prospective candidates to sign up members to help out at the nominating meeting. In between elections the party organization at the local level is often non-existent, and what does exist consists entirely of volunteer labour. There are no paid constituency agents. During the 1960s the federal Liberal party embarked on a program of 'participatory democracy' in order to both broaden and expand the organizational base of the party. But the experiment, rather than engendering more participation, effectively cut off input at the grassroots level. Links with provincial organizations were shattered and decision-making ended up being centralized within a small group of professionals in Ottawa. These reforms hastened the demise of the Liberals in western Canada and more generally helped reinforce the longstanding division in Canadian politics between elite and mass (Smith 1981, 1985). There are surprisingly few intermediary links or organizations which help mediate relations between top leaders and ordinary citizens.

The major parties lack both formal and informal connections to other organizations or social groupings which can be used to help mobilize support or aid in other ways. In the case of the major parties, even the connections with business interests are not as strong as one might think (Gillies 1982), in part because of Ottawa's distance from the major business centres. The lack of intermediary links may explain why party leaders often depend on a populist or plebiscitarian style during election campaigns. Despite differences in personality and style both Diefenbaker and Trudeau depended on direct appeals to ordinary citizens in most of their campaigns. Only the NDP has formal ties with an outside organization, the Canadian Labour Congress (CLC) which involve financial support for the party. This connection with the CLC, however, has been of only limited utility. Union members are still more likely to vote either Liberal or Conservative, and efforts to mobilize CLC members at election time have had only limited success (Archer 1985). Indeed there have been suggestions that the NDP-CLC connection has hurt the party among non-union voters.

Patronage continues to be an important part of Canadian political life, but its role in bolstering party support is problematical. At the local level it can be used to good effect to ensure support not only for the incumbent party but also for the opposing party by offering prospects of gain should it be elected. The sudden increase in road paving in crucial constituencies or employment with the highway department are practices typical at the provincial level, particularly in Quebec and Atlantic Canada. Available at the federal level are items such as judgeships, legal work, advertizing contracts, appointments to a host of boards and commissions, and appointment to the non-elected Senate. These items number in the thousands, but ironically they have distinct liabilities as political resources. 'Modern Canadian politics is characterized more by patronage at the top of the party hierarchy than at the bottom', writes David Smith (1985:53). While important as means for rewarding party activists at the higher levels, thereby helping to preserve the rudiments of the party's election machinery, patronage also feeds public cynicism. Appointments of Liberal party stalwarts to high level positions became an issue in the 1984 election. The practice, however, has been continued by the Conservative government, and has drawn considerable press coverage and opposition criticism. It is doubtful whether current patronage practices help bond ordinary individuals or groups to political parties.

Thus party leadership constitutes the primary focal point of party organization and electioneering activities; party conventions, other than leadership conventions, are of secondary importance. National election campaigns are centred on the leader; when this is not the case, it is usually a sign of serious difficulties in a campaign. Such a focus, in turn, is highly dependent upon media coverage, television advertising, and carefully orchestrated personal appearances by the leader. If only by default, the role of party leader looms much larger in Canada than elsewhere.

The electioneering strategies employed by leaders do not vary greatly from those in practice at the beginning of confederation. But with the constant attention focussed by both the print and electronic media on party leaders on the campaign trail, it has become much more difficult for leaders to say or promise one thing on one side of the continent and quite the opposite three thousand miles away the following morning. David Smith (1985) has argued that beginning with John Diefenbaker, campaigns have become much more national in scope, dependent upon a 'pan-Canadian approach' which differs from older brokerage-style techniques. According to Smith, the three most recent prime ministerial practitioners of this approach - Diefenbaker, Pearson, and Trudeau - sought to establish direct links with individual citizens using as touchstones national public policies concerning language, medicare and the Constitution.

Yet it can be argued that the brokerage strategy has been neither entirely displaced nor even significantly diminished by these pan-Canadian approaches. The three examples cited by Smith all had different foci. While Diefenbaker stressed one Canada and un-hyphenated Canadianism, the 1968 Trudeau campaign had as its motif the just society, the modernizing and streamlining of government, and the beneficial uses of technocracy, which had particular appeal to urban middle classes, resident for the most part in Ontario and Quebec. This coalition, which drew in recent immigrants as well as small 'l' liberals, was not all that far removed from the centrist coalition 'brokered' by Mackenzie King during his lengthy tenure as Liberal leader.

Furthermore, one can also point to examples of campaigns during this period with distinctly regional orientations: to wit the 1957 Diefenbaker campaign employing the 'Churchill strategy' and the 1980 Liberal campaign fought over energy policy, both mentioned earlier. They are perhaps better put under the heading of what Cairns (1968) terms 'sectional' rather than brokerage politics, but they barely qualify as pan-Canadian. However, even these sectional campaigns have to be cast broadly enough to encompass more than one region. Usually the interests of one major region, typically Ontario, are then linked to those of another, either Quebec or western Canada with secondary support in Atlantic Canada. Efforts to forge an alliance between Quebec and the west have not been feasible, although in theory they should be possible.

Probably the best example of efforts to link together all regions would be the 1984 election campaign waged by the Conservatives; Brian Mulroney, a former labour lawyer, made 'national conciliation' his campaign theme, deftly blending brokerage and pan-Canadian elements. During the 1984 campaign commitments were made to both broad national constituencies (e.g. on medicare) and more specific regional constituencies (e.g. a promise to alleviate unemployment in Cape Breton). As well, his personal style leads him to almost continual telephone consultation with individuals he knows well and who have connections with or insight into groups and constituencies across the country (Aucoin 1986). For the first time since the Diefenbaker sweep of 1958 the Conservatives succeeded in wresting the political centre away from the Liberals, if perhaps only temporarily, and they did so using techniques resembling those perfected by Mackenzie King.

Parties then, have a number of options available to them, ranging from specific sectional appeals to broad pan-Canadian approaches. In practice any campaign strategy will combine elements of all of these. The centrality of leadership, the very limited ties to specific groups and organizations, and the negligible importance of ideology, permit parties considerable flexibility in responding to short term political forces and opportunities. For example, it has been argued by some that Mulroney succeeded in capturing the political centre by moving to the left of Liberal leader John Turner on a number of issues.

Leadership looms as the single most important factor in Canadian party politics. It is also the factor that can cause most grief to a party seeking to adapt to changing conditions. There tend to be two basic problems: (1) overcoming internal considerations to select a leader capable of winning an election; and (2) removing a leader whose usefulness has passed without too much public bloodletting. The Conservatives, the perennial opposition party during much of the post-war period, have gone through a large number of leaders in quest of victory, and in doing so have created a number of intense personal rivalries (Perlin 1980). Diefenbaker's ousting in 1967 left a bitter legacy which severely hampered the efforts of two successors to unify the party. The Liberals have generally been considered immune from the 'Tory syndrome', but from 1978 onwards there were rumblings about Trudeau's leadership (Wearing 1981). The leadership factor is therefore very much dependent upon other factors, chief among them being internal party dynamics.

Conclusion

We return to the paradox posed at the beginning: why relative stability and continuity despite weak anchoring of the electorate? Stress should be placed on the adjective 'relative' for at intervals there have been pronounced shifts in party support, though not necessarily resulting in permanent realignment on a national scale. If we have made any progress in resolving our paradox it lies in the elimination of a number of factors which could conceivably account for the stability of the system. Sociological factors such as religion have only a limited effect. The electoral system, while helping to create parliamentary majorities also facilitates entry of regionally based third parties. Such parties have been limited in number, but their paucity is not necessarily due to obstacles built into the electoral system.[7] Patronage, in turn, may actually widen the division between party and voter. Party leadership appears to be a critical factor, but by its very nature it is fleeting and fickle. Leaders come and go while parties continue. While certain figures, among them Sir John A. Macdonald, Sir Wilfrid Laurier and Mackenzie King, showed themselves unusually astute in mobilizing both party and electorate over sustained periods, others have been much less adept.

A possible resolution to the puzzle runs counter to current

thinking. The explanation rests, I would argue, on two factors: the structure of opportunities provided by the simultaneous existence of federal and provincial party systems and the nature of the electorate itself. The arrival of new parties is frequently seen as major factor contributing to volatility and change in any given party system. However, in the Canadian context those seeking to enter the parliamentary arena are much more likely to make the effort at the provincial level. Provincial legislatures and governments represent important bases for opposing the federal government and provinces are smaller and more homogeneous in population, factors which make it more likely that those dissatisfied with mainline parties will launch new political movements at the provincial rather than federal level. The massive financial outlay required for running a national campaign and the limited opportunity for recouping expenses probably plays a role here.[8] But even at the provincial level, with the exception of the Parti Quebecois formed in 1968, new parties and movements have been neither numerous nor very successful in recent decades.

Thus there may well be something in the electorate itself that limits support for such parties and, in turn, inhibits political entrepreneurs from launching new political ventures. While strong loyalties to established parties exist within only a limited proportion of the electorate, there appears to be a more generalized loyalty to the party system as a whole (as distinct from the state, or, in Eastonian terms, the political system). Conversely, it could be argued that there is a basic aversion to parties other than the two major and one minor party presently entrenched in the system. Thus dissatisfied Canadian voters may be more likely to switch parties or perhaps sit out elections than elsewhere, but this behaviour is confined to those two options. Supporting a fourth party is a non-starter for most Canadians. Roger Gibbins (1981), in his book on regionalism and party politics, notes that in western Canada support for the major parties has gradually increased. This is despite efforts by minor fringe parties such as the Western Canada Concept to obtain even minimal electoral success at the federal and provincial levels.

The paradox, and the resolution being mooted here, has broader relevance. In the literature on electoral stability and change it is often implied that volatility or even fragmentation of the party system can result from the lack of either strong partisan loyalties or well organized and cohesive subcultures (Bakvis 1981). The Canadian party system would seem to suggest that this is not always the case.

The Canadian paradox is a long standing phenomenon and may offer insight into the workings of those party systems now losing their structural underpinnings. In a number of countries old cleavages are receding, leaving voters with neither specific cues from traditional subcultures nor direct loyalties to new or old parties. Parties have sought to cope by adopting variations on the catch-all theme, attempting to cast a wider net or merging with other parties, but European parties still compete within a restricted ideological space. Canadian parties have less ideological baggage and hence greater flexibility in responding to perceived needs in the electorate. The Canadian case, therefore, may not be wholly applicable.

If there are possible lessons they relate to the building of coalitions. In Europe these apply mainly to cabinet formation and bargaining among parties after the election, a process which usually takes place behind the scenes. In Canada, the task of party leader is to bring together disparate groupings through a combination of a vague common denominator and specific promises. Needless to say this is a different kind of coalition building, in which connections are made, often in highly public fashion through the media, with groups that may not exist in any formal, organizational sense but which none the less constitute important constituencies.

Whether leaders and their parties in other systems can use these techniques or make the transition is a question which cannot be answered here. But the Canadian political style does suggest that the identification of key constituencies, and the development of election promises that allow the interests of these constituencies to be linked together, is a necessary and perhaps even central component in the conduct of catch-all politics in weakly aligned systems. To be sure this kind of politics is tricky, not least for the politicians. But it should be emphasized once more that the Canadian system is far from the brink of disintegration. Fluctuations, or rapid changes when they do occur, are likely to be confined within the limits of the current system and rebound to the benefit of one or more of the established parties.

Notes

1. All in all, one-party dominance fits more closely with provincial experience. The best example is probably Alberta where Social Credit (1935-71) and the Progressive Conservatives (1971-present) have enjoyed long tenure. Provinces such as British Columbia and Ontario have also seen single parties dominate over long periods of time.

2. The reasons for the sharp differences between federal and provincial systems

can only be hinted at here. On the extent of these differences see Elkins and Simeon (1980). For many, the differences reflect the nature of Canada's political economy, particularly its effects on western Canada. Centre-periphery rather than class conflict is a dominant theme in Canadian politics, and conflicts from this source tend to be fought out directly between the federal government and the provinces. The resource and agriculturally rich prairie provinces, dependent upon export markets and favouring cheap imports, have always been at odds with central Canadian financial and manufacturing interests. See Smith (1981).

3. This reversal is due to a particular historical legacy. Because Newfoundland did not join confederation until 1949, its political parties developed separately from those on the mainland.

4. Data is from the 1974 election survey. See Clarke *et al.* 1979. Brodie and Jenson (1980), using a variation of the class consciousness argument, claim that the major parties, the Church and economic elites have obfuscated the class cleavage. However, this would not explain why the strategy was successful in most of the provinces and Canada as a whole but not in British Columbia, or why voters in British Columbia are more likely to vote on the basis of class in provincial elections but less so in federal elections. See Blake (1985:181-82, note 12).

5. When religious conflict does arise it is more likely to do so at the provincial level. Provincial governments have jurisdiction over education and are subject to forces favouring, or opposing extension of government financing to Catholic schools.

6. At the time of the 1958 Diefenbaker sweep the CCF received 9.5 per cent of the vote and only 8 of the 267 seats in the House of Commons (3 per cent of the total) compared to 10.7 per cent of the vote and 25 seats (9.4 per cent of the total) in the 1957 election. The NDP also found itself squeezed in 1974 and 1980.

7. There is an extensive literature on Canadian third parties, both provincial and federal, for example C.B. Macpherson (1953) on Social Credit in Alberta and Pinard (1971) on the federal Creditistes. Pinard puts forward an elaborate framework based on the notion of 'structural conduciveness' to account for the Poujadiste-like rise of the Creditistes in Quebec during the 1960s. There has been considerable debate about the Pinard model, but overall the discussion suggests that the conditions giving rise to third parties, particularly at the federal level, are both specific and limiting. This in turn suggests that under normal circumstances voters do not easily turn to third party alternatives.

8. The rules governing the financing of political parties play a role in preserving the integrity of the current system. Election campaigns are enormously expensive, given the vast geographical terrain and the extensive costs associated with advertising in the electronic and print media. A typical campaign involves the lease of a passenger jet to transport the leader, his staff, as well as an entourage of reporters. The Canadian election expenses act subsidizes campaign expenses and makes donations to political parties partially tax deductible. As Paltiel (1985) has noted, much of the financial burden of elections has been transferred to the state. This primarily

benefits the three established parties, that is those having a basic minimum number of seats in the House of Commons (for the allocation of television time) and those whose candidates obtain at least 15 per cent of the vote in their riding (for partial reimbursement of election expenses). These provisions came into force for the first time in the 1979 election. The effects on the NDP have been dramatic, allowing the party to move into the jet age along with the two major parties. It also means that it will be more difficult for any new party or movement to displace or join the three existing parliamentary parties.

References

Archer, Keith (1985) 'The Failure of the New Democratic Party: Unions, Unionists, and Politics in Canada', *Canadian Journal of Political Science 18*, 353-366

Aucoin, Peter (1986) 'Organizational Change in the Machinery of Canadian Government: From Rational Management to Brokerage Politics, *Canadian Journal of Political Science 19*, 3-27

Bakvis, Herman (1981) 'Electoral Stability and Electoral Change', *Canadian Journal of Political Science 14*, 519-555

Beck, J.M. (1968) *Pendulum of Power: Canada's Federal Elections*, Prentice-Hall, Scarborough, Ontario

Blake, Donald E. (1972) 'The Measurement of Regionalism in Canadian Voting Patterns', *Canadian Journal of Political Science 5*, 55-81

Blake, Donald E. (1979) '1896 and All That: Critical Elections in Canada' *Canadian Journal of Political Science 12*, 259-79

Blake, Donald E. (1982) 'The Consistency of Inconsistency: Party Identification in Federal and Provincial Politics' *Canadian Journal of Political Science 15*, 691-710

Blake, Donald E. (1985) *Two Political Worlds: Parties and Voting in British Columbia*, University of British Columbia Press, Vancouver

Brodie, M.J. and Jane Jenson (1980) *Crisis, Challenge and Change: Party and Class in Canada*, Methuen, Toronto

Cairns, Alan C. (1968) 'The Electoral System and the Party System in Canada' *Canadian Journal of Political Science 1*, 55-80

Clarke, Harold D., Jane Jenson, Lawrence LeDuc, and Jon H. Pammett (1979) *Political Choice in Canada*, McGraw-Hill Ryerson, Toronto

Clarke, Harold D., Jane Jenson, Lawrence LeDuc, and Jon H. Pammett (1984) *Absent Mandate: The Politics of Discontent in Canada*, Gage, Toronto

Corry, J.A. and J.E. Hodgetts (1966) *Democratic Government and Politics*, University of Toronto Press, Toronto

Dawson, R. MacGregor (1970) Rev. by Norman Ward *The Government of Canada* 5th ed. University of Toronto Press, Toronto

Deutsch, E., D. Lindon, and P. Weill, *Les familles Politiques aujourd'hui en France*, Minuit, Paris

Elkins, D.J. and R. Simeon (1980) *Small Worlds: Provinces and Parties in Canadian Political Life*, Methuen, Toronto

Gibbins, Roger (1981) *Prairie Politics and Society*, Butterworths, Toronto

Gillies, James (1982) *Where Business Fails*, Institute for Research on Public Policy, Toronto

Irvine, William (1974) 'Explaining the Religious Basis of the Canadian Partisan Identity: Success on the Third Try', *Canadian Journal of Political Science 7*, 560-63

Irvine, William P. and Hyam Gold (1980) 'Do Frozen Cleavages Ever Go Stale? The Bases of the Canadian and Australian Party Systems', *British Journal of Political Science 10*, 187-218

Johnston, Richard (1985) 'The Reproduction of the Religious Cleavage in Canadian Elections' *Canadian Journal of Political Science 18*, 99-113

LeDuc, Lawrence (1984) 'Canada: The Politics of Stable Dealignment' in R.J. Dalton (ed.) *Electoral Change in Advanced Industrial Democracies: Realignment or Dealignment* Princeton University Press, Princeton, N.J.

LeDuc, Lawrence (1985) 'Partisan Change and Dealignment in Canada, Great Britain, and the United States' *Comparative Politics 17*, 379-98

Lipset, S.M. (1968) *Agrarian Socialism: The Co-operative Commonwealth Federation in Saskatchewan*, Anchor Books, New York

Lipset, S.M. and S. Rokkan, 'Cleavage Structures, Party Systems and Voter Alignments', in Lipset and Rokkan (eds.) *Party Systems and Voter Alignments: Cross-National Perspectives*, Free Press, New York

Lorwin, Val R. (1971) 'Segmented Pluralism: Ideological Cleavages and Political Cohesion in the Smaller European Democracies', *Comparative Politics 3*, 141-75

Lovink, J.A.A. (1973) 'Is Canadian Politics too Competitive?' *Canadian Journal of Political Science 6*, 341-79

Macpherson, C.B. (1953) *Democracy in Alberta: Social Credit and the Party System*, University of Toronto Press, Toronto

Meisel, John (1973) *Working Papers on Canadian Politics*, McGill-Queen's University Press, Montreal

Paltiel, K.Z. (1985) 'The Control of Campaign Finance in Canada' in H. Thorburn (ed.) *Party Politics in Canada*, Prentice-Hall, Scarborough, 115-127

Perlin, George (1980) *The Tory Syndrome: Leadership Politics in the Progressive Conservative Party*, McGill-Queen's University Press, Montreal

Pinard, Maurice (1971) *The Rise of a Third Party: A Study in Crisis Politics*, Prentice-Hall, Englewood Cliffs, N.J.

Porter, John (1965) *The Vertical Mosaic*, University of Toronto Press, Toronto

Simpson, Jeffrey (1980) *The Discipline of Power*, Personal Library, Toronto

Smiley, Donald V. (1958) 'The Two-Party System and One-Party Dominance in the Liberal Democratic State', *Canadian Journal of Economics and Political Science 24*, 312-22.

Smiley, Donald V. (1980) *Canada in Question: Federalism in the Eighties*, McGraw-Hill Ryerson, Toronto

Smith, David E. (1981) *The Regional Decline of a National Party: Liberals on the Prairies*, University of Toronto Press, Toronto

Smith, David E. (1985) 'Party Government, Representation and National Integration in Canada', in P. Aucoin (ed.) *Party Government and Regional Representation in*

Canada Vol. 36 in the Research Studies conducted for the Royal Commission on the Economic Union and Development Prospects for Canada, University of Toronto Press, Toronto, 1-68

Sniderman, Paul M., H.D. Forbes, and Ian Melzer (1974) 'Party Loyalty and Electoral Volatility: A Study of the Canadian Party System' *Canadian Journal of Political Science 7*, 269-288

Wearing, Joseph (1981) *The L-Shaped Party: The Liberal Party of Canada 1958-1980*, McGraw-Hill Ryerson, Toronto

Whitaker, Reginald (1977) *The Government Party: Organizing and Financing the Liberal Party of Canada, 1930-1958*, University of Toronto Press, Toronto

Chapter Twelve

The United States: A Comparative View

Steven B. Wolinetz

The United States provides an intriguing setting for examining party system change. In contrast to the other party systems treated in this volume, the American party system has been characterised by periodic realignments in which party positions have changed, partisan loyalties have shifted and the content of two-party competition has been redefined. Students of American politics have identified five distinct 'party systems' since the beginning of mass politics in 1800. In the first, incipient competition between Federalists and Democratic-Republicans culminated in the victory of the latter and a temporary eclipse of party politics. In the 1820s, a second and more locally-based party system emerged in which Democrats battled Whigs; it was in this period that many basic features of American party politics were established.

Thirty years later, divisions over slavery resulted in the formation of the Republican Party and the brief emergence of multiparty competition. Founded in 1856, the Republican Party replaced the Whigs and emerged as the majority party when two-party competition was re-established after the Civil War. However, after 1876, the end of the Reconstruction, the re-entry of former confederate states and the disenfranchisement of southern blacks resulted in a finely balanced competition between Republicans and Democrats. In the 1890s agrarian dissent and divisions over tariffs precipitated another realignment and a prolonged period of Republican dominance. Lured by high protective tariffs, urban groups - including both business and organised labour - gravitated to the Republicans, reducing the Democrats to an agrarian and western party. Relatively small electoral swings (Clubb, Flanagan and Zingale 1980) redrew the political map of the United States: one-party dominance was prevalent in both the north (where many states were now Republican) and the solidly Democratic south. Republican dominance survived the emergence of the Progressive Movement and Theodore Roosevelt's third party candidacy in 1912. However, in the 1928-1936 period, the pronounced sectionalism of 'the system of 1896' (Burnham 1970) was supplanted by a class-based alignment. Rallying farmers, immigrants and labour behind the New Deal, the Democrats forged a new coalition and established themselves as the majority party. The Roosevelt coalition remained intact until the late 1960s. (Sundquist 1983)

Since then, party positions have changed, party and group attachments have weakened, and Democratic dominance has given way to a more divided pattern in which Democrats control Congress while Republicans often capture the Presidency. Changes in party organisation are even more striking: presidential nominating processes have changed, parties have become more open and divided, and candidate-centred organisations guided by professional consultants have supplanted local party organisations in battles for nomination and election. In addition, a new wave of actors, political action committees (PACs), have gained prominence and increasingly proficient national committees, once described as committees without power (Cotter and Hennessy 1964), have become involved in raising funds, training campaign personnel, and providing support and assistance to candidates.

Recent changes diverge from previous realignments. Although patterns of change vary, previous realignments entailed both extensive electoral changes and changes in the content of party alternatives (Burnham 1970). Fueled by electoral changes and the presence of divergent interests within parties, realignments gave one party decisive control of Congress and the executive and the opportunity to implement new programs and win additional support (Brady 1985). However, although party alternatives and coalitions have been redefined in the last two decades, massive electoral changes have not followed. Nevertheless, recent changes are far-reaching and include major changes in the ways in which parties and political activity are organised: the highly decentralised and locally based pattern of party organisation in place since the 1830s is being displaced not only by candidate-centred organisations, but also by nationally based actors, including party factions, political action committees, and more recently, national party organisations themselves.

This chapter will examine recent changes in light of the competitive dynamics of the party system and the ways in which different elements have been contained within it. Assembling divergent elements within two large parties has been a source of the generational realignments for which the American party system is noted. However, recent changes reflect not only internal diversity but also the ways in which individual candidates have sought to secure their nomination and election in a loosely structured party system.

Shaping the American Party System

Contemporary changes are best understood in light of the institutional architecture of the American system and the ways in which parties have adapted to competition in a federal and presidential system. Facets relevant to our analysis include the setting in which parties emerged, the persistence of two-party competition and the impact of reforms.

American parties developed in a decentralised federal system with a pronounced separation of powers. In contrast to the twentieth century, the federal government was weak and had little power or influence. Although parties initially emerged in legislative caucuses, by the 1830s control of nominations had shifted to state and local parties whose principal concerns were winning elections and securing patronage. National parties took root as loose confederations of state and local organisations which came together for the limited purpose of designating presidential candidates (Ranney 1975). In the absence of a well-developed administrative apparatus, parties staffed local, state and national governments with their own appointees and used patronage to build party organisations (Lowi 1985; Skowronek 1982).

Despite regional differences and the periodic appearance of third parties, the United States has maintained a two-party system. Its persistence reflects the broad coalitional character of American political parties, which enables divergent interests to coexist within a single party, and the institutional setting in which competition has taken place. Competition for single indivisible offices, such as state governorships or the Presidency, and the patronage which they could provide encouraged divergent groups to come together within one of the two parties. Later, ballot reforms and direct primaries reinforced two-party competition by broadening opportunities for internal contestation and making it more difficult for third parties to gain access to the ballot (Rosenstone *et al.* 1984; Scarrow 1986). As a result, forces which in a different institutional context might have established separate parties frequently found themselves compelled to work within or on the margins of established parties.[1]

In addition, both because of the hold which they exerted on nominations and elections and the style of politics which they practiced, American parties have been the subject of periodic reforms intended to limit patronage, break the grip of political machines, and democratise political processes. In the late nineteenth and early twentieth centuries, civil service reforms, the introduction of the Australian ballot, and the spread of direct primaries altered the frameworks in which parties operated (Ranney 1975). Nineteenth century political parties often had well-developed organisations capable of mobilising large numbers of workers to distribute ballots, win office, and secure patronage. By mandating the election of candidates and party officials, primary laws not only subjected parties to legal regulation, but deprived them of full control over organisation and recruitment. At the same time civil service reforms narrowed, but did not eliminate, the patronage on which traditional party organisations relied. This reinforced the organisational diversity of American parties. Entrenched organisations in the older eastern and midwestern states were often able to extend their control to primary elections. However, where parties were weaker, organisations often atrophied or failed to develop in the first place. (Shefter 1983; Mayhew 1986)

Thus, parties which were already coalitions of divergent interests ended up as coalitions containing very different organisational forms. Depending on where one looked, the local organisation might mask a well-developed electoral machine, competing clubs or factions, the loosely integrated stratarchies which Samuel Eldersveld (1964; 1982) has described, or no organisation at all (Mayhew 1986). The result was a party system with wide scope for individual action and internal competition. In subsequent sections, we will examine the ways in which the presence of divergent groups have contributed to the reorientation of both political parties and the ways in which individual candidates, political action committees and, more recently, national party committees have exploited new techniques and technologies and revolutionised election campaigning.

Changing Party Coalitions

Since the 1960s, important changes have taken place in the orientation and organisation of both parties. The Democrats, the majority party since the 1930s, have become more divided and less certain about how to position themselves. In the Republican party, longstanding divisions between liberal and conservative wings have given way to conservative predominance. Presidential nominating processes in both parties have become more open and less predictable.

Yet at the same time, national organisations have gained influence *vis-à-vis* state and local parties.

The Democrats

The nineteenth century core of the Democratic Party consisted of the south, as well as Catholics and some other ethnic groups in the north. However, the realignment of the late 1920s and the 1930s brought a broader range of interests into the Democrat fold. The New Deal coalition included not only the white south, but also some blacks, organised labour, farmers, Catholics and Jews. This diverse coalition was held together by a mixture of earlier allegiances, commitment to active government, and a sense that group interests were better represented by the Democrats. As such, the Democrats were a multi-faceted coalition capable of being described in ethnic, religious, or economic terms. A confederation of state and local parties, the party embraced different organisational forms, including some surviving political machines in the north and midwest, a few strongly organised state parties, such as Connecticut or Rhode Island, and a number of more loosely structured entities (Mayhew 1986). In order to win nomination, a presidential candidate had to assemble a broadly based coalition and demonstrate that he was acceptable to party regulars and the interests which they represented.

The Democratic coalition contained a number of potential fault lines. One was race and the extent to which the party would tolerate segregation, the second, domestic policy and the extent to which the party would champion social and economic reform, and the third, latent until the Viet Nam War, foreign policy. Racial issues divided the party in 1948, when adoption of a civil rights plank at the 1948 convention resulted in the Dixiecrat revolt and Strom Thurmond's candidacy, and became a salient source of division in the 1960s, when the party had to decide whether it would accept racially segregated delegations to its national convention and how far it would go in pressing racial desegregation (Sundquist 1983).

The Democratic coalition remained intact until the late 1960s. Kennedy's assassination, Johnson's assumption of the Presidency, and his landslide victory over Goldwater in 1964 were turning points. Johnson's victory gave the Democrats an enlarged Congressional majority and an opportunity to press civil rights legislation and new programs of social reform. The former not only enfranchised black voters but also alienated white southerners, providing the basis for the electoral realignment of the south. The latter, compounded by court-ordered desegregation programmes, antagonized lower middle-class voters in the north. (Ginsberg and Shefter 1985). However, although racial and social issues eroded the electoral base of the Democratic Party, it was not the war on poverty, but rather the war in Viet Nam which most severely ruptured the Democratic coalition.

By 1968, the war and military conscription were the objects of rising protest. Opposition to the war resulted in an unprecedented challenge to the renomination of a sitting president. Senator Eugene McCarthy's showing in the New Hampshire primary resulted in the entry of a second challenger, Robert Kennedy, and Lyndon Johnson's decision not to seek renomination. However, this did little to reduce divisions within the party. Following the assassination of Robert Kennedy, the Democratic convention met in Chicago. Surrounded by anti-war demonstrators, the Democrats nominated Johnson's vice-president and heir-apparent, Hubert Humphrey, rather than McCarthy, the remaining candidate of the peace movement. This opened up a major rift between advocates of a new politics on one side and party regulars on the other. McCarthy supporters complained that delegation selection procedures had denied them the opportunity to present their case. Although unable to win the nomination, they were able to secure the passage of resolutions requiring that delegates to the 1972 convention be selected by open procedures in the same calendar year as the convention and the establishment of committees to investigate delegate selection procedures and party rules. The first of these, the Commission on Party Structure and Delegate Selection, more commonly known as the McGovern-Fraser Commission, recommended sweeping changes. Adopted and implemented by the Democratic National Committee, these not only transformed presidential nominating politics but also the distribution of power and influence within the party. (Shafer 1983)

Previously, delegates to the Democratic National Convention had been selected according to procedures determined by state party organisations and state law. The McGovern-Fraser Commission required that delegates be selected either in open party caucuses or primary elections, and that delegates be selected according to publicly known procedures. Delegates' commitments (or lack thereof) were to be known in advance, and 75 per cent of the delegates were to be elected at the level of the congressional district or below. In addition, *ex officio* delegates were eliminated and a maximum of 10 per cent of the delegation were to be selected by party committees, and party officials who had been not been elected in the same calendar year as the convention were barred from participating in the selection of delegates. Finally, state parties were enjoined to ensure the representation of blacks, women and youth in 'reasonable' proportion to state population. (Price 1984)

The McGovern-Fraser reforms altered the ways in which presidential candidates in both parties gained their nominations. Forced to comply with the new procedures or risk having their delegates denied seating at the national convention, many state parties used their control of the legislature to institute delegate selection primaries (Ranney 1975).[2] Prior to 1972, 35-40 per cent of the convention delegates had been elected in primary elections, but with the expansion in the number of primaries to as many as 34, by 1980, three quarters of the convention delegates were selected in primary elections (Reiter 1985). The increased number of primaries generated a new and different series of hurdles which candidates had to leap in order to win the nomination. Prior to 1972, a candidate could attempt to win nomination by entering some or all primary elections, seeking the support of state and local leaders or combining the two strategies. However, expansion in the number of primaries not only made entry into primary elections unavoidable but also made a strong showing in early primaries essential if candidates were to have sufficient finances and momentum to win the nomination.

Changes in party rules have decreased the influence of party leaders and elected officials in the nominating process. The new by-laws preclude unit rules, favorite-son strategies and other devices previously used to control state delegations. Although subsequent commissions have attempted to expand (though not fully restore) the role of party leaders and elected officials, rules requiring proportional allocation of delegates to candidates receiving more than a fixed percentage of the vote (initially 10 per cent and later 20 per cent) and granting candidates the right to approve delegates nominated on their behalf ensure that candidate organisations will dominate delegate selection.[3] Moreover, representatives of prospective candidates have played a prominent role on party reform commissions. Their presence, along with state chairmen and other interests, not only indicates that candidates and their organisations have become important constituencies within the party, but also ensures that their interests will be taken into account in debates on party rules. (Price 1984)

The character of the Democratic coalition has changed as well. Since 1968, reform and the representation of different groups have been the subject of ongoing debate. Successive commissions have not only mandated changes in rules but, in doing so, have also asserted the primacy of national party rules over state laws and state organisations. However, this is not the only consequence: reforms have cut the party loose from the few political machines still in operation and have given the new politics movement a substantial foothold within the party. Representation of older elements such as white ethnic groups or organised labour has become less important, representation of new movements, women, blacks, hispanics and the poor, more important.

Both the initial New Deal coalition and the current version embraced diverse elements. However, the earlier coalition was held together by a mixture of brokerage, tradeoffs, and agreement on policy. Party leaders sought presidential candidates who were capable of winning the election and acceptable to most, if not all, elements within the party. Contemporary party leaders are also anxious to win and are frequently willing to make compromises, but the element of brokerage, prominent within pre-1968 presidential nominating politics, is conspicuously absent. Because recent nominations have been determined in multi-candidate primaries, it is possible for candidates who lack a broad base of support within the party to win the nomination (Polsby 1981). Unless the convention deadlocks, there is little opportunity for bargaining and, in the absence of any experience, little evidence that candidates could throw support to each other.[4] Instead, the media have become a major arbiter of the process: pronouncements on whether candidates are doing better or worse than expected can make or break a candidacy (Orren 1985).

Finally, because of the openness of the process, the positions of party standard-bearers can shift from election to election. Hubert Humphrey, representative of older New Deal elements but unacceptable to the new politics movement was the last product of the unreformed nomination process. In the first post-reform convention, 1972, George McGovern, favoured by new politics groups but anathema to many others, won the nomination. Four years later, the candidate was Jimmy Carter, an outsider free of ties to Washington. Narrowly elected, Carter sought and won nomination for a second term, but not without a challenge from Senator Edward Kennedy. In 1984, the nominee was Carter's vice-president, Walter Mondale. Broadly representative of the party's middle, Mondale was tarnished by his association with the labour movement, a group once said to have exercised a veto on Democratic nominations.

The Republicans

Changes within the Republican party have been less dramatic but no less important. The Republicans have been attempting to make themselves the majority party in a redefined party system. In the process, the Republicans have not only become more conservative but also emerged as a nesting ground for new right groups.

We can trace changes within the Republican party to longstanding factional differences and economic and demographic changes which have enhanced the influence of the south and west. The Republicans were divided between a more liberal wing, with strength in the north and east, as well as the progressive areas of the west, and a conservative wing, stronger in small towns, the midwest and west. The latter were numerically stronger, but in light of Democratic majorities and the biases of the electoral college - winning the larger and more urban states was vital to securing a majority of the electoral votes - Republicans often felt constrained to nominate presidential candidates likely to attract independents and weakly attached Democrats. As early as 1940, Republicans nominated an outsider, Wendell Wilkie. Four years later they chose Thomas Dewey, governor of New York. Defeated in 1944, Dewey won the nomination in 1948 against Senator Robert Taft of Ohio. In 1952, Dwight Eisenhower, a war hero and a non-partisan figure, defeated Taft, the choice of the conservatives. As John Kessel (1968) points out, Republican governors were instrumental in swinging the nomination to the more liberal candidate.

In the 1960s and 1970s, control shifted to the conservatives. Goldwater's nomination in 1964 was a crucial turning point. Previously, conservatives had argued that Republicans had failed to mobilise a hidden conservative majority, available if they were to nominate a conservative candidate. The 1964 election provided a test of this. Following Richard Nixon's defeat in 1960, conservatives became active in Republican parties in the smaller states, enabling them to select pro-Goldwater delegates to the 1964 convention through the indirect caucus systems still in effect in many jurisdictions. Victory in the California primary and divisions among liberal Republicans, unable to group themselves around a single candidate, enabled Goldwater to capture the Republican nomination. (Kessel 1968)

Although Goldwater's defeat put the notion of a hidden conservative vote to rest, the balance within the Republican party was shifting toward the conservatives. The Democrats' embrace of black causes and Goldwater's stance on states rights made the Republican Party more attractive to white southerners. In addition, conservative activists had taken control of some local Republican organisations and constituted a bloc which could be mobilised for future conservative candidates (White and Gill 1981). Finally, liberal Republicans remained divided, without a single standard-bearer around whom they could rally. However, the consequences of this were not immediately apparent. In 1968, the Republicans nominated Richard Nixon, a centrist, who had built up support among party regulars, over liberal Nelson Rockefeller and conservative Ronald Reagan; Nixon defeated Hubert Humphrey in the presidential election and had little difficulty in securing renomination in 1972. But, four years later, in the aftermath of Watergate and withdrawal from Viet Nam, Reagan was able to mount a strong challenge to Nixon's successor, Gerald Ford. Although Ford won the nomination (but not the election), Reagan's challenge demonstrated the growing strength of the right within the Republican Party.

By this time, economic and demographic changes, reactions against the anti-war movement, school desegregation and changing social mores had made a conservative candidacy more credible than before. The south and southwest were growing, southern conservatives were gravitating toward the Republicans, and Democrats were increasingly divided. Moreover, Republican nominating processes - already open and penetrable - had been affected by Democratic Party reforms, which resulted in a drastic increase in the number of primary elections. In 1980, Reagan won the nomination in a wide field of candidates, few of whom could be described as liberal.

Conservative predominance has transformed, but not fully eliminated divisions within the Republican party. Although the previous divisions have faded, new ones have emerged between economic conservatives - whose principal concerns have been a reduction in taxes and government activity - and elements of the new right and moral majority active within the party. However, these are not as sharply defined as the former liberal-conservative split. Nevertheless, the openness of presidential nominating processes makes the outcome of future conflicts uncertain.

Thus, maneuvers of divergent groups within each coalition resulted in changes in party positions and party rules. Despite the occasional appearance of third party candidacies - George Wallace in 1968 and 1972, Eugene McCarthy in 1976, and John Anderson in 1980 - dissident elements generally have preferred to work within the major parties. Although this had already been the case before 1968, changes in Democratic Party rules and the resulting expansion in the number of primary elections widened the scope for intra-party competition in both parties, disengaged state and local parties from delegate selection processes and expanded the already considerable role of candidate organisations in presidential nominations. In doing so, the Democrats asserted the priority of national party rules over state parties and state law (Wekkin 1984). Although the Republicans declined to make a similar leap, the Republican National Committee gained influence by establishing itself as a highly proficient fundraising organisation.

Campaign Finance and Party Organisation

Changes in presidential nominating politics are only one of several changes occurring in the American political system. Substantial changes have also taken place in election campaigning, finance, and party organisation. Campaigns organised and executed by state and local party organisations have been supplanted by candidate-centred campaigns, managed by professional consultants. At the same time, political action committees (PACs) have assumed an increasingly prominent role in election finance and national committees have assumed a new role in fundraising, coordinating election campaigns, providing information and services to candidates, and more recently, building up state and local parties. The expanded role of national party committees, spearheaded by the Republicans, has not only injected an element of coordination into an increasingly decentralised universe of political campaigning, but has also provided the impetus for the reconstruction of party organisation from the top down.

Changes in election campaigning, finance, and party organisation reflect the uneven development of state and local party organisation, the emergence and exploitation of new techniques, and changes in election finance laws. In addition, competition between individual candidates and, more recently, the national parties has played an important role.

We can trace the emergence of candidate-centred campaigning to the variegated development of party organisation described earlier. Late nineteenth and early twentieth century reforms produced an unevenly developed pattern of party organisation in which parties were weak in some areas but stronger in others. Primary elections, the large number of elections contested in intersecting and overlapping districts, and variations in the strength of party organisations meant that in some areas candidates had to rely on their own resources in order to ensure their nomination and election. This was particularly true of Congressmen, whose districts frequently cut across other jurisdictions. (Salmore and Salmore 1985)

Although some degree of candidate-centred campaigning was built into the structure of American party system, this did not become a widespread phenomenon until the 1960s, when techniques first used in Presidential elections were translated to state-wide campaigns (Salmore and Salmore 1985). By this time, state and local party organisations in many areas had weakened and voters were increasingly demonstrating their independence from party. The use of opinion polls and television advertising provided candidates with alternate sources of information and alternate means of reaching voters (Agranoff 1976). However, applying the new techniques required different forms of expertise than those supplied by old line party organisations. Candidates increasingly relied on paid consultants, pollsters and media experts and built their own campaign organisations (Sabato 1981). Doing so enabled candidates to circumvent regular party organisations - which might or might not have been adequate to the task - and secure election in their own right. Bypassing local party organisations contributed to their further decline. (Ware 1985)

Techniques initially exploited by a few candidates were imitated by others. By the 1970s, candidate-centred campaigns employing professional consultants had become the norm not only in senatorial and gubernatorial elections, but also in state-wide campaigns for lesser offices (Agranoff 1976). By the early 1980s, Congressmen, who had previously relied on their own staffs to cultivate their districts, were employing professional consultants as well (Salmore and Salmore 1985).

Thus, instead of drawing on state or local party organisations, candidates rely on a mobile campaign industry, parachuted in to handle specific campaigns. Strategies are mapped by professional consultants on the basis of opinion polls. Voters are reached by a variety of techniques including direct mail and telephone appeals, carefully prepared spot advertisements, and contrived media events focussing attention on the candidate. In addition, in well-financed campaigns tracking polls are used to monitor the impact of campaigning and revise strategies in light of the results. (Salmore and Salmore 1985)

Recourse to these techniques requires large amounts of money. Until the 1970s candidates relied either on their own resources or wealthy donors.[5] However, the Federal Election Campaign Act (FECA, first passed in 1971, but modified in the aftermath of the Watergate affair) redirected the flow of money by limiting the amounts which individuals and party and other committees could contribute to individual candidates. Individual contributions to candidates were restricted to $1000 per primary or general election campaign, contributions to non-party committees to $5000 per committee, and contributions to political parties to $20,000. However, total donations in any year were limited to $25,000. In addition, non-party committees were permitted to donate up to $5000 to individual candidates or party committees, but, according to court interpretations, are allowed to make unlimited 'independent' expenditures (i.e., made without any coordination with the official campaigns) on behalf of candidates. Finally, the legislation limits contributions by party committees to individual candidates to $5000 per election campaign (for House candidates), but allows party committees to spend larger amounts, pro-rated according to the number of voters and adjusted for inflation, on 'coordinated' expenditures made in conjunction with candidates' campaigns. House and Senate campaign committees are allowed to make separate donations. National party committees can also expand the value of their contributions by providing lower cost services-in-kind to candidates and donating money to state parties, which are allowed to make separate contributions (Adamany 1984; Epstein 1986).

Limits on the size of individual contributions not only forced candidates and parties to rely on smaller contributions but also provided substantial opportunities for expansion in the activities of political action committees and national party committees. Until the 1970s, the device of organising committees to raise and expend funds and participate in election campaigns had been exploited largely by unions in support of Democratic candidates. However, provisions allowing non-party committees to receive up to $5000 from individuals and contribute similar amounts to candidates, inserted in the legislation at the behest of the AFL-CIO, made political action committees an attractive channel for donations. During the 1970s, numerous corporations, trade associations, unions, and unaffiliated (non-connected) groups formed political action committees. (Sabato 1984) The number of PACs expanded from 608 in 1974 to 4009 in 1984, and PAC expenditures increased from $19,100,000 in 1972 to $267,000,000 in 1984. A disproportionate share of the increase was in corporate PACs. (Epstein 1986)

Political action committees assemble large numbers of individual donations and channel them to selected candidates or political parties. Typically corporate, labour, and trade PACs raise funds among a select group - e.g., the employees of an individual corporation, the members of a union or an association - and donate funds to Congressmen or Senators active in areas of legislation of interest to them. In contrast, unconnected PACs are typically more ideologically oriented. Funds are raised through direct mail, often on the basis of ideological appeals, and then either donated to candidates sympathetic to the PAC's point of view, or, expended independently - in support or opposed to particular candidates but without any coordination with official campaigns. (Sabato 1984) Corporate, labour, and trade PACs contribute heavily to incumbents. However, unconnected PACs are more likely to support challengers and at times (for example, 1980) have been involved in the defeats of well-known incumbents. (Jacobson 1985-86)

Political action committees contributed nearly 30 per cent of the funds spent on House and Senate campaigns in 1984 (Adamany 1986). However, the impact of political action committees on either party organisation or election campaigning cannot be assessed without exploring the new roles which national party committees have assumed. National Committees have been increasingly engaged in fundraising, training, the provision of information, advice and services to individual campaigns, as well as efforts to build up state and more recently local party organisations. Like the PAC phenomenon, the changing role of national committees reflects both technological developments - which among other things facilitated direct mail appeals - and election finance legislation which forced parties and candidates to rely on smaller donations (Adamany 1986). However, party competition has also played a role: Republicans, particularly in the aftermath of Watergate and election defeat, have pioneered many of the new tasks and Democrats have followed, generally on a smaller scale.

Innovations in the Republican Party stem both from minority status and the setbacks which the party suffered in the 1960s and mid 1970s. Following Goldwater's defeat in 1964, the Republican National Committee (RNC) began to expand its activities and explore direct mail fundraising. Although party-building, initiated under the chairmanship of Ray Bliss, stalled during Nixon's presidency, the Watergate affair and Republican defeats in 1974 and 1976 spurred renewed efforts. These intensified when Senator William Brock became the national chairman in 1977. Under Brock, the RNC invested heavily in the development of direct mail lists and the expansion of the party's fundraising base. (Kayden and Mahe 1985) The moneys raised have been used to finance election campaigns, recruit candidates for lower offices, and expand the party's capabilities at the national, state and, more recently, local levels. Imitating the British Conservatives, the RNC launched an extensive 'institutional' advertising program urging voters to support the Republicans. At the same time, expansion of the national party's staff, research, and data processing and communication facilities has enabled the RNC, along with House and Senate campaign committees to provide a wide range of services to candidates. These include advice and assistance, information on opponents' positions, survey data, guidance on the use and interpretation of polls, position papers, campaign literature, and help in the preparation of media spots (Reichley 1985). National party committees monitor individual campaigns and attempt to channel party funds and PAC donations to campaigns where they are likely to make the most difference (Sabato 1984). The Republicans have also been adept in finding ways to work within and expand FECA spending limits, for example, by channeling funds to state parties, which are allowed to make separate contributions, and by supplying 'depreciated' services (such as opinion polls) to candidates (Adamany 1984; 1986).

Republican National Committee activities extend well beyond providing support services for campaigns. In addition to recruiting candidates for lower office, the RNC operates campaign schools and workshops, and has encouraged state and local parties to expand their staffs and capabilities. As Epstein (1986) points out, assistance to state and local parties has taken the form of grants-in-aid requiring that they modernise in order to receive funds. As such, the Republicans have been reinforcing trends toward greater professionalisation underway since the 1960s (Cotter *et al.* 1984).

Since the 1980s, the Democrats have been imitating Republican techniques. However, saddled with debts from earlier campaigns, the Democrats have been unable to invest as heavily in the development of mailing lists or match Republican spending. Nevertheless, the Democrats have established a permanent national headquarters with their own media production facilities and have been running campaign seminars and providing services such as assistance in the production of media spots. The House and Senate Committees have also become more active. However, Democratic National Committee spending and activities lag far behind those of the Republicans. In the 1982 elections, the two parties spent a total of $254 million, of which $215 million was spent by Republicans. In 1984, Democrats boosted their spending to nearly $100 million, but Republican spending increased to $300 million. (Epstein 1986)

The activities of the national party committees provide an element of coordination to the candidate-centred campaigning prevalent in the United States. Because of its fundraising base, the Republican National Committee (and increasingly, its Democratic counterpart as well) can provide a formidable array of services to their candidates. Although federal regulations limit the amount which party committees can contribute to separate campaigns, provisions for coordinated expenditures and the ability of both parties to provide candidates with discounted services-in-kind extend the value of national party services. Nevertheless, national party committees supply only a small proportion of the funds which candidates spend. As Epstein (1986) points out, Senate and Congressional candidates raise the bulk of their campaign funds from individual donations. Political action committees constitute the second most important source: PACs supplied 31 per cent of House candidates' receipts and 18 per cent of Senate candidate receipts in 1982, and 34 per cent and 17 per cent in 1984, considerably more than the proportion supplied by national parties. However, coordinated expenditures and provision of services in kind increased the weight of party contributions.

Although the professionalisation of the national party committees introduces an element of centralisation into American party politics (Adamany 1984), the extent of change should not be overstated. Thus far, national party services have been more important for first-time candidates than for incumbents. Party funds not only induce candidates to run but, by demonstrating the viability of the campaign, encourage others to contribute (Cohen 1986). Incumbents can draw funds from a wider range of sources, particularly political action committees. Nor can national committee funds be used to intervene in primary elections or enforce party discipline.[6] Nevertheless, efforts by the Republicans to build up state and local organisations constitute a major effort to reconstruct American political parties along new lines. However, the new-style party is being constructed from the top down, and functions more like a professional service bureau than an organisation with distinct roots or membership. (Arterton 1982; Epstein 1986)

Voting Patterns and Electoral Change

Changes in presidential nominating processes, national party orientation, the rise of candidate-centred campaigning, and the professionalisation of national party organisation constitute major changes in the ways in which American parties approach the electorate. Although it is difficult to draw a direct connection between changes in party organisation and changes in the electorate, there are distinct parallels between the changes which we have described and increases in ticket-splitting and independent voting and, more generally, the weakening of the New Deal alignment.

The problem of electoral realignment provides a useful focus. Since V.O. Key's seminal article on critical elections (Key 1955), considerable attention has been devoted to recurring realignments which appeared to be part of the rhythm of American politics. Realignments were considered to be important not only because they

Figure 12.1 Percentage of the Popular Vote in Presidential Elections and Elections to the House of Representatives, 1952-1986

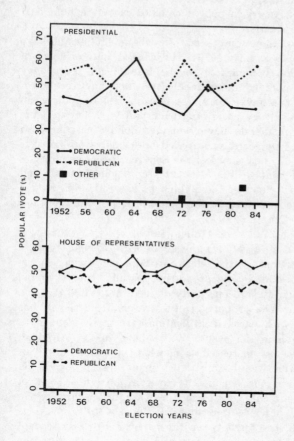

Source: Rose, Richard and Thomas T. Mackie *International Almanac of Election History*, 2nd ed., (Facts on File, New York) 1982; Mann, Thomas E. and Norman J. Ornstein, *The American Elections of 1982* (American Enterprise Institute, Washington) 1983; U.S. Bureau of the Census, *Statistical Abstract of the United States* 75th edition (1954) and 106th edition (1987); *Congressional Quarterly Weekly Report, 45*, no. 11, March 14, 1987, 484.

Note: Other: in 1968 and 1972, George Wallace, American Independent Party, in 1980, John Anderson, Independent.

provided a useful way of demarcating one period from another, but also because the interplay between electoral changes and changes in party coalitions usually gave one party decisive control of Congress and the Presidency and the opportunity to implement new policies (Brady 1985). Because major realignments occurred every thirty to forty years, students of American politics came to expect realignments to occur once per generation.

Had this been so, then some kind of realignment should have occurred in the late 1960s or early 1970s. However, despite evidence of dealignment, no changes comparable to the Republican ascendancy after 1896 or the Democrats' dominance after 1932 have occurred. Although the Republicans have won six of the nine elections between 1952 and 1984, the Presidency has swung back and forth between the two parties and the Democrats have remained solidly ensconced in Congress (figure 12.1). Democrats controlled both houses of Congress from 1954 through 1980, when they lost the Senate. Reagan's victories in 1980 and 1984 have enabled him to assert a new policy agenda and bring about important changes in public policy. However, the Democrats retained their majority in the House of Representatives and regained control of the Senate in 1986.

The absence of any full scale realignment is apparent in survey data. Regular election studies since the 1950s have demonstrated a decline in the proportion of the electorate holding strong party identifications and increases in the proportion of independent voters, particularly those leaning toward one party or the other (table 12.1).

At the same time, the proportion of voters splitting tickets has increased, and voters with party identifications are more inclined to deviate from them than in the past. (Wattenberg 1984) Although Republican identifications increased somewhat in the mid-1980s (Epstein 1985) and the Republicans have made decisive gains in Presidential elections in the south, the overall pattern is one of weakened electoral alignment: groups such as Catholics once solidly in the Democratic fold, now deviate more frequently from previous loyalties and divide their votes between the parties. However, except for the shift of blacks to the Democrats and southern whites to the Republicans in presidential elections (Ladd 1985; Axelrod 1986), there is little evidence of durable shifts between the parties.

The absence of any large-scale realignment has been the subject of considerable debate. Some observers of American politics, such as Kevin Phillips, have argued that the generational realignment which had been expected in the late 1960s and 1970s was delayed by the turmoil of Watergate and the Nixon presidency (Phillips 1975).

Table 12.1 Party Identification in the United States, 1952-84 (in percent)

	1952	1956	1960	1964	1968	1972	1976	1980	1984
Strong Democrat	22	21	20	27	20	15	15	17	17
Weak Democrat	25	23	25	25	25	26	25	23	20
Independent Democrat	10	6	6	9	10	11	12	11	11
Independent	6	9	10	8	11	13	15	13	11
Independent Republican	7	8	7	6	9	11	10	10	12
Weak Republican	14	14	14	14	15	13	14	14	15
Strong Republican	14	15	16	11	10	10	9	9	12
Apolitical, Don't know, other	3	4	3	1	1	1	1	3	2

Source: Epstein (1986), table 8.1., p. 256. The data are from Center for Political Studies/Survey Research Center.

Others, such as Ladd (1985) or Petrocik (1981), have challenged the emphasis, common in the realignment literature, on one party gaining ascendancy over the other and have argued that important changes in the composition of party coalitions have occurred, resulting in what Ladd (1985) termed a 'two-tier' alignment in which Republicans usually control the Presidency while Democrats control Congress. However, although changes in the composition of party support have indeed occurred, this does not explain why more thoroughgoing changes, comparable to earlier realignments, have not occurred.

Part of the explanation lies in the changes in party organisation and election campaigning which we have described. Realignment in the 1890s and in the 1930s took place in periods when state and local party organisations were stronger and changes in presidential voting translated into changes in Congressional elections. Control of the executive and legislative branches enabled governing parties to implement new programmes, which in turn helped to solidify emergent loyalties, particularly among newer voters. In contrast, recent changes have taken place in a period when party organisations have weakened, candidate-centred campaigning has become the rule, and congressional elections have become increasingly insulated from presidential trends (Chubb and Peterson 1985). Each has had an effect. As Martin Wattenberg (1984) has noted, media coverage of election campaigns since the 1950s has paid more attention to candidates than parties and has de-emphasised links between candidates and their parties. The prevalence of candidate-centred campaigning means that voters receive a variety of different messages and can readily be encouraged to split their votes among candidates of different parties (Arterton 1982).

Separation between congressional and presidential voting has been further reinforced by congressional reforms in the 1970s. Seniority has been weakened and legislative caucuses have assumed greater control over committee assignments. However, a proliferation of subcommittees in the House of Representatives has led to a greater fragmentation of power and increased the opportunities for individual congressman to nurse their constituencies and develop support across party lines (Ferejohn and Fiorina 1985). Through the 1970s, the proportion of elections decided by close votes decreased and the proportion of incumbent congressman securing re-election was greater than 90 per cent in all elections except for 1974 when it dipped to 87.7 per cent (Mann and Ornstein 1983:165; Ferejohn and Fiorina 1985). Only in the 1980s, when the activities of more ideologically oriented political action committees and new campaign techniques such as negative advertising weakened the positions of some incumbents, did this pattern show signs of changing (Jacobson 1984; 1985).

The prevalence of candidate-centred campaigning and the ability of incumbents to secure their own re-election have insulated congressional elections from swings in presidential elections and decreased the likelihood of decisive realignments taking place. Divided control of the executive and legislative branches means that opportunities to implement decisive changes in public policy, attracting or repelling large numbers of voters from one party to another are more limited than they might otherwise be. In addition, the prevalence of candidate-centred campaigning is yet another obstacle to a massive electoral realignment. So too is the vulnerability of the presidency to policy failures and exposure in the media. Although this does not preclude large scale realignments, it does suggest that processes of electoral change and realignment will proceed more gradually and less uni-directionally than in the past. In some ways, the Reagan presidency is a testimonial to this: a popular president, skilled in the use of media, Reagan has succeeded in bolstering his party and putting the Democrats on the defensive. Nevertheless, despite the changing preferences of southern whites, a major shift in underlying loyalties, benefitting Republican House and Senate candidates or state and local parties, has yet to occur.

Change Further Considered

Let us draw our argument together. We have explored changes in party coalitions, organisational developments, and electoral change in light of institutional structures and the competitive dynamics of the party system. Factors central to our analysis have included (1) the ways in which divergent interests have been contained within two broadly based parties, (2) the impact of earlier and recent reforms, and (3) the uses which candidates, political action committees and, more recently, parties have made of new techniques and technology. The first has led to the occasional redefinition of party-based coalitions and the periodic realignments for which the United States has been noted; the second to the virtual disappearance of old-style political machines, expanded opportunities for internal contestation, and changes in campaign finance; the third to the professionalisation and streamlining of national party bureaucracies.

These have had substantial impact on the ways in which parties have responded to social change. In contrast to Western Europe, where the emergence of new forces, both in the past and in the present, often resulted in the formation of new parties, in the United States, new groups have usually been contained within the two-party system. However, despite the coalitional character of the parties and the opportunities which primary elections provide, this has not always been a smooth process: new demands have often led to substantial intra-party conflict and occasional third party candidacies, and all demands have not necessarily been addressed to the satisfaction of their claimants. Nevertheless, despite the weakening of party loyalties and the widespread diffusion of campaign technologies, few durable third parties have emerged. Instead, in most cases, opportunities for contestation and influence within one or both parties have discouraged all but the most discontented from joining or establishing third parties.[7]

Inter- and intra-party competition, reforms, and the application of new technologies have resulted in a party system changed in some respects, but not in others. The United States retains a two-party system and parties retain their broad, coalitional character. However, party positions have changed and parties are far more open and penetrable than before. Locally based organisations have been displaced by actors as diverse as candidate organisations, professional consultants, political action committees, and reconstituted national committees. Old-style party organisations relied on party workers whose jobs depended on mobilising the vote, or failing that, volunteers. In contrast, the new-style organisations substitute money, machines, and technological proficiency for manpower.

These changes have both strengthened and weakened parties. On one hand, the spread of delegate selection primaries and plebiscitary nominating processes has eroded parties' control over presidential selection. On the other, the development of technologically proficient national committees has given the national parties an unprecedented capacity to assist candidates and state and local organisations. Even so, the influence of these new-style professional bureaucracies is limited. Despite their proficiency in fundraising and delivering services, national committees exert scant control over either the designation of candidates or the ways in their nominees behave once they are in office. The widespread use of primary elections and jealousies between national and state parties inhibit control over recruitment; moreover, incumbents can either raise their own funds or rely on the support of political action committees, which are also adept at raising funds.

Paradoxically, the emergent strength of national party committees is based on techniques first exploited by candidate organisations and political action committees. Although there may well be economies of scale in the construction and manipulation of large data bases and the delivery of some services, such as institutional advertising, the techniques and equipment required to establish separate operations are widely diffused. Because of the separation of powers, the advantages of incumbency, and the liberties granted to political action committees - in effect, electorally-oriented interest groups with large numbers of contributors - national party committees have no monopoly on the resources or services which they supply, but rather operate in a pluralistic universe in which non-party groups can exert substantial influence in election campaigns.

American parties and the universe in which they operate have been the objects of considerable concern. Well before the decline of old-style party organisations, political scientists debated the need for more responsible parties. Recent changes have widened the discussion. Although increased capabilities have generally been applauded, alarm has been expressed about the growing detachment of the electorate, low turnout rates and the failure to mobilise non-voters or the poor (Burnham 1970; 1982), the decline of 'collective responsibility' in a system in which candidate-centred contests predominate (Fiorina 1980), the inability of parties to perform the brokerage and mediation functions once attributed to them (Polsby 1983), the accountability of political actors (Epstein 1986; Adamany 1986) and the large amounts of money spent in American politics.

Although it is impossible to comment on these deficiencies here - other than to note that the party system meshes with its institutional setting (Epstein 1986) and manages to designate candidates despite its apparent defects - it is important to note that future reforms, along with inter- and intra-party competition, are likely to remain major sources of party system change. Where then, is the American party system headed? Past experience suggests that American politics will continue to fit a two-party mold, that parties will continue to be battlegrounds on which divergent groups compete, and that parties - because they cannot at one and the same time be popularly controlled, responsive to conflicting interests, yet cohesive and responsible - will continue to be the objects of criticism and reform.

Ironically, many of the ostensible problems which conflicting demands create could be resolved if there were more than two parties. However, multi-party competition is so far removed from American institutions and experience that it cannot readily be contemplated as an option for change. That means that change will continue to take place within and between the parties. Whether this will take the form of 'grand' realignments, analogous to those of the past, or less extensive changes, comparable to those of the 1970s and 1980s, remains to be seen. However, the prevalence of candidate-centred campaigning and the continuing ability of incumbent congressman to insulate themselves from national electoral trends suggests that in the absence of either major institutional reforms strengthening parties *vis-à-vis* candidates and elected representatives, or a president capable of mobilising large segments of the electorate in support of his party, the latter are more likely than the former.

Notes

1. Third parties were a regular phenomenon in the late nineteenth century. However, many of these were established in order to influence the Democrats or the Republicans and often nominated fusion candidates (i.e. designated in common with other parties) in order to avoid throwing the election to other candidates. The number of votes a candidate received on a party's ticket served as a measure of its strength (Scarrow 1986; Rosenstone *et al.* 1984).

2. The Democratic National Committee and subsequent party commissions exerted considerable effort to ensure that state parties complied with the new rules (Shafer 1983). Although some delegations (Illinois, controlled by Chicago Mayor Richard Daley, was a notorious example) were not seated at the national convention, most states were in compliance by 1972; however, their compliance was sometimes secured by tolerating exceptions (Wekkin 1984). Members of the McGovern-Fraser Commission, including political scientist Austin Ranney, had hoped that state parties would establish open caucuses; however, many opted for primaries in order to avoid extensive changes in their rules (Ranney 1975). Polsby (1983) suggests that this also helped to insulate state parties from national conflicts.

3. The details are too complex to report here. For a succinct overview, see Price (1984).

4. Price (1984) notes that in recent conventions candidates have had difficulty in controlling their delegates on votes on party platforms.

5. Previous restrictions on the amounts given to candidates could be circumvented by making donations to numerous campaign committees operating on behalf of the same candidate (Sabato 1984).

6. There is a difference in this regard between national committees and House and Senate campaign committees. The Republican National Committee has been enjoined from intervening in primary elections unless the three national committeemen from the state consent. In contrast, the Congressional campaign committees may intervene on behalf of incumbents in primary elections.

7. Access to the ballot has been a formidable obstacle. In many states, 'spoiler' provisions prevent candidates for nomination in Democratic or Republican primaries from running on other tickets. In addition, deadlines for filing for nomination often precede primary elections or conventions. Difficulties in gaining access to state ballots has often forced candidates to run on several different tickets. (Rosenstone *et al.* 1984). However, lawsuits on behalf of Eugene McCarthy and John Anderson have recently eased access to the ballot. Nevertheless, federal financing works to the disadvantage of third party candidates: in contrast to Democratic or Republican nominees, whose primary election expenses are eligible for subsidy and who receive matching funds during the campaign, third party candidates must obtain five per cent of the vote in order to receive funds after the election. However, a candidate receiving more than five per cent would be eligible for funds in the next election (Epstein 1986).

References

Adamany, David (1984) 'Political Parties in the 1980s' in Michael J. Malbin, (ed.) *Money and Politics in the United States*, American Enterprise Institute, Washington. D.C., 70-122

Adamany, David (1986) 'The New Faces of American Politics' in *Annals of the American Academy of Political and Social Science, 486*, 12-34

Agranoff, Robert (1976) 'The New Style of Campaigning: The Decline of Party and the Rise of Candidate-Centered Technology' in Robert Agranoff, (ed.) *The New Style of Election Campaigns*, 2nd edition, Holbrook, Boston, 3-48

Arterton, F. Christopher (1982), 'Political Money and Party Strength' in Joel L. Fleishman (ed.) *The Future of American Political Parties*, Prentice Hall (The American Assembly), Englewood Cliffs, N.J., 101-39

Axelrod, Robert (1986) 'Presidential Election Coalition in 1984' *American Political Science Review 80*, 281-4

Brady, David (1985) 'A Re-evaluation of Realignments in American Politics: Evidence From the House of Representatives', *American Political Science Review, 79*, 28-49

Burnham, Walter Dean (1970) *Critical Elections and the Mainsprings of American Politics* Norton, New York

Burnham, Walter Dean (1982) *The Current Crisis in American Politics*, Oxford University Press, Oxford

Chubb, John E. and Paul E. Peterson (1985) 'Realignment and Institutionalization in American Politics' in John E. Chubb and Paul E. Peterson (eds.) *The New Direction in American Politics*, The Brookings Institution, Washington, D.C., 1-30

Clubb, Jerome M, William H. Flanagan, and Nancy H. Zingale (1980) *Partisan Realignment: Voters, Parties, and Government in American History*, Sage Publications. Beverly Hills.

Cohen, Richard E. (1986) 'Party Help' *National Journal*, Aug. 16, 1998-2004

Cotter, Cornelius P., James L. Gibson, John F. Bibby, and Robert J. Huckshorn (1984) *Party Organizations in American Politics*, Praeger, New York

Cotter, Cornelius P. and Bernard C. Hennessy (1964) *Politics Without Power: The National Party Committees*, Atherton Press, New York

Dodd, Lawrence C. and Bruce Oppenheimer (1985) 'The Elusive Congressional Mandate: The 1984 Election and its Aftermath' in Lawrence C. Dodd and Bruce I. Oppenheimer (eds.) *Congress Reconsidered*, CQ Press, Washington, D.C., 1-10

Dodd, Lawrence C. and Bruce Oppenheimer (1985) 'The House in Transition: Partisanship and Opposition' in Lawrence C. Dodd and Bruce I. Oppenheimer (eds.) *Congress Reconsidered*, CQ Press, Washington, D.C., 34-64

Eldersveld, J. Samuel (1964) *Political Parties: A Behavioral Analysis*, Rand McNally, Chicago

Eldersveld, J. Samuel (1982) *Political Parties in American Society*, Basic Books, New York

Epstein, Laurily K. (1985) 'The Changing Structure of Party Identification' *PS, 18*, 48-52

Epstein, Leon D. (1986) *Political Parties in the American Mold*, The University of Wisconsin Press, Madison

Ferejohn, John A. and Fiorina, Morris (1985) 'Incumbency and Realignment in

Congressional Elections' in John E. Chubb and Paul E. Peterson (eds.) *The New Direction in American Politics* Brookings, Washington, D.C., 91-115

Fiorina, Morris P. (1980) 'The Decline of Collective Responsibility in American Politics' *Daedelus, 109,* 25-47

Ginsberg, Benjamin and Martin Shefter (1985) 'A Critical Realignment? The New Politics, the Reconstituted Right, and the Election of 1984' in Michael Nelson (ed.) *The Elections of 1984,* Congressional Quarterly Press, Washington, D.C., 1-26

Jacobson, Gary C. (1984) 'Money in the 1980 and 1982 Congressional Elections' in Michael J. Malbin, (ed.) *Money and Politics in the United States,* American Enterprise Institute, Washington, 38-69

Jacobson, Gary C. (1985) 'The Republican Advantage in Campaign Finance' in John E. Chubb and Paul E. Peterson (eds.) *The New Direction in American Politics* Washington, D.C., Brookings), 143-73

Jacobson, Gary C. (1985-86), 'Party Organization and Campaign Resources in 1982, *Political Science Quarterly, 100,* 603-26

Jones, Charles O. (1931) 'Nominating "Carter's Favorite Opponent"' in Austin Ranney, (ed.) *the American Elections of 1980* American Enterprise Institute, Washington, D.C. 61-98

Kayden, Xandra and Eddie Mahe, Jr. (1985) *The Persistence of the Two-Party System in the United States,* Basic Books, New York

Kessel, John H. (1968) *The Goldwater Coalition: Republican Strategies in 1964,* Bobbs-Merrill, Indianapolis

Key, V.O. (1955) 'A Theory of Critical Elections' *Journal of Politics 17,* 3-18

Ladd, Everett Carl (1985) 'On Mandates, Realignments, and the 1984 Presidential Election', *Political Science Quarterly, 100,* 1-26

Ladd and Hadley (1978) *Transformations of the American Party System,* 2nd ed., W.W. Norton, New York

Lowi, Theodore J. (1985) *The Personal President: Power Invested, Promise Unfulfilled,* Cornell University Press, Ithaca

Malbin, Michael, ed. (1984) *Money and Politics in the United States,* American Enterprise Institute, Washington, D.C.

Mann, Thomas E. and Ornstein, Norman E., eds. (1983) *The American Elections of 1982,* American Enterprise Institute, Washington, D.C.

Mayhew, David R. (1986) *Placing Parties in American Politics: Organization, Electoral Settings and Government Activity in the Twentieth Century,* Princeton University Press, Princeton

Orren, Gary R. (1985) 'The Nomination Process: Vicissitudes of Candidate Selection' in Michael Nelson, (ed.) *The Elections of 1984,* Congressional Quarterly Press, Washington, D.C., 27-82

Petrocik, John R. (1981) *Party Coalitions and the Decline of the New Deal Party System,* University of Chicago, Chicago

Phillips, Kevin P. (1975) *Mediacracy: American Parties and Politics in the Communications Age,* Doubleday, Garden City, N.Y.

Phillips, Kevin P. (1982) *Post-Conservative America: People, Politics and Ideology in a Time of Crisis,* Random House, New York

Polsby, Nelson W., (1981) in 'The Democratic Nomination' in Austin Ranney (ed.) *the American Elections of 1980,* American Enterprise Institute, Washington, D.C., 37-60

Polsby, Nelson (1983) *The Consequences of Party Reform*, Oxford University Press, Oxford

Price, David E. 1984, *Bringing Back the Parties*, Congressional Quarterly Press, Washington, D.C.

Ranney, Austin (1975) *Curing the Mischiefs of Faction*, University California Press, Berkeley

Reichley, A. James (1985), 'The Rise of National Parties' in John E. Chubb and Paul E. Peterson (eds.) *The New Direction in American Politics*, Brookings, Washington, D.C., 177-200

Reiter, Howard L. (1985) *Selecting the President: The Nominating Process in Transition*, University of Pennsylvania Press, Philadelphia

Rosenstone, Steven J, Roy L. Behr, and Edward H. Lazarus (1984) *Third Parties in America: Citizen Response to Major Party Failure*, Princeton University Press, Princeton

Sabato, Larry J. (1981) *The Rise of Political Consultants*, Basic Books, New York

Sabato, Larry J. (1984) *PAC Power: Inside the World of Political Action Committees*, W.W. Norton, New York

Salmore, Stephen A. and Barbara G. Salmore (1985) *Candidates, Parties, and Campaigns: Electoral Politics in America*, Congressional Quarterly Press, Washington, D.C.

Scarrow, Howard A. (1986) 'Duverger's Law, Fusion, and the Decline of American 'Third' Parties' *Western Political Quarterly, 39*, 634-47

Schlesinger, Joseph A. (1984), 'On the Theory of party Organization' *Journal of Politics, 46*, 369-400

Shafer, Byron 1983, *Quiet Revolution: The Struggle for Democratic Party Reform and the Shaping of Post-Reform Politics*, Russell Sage Foundation, New York

Shefter, Martin (1983) 'Regional Receptivity to Reform: The Legacy of the Progressive Era' *Political Science Quarterly, 98*, 459-483

Skowronek, Stephen (1982) *Building a New American State: The Expansion of Administrative Capacities, 1877-1920*, Cambridge University Press, Cambridge

Sundquist, James L. (1983) *Dynamics of the Party System: Alignment and Realignment of Political Parties in the United States*, (Revised Edition), Brookings Institution, Washington, D.C.

Ware, Alan (1985) *The Breakdown of Democratic Party Organization, 1940-1980*, Clarendon Press, Oxford

Wattenberg, Martin (1984) *The Decline of American Political Parties 1952 to 1980*, Harvard University Press, Cambridge

Wekkin, Gary D. (1984) 'National-State Party Relations: The Democrats' New Federal Structure', *Political Science Quarterly 99*, 45-72

White, F. Clifton and William J. Gill (1981) *Why Reagan Won: A Narrative History of the Conservative Movement, 1964-1981*, Regnery Gateway, Chicago

Chapter Thirteen

Party System Change: Past, Present and Future

Steven B. Wolinetz

Party systems today are different than in the past. Writing in the mid 1960s, Lipset and Rokkan (1967) could characterise most Western European party systems as frozen. With the exception of France, Germany, and Italy, party alternatives and cleavage structures resembled those of the 1920s. Twenty years later, it is difficult to reach a similar conclusion. Despite variations among countries, party systems display considerably more change than they did in the 1960s. Electorates have become more volatile and party strengths are no longer as constant as they were in the past.[1] In many instances, party positions have shifted and new parties have wedged themselves into existing party configurations. Coalition patterns have also changed. Examples of the rigid continuity which Lipset and Rokkan described are harder to find, instances of change much more apparent. Of the countries examined in this volume, Austria, Sweden, and postwar Italy (previously an exception to the generalisation) best fit Lipset and Rokkan's metaphor. But even in these countries changes are becoming more apparent.

Even if change is widespread, it is important not to overstate its extent. Although few party systems have been as constant as they once appeared to be, all exhibit substantial elements of continuity. In each of the countries we have considered, established parties not only survive, but also govern. Exploring why so much has changed and why so much remains the same are the central foci of this chapter.

What Has Changed: An Overview

Patterns of continuity and change vary considerably among geographic areas, size and type of country. The similarity of the three Scandinavian party systems and the societies in which they operated permitted Einhorn and Logue to consider them within a single chapter. Yet one of the most salient features of their chapter is the growing divergence of the three party systems. Only the Swedish party system remains relatively unchanged, with few changes in party strengths, the number of parties or the division into Social Democratic and bourgeois blocks. The same cannot be said of Denmark or Norway. The former has become more fragmented, with nine to ten parties regularly represented since 1973. In the latter, the Liberals have virtually disappeared, leaving the Conservatives as the dominant force within the bourgeois bloc.

Trends among the other smaller democracies are no more apparent. The Austrian party system has been one of the most stable party systems of those which we have been considering: until the recent entry of the Greens, there were no new parties, few changes in coalition patterns, and virtually no changes in party strengths. In contrast, both the Netherlands and Belgium experienced waves of minor parties, many of which gained support in the late 1960s or 1970s and subsequently declined, without entirely disappearing. But even here, patterns differ. In the Dutch case, diminishing support for established parties facilitated the reorientation of the left, the regrouping of the three religious parties, and the emergence of a three-party predominant system, albeit one surrounded by a large number of smaller parties. In Belgium, with the exception of the Volksunie, the linguistic and communal parties which gained support in the 1960s have waned, but the Socialists, Christian Democrats, and Liberals are now divided into distinct Flemish and Wallonian parties.

We come no closer to common trends if we consider the larger continental European countries. The Italian party system, firmly established only after World War II, has been very stable in the postwar period. Although there have been long term changes, such as the growth of Communist support through 1976, the format of the party system (the number of parties and their relative strengths) has been fixed; the principal changes have been in coalition patterns and in relationships within and among parties and their internal factions. In contrast, the West German party system, reflecting both the effects of the 5% rule and the way in which the Christian Democrats absorbed smaller parties on the right and the centre, underwent substantial changes in the 1950s. By 1959, a three-party configuration had supplanted the multiparty system which had re-emerged in 1949. Despite two major shifts in governing coalitions, the three-party system remained intact until the 1983 incursion of the Greens. France exhibits yet another pattern: considerable variation in the 1950s; the entrenchment of a four-party configuration in the 1960s; relative continuity through the 1970s and early 1980s; and more recently, the decline of the Communists and re-emergence of the extreme right.

Trends in Britain, Ireland, the United States or Canada are equally problematic. Changes are readily apparent in Britain: the Labour and Conservative parties have moved farther apart, and the Liberals, in alliance with the newly established Social Democrats, have been trying to capture the centre, raising questions about the future of the two-party system and the class alignment on which it was based. In Ireland, catch-all parties rooted in independence struggles and parish pump politics persist, but changes in coalition patterns, along with internal factional competition in Fianna Fail, have transformed an asymmetrical bipolar system into a more balanced one in which elections make a difference. Whether the Irish party system will revert to one-party dominance, as the 1987 elections suggest, remains to be seen.

Across the Atlantic, Canada continues to display a pattern of weak electoral alignment, in which a loosely attached electorate nevertheless assigns its support to a limited number of political parties: although voters shift their allegiances (and the parties which predominate either nationally or in different provinces may change), the party configuration remains the same. Finally, in the United States, the two-party system remains intact. However, presidential nominating processes have changed, parties have become more open and divided, and national parties have gained strength *vis-à-vis* state and local organisations. Amid all of this, a 'split-level' realignment has occurred, in which Republicans frequently win the presidency but Democrats remain solidly ensconced in the House of Representatives.

Many party systems have undergone modification without radical restructuring. All in all, there have been few major realignments, and all the party systems which we have been examining display substantial continuity. New parties have emerged but, thus far, their impact has been limited. Except in rare instances where parties have merged (the confessional parties in the Netherlands) or faded into insignificance (the Popular Republican Movement (MRP) in postwar France) few *established* parties have disappeared[2] or even lost their parliamentary representation (the Norwegian Liberals are unusual in this regard[3]). Equally, with the exception of the Gaullists, who supplanted several loosely organised parties on the right and centre in the early days of the Fifth Republic, none of the newer parties has succeeded in displacing previously established parties:[4] In Britain, the two-party share of the vote has declined but the Conservatives and Labour remain the principal parties of government and opposition. In the United States, the composition of party coalitions has changed, and the Republicans have become more conservative, but the Democrats and Republicans continue to monopolise party competition. In Belgium, the established parties - now divided on regional and linguistic lines - retain their previous position. We find similar phenomena in the Netherlands and Denmark: although newer parties crowded the political spectrum, for the most part they have played no more than a marginal role in cabinet formations or policy-making. Instead, we must look hard to find examples of *major* realignments substantially altering the format of party competition or redefining party alternatives. In the Western European context, the most prominent cases remain the reshaping of the West German party system in the 1950s and the restructuring of the French party system in the 1960s, following constitutional changes and the advent of strong Presidential government. Significantly, Lipset and Rokkan included both among the 'few but significant exceptions' to their comments on the durability of cleavage structures and party configurations.

But, even if few major realignments have occurred, party systems are no longer as static as they appeared to be in the 1960s. If we look at party systems in the 1980s, we can still detect the party configurations of the 1920s, but the exceptions are growing more numerous and the image is no longer as sharp as it once was. We can no longer justify metaphors of ice age rigidity. Instead, in country after country, we find variants of continuity amid change.

Explaining Continuity Amid Change

Lipset and Rokkan's (1967) observation that many Western European party systems had remained frozen since the completion of suffrage extension in the 1920s came at the end of an essay on the development of cleavage structures in Western Europe. Tracing the emergence of cleavages over several centuries, they concluded their discussion with the 1920s because despite the depression, war, and postwar affluence, few changes in party systems had occurred since then. Lipset and Rokkan suggested that this phenomenon, surprising at the time, reflected the entrenchment of local party organisations.[5] Our task, two decades later, is more complex. We must account not only for the underlying continuities still evident in many party systems, but also the divergent patterns of change which we have detected.

There are ample reasons for expecting change. Important changes in social structure, relationships between citizens and governments and the structure of the media have taken place. Increased education, declining religiosity and changes in occupational structure - the growth of the service sector and the decline of smokestack industries - have altered the social composition of electorates. Governments have assumed responsibility for economic management and the social insurance of their citizens. In many countries the partisan press has weakened, if not vanished, and television has supplanted newspapers as a source of information. Finally, as Inglehart (1977) has argued, older generations raised in an atmosphere of scarcity are gradually being replaced by younger generations accustomed to affluence. Although one may question the extent to which post-material or quality of life values have supplanted materialist values, there can be little doubt that changes in the mixture of public values have occurred. Particularly since the late 1960s, some citizens and many political activists have shown themselves increasingly concerned about the quality of the environment, the ability of citizens to control their surroundings, and the dangers of war and nuclear power.

Far more elusive are the ways in which these changes affect parties and party systems. The effects, even in relatively similar societies like Denmark, Norway and Sweden, have not been uniform. Moreover, if social changes have been as extensive as suggested, then we need to ask why changes in party systems have not been more thoroughgoing than those we have observed.

One answer is that parties and party systems are more resilient than some might have suspected and that durability of party systems depends on multiple sources of stability: voter loyalties, the ability of parties to adapt, organisational resources, and institutional constraints such as electoral laws. In subsequent sections, we will examine the ways in which these have contributed both to the freezing of party systems and to more recent patterns of continuity amid change.

The Cumulation of Electoral Loyalties

The most widely accepted explanations of the stability of party alignments derive from aggregate analysis and survey research. Parties are seen either as rooted in social structure and enjoying the support of specific classes, strata or religions or stabilised by party identifications predisposing voters to choose one party rather than another; in addition, political socialisation serves as a major vehicle ensuring the continuity of parties and party systems. Although the two emphases differ, both provide a 'bottom-up' view of stability in which the continuity of the party systems depends on the accumulation of voter loyalties and the concomitant narrowing of proportion of the electorate available for either shifts in the party balance or the entry of new parties. (Dalton, Flanagan, and Beck 1984) Let us consider the argument from the perspective of party identifications.

Students of voting behaviour have argued that party identifications, usually inherited from parents, form at an early age and intensify over time. Passed down from generation to generation, party identifications provide parties with stable bases of support. Once party identifications solidify (this would not occur immediately) change would necessarily be gradual, reflecting the death of older voters and the entry of younger ones whose attitudes and perspectives differed from their elders. Thus, although one could initially expect considerable volatility, once loyalties developed, voting patterns would stabilise, reducing the potential for party system change. The result - until something happened to undermine existing identifications - would be a freezing of the party alignment. (Campbell *et al.* 1960, 1966; Converse 1969; Butler and Stokes 1969)

Ironically, the replication of voting studies in successive countries cast doubt on the extent to which voters outside of the United States actually identified with particular parties. Studies of voting behaviour in the Netherlands showed that voters changed party identifications as rapidly as their vote, suggesting that questions tapping party identifications measured little more than voters' preferences or loyalties at the moment (Thomassen 1975). Evidence from survey and aggregate research elsewhere raised similar doubts (Budge, Crewe and Farlie 1976). In contrast to the United States, where voters were assumed to need party identifications to thread their way through frequent elections for large numbers of offices, scholars argued that class and group loyalties (Shively 1972) or voters' perceptions of party space (see Budge *et al.* 1976) shaped electoral choices in Europe.

The debate on party identifications has important ramifications for our argument. If voters do develop strong party identifications, and if these harden with age and length of psychological membership and are passed on from generation to generation, then it is not difficult to account for the freezing of party alignments or the considerable continuity still visible in many party systems today. But, if party loyalties are far more fragile and tenuous and fade when class or group attachments weaken, then the continuity of party systems is problematic. In the absence of strong party identifications or deep-seated class or group attachments, we would have to assume either that the continuity of party alignments was coincidental - i.e. electorates were more volatile than suspected, but that changes somehow cancelled each other out - or that other factors intervened. The latter is more probable than the former. Let us consider this in terms of the ways in which parties bid for support.

Parties and How They Seek Support

Parties seek to win public support in different ways. These include selecting issues and programmes thought to have popular appeal, catering to particular classes or groups, and using their access to government in order to reward client groups. In the first instance, parties offer general policies - broad public goods - which they hope will appeal to substantial portions of the electorate. In the second, parties target specific segments of the population - typically a class, denomination, or an ethnic or linguistic group - whose interests they defend. In the third, parties exchange jobs and favours for the support of individuals or groups.

Parties often mix these tactics. Patronage has been important in settings as diverse as eighteenth and nineteenth century Britain (the original title of the party whip was patronage secretary), American cities (and some states), where urban political machines once flourished, twentieth century Italy, and many third world countries. However, few parties rely solely on patronage. As Carty notes, parties such as Ireland's Fianna Fail not only engaged in parish pump politics but also proffered nationalist symbols and characterised themselves as the only party capable of governing. Equally, as Amyot and Covell point out, parties in Italy and Belgium have combined the use of patronage with ideological appeals and the demarcation of political subcultures. The Italian Christian Democrats have not only used their control of the regime in order to generate patronage, but have simultaneously played on anti-Communism and their ties to the Church to ensure additional support. Ideological appeals have been far more muted in Belgium, but the established parties and the spiritual families which they represent have colonised the state apparatus and parceled out its rewards among their followers. As Covell argues, this makes it very difficult to resign from one's party.

Other parties have used different approaches. Some, such as the Dutch Liberals and many of the bourgeois parties in Scandinavia cast themselves as the representatives of particular classes or strata, but often did so without developing specific organisational ties. Others, typically Christian Democratic or Social Democratic, gained support not only by taking specific positions or representing particular classes or groups, but also by cultivating political subcultures based on networks of religious or ideologically based organisations. In a different vein, parties in North America have avoided appeals to specific classes or groups and sought instead to assemble broadly based and often heterogeneous coalitions around loosely defined programmes. However, such appeals have often been supplemented by patronage.

The diverse tacks employed by parties in Western Europe contributed to the freezing of party systems. The development of political subcultures in Scandinavia, Austria, Germany, the Low Countries and Italy played a major role in shaping political loyalties. Political subcultures were either built around early working-class movements or developed as an extension of church-related organisations. Parties and their affiliated organisations provided their members not only with services such as housing and health benefits, but also with a sense of identity and belonging and a frame of reference with which to understand the world around them. Einhorn and Logue argue that working-class movements provided strong bases of support for Social Democratic parties in Scandinavia, and that farmers organisations did the same for agrarian parties. Political subcultures elsewhere - the Catholic and Socialist *Lager* in Austria; the 'spiritual families' in Belgium and the Calvinist, Catholic, and Socialist pillars in the Netherlands - performed similar functions. Although the evidence is fragmentary,[6] there are ample reasons for suspecting that political subcultures played an important role in mobilising the vote, shaping electoral preferences, and reinforcing emergent patterns of political cleavage (see Rokkan 1977). This would have occurred not only because political subcultures inculcated specific doctrines and deep loyalties to parties and/or subcultures, but also because homogeneous milieus filtered out other points of view. For those less ideologically motivated, unemployment insurance, cooperative housing, health benefits, and other services provided an alternate source of attachment (Bakvis 1981).

The elaboration of distinct political subcultures was more typical of working-class movements and some Catholic or Christian Democratic parties (particularly in minority or beleaguered settings) than Liberal or Conservative forces. However, even in the absence of well-developed political subcultures, close ties often developed between particular parties and classes or strata within a society. The sharpness of class divisions and the apparent connections between parties and the interests of specific groups undoubtedly propelled voters toward certain parties and away from others. As more and more voters were mobilised and made aware of their class or group identification, this - like the construction and elaboration of political subcultures - would contribute to the narrowing of the electoral market and the freezing of party alignments. Well-developed patronage networks tying voters to certain parties would have a similar effect.[7] So would a partisan press.

Thus, the freezing of party systems which Lipset and Rokkan described - in some respects, a condition of extreme or hyper-stability - rested on multiple sources of continuity. Party systems were stabilised not only from the 'bottom up' by strong electoral loyalties but also from the 'top down', by organisational networks, patronage and other benefits, and the ability of parties, through a partisan press and homogeneous milieu, to define and interpret social change.[8] This explains the freezing of party systems, but not their continuity in a period when important social changes have occurred. It is to this problem that we now turn.

Parties as Adaptive Organisations

The notion that parties are adaptive organisations, provides yet another 'top-down' explanation for the durability of party configurations. If parties are adaptive organisations, adjusting their appeals to the audiences whose votes they seek, then the continuity of party systems need not be seen in terms of (shifting) electoral attachments, the pressures of (often lapsed) organisational networks, or the filtering effects of (disappearing) partisan presses. Instead, parties and party systems may survive because parties adjust their appeals to the changing predilections of their electorates.

Characterisations of parties as adaptive organisations evoke conflicting images. One depicts parties as organisations which are flexible and opportunistic, capable of changing positions in order to ensure their survival and success. This conforms closely to Anthony Downs' (1957) model of parties as rational actors, continually adjusting and fine-tuning their positions in order to maximise support. Parties' ability to adapt is constrained only by the availability of information and the need to maintain consistency. This contrasts sharply with a second image in which parties are not always capable of adapting successfully. Parties try to maximise support, but their ability to do so is limited by the constraints of party ideology, the demands of followers, the pressures of factions, and the inertia of ongoing organisations (see Hirschman 1970). Human error may also make a difference. As a result, parties are sometimes but not always flexible, and the willingness and ability of parties to adapt varies considerably.

It is with this second image, depicting parties as imperfect maximisers of votes, that we are concerned.

Adaptation and change have been recurring themes in the literature on North American party systems but play a less prominent role in the Western European literature. As Bakvis and Wolinetz point out, Canadian and American parties are thought of as broadly-based coalitions, weaving together a diverse (and sometimes very heterogeneous) collection of interests. Parties, typically more interested in winning elections and enjoying the fruits of office than implementing ideological designs, tailor their appeals to attract the support of a broad majority. Realignment occurs only when very divisive issues emerge, forcing one or both parties to take a stand and recast their appeal. In the process, third parties may appear, but in the United States the most common outcome has been a redefinition of the two-party system, encouraged by - but also resulting in - changes in electoral alignments (Sundquist 1983). However, in Canada similar divisions have led to the entrenchment of third parties. Although adaptation and change have been more muted in the European literature, both figured prominently in Otto Kirchheimer's assertion that a transformation of Western European party systems was taking place. Kirchheimer (1966) argued that parties of mass integration, confronted with affluent and consumer-oriented societies, were transforming themselves into ideologically bland catch-all parties. Rather than attempting to represent particular groups or classes or advance distinctive points of view, parties stressed the qualities of their leaders and bid for the support of interest groups. In doing so, parties abandoned 'attempts at the intellectual and moral *encadrement* of the masses' (Kirchheimer 1966:184) and sought votes where they could be found - in the centre. This in turn transformed the party system: the success of one catch-all party forced others to adopt similar tactics, altering the style of party competition. (Wolinetz 1979)

Although there is little evidence that the *entire* dynamic which Kirchheimer sketched applied beyond the West German case on which he based his scenario, his characterisations of parties downplaying or modifying their doctrines and bidding for broader support summed up changes occurring throughout the political spectrum. Many Social Democratic parties were indeed revising party programmes, deleting references to class conflict and abandoning commitments to nationalisation in favour of a mixed economy. The SPD's 1959 Bad Godesberg programme is only one such example. Parties in the Netherlands, Denmark and Austria also revised their programmes and the British Labour Party attempted to do so. After successive defeats, the latter was anxious to abandon its cloth cap image and broaden its appeal (Butler and King 1965). However, changes were not confined to the left: as Breckenridge, Einhorn and Logue and others indicate, parties on the right were also modifying their positions and endorsing the postwar welfare state and the idea of a managed economy.

Assessing the impact of such changes is difficult. We can surmise that some parties gained - or at least maintained - support because they modified their positions. In power from 1951 to 1964, the British Conservatives characterised themselves as the most effective managers of the new welfare state and told voters in 1959 that they 'had never had it so good' (Butler and Rose 1960). But in Scandinavia the bourgeois parties were unable to displace the ruling Social Democratic parties. Chandler suggests that the German Social Democrats benefitted by adopting the reformist Bad Godesberg programme in 1959; nevertheless, ten years elapsed before the SPD gained sufficient support to win the chancellorship. However, parties such as the Dutch Socialists (in decline through the 1960s) did not fare as well. Particularly where smaller parties could establish themselves to the left of dominant Social Democratic parties (e.g., the Netherlands, Denmark, and Norway) abandoning or downplaying of previous positions may have cost them support. Equally, parties may have retained votes not so much because of the positions which they assumed but rather because they remained able to define and interpret issues.

These changes, in which parties de-emphasised ideology in order to respond to the perceived demands of an increasingly affluent electorate, constitute only one kind of adaptation occurring within a limited and unusual period. Although these maneuvers, along with continuing party or group loyalties, helped to sustain many party systems through the 1960s, we need to consider changes over a longer period whose central features are not a sustained economic growth, full employment and increasing affluence, but rather stagnation, inflation and growing unemployment amid continued affluence. Two facets are central: parties' response to resurgent political activism and demands for an improved quality of life, and more recently, their response to economic decline.

Hard Times and Conflicting Demands

The end of ideology debate was cut short by student activism and renewed political conflict in the late 1960s. Student protest, anti-war demonstrations and the reappearance of ideological rhetoric made it apparent that no end to political conflict had occurred. Social scientists directed their attention to resurgent activism and sought to explain it not only in terms of the issues and events which had spurred it, but also by the advent of post-industrial societies, characterised by an increasingly large service sectors and the entry of new generations raised in affluence rather than scarcity. According to Inglehart (1971, 1977), a 'silent revolution' was underway, producing new bases of political cleavage: younger voters, many of whom were thought to be more concerned with 'post-material' or quality of life values, were gradually supplanting an older generation primarily concerned with economic security and other 'materialist' values.

Inglehart argues that younger middle-class voters should be attracted to parties of the left while security-minded working-class voters should gravitate to the right. This assumes, however, that parties retain previous positions, or only modify them slightly, and that few changes in the number of parties and the format of the party system take place. Our chapters suggest that this is not always the case. Although some party configurations have remained largely the same - e.g. Sweden, as well as Austria and West Germany until the rise of the Greens - others changed because of the ways in which parties, new and old, took up new issues and fused them with older concerns. In many instances new demands were initially expressed outside of the party system by groups bent on direct action and immediate results. However, sooner or later parties had to deal with them. In countries such as the Netherlands, new parties were established in order to represent concerns deemed to be inadequately expressed by existing parties, while in others, activists' demands were taken up by smaller parties to the left of social democracy.

The establishment of new parties and the growth of smaller ones narrowed the base of existing parties and forced many to consider the ways, if any, in which they might adapt. However, their task was not an easy one: as the Dutch Socialists discovered, catering to the demands on one flank (in this case the left) risked alienating supporters on the other. Post-industrial demands were not the only ones which parties had to worry about. By the early 1970s, reactions against the high costs of the postwar welfare state were also becoming apparent, feeding the growth of anti-statist forces such as the Progress Party in Denmark. Authorities' willingness to tolerate abortion and ease restrictions on the distribution of pornographic materials also provoked the formation of new religious parties in settings as diverse as Denmark (where the Christian People's Party was established) and the Netherlands (where in addition to the ultra-orthodox Calvinist parties, a dissident Catholic party briefly appeared).

The suddenness with which new demands appeared and the vehemence with which they were expressed made it difficult for established parties to absorb them. On the left, demands for greater participation and popular control combined with fears of uncontrolled economic growth and environmental disaster to challenge both the centralised states which social democrats had been instrumental in constructing and the economic growth on which the postwar economic miracle had been based. Conflicts were exacerbated by differences in political style and temperament: younger activists' penchant for direct action clashed with older party members' inclination to work within established channels. Nor were conflicts confined to the left. Although there have been fewer new forces on the right, the sudden emergence and success of the Progress Party in Denmark (and its smaller counterpart in Norway) threatened the position of the bourgeois parties. Because they had accepted major facets of the welfare state, the bourgeois parties found it difficult to concur with the Progress Party's wholesale attacks on it. Nevertheless, Scandinavian Conservatives began talking more assertively about the need to revise government programmes and restrain expenditures. Other parties soon followed suit.

Despite initial difficulties, parties in some countries have succeeded in incorporating elements of left- and right-wing protests in their appeals. In part, this could occur because earlier protests dissipated or were absorbed in the face of changing economic conditions. In many countries rising inflation and economic stagnation legitimised right-wing attacks on the welfare state and facilitated the resurgence of free market ideologies. Perceived needs to deregulate the economy and cut the size of the public sector in order to facilitate market-led recovery enabled parties of the right, such as the Liberals in Belgium and the Netherlands, to channel and absorb protests against the welfare state, while parties of the centre (Christian Democrats in these same two countries) began stressing 'responsible' fiscal management, particularly the need to trim the welfare state while retaining its more essential features. However, developments did not work to the total disadvantage of the left. The worsening economic situation enabled Social Democratic parties to emphasise less divisive themes, such as employment and maintenance of the social welfare programmes. This allowed parties like the Dutch Socialists to begin reconstructing previous bases of support, weakened by the decline of older industrial working classes, around a defense of the public sector and its beneficiaries.

Even so, economic factors constitute only one set of factors encouraging the incorporation of dissenting points of view. Internal party politics also play a role. In some instances, such as the Socialist Party in the Netherlands, British Labour, and Democrats and Republicans in the United States, dissident groups gravitated to the party - or were already active within it - and gained greater influence. In others, such as the British Conservative Party and the Republican Party, changes of leadership (the selection of Margaret Thatcher in 1975, the nomination of Ronald Reagan in 1980) were decisive. Often, changes were made more urgent by a sense of crisis within the party or the country as a whole: in the Netherlands, electoral decline, exclusion from the cabinet in the 1966, and the emergence of new parties facilitated New Left penetration of the Socialist Party. In Britain, economic decline and the inability of either Labour or the Conservatives to arrest it strengthened demands for changes in party strategies and government policies.

Such processes were often disruptive. Conflicts were frequently resolved either by absorbing dissident elements and grafting their claims onto established party positions (e.g. the Dutch Socialists and the Democrats in the United States) or by one side gaining ascendancy over the other (Labour and Conservatives in Britain and the Republicans in the United States). Nevertheless these 'solutions', involving the recasting of least one party alternative, have frequently led to other changes. In Britain, the movement of the Conservatives to the right and Labour to the left opened a gap in the centre, where the Liberals and Social Democrats have been attempting to establish themselves as a viable alternative. In the Netherlands, the changing style and posture of the Socialist Party assisted the coming together of the Christian Democrats and contributed to the growing polarisation of the political system.

Not all parties felt constrained to react. In Germany, the Social Democrats - then a governing party - fended off attacks from extra-parliamentary opposition and Young Socialists (Jusos) through the 1970s, maintaining a staid and relatively conservative posture on domestic and international issues. In contrast to the Netherlands, where the Socialists took up the claims of the peace and environmental movements, the failure to incorporate or anticipate Green views on peace or the environment opened up a space to the left of the SPD. Although the five per cent electoral threshold had previously protected established parties from challenges on their flanks, the Greens leapt this barrier in 1983. Parallel developments occurred somewhat later in Austria: confronted by a ruling socialist party closely identified with the existing regime, two separate Green lists entered the 1983 parliamentary election and won 3.3 per cent of the vote. Although their division into two competing lists prevented them from winning any seats in 1983, three years later a united Green list won 4.6 per cent of the votes and eight seats. Pro-NATO Social Democratic Parties in Denmark and Norway have also experienced difficulty in incorporating dissidents on their left. Only in Sweden, a neutral country in which the ruling Social Democrats have been more adept in manipulating class issues and maintaining themselves in power (Esping-Andersen 1985), have Socialists been able to minimise competition on their left.

The ability of many (but by no means all) parties to adapt and respond to change - contributes to the continuity of party alignments. However, this is only part of the story: because spaces along the political spectrum are vacated or new dimensions of conflict are opened up, and because voters may respond differently to changing political alternatives, adaptation often leads to further change.

Organisational Resources and Electoral Laws

New concerns, reactions against government policies, and processes of adaptation create opportunities for both old and new parties. However, although new parties have been quicker to mobilise protest and raise new issues, in virtually all the cases we have considered, established parties not only survive, but continue to dominate political life. This reflects not only their ability to adapt (which is sometimes limited) but also the organisational resources which they can command and the ways in which electoral laws protect them.

Established parties are ongoing organisations with multiple resources at their disposal. These include knowledge and experience, an ability to mobilise supporters and mount election campaigns and, in most instances, legislative seats and control of some public offices at local, regional and national levels. In addition, despite the general loosening of electoral attachments, established parties can generally count on the loyalty of some of their supporters. These often form a cushion for parties in decline.

In contrast, new parties are less well equipped to survive the vicissitudes of electoral competition. Propelled into office on the basis of a particular issue or concern, such parties lose their initial momentum. Given sufficient time to react, older parties often manage to incorporate protests and merge older and newer demands. Nor can new parties rely on the residual resources that established parties have at their disposal. New parties often attract extremely diverse groups of voters, ranging from the highly committed to those barely interested at all.[9] Some are one-time supporters, 'absent on leave from their regular parties' (to paraphrase Covell), while others are *en route* to other political homes. If Dutch experience is any guide, unless the party is linked to highly cohesive social groups such as the Calvinist churches on which the smaller religious parties draw, then the proportion of loyal supporters is likely to be considerably lower than that of established parties (Irwin and Dittrich 1984). In addition, new parties are often run by amateurs, whose interests and energies run out after one or two election campaigns. In contrast to larger and better established parties, new forces cannot rely on large numbers of office holders at national, local, or regional levels to keep the party going when its fortunes ebb. Although new parties can survive - consider the Progress Party in Denmark or Democrats '66 in the Netherlands - the deck is stacked in favour of established parties.

Electoral laws also facilitate the survival of established parties and the continuity of party systems. More often than not these are designed to preserve the position of existing parties, but they sometimes do so in paradoxical ways. The standard arguments concentrate on the effects of single member plurality systems and diverse forms of proportional representation. However, for our purposes, the most important, but not always readily measurable phenomenon (Rae, Hanby and Loosemore 1971; Lijphart and Gibberd 1977) is the extent to which formal or informal thresholds limit the representation of new parties and protect established parties when they are in decline. As is well known, high thresholds, resulting from either formal barriers such as Germany's five per cent rule or Sweden's four per cent provision or the effects of single member districts (in the absence of strong regionally concentrated parties or a large number of parties competing in a given district), limit the entry of new parties.[10] This not only protects established parties from new competitors but also eases the process of adjustment: established parties are freer to ignore the demands of groups unlikely to deprive them of seats.

Far less attention has been paid to the effects of lower thresholds. The standard wisdom, borne out by countries such as the Netherlands, Israel or Denmark, with effective thresholds of 2/3 of one per cent, 1/120 of the popular vote, and 2 per cent respectively, is that low thresholds encourage the entry and survival of smaller parties.[11] *However, low thresholds also protect parties in decline.* This occurs not because of any positive or active effect, but rather because low barriers do little to force the amalgamation or merger of parties or exclude parties which are losing support.[12] In contrast to single member district systems, where parties without regional concentrations of support can be sent to the political wilderness (consider the fate of the British Liberals from the 1930s to the 1970s) or proportional systems with high formal barriers such as West Germany, low thresholds allow parties in decline to hang in and recover at a later date: the Danish Conservative Party, which dipped from an all-time high of 20.4 per cent in 1968 to 5.5 per cent in 1975 but subsequently rebounded to 14.5 per cent in 1982 and 23.4 per cent in 1984 is a notable example. Even so, neither the survival nor the political importance of parties in decline is guaranteed. As Wilson (this volume) suggests in his discussion of Communist parties, there is a point at which parties atrophy and become marginalised. But, this has been a fate more common to smaller than larger parties and more common in systems with higher thresholds or other mechanisms, such as the presence of indivisible offices or double ballot electoral laws, which reward alliances and cooperation, but work to the disadvantage of smaller parties competing by themselves.

Conclusion

Let us draw our argument together. We have reviewed changes in eleven Western European countries plus the United States and Canada and argued that the durability of parties and the party systems in which they find themselves depends on multiple sources of continuity, including electoral attachments, ongoing adaptation, organisational resources, and the cushioning effects of electoral laws and residual loyalties. A number of factors, including patronage, ties between parties and particular groups and classes, and the pressures of organisational networks link voters to political parties and reduce the number of votes available for either shifts in the party balance or the entry of new parties. But not all of these are necessarily active at the same time, and some are more prominent in some parties and party systems than in others.

However, the accumulation of electoral attachments is not the only factor accounting for the continuity of many party systems. Even if voters are less firmly attached to political parties as a result of social and economic changes - or because they were never mobilised in the first place - the deck is still stacked in favour of the continuity of parties and party systems. In the past, many parties were well-positioned to define and interpret social change. Although changes in the structure of the media, particularly the decline of a partisan press and the advent of electronic media, have weakened parties' previous control over voters' agendas, parties in most countries

- the United States would have to be considered an exception - still retain some ability to define and redefine issues and shape voters' perceptions.

In addition, parties are adaptive organisations, sometimes but not always capable of adjusting to changes in the competitive environments in which they find themselves. Although the jolt of successive defeats may be required before parties adopt new strategies, parties adapt in a variety of ways, merging newer issues with older concerns or finding new ways of re-emphasising older themes. However, the process is anything but smooth. New parties are often more adept at raising new issues, and the ways in which established parties respond may alienate loyal supporters. Both provide opportunities for the entry and success of new parties and shifts in the party balance. Nevertheless, powerful forces favour the continuity of party systems, even if in a modified form. Electoral laws and regulations governing campaign finance are often written in ways which protect established parties. Finally, established parties command organisational resources which enable them to survive despite momentary, and sometimes long-term, decline.

This has implications for the way in which party systems change. We have been accustomed - and this book is no exception - to think of party system change in stark terms: party systems are regarded as frozen or 'fluid', or in the American case, subject to massive realignments in which parties and party coalitions are redefined and the electoral map is rewritten. However, few contemporary party systems exhibit either the extreme rigidity which Lipset and Rokkan's metaphor suggests, or the grand realignments which once characterised the United States. Instead, changes in coalition patterns and the strengths of one or more parties have occurred in more 'frozen' periods, and party systems undergoing change - a condition which describes many countries today - still exhibit considerable continuity.[13] Smaller changes - changes in coalition patterns, shifts in party strengths, or the growth or decline of individual parties - are more prevalent than grand realignments.

The absence of grand realignments is not surprising if we consider parties as organisations and actors, responding to and influencing the environment in which they operate. As Sartori (1969:90) points out, party systems, once they are established, act as 'independent system[s] of channelment, propelled and maintained by...[their] own laws of inertia.' Parties develop and maintain their own roots in social structure, and in doing so, inhibit the kinds of changes which can occur. Similarly, their ability to adapt limits the extent of change which is likely to occur. By adapting or modifying positions, pressures can be deflected or absorbed, preserving the underlying format of the party system despite social change or the emergence of new issues. Changes in governing coalitions are yet another means of responding to new situations or demands for change. If few grand realignments have occurred, it is because many parties and party systems have, thus far, proved to be resilient, and because the kinds of changes most likely to produce grand realignments - changes in institutional structures or electoral laws altering the circumstances under which parties compete for office (see Wilson, this volume) - have been relatively rare in the countries which we have been considering. Only in the United States, where competition for indivisible offices such as the presidency or governorships has forced divergent elements to come together in the same party, have grand realignments, reshuffling the coalitions behind each party label, been at all common. But even in the United States, institutional changes - in this case, the expansion in the number of primary elections - have so expanded the space for intra-party competition that dramatic realignments are less probable than before.

Future Changes

In concluding, it is useful to consider both where party systems have been and where they are going. In the period which Lipset and Rokkan considered, the 1920s through the 1960s, the durability of most Western European party configurations depended both on the ways in which parties were anchored in class and religious divisions and, in several instances, on the existence of political subcultures and party-dominated presses. Because parties monopolised most of the electorate, change could only occur at the margins. In many countries, there were sufficient votes available for the entry and occasional success of minor parties, rooted in ideological or religious divisions, but not enough for dramatic changes in either electoral alignments or the format of the party system. This was particularly true in the postwar period, when party systems and electoral alignments were remarkably stable. As Rose and Urwin (1970a) demonstrate, inter-war party systems were more fluid, both because party systems in some countries were not firmly entrenched and because of the greater turmoil of the period. Even so, the greater continuity of the postwar period may have been more contingent than we normally suspect. It is difficult to known whether greater changes would have occurred if, for example, prolonged depression rather than unprecedented affluence had emerged from the postwar reconstruction.

The period since the 1960s has been different. Although the durability of parties and party systems still depends on multiple sources of continuity, these no longer operate as strongly or uni-directionally as in the past. Parties have been less firmly anchored in social structures, and their continuity has depended less on voter loyalty and party identification and more on accumulated experience, organisational inertia, and their ability to market issues and adapt to changing demands.

What of the future? Making predictions is a risky business, but our argument suggests that any return to the hyper-stability of the past is improbable. Although galvanising issues could produce renewed allegiance to parties, the freezing of earlier party systems rested on patterns of mobilisation unlikely to be repeated. Because the stability of contemporary party systems rests on shakier foundations, party systems are likely either to display more of the same - i.e., continuity amid considerable change - or else undergo more extensive realignments.

Changing campaign techniques and the weakening of electoral attachments make more extensive changes in party systems more probable than in the past. Parties in Canada and Western Europe increasingly employ campaign techniques similar to those used in the United States. Although campaigning is usually party- or leader-centred rather than candidate-centred, recourse to new techniques makes parties' clienteles increasingly available to each other. Moreover, rapid communications make it relatively easy for political activists to organise new political parties or inject themselves into the political process through action groups or political movements. Although established parties have generally been able to adapt, there is no guarantee that they will be able to do so in the future.

Will changes occur? Our argument suggests that new patterns will depend on the skills of politicians and the ways in which they respond to the situations confronting them. In Sweden, the Social Democrats were able to use their control of government in the 1930s to forge a base of support durable enough to keep them in power for all but six years since then. However, such opportunities are rare. In contemporary Western Europe, parties of the right and the centre are currently better placed to bring about electoral changes than parties of the left. In contrast to the situation a decade ago, they govern in most countries north of the Mediterranean rim. The principal exceptions are Sweden and Austria. In many instances, commitment to an agenda of retrenchment and market-led recovery has provided the right with a sense of cohesion and purpose which it did not previously enjoy. In contrast, the left in many countries is divided and on the defensive. Although rising unemployment and attacks on the public sector have permitted many parties to rally to the defense of the welfare state, environmental questions and issues such as the deployment of cruise missiles and the position of Western Europe within the NATO alliance continue to divide the left. Green parties have eroded Social Democratic strength in West Germany and Austria. Moreover, in countries where Social Democrats have gained votes, such as the Netherlands, they have not always been able to translate increased support into government power. Were parties in the left in power, decisions about the allocation of scarce resources - for example, whether to subsidise declining industries or whether to restrain government spending - could cause further divisions. As a result, it will be difficult, but by no means impossible, for parties of the left to forge new policies which would expand their bases of support.

What does this mean for party system change? One possibility is that in a situation of weakened electoral attachments and changing methods of campaigning, parties of the left or right could use their control of government policy to forge new electoral alignments. Another possibility is that divisions over these issues will strengthen loyalties to parties of the right and the left without forging new alignments. A third, and more probable outcome, is that party systems will continue more or less as they are now, with established parties, and occasionally new ones, competing for loosely aligned electorates. The Canadian case suggests that party systems can be quite durable despite weak electoral alignment.

What difference does this make? It has become common in a period of loose electoral attachments to argue that parties are in decline. Burnham takes this view and, in a different way, so did Kirchheimer. However, although parties do not necessarily perform all the functions once attributed to them - particularly if these are taken to include providing spiritual homes for classes or religious groups - parties still provide alternatives (even if they are not always clear) and referents through which voters can understand the political world. Voters may be more detached and loosely aligned than a generation ago. But one consequence of this is that elections in many countries are more momentous and decisive. That is an encouraging development.

Notes

1. Other authors have reached similar conclusions. See Maquire (1983); Pedersen (1983); Dalton, Flanagan, and Beck (1984) and Crewe and Denver (1985).

2. Most of the instances in which parties have disappeared took place in party systems, such as the French and the West German, which underwent considerable change in the earlier postwar years. In France, many parties of the right and centre were supplanted by the Gaullists. However, all were loosely organised parties of local notables and, unlike the MRP, none had a mass base of support. In the German case, several parties, including the Communists (KPD) before they were banned, fell victim to the five per cent threshold in the 1950s. See Chandler (this volume).

3. The Norwegian Liberals were a viable force in both the interwar and postwar periods. However, the question of entry into the European Common Market in 1973 divided them into two separate parties. The split weakened both parties and placed the surviving 'old' liberals at a disadvantage in parliamentary elections, conducted for the most part in relatively small multi-member districts. In the 1985 elections, the Liberals failed to secure any parliamentary seats.

4. However, the Gaullists do not fully qualify as a new force in the Fifth Republic. A Gaullist party, the Rally for the French People (RPF,) was active in the earlier years of the Fourth Republic and won nearly 21.7 per cent of the vote in 1951, but General de Gaulle ordered the party to disband in the early 1950s. The Christian Democratic Union in Germany might be considered to be a second exception to the statement. However, the CDU was built on the base of the Centre Party (Zentrum), the former Catholic party in the imperial and interwar party systems. Both the Gaullists and the German Christian Democrats differ considerably from the minor parties established in the 1960s and 1970s.

5. Not everyone was surprised. As Mair (1983) notes, Sartori took a different view. According to Sartori, 'the 1920 freezing of party systems and alignments is intriguing only as long as we persist in understanding party systems as dependent variables. It is not intriguing, however, if we realize that a freezed party system is simply a party system that intervenes in the political process as an independent system of channelment, propelled and maintained by its own laws of inertia.' (Sartori 1969:90) Sartori has been particularly concerned about impact of electoral laws and the circumstances under which the formats of party systems might be manipulated (Sartori 1966), but aside from his work on electoral systems, Sartori has not explored the implications of his concept of channelment for party system change.

6. The available evidence consists of memoirs, aggregate analyses and, more recently, some survey evidence. Recent studies, such as Bakvis (1981) or Houska (1985), suggest a strong relationship. More studies relating the extent and density of political subcultures to aggregate voting patterns in a wider range of countries are needed.

7. This was particularly notable in the nineteenth century United States, where the strength of state and local political machines blocked the emergence of class-

based parties. See Shefter (1986). Patronage alone may be a weak source of continuity because allegiances should last no longer than the flow of benefits; however, in areas in which political machines are entrenched, or alternatively, in regime party systems such as Italy, this could be a considerable length of time.

8.. For a parallel argument on the ability of parties and related organisations to define and interpret change, see Mair (1983).

9. Examining the support of the Progress Party in Denmark in the early 1970s Borre (1977) found that the only characteristic its voters had in common was that most were employed in the private sector.

10. However, the five per cent threshold in West Germany may have an opposite effect, legitimating parties which are able to surmount it. Recent experience suggests that once a party, such as the Greens, surpasses this barrier, it becomes 'established' in the public mind.

11. Italy could also be included in the list. In this case, the use of larger (the average district size is 19.1) rather than smaller multi-member constituencies produces a low effective threshold. On the impact of district magnitude, see Rae (1971).

12. The point is not a new one. As Covell (this volume) indicates, one reason for the 1899 adoption of proportional representation in Belgium was to keep the Liberals, weakened by the rise of the Socialists, from extinction. See also Duverger (1951).

13. As Mair (1983) points out, change need not take place throughout the party system, but can be confined to one or more sectors, leaving the format and other characteristics of the party system intact.

References

Bakvis, Herman (1981) *Catholic Power in the Netherlands*, McGill-Queen's University Press, Kingston and Montreal

Borre, Ole (1977) 'Recent Trends in Danish Voting Behavior' in Karl H. Cerny (ed.), *Scandinavia At the Polls*, American Enterprise Institute, Washington, 3-37

Budge, Ian, Ivor Crewe and Dennis Farlie, eds. (1976) *Party Identification and Beyond: Representations of Voting and Party Competition*, John Wiley & Sons, London

Butler, D.E. and Anthony King (1965) *The British General Election of 1964*, Macmillan, London

Butler, D.E. and Richard Rose (1960) *The British General Election of 1959*, Macmillan, London

Butler, David and Donald Stokes (1969) *Political Change in Britain: Forces Shaping Electoral Choice*, St. Martin's, New York

Campbell, Angus, Philip E. Converse, Warren E. Miller, and Donald E. Stokes (1960) *The American Voter*, John Wiley, New York

Campbell, Angus, Philip E. Converse, Warren E. Miller, and Donald E. Stokes (1966) *Elections and the Political Order*, John Wiley, New York

Converse, Philip E. (1969) 'Of Time and Partisan Stability' *Comparative Political Studies, 2*, 139-71

Converse, Philip E. and Georges Dupeux (1962) 'Politicization of the Electorate in the United States and France', *Public Opinion Quarterly 26*, 1-23

Crewe, Ivor and David Denver, eds. (1985) *Electoral Change in Western Democracies: Patterns and Sources of Electoral Volatility*, Croom Helm, London

Dalton, Russell J., Scott C. Flanagan and Paul Allen Beck (1984) *Electoral Change in Advanced Industrial Societies: Realignment or Dealignment?*, Princeton University Press, Princeton

Downs, Anthony (1957) *An Economic Theory of Democracy*, Harper and Row, New York

Esping-Andersen, Gøsta (1985) *Politics Against Markets: The Social Democratic Road to Power*, Princeton University Press, Princeton

Houska, Joseph (1985) *Influencing Mass Political Behavior*, Institute of International Studies, Berkeley

Hirschman, Albert O. (1970) *Exit, Voice, and Loyalty: Responses to Decline in Firms, Organizations and States*, Harvard, Cambridge, Mass.

Inglehart, Ronald (1971) 'The Silent Revolution in Europe: Intergenerational Change in Post-Industrial Societies', *American Political Science Review 65*, 911-1017

Inglehart, Ronald (1977) *The Silent Revolution: Changing Values and Political Styles Among Western Publics*, Princeton University Press, Princeton

Irwin, Galen and Karl Dittrich (1984) 'And the Walls Came Tumbling Down: Party Dealignment in The Netherlands' in Russell J. Dalton, Scott C. Flanagan and Paul Allen Beck, (eds.) *Electoral Change in Advanced Industrial Societies: Realignment or Dealignment?*, Princeton University Press, Princeton, 267-98

Kirchheimer, Otto (1966) 'The Transformation of Western European Party Systems' in Joseph LaPalombara and Myron Weiner (eds.), *Political Parties and Political Development*, Princeton University Press, Princeton, 177-200

Lijphart, Arend and Robert W. Gibberd (1977) 'Thresholds and Payoffs in List Systems of Proportional Representation' *European Journal of Political Research, 5*,219-44

Lipset, Seymour Martin and Stein Rokkan (1967) 'Introduction' in Seymour Martin Lipset and Stein Rokkan (eds.), *Party systems and Voter Alignments: Cross-National Perspectives*, Free Press, New York

Mair, Peter (1983) 'Adaption and Control: Towards an Understanding of Party and Party System Change' in Hans Daalder and Peter Mair (eds.) *Western European Party Systems: Continuity and Change*, Sage, London, 405-29

Maquire, Maria (1983) 'Is There Still Persistence? Electoral Change in Western Europe, 1948-79' in Hans Daalder and Peter Mair (eds.) *Western European Party Systems: Continuity and Change*, Sage, London, 67-94

Pedersen, Mogens N. (1983) 'Changing Patterns of Electoral Volatility in European Party Systems, 1948-1977: Explorations in Explanation' in Hans Daalder and Peter Mair (eds.) *Western European Party Systems: Continuity and Change*, Sage, London, 29-66

Rae, Douglas (1971) *The Political Consequences of Electoral Laws* (rev. ed.), Yale Press, New Haven

Rae, Douglas, V. Hanby and D.W. Loosemore (1971) 'Thresholds of Representation and Thresholds of Exclusion: An Analytical Note on Electoral Systems', *Comparative Political Studies, 3*, 479-488

Rokkan, Stein (1977) 'Towards a Generalised Concept of *Verzuiling*', *Political Studies, 25*, 563-70

Rose, Richard and Derek Urwin (1970a) 'Persistence and Change in Western Party Systems Since 1945', *Political Studies, 18*, 287-319

Rose, Richard and Derek Urwin (1970b) 'Persistence and Disruption in Western Party Systems Between the Wars' (paper presented at the World Congress of the International Sociological Association, Varna)

Sartori, Giovanni (1966) 'European Political Parties: The Case of Polarized Pluralism' in Joseph LaPalombara and Myron Weiner, (eds.) *Political Parties and Political Development*, Princeton University Press, Princeton, 137-76

Sartori, Giovanni (1969) 'From the Sociology of Politics to Political Sociology' in Seymour Martin Lipset, (ed.) *Politics and the Social Sciences*, Oxford University Press, New York, 65-100

Sartori, Giovanni (1976) *Parties and Party Systems: A Framework for Analysis*, Cambridge University Press, Cambridge

Shefter, Martin (1986) 'Trade Unions and Political Machines: The Organization and Disorganization of the American Working Class in the late Nineteenth Century' in Ira Katznelson and Aristide R. Zolberg, (eds.) *Working-Class Formation: Nineteenth-Century Patterns in Western Europe and the United States*, Princeton University Press, Princeton, 197-276

Shively, W. Phillips (1972) 'Party Identification, Party Choice, and Voting Stability: The Weimar Case' *American Political Science Review 66*, 1203-25

Sundquist, James L. (1983) *Dynamics of the Party System: Alignment and Realignment of Political Parties in the United States* (rev. ed.), Brookings, Washington

Thomassen, J.J.A. (1975) 'Party Identification as a Cross-Cultural Concept: Its Meaning in the Netherlands' *Acta Politica, 10*, 36-56, reprinted in Budge, Crewe and Farlie (1976), 63-80

Wolinetz, Steven B. (1979) 'The Transformation of Western European Party Systems Revisited', *West European Politics, 2*, 4-28

Index

Index

Index

Index

Index

Eisenhower, Dwight 277
Elchardus, M. 117
Elder, N. 186
Eldersveld, S. 272
Electoral laws 5
    thresholds 311, 312
Electoral volatility 3
Engelmann, F.E. 92, 93
Epstein, L. 281, 283, 284, 291, 292
Epstein, L.K. 286
Ergas, Y. 54
Esping-Andersen, G. 310
Ethnic cleavages
    See also linguistic cleavages
Eurocommunism 178
European Economic Community 230

Fälldin, Thorbjörn 196, 198
Falklands War 217
Falter, J. 63
Farlie, D. 301
Farrell, B. 231
Feist, U. 69, 71, 73, 74, 77
Ferejohn, J. 288
Fessel Institute 101
Figl, Leopold 94
Fiorina, M. 288, 291
Fisher, S. 63
FitzGerald, Garret 235, 236, 237, 242
Five per cent threshold
    See also Germany, West - electoral
    law
Flanagan, S. 4, 6, 301, 317
Flanagan, W. 269
Fogt, H. 76, 78
Foot, Michael 217, 218
Forbes, H.D. 250
Ford, Gerald 278
Fordism 40, 56
France
    1981 Presidential Election 20
    austerity policies 19
    cabinet formation 26
    centrism 21
    centrists 14
    cohabitation 22, 29
    constraints on government policy 27
    decentralisation 28

dualism 20
economic conditions and electoral
    change 23
electoral law 14, 15, 20, 29
flash parties 18
front de classes 19, 22
Front Nationale 3, 18, 28
ideological change 18, 19
impact of parties 25, 27
inter-bloc conflict 20
interest groups 25
left-wing unity 20
nationalisation of parties 16
neo-corporatism 25
new social movements 24
polarisation 15, 16
racism 18
right-wing unity 21
social policy 28
Socialist government policies 16, 18
Socialist Party ideology 18, 19
Socialist Party, base of support 22
trade unions 24
Unified Socialist Party 14
voting patterns 23
Franssen, P. 115
Free Democratic Party, West Germany
    239
Freemasonry 110, 113

Gaitskell, Hugh 211, 209, 211, 212, 216
Gallagher, M. 222, 225, 231, 236, 237,
    238
Gallagher, T. 232
Gardiner, Jimmy 258
Garvin, T. 233
Generational change 300
Genscher, H. 77
George, Henry 162
Germany
    Nazi Regime 61
    postwar period 61, 62
    reunification 65
Germany, East 65
Germany, Federal Republic of
    See Germany, West
Germany, interwar
    See Weimar Republic

Index

Index

Index

Index

Index

Index

Index

Sniderman, P. 250
Social Democratic Party (Britain) 3
Socio-economic change
    impact of 300
Søe, C. 65, 75
Sorauf, F. 4
Spencer, R. 62
Stanfield, Robert 257
Statistisk Sentralbyrå 173
Stauning, Thorvald 162
Steger, Norbert 93, 102
Steiner, K. 92, 103
Stokes, D. 2, 69, 207, 301
Stouthuysen, P. 118
Strauss, Franz Josef 74, 75, 77
Strobl, H. 99
Ström, F. 171
Sundquist, J. 1, 6, 270, 273, 305
Survey research 4
Sweden
    cleavage structure 163
    coalition patterns 185, 191
    electoral law 161
    environmental issues 192
    labour movement 170
    minority parliamentarianism 163
    nuclear power 191
    parliamentary democracy, origins of
        160
    Red-Green alliance 163
    suffrage extension 161
    voting patterns 174
    See also Scandinavia
Sylos Labini, P. 43, 44

Taft, Robert 277
Tarschys, D. 177
Terlouw, Jan 144
Terwey, M. 69, 79
Thatcher, Margaret 215, 217, 218, 309
Therborn, G. 44
Thomas, A.H. 186
Thomassen, J. 155, 301
Thurlings, J.M.G. 137
Thurmond, Strom 273
Togliatti, P. 49
Trudeau, Pierre 259, 260, 262
Turner, John 262

Turning Point 143

Ulram, P.A. 100, 101, 103
Union of the Oppositions 109
United States
    ballot reforms 271, 272
    brokerage politics 276
    candidate-centred campaigning 279,
        280, 288
    civil rights legislation 273
    civil service reforms 272
    Congress, organisation of 288
    congressional elections 288
    conservatism, rise of 277, 278
    consultants, use of 280
    delegate selection procedures 274, 275
    Democratic National Convention,
        1968 274
    Democratic Party rules 275
    election campaigns 279, 280, 288
    election expenditures 283, 284
    election finance 282, 283
    election finance legislation 280, 281
    electoral change 284
    electoral law 271, 272
    electoral realignment, absence of 286,
        287, 289
    Federal Election Campaign Act 280
    generational realignments 269, 286
    Great Society programmes 273
    institutional setting, impact of 271
    intra-party conflict 274, 277, 278
    McGovern-Fraser reforms 274, 275
    media, impact of 276, 288
    national party committees 282, 283,
        290
    New Deal Coalition 273, 276
    partisan stability 250
    partisanship 251
    party coalitions 273, 275, 276, 277,
        289
    party identification 286
    party organisation 270, 272, 290
    party organisation, professionalisation
        of 283
    party origins 271
    patronage 271
    political action committees 279, 281

Index